"Dr. Williams has accomplished a 'tour de force' in covering the lives of five generations of the Wilson family, which has had such an impact on world-wide administrative leadership in the SDA Church. Williams has a pleasant, easy style as he writes about the dedication and gifts of the three 'N C Wilsons' in the proclamation of a soon coming Lord and Savior. The author has done a wealth of careful research in correspondence, archives, and articles, which give validity to his writing based on many interviews. The reader will be enriched by a wealth of historical information, not just about the Wilson family, but about the world-wide mission field in Africa, India, the Middle East and the United States. Many 'golden opportunities for God's cause' are presented in the context of an uplifting story of commitment to the church of the Remnant."

—Dr. BERT BEACH
Retired church administrator

"How effective is one convert? In this book, which both historians and casual readers will enjoy, we learn that one E.G. White convert has impacted the history of our church for five generations! For me it carries a deeply personal message: Am I carrying on the family tradition of giving my all for my Lord and Savior? I believe that all who read this book will be blessed."

—JAN WILSON KAHLER
Great granddaughter of William Henry Wilson

"This book on one of Adventism's outstanding families is high in personal interest. Dr. DeWitt S. Williams researched widely and draws upon first-person accounts and recollections of those who knew each of the Wilson leaders. I found the work interesting and informative."

—WILLIAM G. JOHNSSON
Former editor, *Adventist Review* and *Adventist World*.

"DeWitt Williams has developed a compelling, well-researched, and insightful history of one of the most influential families in the Adventist Church. His attention to detail as well as his depictions of individual personalities throughout five generations of the Wilson family bring the stories to life and provide a fascinating read. Of particular interest is the experience of Isabella and William Henry Wilson, the first members of the family to accept the Adventist message and dedicate their lives and children to the Lord and His church. This book inspires us to greater faithfulness and trust in God's guidance and love."

—SANDRA BLACKMER
Features editor, *Adventist Review*

"Dr. DeWitt S. Williams has done an outstanding job of weaving together personal and professional accounts of several generations of the Wilson family, showing how God has used them throughout these several generations. The time he invested in his research shines through, and the final product shows the power that resides in a family unit when a commitment exists to serve God and humanity

—WILLIE E. HUCKS II, DMin,
Associate Secretary, General Conference Ministerial Association,
Associate Editor, *Ministry Magazine*

"Dr. Williams' depth of experience in ministry and his inspired writing skills have served him well for this complicated project. He has successfully chronicled the rich legacy of the Wilson family in Seventh-day Adventist Church history with great care. From an insiders' perspective he has captured and aptly portrayed their many essential contributions to the Church through the faithfulness and sacrifices of five successive generations in ministry and leadership. His credibility is evidenced through his scholarly care in research and insightful analytical interpretations. He leaves the reader expecting great attainments for the Church under the oversight of our current president, Dr. Ted N. C. Wilson, to whom the leadership torch has now been passed. As a child one of my favorite pastimes was to engage in adventure or to journey throughout the world, vicariously of course, through the pages of great, well written histories and biographies. This book brought back memories of those days through the appealing, yet compelling, style Dr. Williams has applied in his dynamic portrayal of the history of this family within the context of the development of the Church. May God continue to bless this gifted author and bless those who read his words. Pray that all will be inspired to use their gifts and talents in the service of the Lord."

—ELLA SMITH SIMMONS, EdD
General Vice President,
General Conference of Seventh-day Adventists

"DeWitt Williams is as highly committed to chronicling the legacy of the Wilson family as the Wilson family is to the Seventh-day Adventist Church. This is the go-to source for information on this exceptional family."

—BENJAMIN BAKER, PhD
Associate Director,
General Conference Archives

"I recommend HIGHLY COMMITTED by Dr. DeWitt Williams. I especially enjoyed the parts about Ted Wilson and his Dad. It encourages me to see how God has led one family through several generations and encourages me that God has blessed the Adventist church with a very committed leader in Ted Wilson."

—PAUL GLENN
Book Manager, Potomac Adventist Book Center

"DeWitt Williams has done an admirable job of chronicling the extraordinary service record of this important Adventist family. *Highly Committed* will interest laypeople and become a handy reference source for scholars."

—DAVID TRIM, Ph.D., F.R.Hist.S.
Director of Archives, Statistics, and Research
General Conference of Seventh-day Adventists

"Highly Committed is a book that should be read by every Christian! It is a remarkable story of transmitted faith, values and mission. More than an inspirational story of a family, it is the story of exceptional multi-generation Christian leadership and mission. You will be inspired to see how God used individuals; leaders will be inspired how to influence and direct God's work; and families will be inspired on transmitting faith, values and mission to their children. The Wilson's have made a huge impact for global Christian mission and all of us will be blessed by reading Highly Committed"!

—BRAD THORP
President, Hope TV Channel Inc.

"I want to commend Dr. DeWitt Williams for writing the book, Highly Committed. We hear a lot about early SDA pioneers such as Byington, Smith, Andrews, White, and rightfully so. However, DeWitt reminds us that God is still using men today to finish His work on earth just as He did to start His work. The Wilsons are such leaders in God's remnant church. Thanks DeWitt."

—JEROME L. DAVIS
Former President, Lake Region Conference of Seventh-day Adventists

"Anyone who relishes Adventist biography, however academic or informal, as I do, will find much to enjoy in DeWitt Williams' study of the Wilson generations. The book is rich in documentation and human interest, drawing heavily from archives and interviews. While obviously focusing on one family's monumental contributions to the church, *Highly Committed* presents an interesting, if necessarily partial, panorama of an amazing era. Both in and between the lines of this story, we see the vigorous commitment to service and leadership that marked so many church workers, including the Wilsons, during what will soon be widely acknowledged by historians as our greatest generation—even as we anticipate and pray for a greater one yet."

—**RONALD KNOTT**
Director, Andrews University Press;
and author, *The Makings of a Philanthropic Fundraiser: The Instructive Example of Milton Murray.*

"I just finished reading *Highly Committed*, DeWitt Williams's new book detailing the history of the Wilson family. I found the book to be most informative and inspirational. Not only did it cover the history of this family, but shed important light on the history of the Adventist church back to the time of Ellen White.

"As I read the history, I was especially fascinated how intertwined and instrumental this family was with Northern California, Madison College as well as ASI.

"I also enjoyed the stories that shed light on the Wilson family's commitment to Bible and Spirit of Prophecy as it relates to: Reaching the big cities, Health evangelism, full message evangelism and more.

"So... buy the book. Read the book. You will be blessed!"

—**DON MACINTOSH**
PR Director, WEIMAR INSTITUTE

"*Highly Committed: The Captivating Story of the Wilson Family and Their Impact on the Adventist Church* is a well-written and nicely illustrated narrative of the relationship that the Wilson family had, and continues to have, with the Seventh-day Adventist Church.

"The two words of the main title articulate the central point of the book. The thesis is that the high commitment of the successive generations of this family to the faith and ministry of the Adventist Church explains their accomplishments and their prominent roles in this denomination.

"For those who are interested in the thinking and values of these prominent religious leaders, this work is fascinating. Indeed, it provides a well-articulated description of the values of the family and how these ideals and beliefs shaped everything else in their lives.

"The book is very easy to read. The author managed to weave together in a very appealing manner the life experiences of four generations of faithful Seventh-day Adventists. The style is more popular than academic. However, the facts and basic information are well documented. Indeed, this work comes with 317 endnotes. This historical account was therefore well-researched.

"The author deserves to be congratulated for a job well done. His work appeals to a wide spectrum of readers."

—**GILBERT ABELLA**
Archives, Special Collections and Reference Librarian Nelson Memorial Library, Pacific Union College

"Brilliantly, I think, Dr. Williams has produced documentation that 5 generations of the Wilson family were instrumental in advancing the work of the Seventh-day Adventist Church around the world. This must-read book, by my friend, DeWitt S. Williams, fully reflects the impact of this 'fully human' family on the church. It is my hope that this book will stimulate further research and study of other leaders in the Adventist Church."

- **MURIEL J. MASSEY-WRAY**
Retired teacher and Pastor's Wife

"I enjoyed the book. I love the stories that illustrate the character of the people. You did an amazing job unearthing their life experiences, and then telling them simply and clearly – but always on focus with helping us know who they are. Good stuff. (But what else would I expect!). I really do like the book."
—**KERMIT NETTEBERG**
Senior Pastor, Beltsville, Maryland Seventh-day Adventist Church

"In *Highly Committed*, DeWitt Williams has again skillfully shaped a substantial body of historical information into a compelling, illuminating story, just as he did more than twenty years ago in *She Fulfilled the Impossible Dream: The Story of Eva B. Dykes*.

"The multi-generational Wilson family saga begins when the Adventist pioneers were still building the movement in America, and then takes the reader to the hey-day of overseas missions in the early and middle decades of the twentieth century, then back to the church's engagement with American society in the latter decades of the century, and finally to the election of a second Wilson in 2010 to lead a rapidly-growing global church.

"Extensive passages from those who experienced the history first hand, both Wilson family members and those associated with them, enrich the narrative and enhance the book's value as a historical resource."
—**DOUGLAS MORGAN, PhD,**
Department of History & Political Studies, Washington Adventist University

"The Wilson family is truly a highly committed family that is greatly loved by the members of the Adventist Church. In my association with Elder Neal Wilson and his son, Ted Wilson, I have found them to be very humble and approachable, a rare quality in the life of current leaders in the Adventist Church. I want to commend Dr. DeWitt S. Williams for writing this book. It is a must read for everyone who desires to serve as leaders in the Adventist church. The life and testimony of the Wilson family will prove to be a blessing for you as a servant leader."
—**PASTOR FRANKLIN DAVID**
Senior Pastor, Southern Asian Church , Silver Spring, Maryland

"Dr. DeWitt Williams has presented a definitive work in the writing of this biography. The Wilson family history is one of ardent service to the Adventist church and depicts the dedication, servant leadership and missionary spirit of their family. The early years of their mission leadership present the hardships encountered in travel, culture challenges and family separations. Yet, their faith and vision never wavered. A vast difference in what is seen today as missionaries travel in what could be called 'luxurious comfort' compared to how they were transported to distant lands years ago.

"The exemplary leadership of Elder Neal C. Wilson is especially noted. Dr. Williams gives space to the realization of racism within the church and the stand Elder Wilson took to insure that this denomination recognized and respected the 'brotherhood of all men' while serving as Columbia Union President, and later as the church's world leader.

"Within the pages of this book, Dr. Williams has compiled the history of a family whose lives were unselfishly dedicated to the growth, development and outreach of the 'Adventist message into all the world.' The final chapter of this remarkable family has yet to be written.
—**CHAPLAIN FRED A. WILLIAMS**
Retired pastor and chaplain

"Dr. Williams you have demonstrated in this unofficial bibliography of the Wilson family that important information is hidden away in the archives, attics and minds of individuals

"Research in future generations would not be able to retrieve and appreciate fully the contributions of the

Wilson family in the formation of the Church nor would the family necessarily be aware of the many interesting facts you have uncovered.

"In reality, history becomes what historians and bibliographers say it is but I think your version of history is more objective than an autobiography usually is. Thanks for the hundreds of hours of your time to make this book meaningful and enjoyable. I have known four generations of the Wilson family but my knowledge of the Wilsons is now enriched greatly from your work."

—STOY PROCTOR
Retired Associate Director, General Conference Health Ministries Department

"'Some men are born great, some achieve greatness and others have greatness thrust upon them.' From the meaningful account of the Wilson family, written from a personal knowledge and careful research, Dr. DeWitt Williams has captured the essence of the total contribution made by the various members of this energetic family.

"Above all else it was made abundantly evident that the Wilson's loved their church and for the most part moved it forward during their tenure. It is true that heredity and circumstances may influence who we are, but we are ultimately responsible for who we become.

"This book will help the reader to realize what has been accomplished by a dedicated family and you will be forced to say, "the Lord hath done great things for us!"

—REG BURGESS
Former Coordinator, Adventist InStep For Life Program

"*Highly Committed*—what an appropriate title for Dr. DeWitt Williams's book that chronicles the Wilson family's contributions to the Seventh-day Adventist Church! Just think, if Dr. Williams had not caught the vision, then took the time to research the family history, and later write the book, this amazing story of the Wilson family's commitment and sacrifices to serve God and humanity might have been unknown. It is significant that they left a legacy of Christian service as they passed the baton from one generation to the next generation.

"Thank you, Dr. Williams, for writing this inspirational book."

—CHRISTINE C. HILL
Elder, Emmanuel, Brinklow, MD Church

"Congratulations. In publishing this inspiring book, *HIGHLY COMMITTED*, you made a tremendous contribution to the history of Adventism. The Wilson family has made a tremendous contribution to this world church and to the world. The book provides delightful and informative reading from beginning to end. The involvement of President Lyndon Johnson and Paul Harvey in Adventist History has not been reported widely in recent years and will be found of great interest to most readers.

"Americans will find the chapter, 'Leadership in North America' of special interest but so will others from the rest of the world. North America is important to the rest of the world just as the rest of the world is important to North America. Your personal experience in Huntsville, Alabama, speaks much about the whole church and about the grace of God working on the hearts of His people. What a team Neal Wilson and C.D. Brooks made!

"Particularly impressive is 'The Final Years' chapter which is filled with honor and glory for God's church and His servant. Great stories are told in photographs throughout but pages 223 and 224 are a history book in themselves. These facts could stand alone as a separate small publication or handout.

"I highly recommend this Heaven-inspired book for every high school and college student and for Christian workers around the world. In my diplomatic travels for the United States, I have encountered a broad interest for this kind of information from every perspective.

"May God bless this book with a broad distribution and may He continue to bless you in your representation of Him and His people."
—Clarence E. Hodges, Ph.D.
www.cehodges.com

"*Highly Committed* is one of the most inspirational books I have ever read. To see how God used four generations of leaders from one family to give significant leadership to His church, with Nathaniel, Neal, and Ted Wilson serving at the General Conference and its Divisions, is a thrilling and awe-inspiring story!

"In the process of chronicling the professional biographies of the Wilsons, Dr. Williams has succeeded in presenting significant chapters of the history of the SDA Church in different parts of the world - Egypt, South Africa, India, Australasia, and America. He has done extensive research using valuable primary sources. In addition, he has supplied a variety of General Conference fact sheets, as well as a treasure of photographs.

"In *Highly Committed*, Williams has also given insights into the church's innovative strategy to turn the setbacks of World War II into steppingstones for post-war Mission advancement. In addition, he has shed light on the little known efforts of Neil Wilson during his presidency of the Columbia Union and onward to deal with the Civil Rights issue which challenged the church in North America in the 1960s.

"One other point that impressed me was the burden that some leaders carried for the completion of the Gospel Commission. I was specially touched by the words of retiring GC President Elder Robert H. Pierson when he told Elder Spangler, 'But the Lord isn't here yet, Bob, and anything short of that is not success.' *Highly Committed* reminds us that the Seventh-day Adventist Church is in God's hands, and He chooses and equips leaders to fulfill His mission.
—**GORDON O. MARTINBOROUGH**
Retired Vice-President, Inter-American Division, Director, Happy Family Bible Seminars International

"Impactful, inspiring and informative.
"These three words capture the essence of Dr. Williams' book on the Wilson family. He chronicles five generations of family members that dedicated their lives to the service of God. They answered the call to serve in diverse places and shared the Gospel of Christ with thousands of people; all the while continuing to nurture their own families so that they too would be ready to serve.

"Dr. Williams has given us a wealth of information about the Seventh-day Adventist church. Did you know that in the 1800's the General Conference sessions were held every year? Sometimes they were held more than once a year for special sessions.

"This book has helped me to become inspired to do more, and to be more active in the soul winning efforts at my church. The Wilson family has made me take a closer look at myself. There must be something I can do to help further the gospel to hasten Jesus' soon coming.

"I commend Dr. Williams for all he has done in gathering this information and providing it to the Adventist community. He too, is a 'highly committed person.'"
—**PEARL JARBOI**
Retired Registered Nurse

Highly Committed

The Captivating Story of the Wilson Family and Their Impact on the Adventist Church

DeWitt S. Williams

TEACH Services, Inc.
PUBLISHING
www.TEACHServices.com

World rights reserved. This book or any portion thereof may not be copied or reproduced in any form or manner whatever, except as provided by law, without the written permission of the publisher, except by a reviewer who may quote brief passages in a review.

This book was written to provide truthful information in regard to the subject matter covered. The author assumes full responsibility for the accuracy of all facts and quotations as cited in this book. The opinions expressed in this book are the author's personal views and interpretation of the Bible, Spirit of Prophecy, and/or contemporary authors and do not necessarily reflect those of TEACH Services, Inc.

This book is sold with the understanding that the publisher is not engaged in giving spiritual, legal, medical, or other professional advice. If authoritative advice is needed, the reader should seek the counsel of a competent professional.

———————————————

Copyright © 2013 TEACH Services, Inc.
ISBN-13: 978-1-57258-848-6 (Paperback)
ISBN-13: 978-1-57258-849-3 (Hardback)
ISBN-13: 978-1-57258-850-9 (ePub)
ISBN-13: 978-1-57258-851-6 (Kindle/Mobi)
Library of Congress Control Number: 2012946579

Published by

TEACH Services, Inc.
PUBLISHING
www.TEACHServices.com

Acknowledgements

Highly Committed is not an "official biography." I was not commissioned by anyone in the Wilson family or in the church to write this book. I took the initiative and began writing it on my own. I have always loved biographies, and I have been impressed by the outstanding contributions of the Wilson family to the Adventist Church and the surrounding community. I knew Neal Wilson personally from the time I first came to the General Conference in 1974, and I valued his counsel and leadership while I was serving as an administrator and departmental leader.

To begin with, I would like to thank God for inspiring me with the desire to undertake what turned out to be a difficult but satisfying task. Although it is not "an official biography" it is a realistic, revealing and carefully researched chronicle of the activities and contributions of the members of a family that have contributed so much to the growth and development of the Adventist Church. I feel that I have uncovered some new information not published about the family and presented an excellent portrayal of the major events in their lives beginning with the conversion of William Henry Wilson in 1904 to 2011 when I ended my research. I was pleased to unearth these stories and accounts that cover more than 100 years as documented in the early editions of the *Advent Review and Sabbath Herald* and other church papers.

Stephen Chavez and Merle Poirier were the first two people who encouraged me to continue writing on this topic. They showed me how to use the online archives and other resources in the *Adventist Review*. Timothy Poirier of the White Estate also provided me with helpful letters and materials.

I want to thank the people in archives for being so helpful. Bert Haloviak, the director at the time I began, Peter Chiomenti, Eucaris Galicia, and Benjamin Baker. They pulled out boxes and hard to find articles time and again.

Many of the members of the Wilson family were also helpful: Ruth Wilson Murrill and Clarice Wilson Woodward, sisters of Neal Wilson, talked with me many times over the phone and provided me with pictures, letters, and family memorabilia. Gwen Schmidt, Clarice Woodward's daughter, provided me with several documents and materials. Jan Wilson Kahler was most helpful in providing the pictures and information about her side of the family.

Shirley Wilson Anderson granted me a solid interview. It was difficult to interview Ted Wilson who had been elected president of the General Conference at the time I was working on the book. His schedule was incredibly busy, but I was eventually able to visit with him on three separate occasions in his office. I thank him for sharing his valuable time with me. Nancy Wilson also granted me a wonderful telephone interview. Eventually, Ted Wilson cleared his schedule to read a rough draft of the manuscript and make needed corrections. I thank him immensely for this. I must also thank Marilyn Perez, his assistant, who kept reviewing his schedule and continued setting up appointments.

Lloyd (Joe) Wilson, son of Robert Ray Wilson, gave me the details of his side of the family, and William

(Bill) Wilson gave me some very helpful information about his side. Bob, Ron, and Ivanette Osborn (niece of Elinor Wilson), Emilie DeVasher, Don Vollmer, and Bruce Wilson all were very helpful in providing me with family information. Phil and Sheila Ward provided me with information about the genealogy of the Scott family. I appreciated the efforts of Larry S. Anderson of the Historic Lodi Memorial Cemetery who supplied me with photos of the grave markers.

I want to thank the following people for allowing me to interview them: Richard and Veda Lesher, Don Roth, Evelyn Zytkoskee, Bert B. Beach, Trevor H. Fraser, Nikolaus Satelmajer, Bradley Booth, Jiggs Gallagher, Bob Nixon, Bryce Pascoe, Harold Burden, David White, Ray Nelson, Gaspar Colón, Charles Bradford, Calvin B. Rock, Ken Singleton, Tony Romeo, Juan Prestol, Robert and Ruth Kloosterhuis, Jerome Davis, Roy Branson, Jon and Pamela Paulien, Ray Dabrowski, Wendell Cheatham, Dale Thomas, Victor Peake, William Johnsson, and Charles D. Brooks.

Special thanks goes to Alvin Singleton who helped me find birth, marriage, and death certificates and many other important documents. I sincerely appreciated the counsel and support of former *Adventist Review* editor William Johnsson and Ansel Oliver for pictures of the Wilson funeral.

My sincere thanks also goes to Rose-lee Power and Laurel Taupongi of the Adventist Heritage Centre at Avondale College in Australia for supplying me with some photos and information from that side of the world; Carolyn Curtis, product development, Pacific Press Publishing Association, for several photos; Gilbert Abella of Nelson Memorial Library, Pacific Union College, for early photos of Neal Wilson; Albert Dittes and Paul Fuqua of the Madison Survey; Paulette Cusick, EASEA and The Layman Foundation; Mary C. Rickelman, reference/instruction librarian; R.A. Williams Library, Florida Hospital College of Health Sciences, for supplying me with information about the Hurlbutt Farm and Madison College; and Bonnie Dwyer for allowing us to reprint the Jiggs Gallagher story from *Spectrum*.

For her professional proofreading and catching all the misplaced commas and other grammatical challenges I salute and thank Kalie Kelch. I also owe a debt of gratitude to my daughter Darnella Williams who gave me many suggestions and encouragement when I got writer's block and my path seemed to be lost. My wife, Margaret, also encouraged and supported me in this endeavor as she has in all my endeavors for the past fifty years. I thank her and love her for inspiring me by her unselfish devotion and praise.

Table of Contents

Chapter One
William Henry and Isabella Wilson–7

Chapter Two
Honoring the Pledge–14

Chapter Three
Nathaniel and Hannah Wilson–29

Chapter Four
Spreading the Gospel in Africa–39

Chapter Five
Evangelism in the Southern Asia Division–53

Chapter Six
Back to the States–63

Chapter Seven
Islands, NAD, Retirement–71

Chapter Eight
Neal Wilson: The Early Years–86

Chapter Nine
In the Land of the Pharaohs—104

Chapter Ten
Leadership in North America—122

Chapter Eleven
World Church President—136

Chapter Twelve
The Final Years—152

Chapter Thirteen
Ted N. C. Wilson: The Early Years—170

Chapter Fourteen
Abidjan, Russia, and the Review—196

Chapter Fifteen
Ted N. C. Wilson: World Church President—212

Endnotes—228

Chapter One

William Henry and Isabella Wilson

"You don't choose your family. They are God's gift to you, as you are to them."
Desmond Tutu

The day was full of surprises. First, the weather had turned hot—really hot for that part of California in 1904. Steam vapors streamed up from the sawdust floor in the worship tent in shimmering wisps. The last of several gifted and long-winded preachers sitting on the raised plank platform had just finished speaking and Mrs. White, dressed in a simple black dress, was being introduced. Ellen White, who lived in St. Helena, California, at that time, was the featured speaker of the day.

Regular church services at Healdsburg usually finished a little after noon, but this was camp meeting, not just church. There were so many outstanding speakers that nobody paid much attention to the time or the heat.

Isabella Scott Wilson sat halfway toward the front with her four sons and her husband, William Henry Wilson. They had married seventeen years earlier in 1887, and Isabella soon accepted the teachings of, and joined, the Seventh-day Adventist Church, but her husband rarely attended the Adventist Church. William Henry was not opposed to church. He didn't use liquor or tobacco or those sorts of things. He didn't party. Maybe on a very rare occasion he went to a wedding. He lived a very thoughtful life and was very close to his wife and their children. But he just didn't want to be involved in religious matters.

Isabella and the four boys had spent the week in a pleasant grove about four miles outside of Healdsburg. They camped under the trees in a tent and enjoyed the spiritual feast. So, when William Henry surprised Isabella by showing up at camp meeting that Sabbath morning, she knew that God was about to do great and mighty things. Her heart filled with anticipation when she saw William Henry drive up to the camp in his spring wagon with two horses pulling it. He tied the horses up, fed them a little bit, came inside the big tent and sat next to his family. Isabella offered another silent prayer that God would speak through Sister White directly to her husband's heart. She didn't know that God was about to answer a prayer whispered daily for many years by a wife who so longed for her husband to be by her side at every church service.[1]

After the introduction was offered, Ellen G. White stood up, opened her Bible, and lifted her voice. Her sermon was not long, about thirty minutes. As she was ending, she stepped down, advanced three or four steps toward the congregation, and extended an invitation to the congregation:

"Today, if you hear His voice, harden not your heart. God wants you to give your heart to Him now. Today, you must prepare yourself for the coming of Jesus. Today, you could die suddenly and your life on this earth would be finished. Would you be ready? Today, you must make your decision to serve God with an undivided heart. Now is the accepted time, now is the day of salvation." A solemnity and urgency mixed with the heat and filled the tent as Mrs. White closed her message.

She paused for a long time and then spoke again, it seemed, directly to William Henry Wilson. "If God is telling you to join His family and prepare for a home in heaven, come down NOW and give your heart to Him!"[2]

Isabella could see from the corner of her eye that William Henry was getting up. Her heart skipped a beat. He walked down the center aisle, and Sister White shook his hand and quietly and solemnly welcomed him into

Highly Committed

the Christian family and the Adventist Church! Isabella's heart was happy with this ultimate surprise, and tears streamed down her face. Other members of the Healdsburg Church who knew her and her family openly wiped tears from their eyes as well.

"Is that Isabella's husband?" they asked in unbelief. Quite a few others came down to stand with Sister White, but most eyes were on William Henry Wilson. They knew that Isabella had lived and prayed and worked daily for the salvation of her husband and four sons: William George, Robert Ray, Nathaniel Carter, and Walter Scott.

In a few weeks the old Healdsburg Church baptized William Henry Wilson. There was joy in heaven but also great joy in the Wilson home![3]

William Henry was a changed man from that day on. Isabella didn't have to pray that her husband would go to church with her; he would begin planning as soon as the sun set on Sabbath evening for the next Sabbath day. He purchased copies of other religious books and read them with purpose and enthusiasm. His faith in the Bible and the Spirit of Prophecy grew stronger and stronger each day. In the evening after supper, he would look for his Bible and copies of his favorite books *The Desire of Ages* and *The Great Controversy*, and he would sit in his comfortable chair by the dining room window and read.

William Henry was born in Donegal County, Ireland, on April 25, 1858. He met Isabella, also from Donegal, Ireland, shortly after coming to America. They married in Eureka, California, on March 10, 1887, and had their first son, William George Wilson, in the same town.[4] William Henry worked as an engineer and businessman, for the most part in Humboldt County, but after doing quite well in these endeavors, he purchased a farm in Healdsburg and became a successful fruit farmer and cattle rancher.

Over the years William Henry had watched Isabella closely and knew that she lived out her faith, and he had come to respect the doctrines of the Seventh-day Adventists. Before joining the church, he had been happy to come to an occasional camp meeting and other services, but he hadn't wanted to commit to Christ or to religion. After his baptism, he pursued religion with vigor.

"Isabella, who's preaching at church this Sabbath? What time do you want to leave for church? Have the boys prepared their Sabbath clothes?"

Noticing his sincerity, his faithfulness, and his zeal, the nominating committee quickly elected him as a deacon, then an elder, and then first elder. Whenever Mrs. White was speaking in the area, he made it a special duty to attend and hear more of her messages. He had joined the church because of Mrs. White's altar call, which was a precious and satisfying thought to him, so it was no surprise that she was his favorite speaker and author. He often mentioned this connection to God's special messenger to the Adventist Church, reminding himself and his family of the significance of her work. The "inspired writings" meant more and more to him and to the Wilson family as time went on. He let others know that God had been wonderful and good in favoring the church with these precious sources of light and truth.

The Healdsburg Church was a busy place, full of constant activity. It had an interesting history. During the summer of 1869 Elders Loughborough and Bordeau held a tent meeting in Healdsburg. Thirty-five people were baptized and indicated that they wanted to form a church. A home and a double lot were purchased, and the tiny group moved into their new church home on December 23 with Elder Loughborough acting as pastor. This was the second Adventist Church west of the Rockies. Santa Rosa beat them by about a month and occupied the first church on November 22, 1869.

In 1871 a church member donated a large lot to the growing congregation and a 30 x 40 feet building was erected, which included a porch on all sides that gave it the appearance of a beehive. Elder Loughborough continued as pastor at this new site. Because of the opening of Healdsburg College in April, 1882, the "beehive" church became inadequate to seat the growing Adventist population. In March 1884 it was decided to push ahead for a new church building whose main auditorium was to be 64 x 96 feet with an additional rear section of 40 x 90 feet. It was completed in 1886 and became the church in which Ellen White frequently spoke to a congregation that at its peak numbered more than 500 members. This third Healdsburg Church was, no doubt, the church in which William Henry served as an officer.[5]

William Henry and Isabella were quite concerned about the four boys the Lord had blessed them with, and they wanted them to be dedicated to the service of the church and trained for usefulness. During the late hours of the night, while the house was quiet, the three youngest boys especially were often a topic of the couple's deep prayers and meditation.

William George, the eldest, had completed his studies at the Healdsburg High School in 1907. He then left home for Western Normal Institute (later called Lodi Normal School). He graduated in 1909 in the very first graduating class.

A young woman caught his eye in the same class, and soon after graduation, in June 1910, he and Edith G. Pierce were married. They both wanted to be teachers, and they sought employment at Mountain View Church School some 100 miles away from Healdsburg. The little school hired William George as the principal/teacher and Edith as one of the teachers.

Robert Ray, Nathaniel Carter, and Walter Scott Wilson were growing rapidly. Nathaniel later reflected on his early boyhood. "I started school in Healdsburg at old Healdsburg College, and I recall those days and years with much joy. When Healdsburg College was closed, I continued school in the school rooms in the big old SDA church. I very well remember Sister White coming to the school and speaking to us and going up and down the aisle and putting her hand on each child and wishing us God's blessings. Yes, indeed, I remember the teachers each one and how thoughtful they were to me. They were most wonderful people."[6]

The parents thought of the tremendous expense it would be to send all three of them to Lodi Normal School. They knew how much it had cost to send William George there.

"Isabella, I think if we would pull up stakes here in Healdsburg and move to the city of Lodi or close by we could possibly afford an education for the boys. Let's go down there and look around." William George, who had attended school there and knew the area, gave them some suggestions on local farms and the best people to contact.

With prayers on their lips and a whisper of hope in their hearts, they visited several prospective farm sites until they narrowed it down to the farm that they thought their growing boys could manage.

They bargained with the owner for a good price and put their house in Healdsburg up for sale. It took a little while for the Healdsburg place to sell. The price they received was more than enough to purchase the

> "Parents, give your children to the Lord, and ever keep before their minds that they belong to Him, that they are the lambs of Christ's flock, watched over by the True Shepherd. Hannah dedicated Samuel to the Lord; and it is said of him, 'Samuel grew, and the Lord was with him, and did let none of his words ... fall to the ground.' 1 Samuel 3:19. In the case of this prophet and judge in Israel are presented the possibilities that are placed before the child whose parents co-operate with God, doing their appointed work" (Ellen G. White, *Counsels to Parents, Teachers, and Students*, p. 143).

Highly Committed

> "What a reward was Hannah's! and what an encouragement to faithfulness is her example! There are opportunities of inestimable worth, interests infinitely precious, committed to every mother. The humble round of duties which women have come to regard as a wearisome task should be looked upon as a grand and noble work. It is the mother's privilege to bless the world by her influence, and in doing this she will bring joy to her own heart. She may make straight paths for the feet of her children, through sunshine and shadow, to the glorious heights above. But it is only when she seeks, in her own life, to follow the teachings of Christ that the mother can hope to form the character of her children after the divine pattern. The world teems with corrupting influences. Fashion and custom exert a strong power over the young. If the mother fails in her duty to instruct, guide, and restrain, her children will naturally accept the evil, and turn from the good. Let every mother go often to her Savior with the prayer, 'Teach us, how shall we order the child, and what shall we do unto him?' Let her heed the instruction which God has given in His word, and wisdom will be given her as she shall have need" (Ellen G. White, *Conflict and Courage*, p. 138).

farm near Lodi and to pay for all of the moving expenses. They felt good knowing that their children would live under their roof while having the privilege of attending an academy and a teacher training school, and the farm would allow them to make a living.

Finally, things came together and on January 11, 1911, they settled into their new home and the boys enrolled in school.

Lodi Normal Academy was a coeducational day school operated by the California Conference on a thirty-eight acre tract just inside the southeast corner of the city limits of Lodi, California. Students came from the surrounding California churches but also from Montana, Kansas, Colorado, Oklahoma, Washington, Minnesota, and Michigan. It began in 1908 as the Western Normal Institute (WNI) but went through a series of name changes. After WNI it changed to Lodi Normal Academy, and then Lodi Normal Institute, and finally Lodi Academy. The school afforded unusual facilities for normal work (or teacher training) because of the large academic school connected with it.

The *Pacific Union Recorder* noted the Wilson family's move to the Lodi Normal Academy area. "We were glad to welcome Mr. W. H. Wilson from Healdsburg among us as a permanent resident. Having purchased a ranch near the normal, tells us that he has come to educate his family. We are glad they saw 'Welcome' written over our doors and entered for training school advantages. We trust that the next discovery will be 'Satisfaction' written in every department with which they may come in contact."[7]

A week after moving to Lodi, William Henry opined to his wife, "Isabella, I don't think I'm going to prayer meeting tonight. I don't feel well. Moving must've been too hard on me. I'm going to lie down for a bit." As the day wore on, he felt worse and worse. Isabella called for a local doctor who came and said that her husband had *la grippe*. All during the next week he rested in bed but seemed to grow worse and worse. There was no thought of him going to prayer meeting that Wednesday either, and again the doctor was called.

"I believe he has spinal meningitis," the doctor said after examining him. "Let him stay in bed, and I'll stop by again in a few days." William Henry got weaker and weaker.

His oldest son was quite worried about him. "Edith, we're right in the middle of the school term. What will they do without us?"

"God will provide," was her quiet answer.

Feeling his strength slip away from him, William Henry called Isabella to his side. "I feel very, very bad, and I think my time here on earth is about to end. Call Ray, Nathaniel, and Walter and tell them to come to my bedside before I lose consciousness and while I still have my faculties. I want to talk to them."

By this time William George, their eldest son, had arrived with his wife, Edith. The family was blessed with a visit from Elder J. N. Loughborough who prayed a fervent prayer for forgiveness of sins, for peace and rest for William Henry, and a special prayer for the three youngest boys standing around their fading father.

The boys saw the seriousness of their father's illness and stood in silence around his bed as he asked them to forgive all they had seen amiss in him. "If I've done anything to you boys that I shouldn't have, forgive me. If I've said anything that I shouldn't have, forgive me. I have tried with all my heart to be a faithful Christian ever since I accepted the Lord as my Savior. Isabella, I love you. Thank you for your witness and your prayers and for introducing me to my Lord and Savior.

"And now my sons I have a request. Promise me; faithfully pledge to me tonight that you will never give up the Sabbath. Do you promise me?" The boys shook their heads up and down. "Promise me tonight that you will faithfully pay your tithes. Do you promise me?"

"We promise."

"And then lastly, will you promise me that you will prepare yourselves as rapidly as possible for usefulness in God's cause?"

The boys shook their heads again and said, "Yes, we promise, we promise." Elder Loughborough prayed another fervent prayer, and they all left the room.

From noon on that Friday, January 27, 1911, until 3:30 on Tuesday, January 31, William Henry lay unconscious. On that fateful Tuesday he turned his head away from the bright light of the window and then slowly closed his eyes forever. Unbelievably, less than a month after getting the family settled and the boys enrolled in school, William Henry Wilson was gone.

A thick silence hung over the Wilson house that Tuesday. Isabella was still disbelieving that her husband was dead. News of his passing spread to the church members, and they offered to bring food and help in other ways. They had the funeral two days later on Thursday at the Lodi Church. The young boys thought about the solemn pledge they had made to their father before his passing.

The funeral was short and sad. The *Pacific Union Recorder* shared this statement of grief: "Sad indeed were the last respects paid our worthy friend and patron Brother W. H. Wilson, who so lately came among us. The normal was silent Thursday afternoon—no sound of hammer or classroom recitation. The students and teachers attended the funeral services in a body, and sat as mourners. The son and daughter-in-law, Mr. and Mrs. W. G. Wilson, who were former students and members of the class of 1909, were also present, having left their school duties in Mountain View, where both have been engaged in teaching for the past year. The family have our deepest and most heartfelt sympathy, and the school will hold out to the younger sons in this family every inducement and encouragement to help them carry out the father's dying request, 'Prepare for service as soon as possible.'"[8]

William Henry Wilson was buried in the Historic Lodi Memorial Cemetery. A passing century has not erased his faith in the church and the truths he believed in. Engraved on his tombstone are the words of the blessed hope that inspired him. "I shall be satisfied, when I awake, in thy likeness."[9]

Isabella Scott Wilson continued to live and work and pray for her sons after her husband died. Born on November 10, 1861, Isabella died in California, near Lodi, on January 30, 1923, almost twelve years after her

Highly Committed

husband. She was buried close by him. In the day of final reckoning, she will be rewarded for her life of faithfulness. The same reward will await untold numbers of wonderful, God-fearing mothers and wives—women of God pleading for their families in persistent prayer. The Wilson family owes their dedication to God and the Adventist Church to Isabella. She was the first Adventist, a pioneer.

William Henry's prayers for usefulness and committed service to the church were answered. Robert Ray Wilson and Nathaniel Wilson both graduated from Lodi Academy in June 1917. Their class aim was "to be missionaries to carry the last message of mercy to a lost world." Their class motto was "Out of the Harbor into the Sea." Their pictures still hang on the walls of Lodi Academy next to their elder brother William George's. Walter Scott would later graduate from Madison College.

No one at that time could have known that generations of dedicated, totally committed workers would come from the Wilson family. Some would serve in the medical field, some in publishing, and some in ministerial and other areas. Three names would especially become highly visible and well-known leaders throughout the Seventh-day Adventist Church: William Henry's son N. C. (Nathaniel Carter) Wilson, his grandson N. C. (Neal Clayton) Wilson, and his great grandson Ted N. C. (Norman Clair) Wilson.

Lodi Academy Class of 1917: (Robert) Ray Wilson (top row), future wife (Melva) Laverne Myers (bottom row), and Nathaniel (Carter) Wilson (bottom row).

William Henry Wilson's final resting place in the Lodi Memorial Cemetery. His hope for the future is expressed in the text on his tombstone. "I shall be satisfied, when I awake, in thy likeness" (Psalms 17:15)

William Henry and Isabella Wilson. Isabella is responsible for introducing her husband and children to Christ and the Adventist Church.

William Henry Wilson's Family

William Henry WILSON
- Born: April 25, 1858, in Donegal County Northern Ireland
- Died: January 31, 1911, in Lodi, California
- Married: Isabella SCOTT, daughter of William SCOTT and Ann Jane LOVE, on March 10, 1887, in Eureka, Humboldt, California. She was born on November 10, 1861, and died on January 30, 1923, in Lodi, California. The couple had four children, who are as follows:

William George WILSON
- Born: March 1, 1888
- Died: February 21, 1915, in Reeves, Georgia, and buried in Lodi, California
- Married: Edith G. PIERCE on June 10, 1910, in California. Edith died in December 1972.

Robert Ray WILSON
- Born: December 1894 in Fields Landing, California
- Died: May 2, 1977
- Married: Melva LaVerne MYERS, daughter of Dr. J. J. MYERS and Grace Harris MEYERS, in 1918. Melva was born on April 26, 1899, in Healdsburg, California, and died on November 1, 1980, in Nashville, Tennessee. She is buried in Woodlawn Cross Mausoleum in Nashville.

Nathaniel Carter WILSON
- Born: February 4, 1897, in Fields Landing, California
- Died: December 1, 1992
- Married: Hannah Myrtle WALLIN, daughter of Louis WALLIN, on October 1, 1919. Hannah was born on February 24, 1898, in Roseau Minnesota, and died on March 18, 1995, in Loma Linda, California.

Walter Scott WILSON
- Born: March 9, 1901, in Lakeport, California
- Died: January 10, 1989, in Hendersonville, Tennessee. He is buried in Spring Hill Cemetery in Nashville.
- Married: Teckla NIMLOS. Teckla died on November 15, 1978.

Chapter Two

Honoring the Pledge

"I have found the paradox that if I love until it hurts, then there is not hurt, but only more love."
Mother Teresa

There was a great void in the lives of the Wilson family as a result of William Henry's premature death. Everyone went about the usual activities of the day, but an aching emptiness filled the hearts of the entire family.

"William, you're the oldest by some seven years," his wife Edith stated matter-of-factly. "Let's move back in and help direct those growing teenagers. It won't hurt to talk it over with your mother." And they were grateful when Isabella approved of this plan. The schedule of household duties was tight and precise: chores to do before school, homework after school, and more chores. The family functioned once again.

Unfortunately, William George was feeling very ill, a physical sickness similar to his father's. "William George, I think you caught whatever your father had. You don't look well, and you're coughing a lot."

It was a difficult time for Edith and William George. Trying to look after the just-widowed Isabella and the three boys was a taxing job. In addition, William George was really feeling poorly. They thought often of the Mountain View School they had left to care for their family.

They had been happy with what was happening at their little Mountain View School. An article signed by them states: "The church school in Mountain View opened September 19, 1910, with an attendance of forty-two, twenty-one in each room. Since then there have been two additions to the number in the advanced department. Two students came from other churches, working their way, to enjoy church school privileges.

"It is encouraging to see the good spirit that prevails, specially among the older ones. Taken as a whole, the students are earnest, industrious, and spiritually inclined. A missionary society has been organized, and aggressive work will be planned.

"The industrial phase has been introduced as an experiment in this place. Students are making good progress in the lines started, and manifest so much enthusiasm in this branch that the teachers have to watch to keep them from devoting too much time to the manual studies and slighting the others."[10]

The couple clearly enjoyed their work and were sad to leave their students and the work of teaching them. But they were committed to their family and helping Isabella with the task of keeping the household running and training the boys to serve the Lord.

William George and Edith attended the Lodi Normal Academy graduation of 1911 along with other family members. Prescott Pierce, the president of the class and the brother of Edith Wilson, made them feel proud. He gave challenging marching orders to the twenty-eight students receiving diplomas.

On Monday evening following graduation, the alumni had their first meeting with about fifty people assembled in South Hall. There were representatives from all three previous graduating classes. There were stories about what they were doing, their travels, and recent experiences. "So enjoyable was this reunion of students and teachers that it was unanimously decided to form a permanent organization. Mr. W. G. Wilson, of the class of '09, was elected president of the alumni association for the coming year." There was a great spirit as they mingled and shared light refreshments.

After singing "God be with you till we meet again," William George asked "God to direct in the coming year and keep each graduate true and faithful to the principles for which his Alma Mater was established."[11] William George did not know that he would probably see very few of his classmates again.

Life seemed to be dealing the Wilson family a bad hand because William George was diagnosed with consumption (tuberculosis). Consumption was the leading cause of death in America in the late 1800s and early 1900s. It was called consumption because the disease seemed to consume the patient and caused them to lose weight rapidly and cough incessantly. Doctors told their patients to move close to nature at higher elevations with drier climates. Sanitariums with screened porches and outdoor tent cities sprang up in Boulder, Colorado Springs, and Denver to accommodate thousands of severely ill Americans who came for a cure. They had heard about a rest cure at a place near Boulder, so Edith insisted that they go there immediately.

Leaving his mother and young brothers was difficult, but Edith thought that was the only way to save her husband's life. They spent the rest of the winter of 1911 and summer of 1912 in Niwot right outside of Boulder, Colorado, getting the "rest cure."

Nine months after his father's death William George was struggling for his life. His strength was ebbing away, and he felt himself getting weaker and weaker. But there was a ray of sunshine that lit up their lives when, on July 27, 1912, they were blessed with their first child, Kenneth William James Wilson. "My birth certificate says I was born in Niwot," said Kenneth. "My parents lived in Niwot, but when labor started, Mother said she boarded a trolley and went to a friend's home in Boulder for the delivery. I was born in a private home at the corner of Fifth Street and First Avenue (now Alpine Avenue)."[12]

Fortunately, the dry air of Colorado was refreshing for William George, and he slowly regained some of his strength. One August afternoon as he was about to open the door to go to the store to get some supplies for baby Ken, William George saw a few letters on the vestibule floor. He reached down, picked them up, and put them on the little table where the mail was always put. There were about five letters. One was still stuck in the mail slot. It was halfway in but had not fallen on the ground like the other mail. He pulled it out of the slot. As he was about to put it on the table, he noticed with surprise that the letter was addressed to him. They didn't get much mail. Most of their friends didn't know their address in Colorado. He thought at first that it was from his mother or one of the boys because he saw a California return address. But when he looked closer, he saw that it was from the Hurlbutts!

Instead of going to the store he turned around and went back up the stairs to their little apartment, sat at the kitchen table, and quickly opened the letter. He read it, and then read it again. Then he knelt to pray. He didn't hear Edith come into the kitchen, bouncing baby Ken to keep him from crying. She was surprised to see William George there, kneeling, his elbows propped on one of the wooden chairs with a piece of paper in his hand.

She waited a few minutes. She didn't want to interrupt his prayer, but she was glad that baby Ken started crying so that William George knew they were in the room. He looked up and slowly got up from his knees. "William, what's wrong? Did you go to the store? William what on earth has happened?"

"No, I didn't go to the store yet. I just got a letter, and I came back to read it," he said solemnly.

"Who is it from?"

"Grandma Hurlbutt. She wants us to come south and build a school, manage it, recruit some students, and teach them. She has just bought a piece of land and needs someone to get it going. It will be a self-supporting school. She wants us to come right away."

Highly Committed

"To build a school?"

"Yes."

"And manage it?"

"Yes."

"And recruit the students?"

"Yes."

"And teach also?"

"Yes."

"William, you are not strong enough for all of that."

"Well, I think we should go. I want to go. I think this is what God wants us to do. If God restores my health, which I think He has, I must go. I feel He is calling me there. I'll let Grandma Hurlbutt know right away."

"Don't you think we ought to go back to Mountain View, the school that we just left? What about your mother and your brothers? William, are you sure?"

"The Hurlbutts want us to come now. Her husband is very sick, and she needs me to be her right-hand man."

The "rest cure" had done its work, and in October 1912, feeling rejuvenated and strengthened, the little family left Boulder. The South was calling them. This was William George's opportunity to fulfill his father's dying request.

William George was the first of the Wilson boys to try to honor the pledge to their father. After making sure that the three younger brothers were securely matriculated in school for the new school year and a routine was set up and that his mother had everything she needed, William George and Edith decided to be "useful" in the South. They headed for the Hurlbutt farm in Reeves, Georgia.

****

Most people don't realize the devastation that the Civil War brought to America. The South, especially, lay in ruins for years. The educational system had been almost completely destroyed. There were a few public high schools, but they were mostly scattered through the richer districts of the South and confined to the large cities. Well into the 1900s poor people in the South were unable to receive a higher education.

Edward A. Sutherland, the president of Battle Creek College (later Andrews University), felt so burdened over what was happening in the South as he studied the educational theories of Mrs. White that he felt compelled to do something about it. Mrs. White emphasized that true education was the harmonious development of the physical, mental, and spiritual powers, and he felt that current education was not following that model.

Early in 1904 he was invited to speak at a meeting at Hinsdale Sanitarium and Hospital near Chicago, Illinois. Afterwards, some young people asked him for an interview. They wanted a college education but didn't have the means to pay for it. So President Sutherland and Dr. David Paulson decided to pray and ask God for counsel as to how they could provide a way for young people who had no means to go to college. They sought out a secluded and quiet place and poured out their hearts to God. The students wanted to work to cover their school expenses so they would not have to pay tuition. They would be educating mind, heart, and hand.

They wanted to follow the example set by Captain Bates, the retired sailor who paid for his own expenses while he was traveling by printing and selling tracts. William Miller worked as a farmer while he preached the coming of Christ. Elder James White worked in the woods, on the railroad, or in the hayfield to support his family while he preached. They wanted to learn by doing.

Sutherland shared his feelings with Professor Percy T. Magan, dean of the college, and they decided to do something about it. Incredibly, Sutherland handed in his resignation as president of Battle Creek College and with Magan, who also resigned, headed South, asking God to help them implement their dreams.

In the spring of 1904 in the company of Ellen G. White and her two sons, J. Edson White and W. C. White, Magan and Sutherland set out on the riverboat the "Morning Star" to look for a place to locate a training school. The Morning Star had a mechanical problem, and they had to stop for repairs at Edgefield Junction Landing, twelve miles up the Cumberland River from Nashville, Tennessee. While waiting for the repairs to be made, Mrs. White and some of the others went up the riverbank and came across a plantation that was for sale. "This is the place the Lord said you should have," said Mrs. White. The men had hoped to buy a small place in the hills because they had limited resources, but Mrs. White encouraged them to buy the 414-acre Nelson place, which was situated twelve miles from Nashville.

They scraped together $100 to put down on the property. The purchase price was $12,723 of which $5,000 was to be paid within ten days. Magan stayed by to develop a plan for the new college, and Sutherland rushed back to Michigan to find the needed money. He returned shortly afterwards with the money and faculty members. The farm contained valuable fruit trees and 100 acres of virgin timber.

Classes started on October 1, 1904. Counting faculty and students. there were fourteen present. Nellie H. Druillard, who had served in Africa as a missionary and had a talent for handling money, was the treasurer. She was an astute well-to-do businesswoman.

It was called the Nashville Agricultural and Normal Institute (NANI) until 1931 when its name was changed to Madison College. Manual arts were to be given a position of equal importance with literary subjects. A sanitarium and hospital were to be built where people could come to learn how to care for the body and care for other sick people. Half of the day was devoted to study and half of the day to work.

The Bible was a prominent feature in the curriculum. In 1907 nineteen buildings, including a rural sanitarium, had been built or were in the process of being built. Before the sanitarium could be finished a businessman came to the president's office. He was in poor health and needed help.

All of the rooms and houses were full, but he insisted on staying. He said the picturesque setting, the sweet spirit of the place, the fresh country air, the quiet, the Christian influence, and the good food all appealed to him, so he offered to sleep on the porch.

His desire was granted. A portion at the end of the porch was curtained off, and an improvised room was created. His recovery was rapid, and his praise overflowed. Many, many patients from all around the area came as a result of his testimony. The experience pushed both Sutherland and Magan to study medicine. While carrying on their administrative and educational work at the new college, they took the full medical course at Tennessee and Vanderbilt universities, graduating four years later as full medical doctors.

The philosophy of Madison College attracted many students, many faculty, and many volunteers. Lida Funk Scott, the daughter of the late Dr. Isaac K. Funk, cofounder of the Funk and Wagnalls publishing company, went to Madison as a patient in 1914.

She had been raised in luxury and was a millionaire. Just before going to Madison her only child, who was just 14 years old, died, and she was all alone. So impressed was she with the practical application of the principles of the campus that she decided to stay and devote the rest of her life and her fortune to the promotion of the objectives of Madison.

Under Mrs. Funk's leadership, the Laymans Foundation came into existence, which was a nonprofit corporation organized under the Welfare Act of the State of Tennessee. Mrs. Funk became a Seventh-day

Highly Committed

Adventist and transferred her fortune of more than $1 million into this organization.

Not only was Madison to have an educational institution different from our other established schools, but through the financial help of Mrs. Funk, it had a sanitarium as well. On a visit to the Madison campus, Mrs. White pointed to a spot and said, "This would be a good place for a sanitarium."[13]

****

The Lord impressed Brother and Sister Hurlbutt, who at that time lived in California, that they should do something about the educational situation in the South. Sister Hurlbutt's mother, before she died, had bequeathed her a legacy to be used in giving care and training to neglected youth. They had purchased a large property and had become wealthy dairy farmers who operated the Hurlbutt Home for orphaned boys and girls.

The Wilson family was very well-acquainted with the Hurlbutts. Before William Henry and Isabella were married, William Henry had stayed with them, and they had treated him as the son they never had. While living there William contracted typhoid fever, and Mrs. Hurlbutt had nursed him back to health. When Isabella and William Henry got married, the Hurlbutts opened up their house to them and shared their home, their means, and their love with the young couple. At that time Isabella and William Henry had only two sons, William George and Robert Ray. When the next boy was born, the Wilsons decided to name him after the head of the household that had been so kind to them.

Nathaniel and Emeline Carter Hurlbutt were proud to know that this little boy would be named after them. He took Brother Hurlbutt's first name (Nathaniel) and Sister Hurlbutt's family name (Carter). Later on Nathaniel Carter Wilson would be accepted as a part of the Hurlbutt family and all of the Wilson family would remain close friends with them. The Wilson children all called her Grandma Hurlbutt.

In 1908 Mrs. White and Dr. Sutherland visited the Hurlbutt Home and shared with them the great needs of the South and the concept of NANI. This account by W. C. White (where he spells Mr. and Mrs. Hurlbutt's name incorrectly) gives the details of that visit:

"Sunday morning, April 19, we started at 4:30 A.M., hoping to reach the home of Mr. N. Hurlburt [*sic*], near Finley post-office, in one day's drive. It is fifty-two miles by the route we had chosen ...

"There were five in our party: Mrs. Ellen G. White and the writer [W. C. White], in a single buggy drawn by a heavy bay; in a strong platform spring wagon, drawn by a span of heavy grays, were Mr. Iram James, of Pratt Valley, Professor E. A. Sutherland, of the Nashville Normal and Agricultural Institute of Madison, Tennessee, and Miss Sara McEntefer, Mrs. White's secretary and traveling companion....

"Over the last ridge, we soon caught sight of Clear Lake, and it, with the rich pasture lands and orchards with which it is surrounded, was in view much of the time during the last two hours of our journey. Just before sunset we passed through the village of Kelseyville, and at seven o'clock we were warmly welcomed at the home of Mr. and Mrs. Hurlburt [*sic*].

"Monday was spent in looking over the large ranch where Mr. and Mrs. Hurlburt [sic] have been conducting an orphanage for several years. The soil is rich and productive, and the large orchards, the broad fields, the pretty wooded lot and the point of land jutting out into the lake are all interesting features.

"Tuesday morning a short service was held at the orphanage, Mrs. White giving a brief address which was followed by a talk to the children from Professor Sutherland....

"We wish the young people much joy as they take up unitedly the responsibility of caring for the big ranch while Mr. and Mrs. Hurlburt [sic] go for a time to the St. Helena Sanitarium to see if the far-famed skill of Dr. Rand and the care of his faithful associates may prove a benefit to Mr. Hurlburt's [sic] health."[14]

The visitors shared with the Hurlbutts the latest news about what was happening in the South and at Madison College. For a while the Hurlbutts wanted to establish a self-supporting institution like Madison in the California area. As soon as they could, they arranged a visit to the South to see what was happening. But after making several visits to Tennessee and Georgia, they decided they would join forces with Sutherland and help the people in the South.

Hoping to establish a farm school and a country sanitarium similar to NANI, the Hurlbutts finally purchased a piece of property in Georgia in 1912 before Brother Hurlbutt's death.

Hurlbutt Farm Sanitarium was situated at Reeves, Georgia, on the main line of the Southern Railway between Chattanooga, Tennessee, and Rome, Georgia. Although in an isolated area and difficult to reach, the Hurlbutt Farm consisted of a large tract of land in a beautiful River Valley, containing at first 480 acres. They purchased more land later to add to the original tract, bringing it closer to 600 acres in all. It was to this property that William George and Edith Wilson came when they left Boulder, Colorado.

"Brother N. Hurlbutt and his wife, of Findley, California, have been stopping at the Rural Sanitarium since the first of May. They are not here for their health only. They are intensely interested in self-supporting missionary work. Though Mr. Hurlbutt is a semi invalid and Mrs. Hurlbutt is far from strong, their interest was so great that they traveled, since coming here, over 150 miles in visiting some of these schools. They are planning to establish a work similar to the Madison School and Sanitarium in California."[15]

Mr. Hurlbutt's Death

Nathaniel W. Hurlbutt had a severe form of rheumatoid arthritis and could hardly walk. Summoning all of his strength, he could get around with great difficulty on crutches. Mrs. Hurlbutt was a petite lady who weighed about ninety pounds and was very forceful in her opinions and manner. When she decided to do something, it was done. Shortly after purchasing the land, Mr. Hurlbutt passed away on December 17, 1912. A large funeral was held for him in California.

Just before he passed away, they had contacted William George and Edith by letter to let them know they had purchased the land and needed them to come and help. The Wilsons left Boulder, Colorado, and began right away to develop the property. After they settled on the property, they sent out some letters to let people know what they were doing and to request help in the form of money and more workers. More workers were desperately needed. Edith sent out this letter, which was published shortly after it was received.

"You will wonder what we have here, and what the needs and opportunities are. There is much more land in the South, but the Lord has given us a valuable asset to begin with in the five hundred acres of exceptionally good land that has been secured. It is mostly river bottom land of the best quality. The climate is very healthful, although at times the temperature goes somewhat in extremes both ways. Most of the work on this farm has been carried on by tenants with one horse implements. Forty acres is a one-mule farm, and there are at present three renters on the place besides the owner. These renters are in a condition bordering on slavery. They don't have money, and would not know how to use it if they had it. If they want something from a store or from a neighbor they 'swap' for it. When the cotton is sold they sometimes get a little money to pay old bills with.

"With the lower classes the ignorance is profound. There seems to be no compulsory education. There is a 'fine' school at this place where some of the more fortunate children attend. It usually runs nearly two months in the year. The lack of education is a hindrance to the progress of the gospel. Even where the children could be spared from work to attend school, the desire for knowledge is small indeed.

"The people here are church members as a rule. They go to church at least once a year, sometimes oftener. The belief of 'once in grace always in grace' is universally held, and if you ever heard of people having the form of godliness, but denying the power thereof this is the place to see it lived out in a new light. I wish you could

Highly Committed

accompany me to church and see all the men chewing tobacco, the minister not excepted. The women do not chew in church, but use snuff freely at home.

"The people are suspicious of newcomers, especially such peculiar people as we are, and it seems as though the most we can do at present is to make our lives 'epistles known and read of all men.' We are fortunate in having associated with us such experienced missionaries as Elder and Doctor Laird, and we hope the way will open soon when some prejudice will be overcome, especially through the medical work. There is great need along this line. The people cannot think of anything curing sickness unless it comes in a bottle labeled, 'shake well before using. Dose one teaspoonful hourly.'

"Of course the people of whom I have written do not represent all the Southern people. There are thousands of our country's best citizens in this section. But even with them, our people have not touched this field with the tips of their fingers."[16] In response, several professional people joined the Wilsons. More help was coming.

"Professor Boynton and wife, instructors in the academy at San Francisco, Calif., have been invited to associate with Brother W. G. Wilson in building up an industrial school on the property purchased by Brother and Sister Hurlbutt near Reeves, Ga. Professor Boynton spent the summer months in the Madison School, for it is the purpose of the founders of the new school at Reeves to make it a school after the Madison order. Professor Boynton returned to San Fernando for the winter, expecting to come South again next spring. Brother W. G. Wilson and family are living on the property at Reeves, and recently Brother J. E. Hanson and wife, formerly of Madison, joined them."[17]

California Youth

They received great encouragement from a special gift that came from California. "Last Monday, June 8, the Madison school family were given the pleasure of an all-day call from a company of 23 California young people who were on their way from the Pacific Coast to the northern part of Georgia where they are to enter the work either as students or as instructors and workers in the new school being started on the property purchased for that purpose by Brother and Sister Hurlbutt near Reeves, Georgia. It is the first time in the history of our work that such a large company has come south at one time to engage in the self-supporting work. It ought to be a source of great encouragement to all of us. May the Lord bless all those who have had the courage to take this step.

"Sister Hurlbutt has been in the truth for a good many years, and has been in the South twice in order to see the needs of the work. The place purchased by her and [her] husband is not far from the city of Rome. It consists of about five hundred acres of land on which she hopes to see a school developed. There are a number of workers already on the farm, several of whom have formally been students of the Madison school. Others expect to join the company at Reeves in the near future. God has said that many schools should be established, and he is showing that his Spirit is at work in the hearts of men. We are living near the end of time and what is done must be done quickly."[18]

"On December 11 [1913] a little daughter arrived at the home of Brother and Sister W. G. Wilson at Reeves, Georgia."[19] The Wilsons were happy to add this special gift to their family. They named their little girl Gladys.

Below is the very last mention of William George in our publications. "Several years ago the Lord impressed a sister and her husband, then living in California, that they should use some of their means for the advancement of the work in the South. As a result of this conviction, they came, and after looking at several locations they purchased a four hundred and eighty acre farm near Reeves, Georgia. It was their plan to establish here a school to prepare teachers and Bible workers for special work in this section.

"A few months after the purchase of the farm, Brother Wilson and his wife, of California, came and began to work the place with a view of having help later to carry on the proposed work. Afterward the writer and his wife joined them, and together we worked, ever looking to the time when something definite for God would be started.

"This sister, Mrs. Hurlbutt, came to join us seven weeks ago, and two weeks later a company of young people, twenty-six in number, came from Southern California to help in the work here, and to prepare themselves to be active missionaries. We are glad to welcome them, and believe that soon northern Georgia will see souls saved in the kingdom of God as a result of the work done by these workers.

"We have organized a Sabbath-school of thirty-two, and at the end of the quarter will be able to send to the Georgia Conference a nice sum of money for mission work.

"This is a needy field, and already our neighbors are beginning to ask about the truths we teach. We trust that many will yet understand the truth and live it, and finally be saved in heaven. Pray for the work, that each one connected with it may do his part well."[20]

Just as the work was progressing nicely on Hurlbutt Farm, William George started feeling poorly again. His coughing returned and his strength diminished. Edith was dismayed to see her husband moving with difficulty. His step was slower, and he didn't have the strength to work all day.

One day one of the local villagers passed away, and William George volunteered to dig the grave. The extra effort of using the pick and shovel caused him to cough up blood again. It was an especially hot and humid day, and digging the grave provoked his condition again.

"William, I have heard that they have an expert on consumption in Tampa Bay, Florida. Let's go down there to see if we can find some treatment for you. It's closer than going all the way back to Boulder for the rest cure again. What do you think?"

"I think you're right. Let's get the children and go there. Hopefully I can be back on the job soon."

Once in Tampa Bay, William George grew worse. The trip there, the heat, the anxiety of not being able to do all of his work, and the care of his family was too much for him.

Death of William George

Janet Wilson-Kahler tells us that her Grandmother Edith told her that as the end drew near she put little Gladys and Kenneth into the bed with their father so that they could spend their final moments together. At that time they did not realize that this action could spread the disease to the children. Fortunately, it did not harm them.

On February 21, 1915, William George died, but records do not indicate if he died in Tampa Bay or if he made it back to Reeves. Florida state vital statistics have no record of his death anywhere in its sixty-seven counties, and Georgia death records are not available before 1919. Edith contacted their relatives, boarded a train with her husband's body and the two little children, and went back to Lodi, California, to bury her husband in the Wilson family plot. It was a quiet family funeral.

Edith was still a very young woman when her husband died, and she returned to her family in Sonoma for awhile before moving to Boise, Idaho, to be with her brother. While in Idaho she met and married a Walter Wetmore, a new convert, in 1918.

Suspecting that she had consumption, her new husband decided to take her back to the good air of Colorado. Together the little family traveled from Boise to Laramie, Wyoming, in a covered wagon and then on to Boulder by train. This was seventy-five years after the Oregon Trail stopped being regularly used, and it had not been maintained for quite a while.

The trip was interesting and exciting, and Kenneth Wilson wrote out many stories that were published years ago in the *Primary Treasure*. After his death, his daughter, Jan Wilson-Kahler, continued the process he had started, reworking his stories by updating and clarifying some of the wording and adding stories and details

Highly Committed

that he had told but were not included when the stories were originally published. Thus the book *1918 Covered Wagon Adventure* was born.[21] Years later X-rays revealed a walled off portion in Edith's lungs, validating her belief that she had contracted consumption from her sweet William George, but the move to Boulder saved her life. Edith and Walter later divorced and she married Clarence Long.

"Edith's first love was always William George Wilson. How she loved him! I believe she mourned his death all her life. In fact, I remember a flower garden she had, where she grew *Sweet Williams*, her favorite flower, and this was after she and Clarence Long had been married for years. Yes, she still called him 'my sweet Wiliam' all her life. One can only wonder how Clarence felt playing second fiddle to a dead man! When she passed away in December of 1972 Edith was finally buried close to her sweet William in Lodi, California, not next to her second or third husband."[22]

William George and Edith's service in the South had ended, but the three other Wilson boys would migrate to Reeves and Madison and continue the work in the South. Their efforts at the Hurlbutt Farm would bear fruit. Later reports in the union papers tell of the slow but steady progress there.

"The approach to the sanitarium is a winding road between the two pine-clad ridges, and I was pleasantly surprised to see on one of these ridges a good looking building which I knew was the new sanitarium. Passing on to the school building, I met many old friends.

"I learned that there were about forty persons living on the farm. Of these about twenty were students. Of the other twenty, nearly half were children, and the others were teachers, mechanics, foremen of various lines of work, and sanitarium patients.

"During the day just closing, Dr. Hayward with two or three of the school boys had been sowing field peas.... As the sun was setting and the Sabbath came on, the whole community gathered in a portion of the big dining-hall for worship. Mrs. Hurlbutt was there with the younger people. Her rickshaw being out of repair she had ridden over from the farm house in a buggy drawn by four or five of the younger boys and girls who delight to render any service they can to 'Grandma Hurlbutt.'...

"Sunday I had a long visit with Sister Hurlbutt. She is full of courage regarding the work she has undertaken and is fostering at Reeves. Her whole life seems to be devoted to making a success of the work of educating and training young people for service in the Southland, and in providing a place for the care of the sick. She says she can sell property, and put on Hurlbutt Farm all such improvements as may yet be necessary to fully equip it for self-supporting work, and this she hopes to do soon."[23]

"Hurlbutt Farm lost its sanitarium by fire but the company in charge looks forward to a renewal of the medical work and recently, in harmony with the idea that each center should be active in health work, the school has linked up with the city cafeteria in Chattanooga."[24] A second fire did even more damage. "Hurlbutt Farm School, Reeves, Georgia, has been unfortunate. On the fifteenth of December a fire, set to burn the grass, from a nearby field, destroyed the barn and granary containing hay and grain estimated at about one thousand dollars. Prof. Boynton writes that while they feel the loss keenly, they are not discouraged."[25]

Mother Hurlbutt continued to be active in the area. She helped run a vegetarian cafeteria in Birmingham and returned to Madison College in her later years. Her final days were spent at Madison.

"Another long life of useful service ended this week in the passing away of Sister Emeline Hurlbutt, formerly of Lakeport, California, who spent the past fifteen years in the South. For years she and her husband were interested in the medical and educational work centering at Madison. They purchased a large tract of land near Reeves, Georgia, dedicating it to a similar work. Since the death of her husband several years ago, she has been actively connected with a number of mission centers. About two months ago, when she found that her health was failing, she came to the Madison sanitarium. She passed away the evening of July 18, [1932], aged 88 years, and was laid to rest in Spring Hill Cemetery near Madison. She was a woman of strong faith and a courageous heart. Those who have known her feel that indeed 'a mother in Israel' has gone to her rest."[26]

Georgia Cumberland Academy, a coeducational boarding school on the senior high school level, opened in 1965. It stands as a tribute to the Hurlbutt family and to Edith and William George Wilson.

"... Nathaniel and Emeline Hurlbutt ... were the first Adventists to operate an institution on the GCA [Georgia Cumberland Academy] property. In 1908, Ellen White encouraged the Hurlbutts to move from California to Georgia and support the work being done by E. A. Sutherland in the South. In 1914, the Hurlbutts followed this advice and bought 500 acres of land in Reeves, Georgia. Over the following years they operated a farm, a school, and a sanitarium.

"The Hurlbutts spent the rest of their life working in the South. Before Mrs. Hurlbutt's death in 1932, she donated her land in Reeves to the Layman's Foundation.

"In 1958, constituents of the Georgia-Cumberland Conference began looking for land to start a boarding school. They eventually purchased the Hurlbutt property. The school was built with help from funds raised in the 1964 Penny Campaign. More than 11 tons of pennies were collected, totaling 3,391,861 pennies."[27]

Wilson Boys

Madison beckoned to the three other Wilson boys. Nathaniel Wilson and his new bride headed South right after they were married in October of 1919. They left California to take up their first post of duty at the school their brother William George had given his life to build on the Hurlbutt Farm in Reeves, Georgia. Nathaniel was the purchasing agent there, and Hannah was a cook. After a few months they went to live with Grandma Hurlbutt, and Nathaniel taught Bible while Hannah taught arithmetic and geography. (The 1920 U.S. Census shows Nathaniel and Hannah living with Grandma Hurlbutt.)

In May they returned to California to help Isabella who was not doing well. Two years later they returned to Madison with their two little children. At first, Nathaniel served as a part-time Bible teacher, but when Elder C. V. Leach, the full-time Bible teacher, left to go to West Virginia, Nathaniel took over as full-time Bible teacher. The General Conference Committee voted that his salary would be $15.00 per week.[28]

One of his duties was to promote the Harvest Ingathering Campaign, which he ably led out in with the Tennessee River Conference President Elder H. E. Lysinger.[29] On one trip with Grandma Hurlbutt, they visited Alabama and returned by way of Huntsville where they visited Oakwood Junior College, the training school for black workers.[30] On another occasion "the ministerial band, a group of twenty young men," held weekly evangelistic meeting with N. C. Wilson directing their study and public speaking.[31] The life of the young Bible teacher was busy with various kinds of missionary activities.

After graduating in 1917 from Lodi Academy with his wife to be, Melva LaVern Meyers, Robert Ray (or Ray as he preferred to be called after that) returned to his alma mater to be the manager of the farm and the dairy. When his other brothers migrated to Georgia and Tennessee, he also moved to Madison and became a faculty member, taking charge of their farm and buildings.

The youngest son, Walter Scott Wilson, sustained a severe injury to his right ankle that refused to heal properly, and physicians in California decided to amputate his foot. Upon learning about the situation, Nathaniel appealed to Dr. E. A. Sutherland for medical advice. Walter was called to come down to Madison. Dr. Sutherland consulted with a colleague in Nashville who operated on Walter and saved his foot. A long and close friendship between Dr. Sutherland and the Wilsons followed, lasting many years until Dr. Sutherland's death in 1955.

Walter Wilson lived at Madison College for 33 years, first as a student and later in various administrative

Highly Committed

positions, the last as purchasing agent for both Madison College and Madison hospital, a position he held for twenty years. He and his wife, Teckla Nimlos, had three children, all born and educated at Madison College: Laverne Wilson Dodd, Patricia Wilson Rushing, and William H. (Bill) Wilson. Bill Wilson distinguished himself as a hospital administrator and served several years at the General Conference before taking a position in the Adventist Hospital System in Florida.[32]

The Wilson boys and their families were now all in the south in Madison, Tennessee. They were often referred to as the three tall Wilson boys from Lodi, California. In a short time Nathaniel Carter Wilson would leave them and travel all over the world to answer the call of the church.

William George Wilson's Family

William George Wilson

- Born: March 1, 1888, in Ferndale, California
- Died: February 21, 1915, in Reeves, Georgia, and buried in Lodi, California
- Married: Edith G. PIERCE on June 10, 1910, in California. Edith was born on December 16, 1884, and died on December 7, 1972, in Sonoma, California. The couple had two children, Kenneth and Gladys.

Kenneth James William WILSON

- Born: July 27, 1912, in Boulder, Colorado
- Died: July 13, 2003, in Selma, California
- Married: Ethel Mae AUSHERMAN on August 30, 1935, in Walla Walla, Washington. Ethel was born on December 28, 1914, in Walla Walla, Washington, and died on July 23, 1987, in Thousand Oaks, California. The couple had four children, who are as follows:

Janet Clarice WILSON Kahler

- Born: November 7, 1937
- Married: Tom KAHLER on April 4, 1971. Tom was born on July 27, 1937, in Minneapolis, Minnesota.

Lois Rachel WILSON Moore

- Born: June 4, 1939, in Pisgah, North Carolina
- Married: Marivn MOORE on December 20, 1937, in Keene, Texas. Marivn was born on December 20, 1937, in Peru.

(cont.)

William David (Dave) WILSON
- Born: January 9, 1941, in Portland, Oregon
- Married: Sharon STODDARD on October 27, 1968, in Denver, Colorado. Sharon was born on May 16, 1943.

Ruth Marie WILSON Robertson
- Born: August 2, 1947, in Bakersfield, California
- Married: John Martin ROBERTSON on September 14, 1969. John was born on December 12, 1946.

Gladys Alibel WILSON Mayes
- Born: December 11, 1913, in Reeves, Georgia
- Died: January 21, 2011, in Sonoma, California
- Married: Orville MAYES in 1931 in Gladstone, Oregon. The couple had two children, who are as follows:

Doris Joan MAYES
- Born: December 6, 1934, in Monterey, California
- Died: December 19, 1981

Donna Jean MAYES
- Born: December 6, 1934, in Monterey, California

Highly Committed

Edith Pierce (1884-1972) and William George Wilson married June 1910.

Nathaniel and Emeline Carter Hurlbutt. This wealthy couple had no children of their own and treated the Wilson boys as their family because William Henry had lived with them when young and Grandma Hurlbutt had nursed him back to health when he had typhoid fever. The Hurlbutts were responsible for getting the Wilson family to move from California to the South.

Pioneering in Reeves, Ga. on the Hurlbutt Farm.

William George Wilson's final resting place in Lodi, CA. Engraved on his tombstone are the words "He giveth his beloved sleep" Ps. 127:2. He is buried next to his mother, Isabella and his wife, Edith.

Honoring the Pledge

William George Wilson-Born March 1, 1888, died February 21, 1915, just 27 years old. The picture was taken by the A. Askin studio in Marksdale, Ontario, Canada.

In 1918 widowed Edith Wilson married Walter Wetmore, who had several horses and a wagon. Edith had symptoms that suggested that she had consumption, which was confirmed years later by x-ray. With the two children and four horses they set out for Boulder, hoping the Colorado "rest cure" would work for her as well as it had for William George. It did! The story is told in an exciting way in the book: 1918 Covered Wagon Adventure.

William George Wilson and wife Edith standing in front of the "Scupernong vine" at Hurlbutt Farm, Reeves GA in 1914. Little Kenneth is standing next to his dad and Edith is holding Gladys.

Highly Committed

Western Normal Institute (Lodi Academy) –Class of 1909- William George Wilson in back row with high hair and wife-to-be Edith Pierce to the far right

Chapter Three

Nathaniel and Hannah Wilson

"If you don't like something, change it; if you can't change it, change the way you think about it."
Mary Engelbreit

The *S.S. Leviathan* slowly rose and sank as it dozed in the New York harbor, seemingly unaware of the commotion all around it. Crew members went in and out. It was Friday, May 1, 1925, and passengers were checking in their trunks and luggage and making final arrangements for the long trip that would begin the next evening.

"When are we getting on?" little Neal quizzed his dad. Four-year-old Neal, dressed like a little sailor, ran up and down on the wooden dock trying to release some of his pent up energy. His two-year-old sister Clarice stood quietly beside her mother.

"When are we leaving?" Neal queried again, a little louder. He wanted to take charge of the situation and get the show on the road. "Daddy, I'm ready to go!"

"We're not leaving until tomorrow night, but we have to get everything ready today, Neal. This is supposed to be the largest ship in America. It will have plenty of passengers and take on a lot of cargo. We must get everything ready today before the Sabbath. We're going to be gone for ten years, so we must take as much as we can."

"Wow! That's a looong time." Precocious Neal dragged out the word "long." He continued talking, "Can't we come back home a little sooner? I'll be almost big by then and all of my friends will be almost big, too." If you were to ask Neal how old he was, he would hold up five fingers and tell you quickly, "Four, but I'm almost five. I'll be five in two months."

"The people need us, so we'll be gone a long time. It's too expensive to keep coming back and forth." Neal was quiet for a while as he pondered this statement.

Nathaniel Carter Wilson and his wife, Hannah, had just returned from a four-week vacation spent at their family home in Lodi, California. The Mission Board had been writing letters back and forth to get the family ready for the overseas trip, and they had instructed them to see their family and friends because a term of service was ten years. So, having made the trip to see family in California, they were ready to go.

The *Southern Union Worker* stated, "Mr. and Mrs. N. C. Wilson, of Madison, are back again from their visit to California. They plan to be at Madison for about a month before leaving for Africa, where Brother Wilson is booked to head to the Bechuana Mission field. We are glad to see these good people back with us again, and will be sorry to have them leave us soon. However, we realize that our loss will be a gain to this African mission field."[33]

While waiting in line, the young pastor pulled out several sheets of paper from his coat pocket. He reread the top letter from Des Moines, Iowa, dated October 22, 1924.

"Dear Brother Wilson: The General Conference secretarial department informed us that you were willing to respond to a call to the mission field. We therefore placed your name before the General Conference Committee, and they have invited you to accept the position of superintendent of the Bechuanaland Mission.

"As you probably know, this is the field where Elder W. H. Anderson has worked for several years, and where Dr. Kretchmar has now engaged in medical missionary work. The field is not very well developed so far as our work is concerned, but the opportunities there are very great. Dr. Kretchmar has a splendid mission started, and other missions are to be opened in the near future. There are a number of native workers employed in the work there, but that portion of the field where Elder Anderson did most of his work is now a part of the Orange River Conference, and the Bechuanaland Mission field is quite largely undeveloped. It presents perhaps the greatest opportunity for mission work of any one section of Africa, because in that field the natives live in large villages, ranging from five to thirty and 40,000, and they are a very good class of natives.

"I hope you will find it in your heart to respond to this call. I assure you that you will receive a hearty welcome by the brethren in Africa. We would like to have you plan to go forward at the earliest possible date. Of course it will be necessary to secure permits, and this will require perhaps two and a half months.

"I should be sailing for Africa November 12, and shall be in Washington at the General Conference Office just before that date. I wish it might be possible for you to write me your decision there.

"You understand, of course, that you will hear from the secretary of the General Conference, with the official notice of this appointment, and with instruction as to how you must proceed as regards medical examination, etc. But if you are clear in your mind concerning the call, I shall be glad for just a word from you.

"Truly your brother, W. H. Branson."[34]

A Letter

Neal and Clarice were busy looking at and counting the ships in the ocean. Nathaniel pulled out another letter and quickly read it through again. This one was dated March 18, 1925.

"Dear Brother Wilson: I have your letter of March 10, raising a number of questions with reference to your appointment to the African field. We are glad to know you are planning to get away about the first of April. Be sure to write Elder J. L. Shaw, the treasurer, as soon as you have definitely made up your mind as to the date of sailing, for at this season of the year travel across the Atlantic is pretty heavy, and he will need all the time you can give him in order to secure suitable accommodations for you.

"I note what you say about Elder Hankins' recommendation of the P. & O. Line from England on to South Africa. Brother Beddoe, who has been in South Africa, tells me that our brethren there have advised our workers to use the Union Castle Line, inasmuch as the P. & O. has such a heavy tourist traffic that the boats are always crowded, especially on the outward trip to South Africa and Australia. Coming from South Africa to England, of course, the traffic is lighter and one is assured of more comfort on the boat. It is because of this condition that the African brethren recommend the Union Castle Line. However, this will be a matter for you to work out with our Transportation Department.

"Now as to your location in Africa. We understand you are to take the superintendency of the Bechuanaland Protectorate Mission Field, and Brother Branson says you will practically have to open up the work in that field. All they have there at present is a little dispensary work carried on by Dr. Kretchmar. Therefore we judge there was no superintendent's home as yet, and of course no equipment. As to the question of taking any equipment, such as desk or typewriter, with you, we here would have no authority to give you advice. Such advice would have to come from the Division. If you already own a typewriter it might be a good thing to take it along, especially if you can do so as part of your luggage.

"As to taking a Ford car, I do not know what the cost would be, but I do not think it would pay to take it. You would not find roads in Bechuanaland such as we have in this country. Your sewing machine of course you should take, that is, a treadle machine. An electric machine would be of no use in that part of Africa.

"You ask if anyone else will be going to Africa when you go. Not if you plan to sail in April. Brother L. L. Moffitt, I think, is planning to sail May 2. Our Transportation Department is arranging for two other families on that same date, Brother and Sister A. V. Edwards, and Dr. and Mrs. Archie Tong. Dr. Tong will go only as far as England, where he will take some postgraduate work before going on to Africa. If you decide you would like to go with this party, better write to Brother Shaw at once, so that he may make reservations for you, for as I have said, traffic toward England at this time of year is heavy, and reservations must be made well in advance.

"Hoping that I have answered your questions in a measure at least, and trusting everything will work out satisfactorily for your journey, I am, yours very sincerely, Elder C. K. Myers, Secretary"[35]

Nathaniel thought about that counsel and was glad that he had packed his typewriter and Hannah had her treadle sewing machine. He and Hannah used the typewriter a lot to send letters back to the States about how the work was progressing. His family said that Hannah used the typewriter the most and that most of the letters and speeches of Nathaniel were typed and perfected by the diligent and multi-talented Hannah.

Nathaniel smiled and poked out his chest a bit as he looked at the news clip he had torn out of his union paper. He was happy to be an ordained minister now, fully qualified to preach the gospel and be a superintendent. The brethren had laid hands on him just before he left the college.

"Special services were held on Sabbath, April 11, when Brother N. C. Wilson was ordained to the gospel ministry. Elder Lysinger delivered the sermon, Professor Thompson offered the prayer, and the charge was given by Elder Wells. On Sunday evening a farewell meeting was held in the chapel. Short talks were made by Brother and Sister Hankins and Mrs. Druillard, former missionaries to Africa, to which field Elder Wilson is going. There were a number of other short speeches. In view of the high esteem in which they are held, and as a small token of appreciation of their valued services here, they were presented with a steamer rug, a brief case, and a purse."[36]

His luggage checked in and his tickets secure, Nathaniel and his family went back to the hotel to get ready for the Sabbath.

50th Anniversary

There was a great emphasis by the Seventh-day Adventist Church leaders to send missionaries overseas into foreign fields in 1924 and 1925–1924 was the fiftieth anniversary of the sailing of John Nevins Andrews to Switzerland as our first overseas missionary in 1874.

"The Autumn Council held in Des Moines, Iowa, October 14–23, [1924], was a memorable occasion. It was a great foreign missionary council, in which the Lord spoke definitely through the leaders present, representing the strength of the homeland with its great resources. We were reminded by the reports given by the division leaders, nearly all of whom were present, that now is the time to finish the work in all the world, for the Lord is creating the opportunity by laying it upon hearts in the most remote parts of the earth to seek in the spirit of inquiry the message that His people have for these days.

"This keynote was struck in the presence of a full attendance of committee members and local conference presidents from North America, with representatives from each of the foreign divisions except Australia....

"Speaking for the African Division, W. H. Branson said that in the short interim between the General Conference session and the present time more believers had been won than in all previous years....

"In the first business session the treasurer was given opportunity to present his report, for it is always recognized in the Autumn Councils that the most important item to consider is the distribution of the means that the faithfulness of our people provides for maintaining and supplying workers for the world field. J. L. Shaw presented an operating statement for the first eight months of 1924. He also presented some interesting facts relative to mission gifts during the last six years. Especially encouraging was the increase of these gifts from our believers during the six years ending with 1923. In 1918 our total gifts to missions, as reported in the Sixty-cent-a-week Fund, were $1,250,990; in 1923 they were $2,307,069, or a gain of more than a million dollars.

Highly Committed

"Words of appreciation of this splendid showing were voiced by representatives of the foreign fields, and it was moved by Elder Evans, of the Far East, and seconded by Elder Branson, of Africa, that we express our thanks to the officers of the General Conference, the union conferences, and local conferences, and also to the donors, for this excellent report, indicating so large an increase in the gifts of our people to foreign missions. The motion was carried unanimously by a standing vote."[37]

"The Autumn Council, held on the fiftieth anniversary of the beginning of our foreign mission work, has had laid before it the most earnest and pressing calls for assistance in holding the ground already gained in foreign lands; and in facing the call of God's providence in the great world field, which is opening before us wider and deeper year by year, bringing us ever into contact with new tribes and tongues and with the needs of newly awakening millions who must hear the message that God has committed to us, we see that the emergencies of one year expand into yet greater emergencies of need the following year. The pressure of the final harvest hour is upon us. The message is winning souls by many thousands every year. We are entering the time long-expected of the 'loud cry' of the third angel. To name but one item, we place on record one appeal that reached us during the Council by cable from the Lake Titicaca Mission field, pleading for help as follows:

"'Two thousand in baptismal classes 1924. Calls beyond us. Situation critical in established work. Consideration needed.'

"Not in that field alone, but literally in all the four quarters of the earth, such a situation has been placed before us at this Council as to indicate clearly that God's providence calls to us to maintain and extend our forces on every missionary front.

"Upon our ears comes the cry of Christ our Leader, saying in the language of the spirit of prophecy:

"'And still our General, who never makes a mistake, says to us, "Advance. Enter new territory. Lift up the standard in every land. 'Arise, shine: for thy light is come, and the glory of the Lord is risen upon thee.'"'–*Testimonies,* Vol. VI, pp. 28, 29."[38]

And in another paper on the same subject titled "The Autumn Council Calls for Help" we find this account:

"We wish every brother and sister could have heard the stirring reports at the recent Autumn Council in Des Moines, Iowa. Surely the message is going.

"Elder W. A. Spicer, president of the General Conference, just returned from Africa, said: 'Hundreds are turning to us. Thousands wait for us to come and teach them.'

"Speaking of the ingathering of souls he said: 'There is another Titicaca interest in Africa.'

"From darkest paganism souls are pressing toward the light, and want the Adventist missionary to come and teach them. This is God's hour of salvation in Africa."[39]

The General Conference did all it could to recruit workers to go overseas and to create an interest and an urgency for finishing the work. The cover of December 4, 1924, issue of *The Advent Review and Sabbath Herald* featured a poem they hoped would catch the spirit of this message.

Heed Ye the Call

Bertha D. Martin

There's a whisper in the air,
O ye sons of mine, and daughters,
Soft and low as from afar,
Like the murmuring of waters;
And my heart has ceased its beating,
Lest I lose the sweet refrain,
Even now I hear repeating,
"Jesus soon will come again."

There's another cry tonight,
O ye sons of mine, and daughters
Loud and arrogant with might,
Like the sound of rushing waters;
And my heart is faint with sorrow,
And the night is filled with pain,
For the millions who are heeding
The alluring cry of gain.

There's a moaning on the air,
O ye sons of mine, and daughters,
Earth's and heaven's mingled there,
Like the sound of troubled waters;
And my heart is racked with anguish,
And my soul is sick with fear,
For my children who are sleeping
As the day of God draws near.[40]

This special emphasis paid off, and a great number of missionaries signed up for foreign service in 1924 and 1925. The assistant secretary of the General Conference in a front-page article announced, "We thank God that each year witnesses marked advance in the movement of heralds of the message into all lands. The record for 1925 is now ready to be reported to our people. There has been a steady movement of missionaries every month of the year. We are greatly cheered as we pause to recount the names in the list given herewith.

"There was a total of 234 who went to the fields during the year. Of these, 175 were recruits; and fifty-nine returned to their mission posts following furloughs. The number of recruits exceeds those of 1924 by thirty-three. How encouraging to know that 175 workers have moved out to strengthen present centers and to establish many new ones!

"North America, Europe, and Australia have shared in supplying these missionaries. Australia supplied nine, Europe thirty-six, and North America 128. These older conferences have given of their best, and at very

Highly Committed

real sacrifice. But 'the liberal soul shall be made fat: and he that watereth shall be watered also himself.' Heaven is blessing every conference that has been releasing these loyal workers for the mission fields.

"To the four winds these workers have gone—to various parts of India, to China, Korea, Japan, Malaysia, and the Philippines. Into Africa they have gone, along both the east and west coast, from Egypt in the north to the Cape in the south; and not a few have gone into the very interior of the Dark Continent. They have entered South America, going to the north, south, east, and west. They have gone to Mexico, Central America, and the West Indies. They went to Iceland in the north and the South Seas in the antarctic, and to islands far and near.

"These recruits are evangelists, teachers, doctors, nurses, and colporteurs. This list includes twelve doctors. And so these workers, with various training and experience, have gone out arm in arm, preachers, medical evangelists, teachers, and salesmen,—all uniting under God to push on the triumphs of the message. We will all join in supporting them with our funds. We will all unite in unceasing prayer that God may keep and strengthen these faithful men and women in their heaven-assigned task."[41]

The Thirteenth Sabbath offering for Africa increased as the members heard of this special emphasis on sending missionaries to the Dark Continent. There was an overflow of more than $18,000. President W. A. Spicer who was visiting in Africa at the time sent the following cable message:

"'Thirteenth Sabbath school overflow set twenty-five languages singing Hallelujah.' Thirty years ago the message was being proclaimed in only two or three languages in Africa. Today thousands of believers scattered over Central and South Africa sing their joy in twenty-five languages because of a surprise gift of over $18,000. We did it through this Sabbath school. This should be an inspiration to us every Sabbath, when the familiar class envelope is passed around."[42]

Hannah's History

It was in answer to the call for missionaries that Nathaniel and Hannah were preparing to embark for Africa. As they boarded the *SS Leviathan,* they began the journey to a new life overseas in service to the Lord. The liner moved ahead at top speed, taking them across the ocean. Neal and Clarice had problems sleeping that night as they tried to get used to the up and down movement of the big ship. They were still excited about going so far. They had met the other missionaries going with them and also found out that the quite famous missionary from China, Dr. Harry Miller, was traveling with them to Europe for some study before he returned to China. The Moffitt's had a little girl, Juanita, who was just about their age, and the Edward's had a little boy named Dean. They were happy to have some friends to play with.

Dr. Archie Tong had been in the same 1917 graduating class at Lodi with Nathaniel, so they already knew each other. The families got better acquainted on the long trip.

"Nat, how did you meet Hannah?"

This was a subject Nathaniel liked to talk about, and he jumped right in. "Hannah was born in Roseau, Minnesota, and I, as you know, grew up in California.[43] She wanted a Christian education, which was difficult since she came from a large family—twelve children, to be exact. Her first schooling was in their family's home with an older brother as her teacher. For a few years as a young girl she walked five miles each way to school, even through rain or snow.

"At thirteen it was necessary for her to live with a family in town where she worked for room and board, enabling her to finish the eighth grade. Anyway, when she was 17, she and her sister Esther left Minnesota for California with only ten dollars between them. Somehow they made it to California. They stayed with an uncle in Turlock for the summer and worked in the orchards picking fruit and in a packing house.

"In September of 1917 she was baptized in a canal and became a member of the Adventist Church. With the money they had earned, they were able to enroll at Lodi Academy. It was her first year at Lodi Academy, and I was a theology student at PUC when we met in 1917. The more I saw her, the more I admired her. She was quiet and very efficient.

"We met again at a party given by my brother Ray and his wife, LaVerne. I came home to Lodi to visit my family at Christmas, and I was invited to a Christmas party at Lodi Academy for the few students who remained to work during Christmas vacation. And there she was. Hannah was in charge of the kitchen and the food services. We had a lovely evening together.

"From then on we corresponded with each other while I attended PUC and Hannah remained at Lodi Academy. The principal soon assigned her to manage the academy cafeteria and help with bookkeeping in the office. While doing all of that, she was able to graduate with her diploma from Lodi Academy." You could see the pride on his face as Nathaniel gave this account.

Hannah chimed in, "Nat was so kind and considerate all the time, and gentlemanly. He started writing me regularly. In one of his letters he told me that Elder W. H. Anderson spoke in one of the evening chapels and he was taken up with the idea of going to Africa. He felt that there was a great need. So I knew that if we married we might end up going to the mission field.

"Shortly after I got to know him a little better at the Christmas party, I was surprised when my professor came to our worship room and in front of all the girls said, 'I have a box of chocolates for Miss Hannah Wallin from President Wilson.' Wow! At first I thought it was from the United States President Woodrow Wilson, and I wondered how he knew me! But then I realized it was from Nathaniel Wilson who must have been dreaming he might become a president of some mission someplace someday. Shortly after that I sent him a thank you note, and we started corresponding regularly. We were engaged only one month before we got married.

"Our wedding was in his brother Ray's home. It was a small wedding with only a few relatives and the faculty from the academy. We were given a set of *Testimonies for the Church* as a wedding present. There couldn't have been a better present. One of the professors sang. We were engaged from September 1 to October 1, 1919, our wedding date. After the wedding, we left that same evening by train for the self-supporting school at Reeves, Georgia. Let's see, that means we've been married for almost six years now, actually five and one half." Hannah laughed as she reflected on this.

Postcards

Their third child, Ruth, likes to joke about the trip to Africa. "I was on the *SS Leviathan,* and no one knew it," Ruth said. My mother was pregnant with me, and I was born shortly after we arrived in Lusaka, Zambia (then Northern Rhodesia) on November 12, 1925. I was the first Wilson child born overseas."

The trip to Africa took more than a month with a short visit in England and a change of ships. They were sorry to leave the *SS Leviathan* for the *SS Saxon,* but each day took them closer to their destination of Cape Town, South Africa.

One postcard dated May 7, 1925, to Inez Wallin gave this information: "We are getting further and further away all the time, but we can hardly realize it. We are enjoying our trip very much as we haven't any of us been sick yet. We will get into South Hampton tomorrow night but won't anchor until Sabbath morning. We have had an unusually smooth sea they say and not so very cold. Everything nice and clean. Boat is 900 feet long and twelve stories above water. Love from all, Hannah."

Another postcard to Enos Wallin dated May 30, 1925, read, "It seems strange to think that we are so far away, almost to Cape Town. Expect to land Monday morning. We have had a very pleasant voyage, fine weather, and have felt well. It was rough for about three days. We have seen a number of whales spouting, also

Highly Committed

a great number of flying fish especially near the equator. It was very hot there for a couple of days, especially in our cabins where the breeze didn't strike us. Of course we spent all our time on deck except for mealtime and at night. Love to all, Hannah and Nat."

They were received with open arms by the leaders in Cape Town, South Africa, when they arrived. They were soon ready to go onward to Bechuanaland. Today Bechuanaland is known as Botswana, which is located south of the equator and is dissected by the tropic of Capricorn. It is in both the eastern and southern hemispheres. It is a landlocked country in southern Africa, bordered by the countries of South West Africa (Namibia), Northern Rhodesia (Zambia), Rhodesia (Zimbabwe), and South Africa.

The overseas missionary experiences of the Wilson family had begun.

Dean Edwards, Juanita Moffitt, Neal Wilson, and Clarice Wilson. May 1925 in New York

Clarice (age 5) and Neal (age 7) in Lusaka, 1927

Nathaniel and Hannah Wilson June 7, 1929.

Nathaniel and Hannah Wilson sailed out of New York for Africa on the largest Ocean liner of that time, the S. S. Leviathan as depicted in this post card sent back to her family.

Highly Committed

Missionary group on the S.S. Leviathan, May 1925. Left to right: L. Moffitt family with Juanita, Dr. and Mrs. Archie Tonge, the Edwards family with Dean, the Wilsons.

Nathaniel Wilson, Superintendent of North Rhodesia Mission Field, and his family, 1925.

Chapter Four

Spreading the Gospel in Africa

"Age considers; youth ventures."
Rabindranath Tagore

William H. Branson stood up quickly from behind his wooden desk and greeted the family who had been ushered into his office. "Welcome Brother and Sister Wilson and family," he added as he looked at Neal and Clarice. "Have a seat. I'm glad you finally made it to Africa. How was your trip?"

The Wilsons gave a short account of their voyage. After leaving New York on the largest ship in the world, the *SS Leviathan,* in May, which took them to England, they continued their voyage on the *SS Saxon* and arrived in Cape Town in early June. Elder Branson had been appointed five years earlier in 1920 by the brethren to be the first president of the newly formed African Division, which was growing rapidly. It then comprised three conferences and sixteen missions, with fifty-two churches and 2,705 members.

Elder Branson would continue to lead that fast-growing field until 1930, when he became vice president of the General Conference and in 1950 president of the General Conference. Branson was a strong administrator, a grounded spiritual leader, and an authority on early missions in southern Africa. He was only ten years older than Nathaniel Wilson, but denominational administration had seen great leadership potential in him. It would prove to be a blessing for the newly ordained Nathaniel to work with him.

"Well, we'll get you settled in Lusaka. We have a decent house for you there. We'll take you on a shopping trip for some beginning supplies and get your family settled in. We'll take you up to Rusangu Mission and a few other places after you get settled in. It's a very challenging work here, but God is blessing!" Branson said.

"Let me tell you a little about the work here," he continued. "The Adventist work in Africa started among the Europeans. Actually, a gentleman by the name of Wilson, imagine that, helped to get our church going here on this continent. Have you ever heard that story?"

Without stopping to find out if they had actually heard the story, Branson continued. "Back in 1878, a man by the name of William Hunt who had heard Elder J. N. Loughborough preach in California came to South Africa with some Adventist literature, *Signs of the Times,* and other pamphlets, and he started prospecting for diamonds in the diamond fields at Kimberley, South Africa. While searching for diamonds, he began to seek for souls.

"Hunt handed out some literature to a man by the name of J. H. C. Wilson who was a former Wesleyan Methodist preacher. That Wilson and several others started studying the literature and decided to keep the Sabbath and become Seventh-day Adventists. They felt that Adventists were correct in their interpretation of the Scriptures and that the seventh day was definitely the Sabbath. That Wilson, J. H. C. Wilson, wrote a letter to the *Review and Herald* telling them that he had read copies of *Signs of the Times* and that he had taken a stand for the truth and was determined, with the help and blessing of God, to keep all His commandments, including the fourth. We don't know anything else about that Wilson or whether he became a member of our church. But we do know that his letter caused the brethren in America great joy, and they forwarded more literature to South Africa and made plans to send some workers to make contact with these believers."

Highly Committed

Branson stopped for a moment to give Neal and Clarice a piece of paper and some pencils because they were getting restless. This done he continued his account. "Seven years later a chain of events began that resulted in the arrival of the first Adventist missionaries in the Cape Colony. Pieter Wessels, a Dutch farmer, became sick with tuberculosis. He read a tract on divine healing and went to a minister to seek healing through prayer and anointing. The minister said that the principle was correct, but he didn't want to carry out the injunction of the Bible.

"Pieter Wessels went home, told the Lord that he had done everything he could, and then asked Him to heal him upon the condition that he would be obedient to all of God's requirements. His prayer was answered. He was miraculously healed. Shortly after that his conscience bothered him about operating his dairy on the Sabbath, which to him meant Sunday, and when he mentioned this to a friend, he was told that if he were so conscientious he ought to keep the Bible Sabbath, which was the seventh day or Saturday.

"Wessels started studying the Bible and became convinced that the seventh day was indeed the Bible Sabbath. And that's when Pieter met this man William Hunt who was passing out literature. When they learned that there was an entire organization back in Washington, an organized church in America where all the members kept the Sabbath, they decided to make a request for a minister to be sent to them. And they sent a check for $250 to defray the expenses of the preacher. When this letter was read at the 1886 General Conference, the audience was so moved that it spontaneously rose and sang the doxology. And they sent some missionaries to get the work going. We are now moving northward up into Rhodesia and Nyasaland and Congo. That's our work. The gospel must go to the nationals. Every nation, kindred, tongue, and people. That's our mission. And God is blessing. If we only had more workers!"

Seeing that the children were getting restless again, Branson stood up, ending his little story. "Let's get you people settled," he said as he ushered them out of his office.

Getting Settled

It is not clear whether the Wilson family ever moved to Bechuanaland. The family remembers their first house in Africa being in Lusaka. Nathaniel may have served only a short time in his first leadership position as superintendent of the Bechuanaland Field before he was assigned to his second position in Northern Rhodesia. A previous leader in the area, Elder Thompson, was ordained and moved to the Zambezi Union, leaving Northern Rhodesia open and in need of leadership. "F. E. Thompson, superintendent of Northern Rhodesia, was ordained, and takes the Zambesi [*sic*] Union. Elder N. C. Wilson, who had just arrived from Tennessee, takes the Northern Rhodesia superintendency, made vacant by this call."[44] In addition to the vacancy, having a pregnant wife and two small children may have influenced the brethren not to send Nathaniel and his family into the deep bush country of Bechuanaland.

After spending six weeks in Cape Town getting oriented to Africa, the Wilson family proceeded northward to Rusangu Mission in Rhodesia. In mid September they made the long trip from there to Lusaka in Northern Rhodesia where Nathaniel took over as superintendent of the Northern Rhodesia Mission field, and Hannah assumed the post of secretary-treasurer.

At first everything was so new and different. They were surrounded by people who spoke different languages in a country where winter was summer, and people drove on the left side of the road instead of the right. But everybody adjusted quickly.

Just about anything anybody needed, or wanted, could be found in the outdoor African market. There was a small market not far from where the Wilsons lived that sold the basics–fruits, vegetables, tea, eggs, and firewood. These small markets were omnipresent in Lusaka, the capital of Northern Rhodesia.

The central market downtown was an amazing hub of activity. Hundreds of stalls, tables, and booths leaned dangerously against each other yet they did not fall. Wagon wheels, bright cloths, jewelry, American dresses,

African art, fish, avocados, nuts, and bananas—absolutely everything could be found there, or bought there, if the price was right. A strange mixture of raw scents, both good and horrible, baffled the nose. No price was fixed even though numbers were written in scrawny characters on pieces of cardboard stuck on each product. Only tourists paid the written prices. The unwritten law was to barter for a better price. Everything was negotiable, and toward the end of the day the tired merchants were willing to part with their products at the cheapest prices so they could go home.

Hannah Wilson became an expert at bargaining and buying food for her family at the market. She was an excellent hostess and always had some visitors sitting around the family table. She also had a plot of ground for a garden in which she planted and harvested most of the food they needed. Her house was surrounded by fruit trees and bushes—pineapples, avocadoes, bananas, guavas, limes, and mangoes.

Snakes

While Nathaniel was out on mission trips often on his 2½ horsepower Raleigh motorcycle (and he must have gone on hundreds of them as reported in the division papers and the *Review and Herald*), Hannah assumed much of the responsibility for the growing family and for the supervision of the mission office. She got the kids up in the morning, taught them their school lessons, took care of their medical needs, and continued to entertain their many visitors. Each evening she made sure the house was free of snakes. She checked in corners and under furniture, stepping on any baby cobras that might have found their way into the house. She also became adept at killing larger snakes. In one place where they lived, baboons would sit in the mango trees near the house. Afraid that they might cause some harm to the family or carry off her little ones, Hannah learned to fire the shotgun to scare the baboons away.

The Wilsons were missed at Madison College. His former president of the Tennessee-River Conference, Elder H. E. Lysinger, wrote in the *Southern Union Worker* that although tithes showed a gain, Harvest Ingathering was down, and it was due in part to the fact that they had lost "Brother N. C. Wilson, the Bible teacher at Madison, who was one of our faithful Harvest Ingatherers, [who] had been called to Africa."[45] Madison College's support of the Wilsons was evident one time when they took up an offering to buy a stereopticon and other evangelistic equipment for the Wilsons when they heard of the need in his field.

Nathaniel was glad he had brought his old typewriter with him, for he sent hundreds of letters all around the world and especially to the leaders of the church to let them know how the work was progressing in Africa. Appeals had to be made for more workers and for offerings to open up new work and new mission stations. Scores of letters from his typewriter were printed in *The Advent Review and Sabbath Herald* and the union papers. Hannah typed most of the letters after Nathaniel gave her a pencil sketch of the thoughts he wanted to express.

One of his earliest letters published in the States gave a report on how God was working through extraordinary ways to tell Africa about Jesus and His soon coming.

"We see many evidences of God's special blessing upon the efforts put forth in this field [Northern Rhodesia]. Truly the seed which has been sown in past years is today springing up and bearing abundant fruit.

"Recently a general meeting was held in a section where a group of our teachers are working. We knew that these teachers have been doing faithful work, but it seemed a little hard to get very accurate reports from them. At the close of one of the meetings, we asked all to stay who had been in the baptismal class for the required two years, and who desired to be baptized. About fifty stayed. I said to Brother W. Mason, who was speaking, 'Surely these people do not understand what your interpreter said,' so it was all again carefully explained. But none went out. So we began examining each one, and found thirty-eight who were ready in every way for the sacred rite of baptism. That afternoon they were baptized, and what a happy group these new members of the church were!

Highly Committed

"In a group of villages far to the west we have a few baptized believers. They are so far away, and the paths to their villages are so rough that our mission workers very seldom visit them. But they have been faithful in attending camp-meeting year by year, although it required a walk of six days. A few weeks ago we asked one of our native ministers to visit these people. He stayed with them for two weeks, preaching in their villages and encouraging them to be faithful. Upon his return the other day, he reported that fourteen have been studying faithfully week by week, although without the encouragement of a teacher, and they have learned so well that they are ready for baptism.

"The faithfulness and loyalty of our native believers, although many times isolated, is a source of joy to us. Interest is springing up and calls are coming from unexpected places. God is making bare His mighty arm in this sin-darkened and superstition-bound land, to save those whose hearts are seeking for truth."[46]

Establishing Schools

The procedure for building up the work was at first to establish a village school with grades one to three with all lessons being taught in the indigenous languages. A number of the small village schools joined together to send their students to a central school where they could finish grades four and five. Then hopefully a mission boarding school and a station could be established. The students would be separated from their home influences, which often included the wrong diet, tobacco, and alcohol and many dangerous philosophies such as spiritism, witchcraft, and animism. They were also taught manual labor and the principles of the Bible.

Many national teachers who went through the schools were given certificates from the government. They could now teach schools, but they were also evangelists. Most of the nationals had extraordinary teaching and preaching abilities. Every other year these workers would meet for an institute that lasted three or four weeks. Problems were discussed, better methods of teaching were demonstrated, doctrinal issues were considered, and plans to strengthen the educational system were adopted.

When the school year was over, there was usually six to eight weeks of opportunity for the teachers to preach in the villages. Candidates for baptism and church membership were carefully instructed and selected. Most were put in a baptismal class that lasted two to four years, and they became prospective members on probation. When they were examined for baptism, they were not asked, "Do you believe in the second coming of Christ?" But they were told to explain in detail the signs and nature of Christ's second coming. Each doctrinal belief had to be explained in a similar fashion. The standards were high, and the nationals were challenged to meet them.

The camp meetings were additional opportunities to teach members about the truth. These were thrilling experiences where sermon after sermon was preached starting early in the morning. Sometimes snakes would creep into the crowd of people sitting on the ground, and there would be a momentary pause as those around jumped up and attempted to kill the intruder. It was thrilling to see thousands of people coming from their villages following the foot trails that had been beaten in the high weeds. The members carried their kettles and "mealies," or cornmeal, for food as they walked to the meetings.[47]

Nathaniel always felt that despite the many difficulties the workers encountered the gospel was winning the day against the forces of darkness and heathenism. He praised God for his workers and the outstanding job they were doing. Sometimes help came from unexpected sources—young school boys, in some instances, who had spent only a few months in one of our village schools shared the joy of the Lord with their family and friends.

The Advent Review and Sabbath Herald gave an account of how this happened. "Brother S. M. Konigmacher, who is pioneering the work between Bechuanaland and Northern Rhodesia, wrote me just a few days ago that he had been out on an extended trip, many miles into the interior, far back beyond any place where he supposed the influence of our work had gone, and was astonished to find four or five companies of believers who were holding their Sabbath meetings. They were worshiping the true God, have thrown away their idols, given up their tobacco, and were struggling toward the light of this truth. He investigated to find out how it came about, and found that some boys who had been in one of the seven or eight outschools established in other parts of the field, had gone through that country, and everywhere told the story of what the Lord had done for them, and the people had accepted their testimony.

"Elder N.C. Wilson, superintendent of the Northern Rhodesia Mission, is visiting a village where one of our mission school boys settled a few years ago, and where, since then, a large number have accepted the truth as a result of his simple teaching. This boy went back home to his village, as many others have gone, and we forgot all about him; but he sent in his appeal, and Brother Wilson finds that a large number there have accepted the message through his efforts. Elder Wilson adds: 'The truth has power. In this district there are many villages calling for schools. They have sent representatives many times during the past year, asking for even one teacher, but we have been unable to answer the calls. Brother Robinson is going with me to this place. I trust we may be able to find one teacher at least for the struggling company of new believers.'"[48]

Nathaniel's optimistic attitude and his emphasis on evangelism persuaded the brethren in October of 1927 to elect him to his third leadership position as the superintendent of a larger territory, the South East African Union, which was headquartered in Blantyre, Nyasaland (Malawi). Hannah served as secretary-treasurer again as well as being a teacher, mother, and doctor for their family. The family moved from Lusaka to Blantyre (Malawi).

Traveling in 1920s

These leadership positions required a great deal of travel. In the mid 1920s travel was a difficult proposition. For trips under 100 miles, Nathaniel usually rode his 2½-horsepower motorcycle. His bed was bundled up, tied down, and carried on the back of the motorcycle. On longer trips, he took the mission's old Ford truck, which he loaded down with his tent and other supplies. Often times they had to take a train to the end of the line and then look for a truck that would take them the rest of the distance.

On one of his postcards to his brother Walter Wilson, he wrote, "I suppose I live in a tent out in the wild about six months each year and about three months at our mission stations. With general meetings out of my territory, I get about two months or six weeks at home." Lake Nyasa had a government boat service once every month, which meant it was not too often. Even then, the schedule was subject to cancellations and changes.

On some of his explorations into North Nyasaland, he found many bridges washed away. "We drove over about 100 miles of trail where only one vehicle had preceded us and that was a Hupmobile car. We were the second machine and the first truck," he wrote on the postcard. Often they had to rebuild bridges that had been washed out or rotted away. Often they would drive the truck into shallow water to cross a river. Fortunately, the nationals pushed them out if they got stuck. The railroads only went so far. Many of the mission stations that were established were 700 or more miles from the last railway terminal and the base of supplies.

Once when he was traveling in his old Model-T Ford, visiting camp meetings and the mission stations, his group found the road very rough, and with the heavy load, the main leaf in the rear spring broke. The body of the car settled down upon the rear axle housing, and the car came to a dead stop.

There were no other cars in that whole district, and it was seventy miles to the nearest garage. Nathaniel had other appointments waiting. If they made camp and sent a runner to Blantyre for a new spring, that would result in a four-day delay while they camped by the roadside. Brother J. I. Robison who was traveling with them improvised with his hatchet. He took the African cook into the forest and asked him to pick out a tree that was tough and strong. He selected a straight limb as big around as his wrist and trimmed and fashioned it down to about the spring size, only thicker. He then asked the boy to get several strips of strong bark from the forest, like that which he had often seen the natives use in tying up their bundles.

Highly Committed

The cook was soon back, and they jacked up the car until the spring was in its normal position, and then with the bark cord, they bound the makeshift leaf firmly to the spring. They then let the weight of the loaded car down on the spring. It held! They carried on, examining the spring at intervals. Needless to say, they were happy to reach Blantyre only about two hours behind schedule.[49]

Hannah recounts in one of her letters to Nathaniel about a scary experience while he was traveling. "Last Tuesday about five o'clock I had a good scare. I was in the office writing, getting the Sabbath School report ready, etc. Neal came running and crying, and the blood was running out of his nose and mouth. He told me he had a stick in his mouth and fell on it.

"I got some salt water quickly and had him gargle. I could see two cuts; only a fraction of an inch and the stick would have gone right down his throat and it might have killed him, so we have much to be thankful for.

"I sent for Dr. McFarlin as I was afraid it might swell badly or something but when he came Neal was feeling much better, and he said that it would be alright. He said all there was to do was to have him gargle with salt water or Boric acid water. He has had a hard time eating, but it is almost healed now, so I can hardly see it." Hannah was coping, but she longed for the help and love of her husband. She ended her letter with this: "We will be looking forward with pleasure to your coming, and surely hope you come on Friday as we miss you so much on Sabbath. Lots of love and kisses from us all."

Entering New Territories

In spite of the travel difficulties, Elder Wilson wrote in one of his letters about the progress of the work in unentered territories. "I am sure there never has been a time during the history of our work in this union when the door stood so wide open for the third angel's message as today. Whichever way we turn we are confronted with most earnest appeals for help from those standing sorely in need of the blessed truth intrusted [sic] to us. In sections long ago entered by our workers, in sections only recently occupied, in vast stretches of unentered country with their unnumbered throngs of judgment-bound souls, the doors stand wide open....

"As our committee meets from time to time, we are confronted with the stupendous task of trying to answer the many calls which are pressed upon us from villages wanting schools, from understaffed mission stations, and from the great unentered parts of our union. Many times we are compelled to turn a deaf ear to these providential openings, due to lack of funds and workers.

"What a golden day of opportunity is this for the cause of God, and how the unentered territory with its wide-open doors urges us onward into new fields! Let us be true to the sacred trust which has been committed to us, of warning earth's inhabitants of coming events, and preparing a people for the coming of our Saviour."[50]

In July of 1928, shortly after being selected as the superintendent of the Southeast African Union Mission, Nathaniel decided to make the long trip of nearly 600 miles to investigate the appeals they had been receiving from former Seventh Day Baptists for teachers and workers. For nearly twenty years some of the Africans had reported that there were thousands of Sabbathkeepers along the lakeshores in North Nyasaland. As early as 1911 some European missionaries from the Seventh Day Baptist Church had taught the natives about the Sabbath, but for financial reasons they had to return to their home base. The Sabbath truth remained behind and lived in the hearts of the people of that region.

The paramount chief of the Atonga tribe wrote Pastor Nathaniel: "I am asking you about your mission. I need your mission in my land to teach my children and my people the word of the living God. Please do not change your mind. Do not fail, but bring the things of God to my people this year. We hope you will come quickly. We will always be looking down the path for your coming."

Unknown to the Adventists, these people sent boys 600 miles to attend the Adventist school in Malamulo to learn about Adventism, and the boys returned to tell their people about the Bible. Nathaniel took Pastor R. G. Pearson and a national worker, Pastor James Malinki, and started on the long journey northward. In many places the bridges were broken. In other places they passed deserted villages where lions had eaten most of the people. They could see nests in the trees where people had found refuge from the lions.

The missionaries walked through the mountainous country and finally found the chief and his people. The lions were very numerous in the area, passing to and fro on and around the mission. The post carrier would often see places where the lions had killed people in the past, but he was never harmed.

It was agreed that R. G. Pearson and James Malinki would stay and pioneer the work there and that their families should remain at Malamulo until they had homes prepared for them. For months Pearson lived in a mud and pole hut. He went out seeking the scattered Seventh Day Baptist members, walking from place to place more than 600 miles. The sun burned hot. "This is not a white man, this is a red man," the people said when they saw his burned complexion. Nathaniel returned home but came back the next year and talked with the district commissioner about opening the work in that district. A mission site was chosen, and the government granted the church 500 acres of land. The Luwazi Mission station opened on that site.

Luwazi and Malamulo

There were hardly any roads around the station. The jungle was thick, and the rainfall was heavy, too heavy to grow good crops. All building materials had to be brought up by rail from Blantyre to the end of the train line, transferred to the lake steamer that came once a month, then carted the last fourteen miles over land, often on the heads of African carriers. Thousands of baboons infested the forests around the mission, raiding gardens and destroying any crops that might survive the heavy rains. The wild pigs were such a menace that a deep trench was finally dug completely around the mission property.

Mrs. Pearson and their four small children finally moved there and lived in a temporary mud and pole building for many months. Food was hard to get since the nearest store carrying regular supplies was about 300 miles away. The mail arrived once each month. But God blessed. The Pearsons and Pastor Malinki continued to be faithful. The support of the union was with them, and a school was finally started on the station. Seventy-five students from a radius of 200 miles enrolled, many being old men and women. Two years before there were no Adventist believers in that area. Suddenly, with the blessings of God and the faith of the leaders, there were nearly 2,000 Adventist Sabbathkeepers. The new members were completely convinced that the seventh day was the Bible Sabbath. Many had to be taught about clean and unclean foods, paying tithes, and abstinence from tobacco and alcohol, but once they learned these truths the majority were eager to follow the truth.[51]

Malamulo Mission station, the oldest and strongest of the mission stations, also came into existence by great sacrifice from an elementary school. It was once called the Plainfield Mission and was established in 1897 by a Seventh Day Baptist group who in 1902 sold it and 2,000 acres to the Adventists. Thomas Branch, a black American minister sent out by the Adventist Church to Malamulo in 1902, gave great attention to manual labor as part of the activities of the school while he taught the people the Ten Commandments. The name of the school was changed from "Plainfield" in 1907 to "Malamulo," the Cinyanja word for commandments.

His daughter, Mabel Branch, taught classes for the girls, and Branch's wife gave simple health treatments. Branch had been a pastor in Pueblo, Colorado, before he was sent to the Plainfield Mission station. He was one of the first African Americans to be sent overseas as a missionary. He returned to the United States in 1908 because of ill health and continued his pastoral work there. Malamulo was the main mission station for the Southeast African Union. During the first years of the work in Nyasaland, Malamulo was recognized as the center. A hospital and leper colony slowly developed there.

Highly Committed

The medical work opened many doors as can be seen in this report from Nathaniel: "I take pleasure in sending on to you a brief report of the progress of the medical work in this union. As we review this important branch of our mission work, our hearts rejoice at the marvelous progress made under Heaven's blessing.

"We have two hospitals in this union field, one at Malamulo Mission (southern Nyasaland) with Dr. C. F. Birkenstock in charge, and the other at Mwami Mission (central Nyasaland) where Dr. Marcus leads out. Rapid growth has taken place at both these hospitals during the last year which has been made possible, to quite a large extent, by the Extension Funds which have been sent over to us. We all greatly appreciate the help which has come to us in this way, and we pledge ourselves to the sacred trusts of appropriating these funds in such a way that the most people may be helped and the most souls saved in the kingdom of God.

"Dr. Marcus is 300 miles beyond the end of the railway. He is in a very needy field, one untouched by us until they went there a year ago. But the progress which has been made in this one year is truly marvelous.

"It means much to go to a new place and start without anything, build right from the ground up. But this is what the doctor has done. He has put up a house and a school building as well as other necessary buildings. Along with all this he has carried on hospital work in an old shed, and traveled by bicycle over the country within a radius of 100 miles, helping those who have called for his assistance.

"Large groups of poor unfortunate natives come to the mission day after day for medical help. It is impossible to describe the conditions under which this work must be done. Delicate operations have been performed. Surely it takes a strong-hearted man, a man of God, to work and keep happy and courageous through it all. Such men deserve our faithful support and prayers.

"I wish you might know the joy and renewed courage which came to Dr. Marcus when he learned that in the 1928 Extension program there would be included a hospital for his station. It is unthinkable to ask him to continue under present conditions. The least we can do is to provide a simple building where he can safely carry on his work. Such a building will exert a powerful influence for the truth in this new section of our field."

Dr. Marcus' Leper Colony

"Dr. Marcus has also started a leper colony at Mwami Mission, where there are many lepers. Just a few grass huts and some defiled, offensive natives constitute the colony. It is wonderful the rapid improvement these lepers make, especially under such unhygienic conditions.

"At Malamulo Mission Dr. Birkenstock is carrying on an aggressive medical work. Last year he treated about 75,000 patients. Many operations were performed with marked success. He visits village schools all over this field, and the native people regard him with profound respect. He has won a remarkably warm place in the hearts of the people. Dr. Birkenstock is carrying on the most successful leper work in Nyasaland. More than ten lepers have been cured and have returned to their homes and families. Could anything be more like the work of the Master?

"But Malamulo Hospital stands in dire need of funds for better buildings. For instance, Dr. Birkenstock is carrying on his general hospital work in an old building with a grass roof with such small windows that the place is dark and dingy. What a blessing it would be if we had funds to build a few suitable wards, and how much easier it would be for Dr. Birkenstock! He is now doing the work of two or three men, and it is not right to ask men to continue until they break in health and are forced to leave the tropics.

"This year G. Pearson and his family are opening work in the very northern part of Nyasaland. They will be the only Seventh-day Adventists in 300 miles, 600 miles from a railway, away up among the raw tribes of the north. Brother and Sister Pearson are active medical missionaries, but we have been unable to provide them with funds for a little dispensary. What a blessing it would be to these faithful workers on this new station if we could in some way arrange for a suitable building for the care of the sick people who will come to them!

"Then Thekerani Mission, where Brother and Sister J. L. Grisham are working, with its thousands of natives within the radius of a few miles, has nothing in the way of the hospital. Mrs. Grisham treats people by the score, but has not even a roof to call a dispensary. The possibilities for the development of the medical work at Thekerani Mission are almost limitless. We could possibly locate a doctor in this place. It does seem that the very least we can think of doing is to provide these people with a little dispensary for their rapidly growing medical work....

"Next year we hope to enter Portuguese Africa with her two and one-half million unwarned people. There is not one Seventh-day Adventists in all this vast territory. We have a call in for a doctor for this field, and we hope he can enter early next year. But I am beginning to think about how we shall ever be able to build him a simple hospital. We can never do it from regular appropriations. We must look to the Medical Extension Fund for this, it seems. Portuguese East Africa, with her unwarned, untold thousands, stands as a mighty challenge to the church of the living God. Let us stand by the doctor when he enters this field.

"Our workers are of excellent courage. We have been able to enter new territory this year. We rejoice in the way God is going before us, and as workers we dedicate our lives to the speedy finishing of the work in this part of the world field."[52]

Thekerani and Matadani

Division President W. H. Branson relayed this message to the public: "I want to pass on some really good news which I have gathered during the past week, and which has brought joy and courage to our hearts here, and I am sure will also be very encouraging to you.

"At our union committee meeting in January we set the goal for new converts in 1928 for south Nyasaland—that is Malamulo Mission, Thekerani Mission, Matadani Mission—at 1,350. The brethren thought at the time that this was a good high goal, and I think it was myself. Well, up to the end of May, or the first five months of the year, we have more than reached our goal for the entire year, having had just about 1,500 new converts enter our Bible classes since January 1.

"When I was adding up the results of our few little evangelistic efforts already held this year, I could hardly believe my eyes, for I had almost been thinking the past few weeks that things were going hard and slow. But we have not really entered into our evangelistic campaigns for 1928 as yet. Our two big months should be July and November, for during these months all our workers, both European and native, will give their entire time to soul winning. I do not care to make a forecast of the final results of souls won in 1928, but if things continue as at present, with Heaven's blessing we should more than double our goal of people won to the gospel in Nyasaland.

"During July we shall have more than fifty evangelistic efforts in progress in south Nyasaland. These efforts will be held at and near our present centers of influence. However, we are holding a number of efforts in quite new territory. I feel greatly encouraged by the way our entire force of workers are taking hold of the evangelistic part of the work. A deep sense of the importance of evangelism seems to be settling on both European and native laborers, and I think that the future of our churches in Nyasaland is very bright indeed. I believe that now is the time for us to 'go up and possess the land.' From south Nyasaland I have been receiving most urgent calls for teachers and preachers during the past month.

"I am happy to think that during July, while Brother Pearson and I will be preaching the first Seventh-day Adventist sermons ever delivered in north Nyasaland, we may be assured that the hills and valleys of south Nyasaland will be fairly ringing with the voices of the Adventist preachers. Please join us in prayer that many honest souls may be gathered out from heathen darkness even in those parts where Christ has been known longer, and that God may give success as we push on to the unentered north."[53]

Highly Committed

On Sunday afternoon, March 2, 1930, a large number of the workers and members of several churches met under some beautiful pines on the Rhodes Estate in Cape Town to bid farewell to Elder and Mrs. Branson and their daughter who were leaving on furlough and to welcome Elder Nathaniel Wilson into his fourth position of leadership in Africa, president of the South African Division. Nathaniel had served faithfully in the Southeast African Union, but the executive committee of the South African Division knew that his leadership would be exactly what was needed during Branson's absence. *The African Division Outlook* gives this picture of the transition.

"Elder N. C. Wilson, who is to act as Division President until appointment to the position is made at the time of the coming session of the General Conference, told of the purpose of our gathering, and referred at length to Elder Branson's connection with the work in Africa for the past ten years. He believes that God, in His plans for the development of the work in Africa, guided in the selection of Elder Branson as leader in this field, and that since the year 1920 He has been pleased to use His servant in directing the affairs of His cause in Africa.... Before closing his remarks, Elder Wilson, on behalf of the workers throughout the Division as well as several of the Peninsula church members, presented to Elder Branson a very handsome kaross. Sister Branson was asked to accept as a parting gift from her many friends in Africa a very nice leather blouse case, and to Lois [their daughter] there was given a photograph album."[54] The Wilson family moved from Blantyre to Cape Town, South Africa.

Elder Benjamin W. Abney, Sr., the son of an African Methodist Episcopal minister, was born in Edgefield County, South Carolina, on November 30, 1883, and was baptized into the Adventist faith by Evangelist Sidney Scott in 1910. He attended Huntsville Training School (Oakwood University today) and became a minister. While there he met Celia Hart of Muncie, Indiana, and they married in 1912. At the General Conference session of 1930, they were invited to serve as a union evangelist to South Africa in response to requests from the African people for an African American to serve their people in their land. By 1931 the family included Celia (who later married evangelist E. E. Cleveland) and Benjamin Jr. In total, the family lived in Africa for seven years, returning to the States in 1938. Ben and Celia became playmates of Neal, Ruth, and Clarice Wilson while living in Africa.[55]

B. W. Abney held a series of evangelistic meetings beginning on Sunday night February 19, 1933. The meetings were held in a tabernacle with a seating capacity of 250 in the thickly populated suburbs of Cape Town. On the opening night the building was full, and the attendance continued to be good thereafter. On the last Sunday night in July when they closed the meetings, many were disappointed because they wanted the meetings to continue. Twenty-five people were baptized, and others began worshiping on the Sabbath and were baptized at a later date. Elder Abney was also teaching Daniel and the Revelation courses in the Good Hope Training School. During the effort, one man and his wife who were attending the services and were quite interested asked for special prayer for their baby who was suffering from pneumonia. As a result, the child recovered, and both the man and his wife were baptized.[56]

The fifth and last position of leadership that Elder Nathaniel Wilson would fill in Africa was president of the South African Union. The family had to move again, this time to Bloemfontein, Orange Free State, South Africa. Nathaniel served there until they went home on furlough in June of 1934. Wilbur Bruce Wilson was born on March 16, 1934, just before they left for the States.

Hannah kept the family together, and she cherished the moments when her husband was at home. One special memory was when the family climbed Table Mountain together in Cape Town. Neal really enjoyed that! Hannah was a wonderful homemaker and hostess. She was able to grow beautiful flowers and plants, even in

Spreading the Gospel in Africa

the most remote areas where she had to use kerosene tins for planters and water them with the dishwater. She believed with all her heart in the health reform message, in a simple, natural diet, and in the healing power of natural remedies. "One of our early memories is of Mom going to people's houses to give fomentations for pneumonia when we lived in Bloemfontein. She believed in God's power to answer prayer, but also felt that we had to do our part," said her daughters, Ruth and Clarice. "Mom could make us feel at home wherever in the world we were. She brought heaven to home."

The family of six left Africa in 1934 and returned home to the States after nearly ten years away from home.

Back Row, left to right: E.D. Dick, Div. Educ. Sec.; S.G. Hiten, Representing Dutch Believers; A.E. Nelson, Div. Sec. Treas.; M.P. Robinson, Pres. Helderberg Coll.; J.I. Robinson, MV & HM Div. Sec.; J.G. Slate, Mgr. Sentinel Pub. Co.; O.R. Shreve, Mgr. Helderberg Coll.; W.R. Commins, Div. SS Sec.; L.A. Vixie, Div. Pub. Sec.
Front Row, left to right: C.W. Bozarth, Sup. Ruanda Union; C.W. Curtis, Sup. Congo Mission; N.C. Wilson, Pres. African Div. (acting); J.F. Wright, Pres. African Div. Conf.; O. Montgomery, Gen. Vice Pres. G.C.; W.H Anderson, Sup. Angola Union, E.C. Boger, Sup. Zambezi Union; O.U. Giddings, Sup. Nyassaland.

Highly Committed

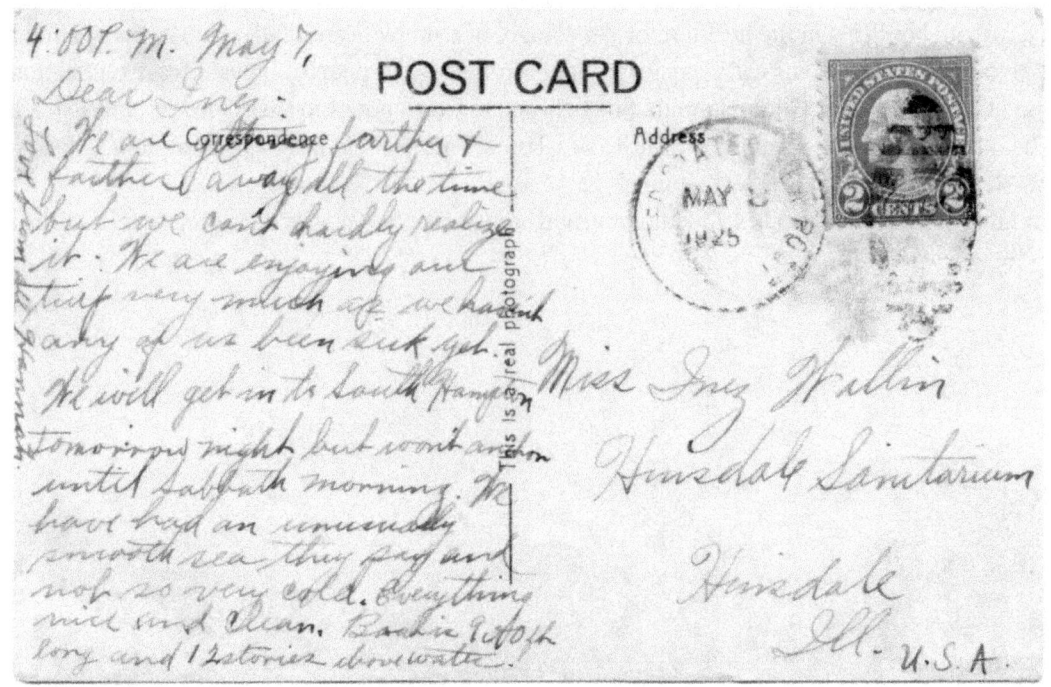

Hannah Wilson sends a post card to her family postmarked May 8, 1925 letting them know about their progress to Africa on the S. S. Leviathan.

North Nyasaland: A Picture of Seventh Day Baptist preachers who have now declared themselves S.D.A. and who are working under our direction although not on the payroll.

Spreading the Gospel in Africa

Traveling in Northern Rhodesia in 1926.

Neal, Ruth, Esther, and Clarice.

Nathaniel Wilson on his little 2-1/2 hp Raleigh motorcycle.

Our camp meeting outfit. My old Ford truck and our tents, etc. The building to the right is the schoolhouse. From left to right are: Prof. Cadwallader, Dr. Birkenstock. N.C.W. and Elder J.I. Robison.

Bro. Wheeler and N.C. Wilson starting out on a village trip. We were gone about three weeks on this trip. Our beds are on the back of our motorcycles. Bro. Wheeler is to your left.

Highly Committed

Our home in Blantyre. The building in the center is the Union Mission Office, and the one to its right is the garage. To the far right is the house with grass roof.

Chief Maukhambe with his son and favorite wife. The chief begged us to start work on his section of Lake Nyasa, and even gave us about 1,000 acres, but we are instead, locating about 15-20 miles away.

Camping at Walamba Siding

Bulawayo, Southern Rhodesia, 1925.

Neal, Nathaniel, and Clarice.

Chapter Five

Evangelism in the Southern Asia Division

"The elevator to success is out of order. You'll have to use the stairs ... one step at a time."
Joe Girard

Rest. Relaxation. Repose. That's what is needed after one spends nearly ten years away from home in a very hot climate. The Wilson family returned to the States in June of 1934 and tried to make provisions for the children to go to school and reconnect with family they had not seen in nearly a decade. Nathaniel had also agreed to visit certain churches and camp meetings to help recruit talented and dedicated workers to go overseas as missionaries. They made plans to visit Madison College where his two brothers lived and California where they planned to put the children in school.

Several letters were sent out from the African Division to make sure that the Wilsons were given time to recuperate before tackling another very difficult mission assignment. One letter stated, "With regard to the time of his furlough we wish to call attention to the fact that the Division committee has authorized eleven months furlough for Elder Wilson rather than ten months as you have been previously informed. This is due to the fact that Elder Wilson's service has been divided between the South East African Union, which is in the tropics, and the South African Union which has a more favorable climate."[57]

A medical report for Nathaniel showed that he had "varicose veins in both legs. The veins are enlarged enough to easily cause him trouble on taking much exercise."[58] He had trekked hundreds of miles in Africa, and his legs never seemed to bother him much. But he still needed rest.

Another letter from the division president recommended, "With regard to Brother Wilson ... He is to attend the Autumn Council and of course will be able to visit some of the conferences in behalf of mission promotion as may be arranged. We do feel to suggest, however ... that Elder Wilson be given a few months' complete rest first of all. He is in quite a rundown condition and needs rest very much. Hence I would like to suggest that whatever may be arranged for Brother Wilson to do while he is at home, his health be taken into consideration, and that he be given time to recuperate so that he will come back to us greatly improved healthwise. I am sure that with this suggestion you brethren will take the matter in hand and do what is right relative to his case."[59]

At the November 1934 Autumn Council, Nathaniel Carter Wilson discovered that he would not be returning to Africa with the nomination of his sixth position of church leadership—the presidency of the Southern Asia Division, where he took the place of A. W. Cormack, who was called to be an associate secretary of the General Conference.

At the end of his furlough, Wilson wrote this letter, "I wish I could tell you what a great blessing our furlough has been to us. After spending ten years in Africa, much of that time being spent in the tropics, one feels the need of a change and a little opportunity of associating with the workers here in the homeland. We go out to India feeling well, and ready for future years of hard service in that very needy field. The thing which has cheered us most during our furlough has been the deep and genuine interest which our people everywhere in

Highly Committed

the homeland have in the great mission program throughout the world field. It seems to me that they are solidly with us in the task of quickly finishing the work. This confidence encourages us as we leave the homeland for Southern Asia with its many and difficult problems."[60]

Having gotten the rest and recuperation the family needed, the Wilsons set out for a new field of labor. "Elder and Mrs. N. C. Wilson and their children sailed from Portland, Oregon, April 23 [1935], on the 'General Sherman,' for India. Brother Wilson and his family spent nine and a half years in missionary service in Africa, coming home for their first furlough last summer. At the Autumn Council he was appointed vice-president of the General Conference for the Southern Asia Division, and it is for this post he and his family have sailed, on the completion of their furlough."[61]

After arriving in India and getting to work, Nathaniel wrote, "We have been here now about two months, and are beginning to feel very much at home. We find a good many conditions quite similar to those in Africa, and this has greatly assisted us in getting settled in our new work. Another thing which has greatly helped is the kindly and cooperative attitude on the part of the brethren here at headquarters and throughout the field. I do not know how one could ask for better cooperation and a more willing spirit on the part of the workers generally than we have found here in Southern Asia.

"A good foundation has been established for the work in this field through the years, and I find the spirit of optimism on the part of the workers, particularly those who have been in the field for many years, and who have had an opportunity to observe things for a long time. It must have taken a great deal of courage and fortitude on the part of the early workers in this field to labor on year after year facing caste conditions, opposition, and many other obstacles. But now the brethren are greatly encouraged in that a new day has arrived for us in Southern Asia, and there are so many calls and providential openings that, rather than finding difficulty in getting a hearing or finding a place in which to work, we are totally unable to answer the urgent calls which come to us. You can imagine the courage and inspiration which this change in the situation has brought to the hearts of our workers generally, and particularly to those who have labored here for many years.

"While the response of the people here in India is not so ready nor so large as it is in some other parts of the world field, nevertheless there is a very apparent seeking after truth and a real earnestness taking possession of the people.

"One thing which has encouraged me as I take up my work in Southern Asia, is the keen interest which the leadership throughout this field has in evangelism, and I believe that the workers, one and all, in this country are anxious to join in gathering in a large harvest of souls during this time of awakening and special opportunity in our field."[62]

Evangelism in India

Nathaniel Wilson's motto became evangelism. "We have only one watchword—evangelism! Lay evangelism, youth evangelism, literature evangelism, and most of all, public evangelism. Evangelism!" These were the words of the new leader of the Southern Asia Division, which brought dramatic changes to caste-ridden India. With this dynamic emphasis, the following year saw twenty-seven new churches added and Sabbath School membership increased by 50 percent. One national leader said, "After twenty-six years of faithful service, all workers rejoiced in being able to report a church membership of just over 1,000. In other words it took twenty-six years of very hard work to build up the church membership to 1,000. How happy we are to report that the past three years, 1934 to 1936 have seen as much accomplished as those first twenty-six years from 1894–1920." Under Nathaniel's leadership division membership passed the 7,000 mark for the first time.[63]

But Nathaniel Wilson didn't just talk evangelism; he practiced it. He made sure he led by example. Three simultaneous meetings started in the middle of August in Lahore, the capital city of the Punjab Province, and were held six nights per week with an average attendance of about 1,200 for the three meetings each night. He led out in the largest of the three. *Ministry* magazine gives an account of one of these efforts. "I am now in Lahore arranging for an evangelistic campaign in this large city of nearly one million population. I have associated with me fourteen Indian evangelists, and we are really making this an evangelistic training school. We shall also keep two other efforts going in the suburbs of the city, with experienced Indian workers in charge. All of us meet frequently to plan the work and pray for its success. This is a new experience for North India, and so we are approaching the problem with humility, but nevertheless with great courage. We recognize that it is only as God pours out His spirit and impresses the hearts of the people that we can hope to succeed.

"I am enclosing the opening announcement for our effort in Lahore. We also have billboards for each of the three tents in the effort. These are attractively painted, size, 10' x 6'. The upper six feet of the billboard has permanent wording. The lower four feet is left blank for daily changes. Each day a local artist advertises our subject on colored paper, and this is placed in position.

"We have arranged with a local music house for a gramophone and an amplifier for each tent, and shall have a good selection of English and Urdu records. The weather is very hot day and night; so we have installed large overhead fans. We also have stereopticon, filmstrip, and moving-picture machines. So our equipment and physical arrangements seem to be satisfactory. This is a large, important campaign, and we are indeed anxious that the work shall be definitely successful. We feel that this kind of program is in harmony with God's plans, and are most anxious to do everything possible to place public evangelism on a firm basis in all parts of this division."[64]

General Conference Sessions

Soon after the organization of the Adventist Church, the leaders recognized that it was essential to have the administrators and pastors come together to discuss problems and progress and hear reports of God's blessings on the work of the church. The first General Conference Session, as they called it, was held May 20, 1863, in Battle Creek, Michigan, with only twenty delegates. The sessions were held every year thereafter at a favorable time and mostly at Battle Creek with the number of delegates generally increasing. In some difficult years the numbers were reduced a bit.

At the twenty-eighth session in 1889 it was voted, because of the expenses of bringing the delegates together (the number had increased to 109), to have the sessions every two years. These biennial sessions continued from the twenty-ninth session until the thirty-sixth session in 1905 when it was again voted, for the purposes of finances (the delegates had increased to 197), to meet every three years. The thirty-sixth session voted to hold the meetings every four years, so the thirty-seventh session with its 328 delegates met in Washington, D.C. in 1909.

The four-year pattern held good until the Great Depression in 1929. The leaders at the 1930 General Conference Session felt that it would be difficult to bring the delegates back in four years. "The first half of the 1930s was indeed a trying time for those responsible for the financial operation of the church. Tithe receipts in the United States declined by 25 percent from 1929 to 1933; total church income in 1934 was only about two thirds of what it had been in 1930. Hard decisions had to be made. Should the number of denominational employees be cut back, salaries reduced, and mission projects delayed? ... The normal quadrennial session of the General Conference regularly scheduled for 1934 was delayed two years as an economy measure."[65]

The forty-third General Conference Session in San Francisco, California, which began on May 26, 1936, was a great experience for the 571 official delegates, which included Nathaniel Wilson. It had been six years since church leaders had met, and they were anxious to hear how God was blessing in spite of great financial difficulties in the world. It would be the beginning of a new trend for Nathaniel and his family. From then on there would be an N. C. Wilson at these world sessions as a delegate and in an administrative position.

Highly Committed

The session revived Nathaniel's spirits and that of the other missionary workers in the Southern Asia Division. His reports were spellbinding and an inspiration to all the delegates. Remarking on the session, he said, "The Conference breathed a spirit of hope and confidence. It could hardly be otherwise as we listened to the story of God's abounding grace in every land. The story of our advance during the past six years at home and across the seas is one of great blessing and victory. The Conference session breathed a spirit of determination to undertake even larger things for God during coming days. No thought of standing still or of retreat found any room at the San Francisco meeting. The very clear and dominant keynote of the entire Conference was 'Onward to Victory.'…

"We return to our task in the distant lands with confidence and courage. We return with a very keen sense of the deep interest taken by our people of the homeland in our great foreign mission task. We in Southern Asia stand with our people in the homeland fields and in the mission divisions in a consecration of our all for a great forward move under God's leadership that shall result in speedily finishing the work."[66]

Greater Evangelism

A resolution was made for a renewed call to greater evangelism throughout the world. Nathaniel Wilson rose to speak to the resolution. "I believe with all my heart in the resolution before us. I am sure that no more important resolution could come before this large body of delegates. I have seen the blessing that has come to our work in Africa and in India, through this program of larger evangelism.

"Dear friends, the work of God in Southern Asia, where we have 400,000,000 people, can never be finished in any other way than through the preaching of the word with greater power. We believe in this program of larger evangelism in the Southern Asia Division.

"I have here a message from the city of Madras, a city of three quarters of a million people, which tells of the program of God's work there. Until recently we have kept a foreign worker in the city of Madras. During the difficulties of the last few years we have been obliged to remove this worker. We have there, however, an Indian brother whose heart is on fire with the spirit of evangelism. A few weeks ago this brother got out some handbills and scattered them over the city, calling the people to meeting. He tried to secure a hall, but was unsuccessful. Finally he decided to hold meetings in an upper room, where our believers meet. As the meetings have gone on, he has been greatly surprised at the crowds that have come to listen. On the third night he had an audience of 400, and about 400 more were turned away. The stairway was full, the balcony outside the hall was crowded, and even the roof was covered with people. There were people standing on the rostrum and in the aisles.

"We do not have to wait until we have a large budget, until we have a great preacher, or elaborate equipment. Simple men who have the Spirit of God and the spirit of evangelism in their hearts can do and are doing a large work for God.

"Six years ago an urgent call to greater evangelism went out to the world field. A great blessing has come to the church of God in every land as a result of the program that was adopted at that time. I feel that in this Conference, with this large delegation present, we should mark another milestone, another great forward step toward world-wide evangelism."[67]

Each division gave a report about the work being done in its territory. Nathaniel Wilson's Southern Asia delegation brought inspiration and joy to the other delegates. It was described this way by Alonzo L. Baker, the reporter for the day:

"Down the long aisle of the Auditorium Arena they came, one hundred of them,–Hindus, Brahmins, Buddhists, Mohammedans, Parsees, zamindars, rajas, purdah women, turbaned men, Telugus, Tamils, Punjabis, Bengalese, Ceylonese, high class, low class, and no class at all.

Evangelism in the Southern Asia Division

"And all of them in full costume—yellows, greens, reds, purples, lavenders—costumes so vivid, so chaste, so graceful. Upon the platform they marched to the rhythmic beat of an Indian drum.

"Who are they?

"Seventh-day Adventist missionaries from India with such veterans as Brother and Sister J. S. James of thirty years' service; Brother and Sister G. F. Enoch with twenty years' service, and all the way down to sixteen little missionary children three to seven years of age.

"So graphic was the evening's program and pageant which the Southern Asia Division put on tonight that the 6,000 people in the audience could almost feel the fetid heat of India's hot, hotter, hottest climate even though sitting here in cool San Francisco.

"Brother John Steeves added to the tang of the Orient in the singing of an Indian hymn. It was in minors, with all the pathos that centuries of sorrow, belief in Kismet, and a blind longing for a living and a loving God have begotten.

"While the program was going on, scores of slides flashed across the big screen in front of the organ's pipes giving us eye pictures of India while word pictures were flung at us in great array. On the screen the Taj Mahal, Everest, Bombay, Benares, the Ganges, Burma, the land of the pagodas, as well as our own institutions, churches, and dear people, were seen.

"When we heard of the subtle philosophies dominating the conservative East, of the barriers of caste, of the utter content of the religionist there, we saw that it is indeed a miracle of God's grace that we have 5,000 baptized believers in that land."

Immense Task

"N. C. Wilson, the division president, fairly stunned us with his description of the immensity of the task there when he said:

"'If Christ had started to preach in the villages of India on the day of His baptism, and had visited one village each day since that time, He would still have 30,000 villages to visit after 1,900 years' work. Southern Asia's population equals that of five of the great division fields—North America, Australasia, Southern Africa, Far East, and South America. If the people of our division stood six feet apart they would encircle the earth seventeen times at the equator. If the workers in our field were equally distributed along this line they would be a distance of over seven hundred miles between workers. Each worker, including school teachers, has approximately three fourths of a million people for whom he is responsible. Such is the magnitude of our task. What a challenge!'

"Surely it is just as W. A. Spicer has so often said, 'It is not time that separates us from the second coming of Jesus Christ, but a task.'

"Brother Wilson says he is confident that we shall be baptizing 1,000 new members annually by the next General Conference. His plea for more evangelistic families for India's 400,000,000 touched every heart.

"As these missionaries marched in, our eyes filled with tears as we thought of that glory day to come when millions from every land shall march across the sea of glass, when the trophies of all the mission programs of the church will present themselves in person before Christ Himself—the first missionary to a foreign land."[68]

Nathaniel Wilson would never forget the 1936 General Conference session.

Back in India the Wilson family was busy going to school and growing up. Hannah saw to it that the family attended school and church and participated in dozens of activities. Donald Wallin Wilson was born January 1938 in Poona while the other children were active at Vincent Hill School. Neal turned 18 in 1938. The division newspaper gives us a few glimpses of the Wilson family. Elder R. H. Pierson gives this account of the children participating in carol singing in Bombay to raise Harvest Ingathering funds: "What a priceless possession

Highly Committed

we have in our children and young people! What potential possibilities for service are bound up in the energies of youth! Now that we are approaching another Uplift season we can profitably plan to harness some of this pent-up energy for the Lord's work in this section of His great vineyard.

"We had some interesting as well as materially profitable experiences in Bombay during the forepart of Christmas week, working with our children and young people in the Uplift work. Sunday afternoon about six o'clock a few of the children went out with capable chaperones to some of the popular 'parades' of Bombay, and returned in about an hour's time with Rupees 45–0. Had we not previously arranged for carol singing at seven o'clock, doubtless this total could have been materially enlarged by a longer stay. At any rate, the children all thoroughly enjoyed the work and are eager to go again to help reach the goal of Rupees 250 which has been set for them. (They raised this amount in the 1937 campaign.)

"Carol singing was something new for most of us in Bombay, so we found it necessary to learn much that was new and also adapt what we did know to the circumstances peculiar to Bombay. We were most fortunate in having the very valuable assistance of some of our good Poona young people, including Pastor and Mrs. Steves and Maxine, Brother and Sister R. J. Ritchie, Neal and Clarice Wilson, and Judson and Charlie Thomas."

From six o'clock in the evening until 7:30 public parades or parks where people went for an evening walk or to sit and visit were good places to go. Children, wearing identification badges, were sent out two by two with chaperones. A prayer was offered at the beginning for God's guidance and a prayer at the end for thanksgiving and praise for what was collected. The little children used cans with a glass front. A lighted electric Christmas candle inside lit up the money that was placed in as an offering.[69]

Clarice Wilson

Around this time Clarice Wilson was the bridesmaid in a wedding. "The church at Salisbury Park witnessed an impressively beautiful marriage ceremony on the evening of February 10 [1936] when Ms. Grace Thomas, daughter of Pastor E. D. Thomas of the Division, was united to Mr. Prasada Rao, teacher in the South India Training School. Pastor J. S. James officiated. Clarice Wilson was bridesmaid, and Walter Mackett best man. The bride's sister, Gloria, was flower girl. The church was tastefully decorated with flowers and a large congregation both from the Estate and Poona attended.... We are sure the blessing of all our workers rests on this happy pair as they begin their united life in God's service.[70]

We have the recorded event of Clarice being baptized in India. "No other occasion is so solemn as the one when a soul takes his stand for Christ, signifying it by being buried in the water with Jesus and coming up from the water being born again.

"The delegates attending the Poona Biennial Council had the privilege of witnessing such an occasion on January 9, 1937. The baptismal service was held at the Poona English Church at 8:30 AM. The church was so full that many could not find standing room inside. After singing a hymn, Pastor J. C. H. Collett led us in prayer, beseeching the Lord to especially bless those who were going to be baptized.

"Pastor W. W. Christiansen preached an appropriate sermon, and all who have been baptized recall the time when they entered upon this sacred rite. At the close of the service, Pastor J. B. Conley baptized thirteen of our young people. These candidates were thoroughly instructed during the Council period in the baptismal class conducted by Pastor Collett and Christiansen. We were glad that we did not have to wend our way to some well or tank, but we have a font right in the church, constructed especially for this purpose.

"The meeting came to a close by singing the hymn, 'I Surrender All.' May the Lord bless these young people who have taken their stand for the master in the new Christian experience." The article gives the names of the newly baptized, and Clarice Wilson was baptized at this time. Neal Wilson was baptized earlier in 1935 at age 15.[71]

Clarice Wilson met her future husband's family at the Vincent Hill School.

She married Ivor C. Woodward in the College View Church in Lincoln, Nebraska, on December 26, 1944, and after finishing nursing school at Loma Linda University, she and her husband returned to teach at Vincent Hill School. Dr. Ivor Woodward later became the dean of Loma Linda University's School of Allied Health Professions.

The Wilson family, now consisting of seven, left India in June of 1940 on their furlough. They traveled from Bombay to Calcutta and then took an Italian boat to Singapore. After staying in Singapore for three days, they took a Chinese freighter to Hong Kong. "It was a really rough trip because of lack of space on the boat," Hannah said. "The quality of food was not good either. After a few days in Hong Kong, we left on an old Dutch freighter, the only thing we could find for Manila, Philippines. We had a very rough trip as there was a number two typhoon, and we got caught in this storm. We arrived in Manila on July 4. In some places the water was three feet deep in the street and the horse drawn carts had a hard time to make it. This was a very crowded time in Manila because so many people from Hong Kong and other places had arrived there because of the war.

"The seven of us had one room in the hospital just above the operating room. After two weeks Elder Figuhr offered to take Clarice and Ruth to their home, which was a great help. In early August we found passage on the 'Empress of Russia' for Canada. We arrived in Victoria, British Columbia, and traveled by train to Stanwood, Washington, and on to St. Helena, California, arriving there in early September just in time for Neal and Clarice to enroll in PUC. The rest of us stayed at St. Helena where Ruth attended school."

It was good to be back in the States again.

Nathaniel Carter Wilson's Family

Nathaniel Carter WILSON
- Born: February 4, 1897, in Fields Landing, California
- Died: December 1, 1992
- Married: Hannah Myrtle WALLIN, daughter of Louis WALLIN, on October 1, 1919. Hannah was born on February 24, 1898, in Roseau, Minnesota, and she died on March 18, 1995, in Loma Linda, California. The couple had five children, who are as follows:

Neal Clayton WILSON
- Born: July 5, 1920, in Lodi, California
- Died: December 14, 2010, in Dayton, Maryland
- Married: Elinor Esther NEUMANN on July 19, 1942. Elinor was born on January 21, 1920 and died June 8, 2011, Dayton MD.

Clarice June WILSON Woodward
- Born: June 7, 1922, in Stockton, California
- Married: Ivor Carey WOODWARD on December 26, 1944. Ivor was born on June 28, 1921.

Ruth Elvira WILSON Murrill
- Born: November 12, 1925, in Lusaka, Northern Rhodesia (Zambia)
- Married: William Lawrence MURRILL on June 28, 1949. William was born on May 28, 1926, in Ripley, West Virginia, and died on December 5, 2011, in Shawnee, Kansas.

Wilbur Bruce WILSON
- Born: March 16, 1934, in Bloemfontein
- Married: Meryl SPRENGLE on May 31, 1954. Meryl was born on July 29, 1932.

Donald Wallin WILSON
- Born: January 9, 1938, in Poona, India
- Died: May 16, 2003
- Married: Kathleen Sue GARNER on December 30, 1965. Kathleen was born on June 28, 1946.

Evangelism in the Southern Asia Division

*The Wilson family in 1940. Back row: Neal, Clarice;
Front row: Ruth, Hannah, Donald (born January 9, 1938 in Poona, India), and Bruce.*

The Wilson family in 1938. From left to right: Hannah, Ruth, Neal, Bruce, Nathaniel, and Clarice.

Highly Committed

The Wilson family in 1936. Back row: Ruth, Neal, Clarice;
Front row: Nathaniel, baby Bruce (born in Bloemfontein, Africa, March 16, 1934), and Hannah.

Chapter Six

Back to the States

"While we are free to choose our actions, we are not free to choose the consequences of our actions."
Stephen R. Covey

General Conference sessions are momentous occasions for the Seventh-day Adventist Church. Besides the high spiritual flavor, they bring together friends and relatives who have not seen each other for many years. The delegates have work to do, but thousands of other onlookers and visitors greet each other in a leisurely fashion during the week and on Sabbath.

The forty-fourth General Conference Session was held in San Francisco, California. This was the fifth time the church had availed itself of the beautiful climate and the services of the civic auditorium. The meeting opened on Monday evening, May 26, 1941, and closed on June 7. The civic auditorium could seat about 10,000 people comfortably. It was a perilous time for the church with war raging on three continents. As they were seating the delegates, they sent up special prayers for the great Australasian field, one of the home bases of the movement, since no delegates were able to attend because of the turbulent war emergency. The president of the Northern European Division and the president of the Southern European Divisions were not able to be there either.

Late in the afternoon, and before even twenty-four hours had passed, the nominating committee brought in its first partial report. Elder J. L. McElhany had been nominated to serve the church for a second term. With a unified spirit, he was unanimously reelected.

The first Sabbath of the conference had been a wonderful day with 15,000 plus people meeting together in the two auditoriums to praise God. The auditoriums were full again that Sabbath evening to hear the report of the Southern Asia Division. Elder Nathaniel Wilson, using graphic pictures, gave an exciting and inspirational report of what was happening in the Southern Asia Division, not realizing that this would be his last report for this division.

At the tenth meeting, which was held on June 2, the nominating committee brought in another partial report. "We recommend as president of the Southern African Division, N. C. Wilson." Elder J. F. Wright, the former president of the South African Division who had served for sixteen years in Africa, eleven of those years as president, had been voted in to be a general vice president of the General Conference, leaving a vacancy in the South African Division. The church would go to a man who had spent nearly ten years of service in Africa and had acted already as division president.

The family had come back to America to attend the General Conference Session, and while there they were required by the mission board to get their physical exams. For Elder Wilson the chief physical handicaps appeared to be varicosities in his leg veins, also apical abscesses. The report on Mrs. Wilson revealed a need for considerable dental attention and treatment for moderate anemia. The examining physician also recommended a blood-building program including iron and vitamin concentrates for Clarice and her sister, Ruth. Neal and Donald were in good health.

However, Bruce was not in good health. "The report of the examining physician in the case of Bruce Wilson would indicate that he is not in good health. It is recommended that he consult a specialist in allergic

Highly Committed

diseases also a skin specialist, and that he also be under close medical supervision seeking to build up his general health. For the present it would be inadvisable for him to return to the mission field. Therefore, further report will be required before making final recommendation. The urinalysis should be repeated, giving study particularly to the specific gravity."[72] The medical report was cause for concern.

Service for the church is hard on families, especially missionary families. A church pastor has many additional spiritual children. If his congregation consists of 200 members, he has 200 additional people to care for, pray for, and see that they are in good spiritual health. Some call in the middle of the night for relief from spiritual pain. Some need visiting in hospitals for physical pain. Others need constant advice. Some PKs (preacher's kids) are resentful of their father's responses to the many calls for help outside the family.

Leaving family and friends for long periods of time is quite a sacrifice. Only a missionary who has gone through the loneliness at Thanksgiving, Christmas, and other important family days knows what it means to give up these special times with friends and family. The Lord usually provides new family and new friends who remain close throughout life. Among the other challenges, medical care in faraway lands in the 1930s and 1940s was completely inadequate, if it existed at all.

Accepting the Call

Nathaniel and Hannah had to make a big decision. Should they take the family back to Africa when Bruce was sick and might need more medical attention that they knew would not be available to them in the mission field? The world was in turmoil, and war was threatening. Could they get passports and travel with safety across the oceans? The call had been voted, but should they accept it? They remembered when they had left India in June 1940 on their furlough that they had booked passage on a Japanese boat, the Assama Maure, but were advised by the American Embassy not to go by a Japanese boat because of the war. They prayed that God would guide them in their decision.

The same month of the session, May 1941, a call was extended to Nathaniel to be the president of the Central Union (Mid-America Union today) headquartered in Lincoln, Nebraska. That settled it. This was God's answer to their prayers. They accepted the call in America and did not go back to Africa.

However, the Sothern African Division was still looking for him. J. F. Wright wrote an open letter in the division paper. "Already a cable has been sent to South Africa relative to the election of your new Division president. Inasmuch as my tenure of office had expired, a change in the leadership of the Division was obvious. Personally, I was very happy when Elder N. C. Wilson, already known to so many of you, was chosen to be the new leader of the Southern African Division. His nine years of service in Africa, as well as the few years he has spent as division president of Southern Asia, will ably fit him for the task which now lies ahead of him in Africa. You will accord him, I am confident, the same loyal, cheerful, co-operation and support, you always so willingly gave to me. Under the Spirit of God, the work should continue to move forward out there without loss or delay. Elder Wilson will give to you his best, I know."[73]

Reluctantly, the Southern African Division gave up hoping for Nathaniel Wilson's presence when they received a cable from the General Conference. "In the cable from Washington it is explained that Elder N. C. Wilson has been released from his appointment to Africa owing to the impossibility of securing transportation for him and his family under present conditions. We deeply regret that circumstances have made it impossible for the Wilsons to come forward ..."[74]

The family moved to Lincoln in early 1942. The Central Union, Nathaniel Wilson's seventh position of leadership, was comprised of four conferences and one mission: Colorado, Kansas, Missouri, Nebraska, and the Wyoming Mission. The state of Wyoming was a large mission field. Their camp meetings were usually held in Casper, Wyoming, and the attendance was growing. They were hoping to organize their membership into a full conference. In July 1945 the Wyoming constituency meeting selected a group to study whether the Wyoming field should be organized into a conference. Wilson chaired the meeting and gave advice to the leaders when it was voted unanimously to form a conference.[75]

Wilson helped facilitate a two-day home missionary convention with the Northern Union in Omaha, Nebraska. The leaders there emphasized that literature was the backbone of soul winning.[76] At the Sabbath School conference hosted in the Central Union, it was brought out that "The study of the Bible is of first and supreme importance.... Sabbath School members everywhere delight to give to help others."[77]

Nathaniel always supported evangelism and was happy to host an evangelistic institute in Topeka, Kansas, with 150 evangelists, pastors, Bible instructors, and other workers. They shared ideas and laid plans to bring the third angel's message to every city in North America.[78]

Within the union, Boulder-Colorado Sanitarium marked its fiftieth anniversary in a unique and happy celebration. It proved to be a truly "golden" anniversary, for funds had been raised, and were in hand, to liquidate the remaining part of the debt of $115,000, which had been hanging over the institution as a dark cloud and a heavy handicap. Nathaniel Wilson was there to celebrate with the hospital officers.[79]

In addition to his other duties, Nathaniel served as the president of Christian Record Benevolent Association, Inc., which was located in Lincoln, Nebraska. In 1942, in order to better meet the requirements of operating such an association for the blind, Elders I. H. Evans, S. A. Wellman, and Nathaniel C. Wilson carried out its incorporation for "charitable, educational, religious, and missionary purposes and to bring the teachings of the Bible, culture, and happiness to blind people all around the world."[80] One of its major projects was to publish free reading material for the blind. It had become the largest publisher of religious literature for the blind in the world. Its name was changed to Christian Record Benevolent Association, Inc., in 1963, and later changed to the name it holds today, Christian Record Services for the Blind.

The Central Union also hosted a Japanese Workers' Council in Colorado from December 14 through 17, 1944, to study the many problems in connection with the Japanese work in America. About 100 had been baptized since the war started, and plans were laid for continuing the work in a more aggressive way. The council recognized that almost 100 years had passed since the memorable day of October 22, 1844, but a century later many Japanese had not found the gospel light. The delegates voted a pledge of consecration: "We still face a tremendous task of telling our race, which includes more than 150,000 in this country, about the nearness of our Lord's return and the impending consummation of all things."[81]

While in his position, Nathaniel Wilson officiated at the dedication of many churches and the ordination of many new pastors.

The forty-fifth session of the General Conference of Seventh-day Adventists was scheduled to take place in the Central Union, the territory under Nathaniel Wilson's leadership. Definite plans had been made for holding the session in St. Louis, Missouri, but at the last minute the leaders were informed that there would not be enough rooms available to house the delegates and the larger crowd expected on the weekends. Some thought was given to changing the time of the session.

After much prayer it was decided that the session would be held June 5–15, 1946, in Takoma Park, Maryland. Takoma Park was a suburb of Washington, D.C., and the church headquarters were located there as well as the headquarters of the Columbia Union and Potomac Conference, Washington Missionary College (Washington Adventist University), Washington Sanitarium and Hospital, the Review and Herald Publishing Association, and the Theological Seminary. It was felt that sufficient sleeping, eating, and meeting spaces could be managed for the accredited delegates and their families. They would try to discourage the general denominational public from attending and emphasize that it was strictly a delegate session. Many who had planned to attend canceled their travel arrangements. The planning committee contacted members about using their private homes, basements, attics, and other sleeping quarters. The Potomac Conference camp meeting tents were pitched on the college campus and the rooms of the dormitory were full.

"Also this will be an air-minded meeting, for most of the delegates from overseas have come either all or part of the way by plane. Just five short years ago, when the last Conference was held in San Francisco, no one even thought of traveling to the session by air!"[82]

Elder J. L. McElhany was quickly reelected as president. Nathaniel Wilson was the secretary of the nominating committee. It was his responsibility in reading a partial report of the nominating committee to read his own name. The nominating committee had selected him as vice president for the North America Division. It would be his eighth position of leadership in the Adventist Church. The North American Division was considered the home base of Adventism. It was the financial and administrative heart of the church. His nomination was quickly approved, and he gave his acceptance speech.

"The present is a time of great opportunity and responsibility in all parts of the North American Division. We face a large task with but little time remaining for its accomplishment.

"The message of God for this hour must be preached in a larger and more fervent manner in the centers of great population, and everywhere throughout the country. Every phase of church activity must be enlarged and extended. Thousands are still to hear and accept the advent message. Our objective is to make every activity of the movement a soul-winning agency. Every church, every school, every sanitarium, and every publishing house must have but one purpose and goal in mind, and that is to contribute just as much as possible to the carrying of God's message to every honest and inquiring heart in our division field.

"And then in this home base division we recognize our privilege and responsibility in helping in a large way to extend the work of God to all parts of the world. Our people in the homeland churches find great joy and blessing in giving and praying for the blessing of God in lands afar. Our people scattered over the North American field are a liberal and large-hearted people, and the success and triumph of God's work throughout the world is a matter of prime concern to them.

"Our task in North America is a great one; our opportunities and blessings are many. We face the future with courageous and earnest hearts, confident that God will speedily lead us on to final victory."[83]

Being vice president of the General Conference responsible for the North American Division or as some would say president of the North American Division, meant chairing many committees, writing many letters, attending many meetings, and preaching in many churches. At a constituency meeting of Madison College, Madison Sanitarium, and other related industries, Nathaniel Wilson was elected chair of the Board of Trustees. He thought about the time he had spent there from 1922 to 1925 as a Bible teacher and how he was ordained there. Madison had become a large and important institution. Its sanitarium and hospital could now accommodate 180 patients. The college was planning to care for 500 students. The food factory, farm, and various other industries were now important enterprises. God had led and directed his life so that he was right back where he started.

One of the most lasting influences to come out of his leadership in the North American Division occurred when Nathaniel Wilson was selected to be the chair of the General Conference Commission on Rural Living. After the cities of Hiroshima and Nagasaki were bombed, many Adventists gave serious consideration to the counsel of Mrs. White urging members to leave the large cities and find homes in the country. Some leaders cautioned against rash, haphazard moves, particularly on the part of those who had no knowledge of farming.

Back to the States

On March 4 and 5, 1947, in Cincinnati, Ohio, Nathaniel Wilson chaired a meeting where approximately fifty representatives and leaders from a large number of self-supporting institutions met together. Various types of missionary enterprises and institutions were represented, including schools, sanitariums, and health centers. The focus changed somewhat into encouraging a stronger tie between laypeople who were businesspeople and the regular organized work of the denomination. Twenty-five institutions became part of the charter group and adopted its constitution and bylaws.

Elder Wilson called the formation of this association "a great day in the history of the church." Some excellent studies on medical and educational needs, with particular emphasis on gardening, and practical courses for the laypeople desiring to leave the cities were given. The name of the Association was to be called the Association of Seventh-day Adventist Self-Supporting Institutions. A nominating committee was set up with Nathaniel Wilson as the chair. Interestingly Walter Wilson, his youngest brother from Lawrenceburg, Tennessee, was chosen as one of the twenty-five charter members.

A follow-up meeting two years later in Grand Rapids, Michigan, further developed the organization. Dr. E. A. Sutherland was chosen as the president of the organization and Dr. J. Wayne McFarland as the secretary.

Today ASI is a membership-based organization of lay business and nonprofit organizations, entrepreneurs, and professionals who support the worldwide mission of the Seventh-day Adventist Church. Its motto is "Sharing Christ in the Marketplace." ASI's history was rooted in Madison College in Tennessee. As Madison expanded, its graduates planted satellite schools and institutions around the country. Thus in 1979, to better reflect ASI's diverse membership, the organization's name was changed to Adventist-laymen's Services and Industries.

ASI members still seek to maintain Christ-centered lifestyles and to experience Christ's love in their own lives, as well as to share that love with people they encounter in their daily business and professional activities. Recognizing that their time, talents, possessions, and bodies belong to God, they use their vocations as ministries to advance the great gospel commission.

The ASI organization exists to challenge and nurture its members in wholeheartedly supporting the mission of the Seventh-day Adventist Church through various outreach programs that focus on health, education, evangelism, community services, family concerns, and special projects. Each year in August ASI holds an international convention that features dynamic speakers and a rich array of seminars on spiritual growth, health, business, nonprofit, and evangelism topics.

Thousands of ASI members and supporters, including many church employees, gather to listen to inspiring testimonies and sermons, attend practical ministry seminars, and wander through an exhibit hall filled with hundreds of Adventist ministry booths.

Other countries have formed their own ASI organizations, including ASI Europe, ASI South America, and ASI Asia. These groups share the same mission and objectives as ASI in North America. The various ASI organizations ultimately bring a large family of like-minded ministries and individuals together to carry out a common goal—to prepare the world for Christ's soon return![84]

Indeed Nathaniel Wilson's leadership and vision in the early establishment of ASI have resulted in a strong organization that is preparing the world for Christ's return.

Sessions of the General Conference of Seventh-day Adventists

Session	Delegates	Opening Date	Place
1	20	May 20, 1863	Battle Creek, MI
2	20	May 18, 1864	Battle Creek, MI
3	21	May 17, 1865	Battle Creek, MI
4	19	May 16, 1866	Battle Creek, MI
5	18	May 14, 1867	Battle Creek, MI
6	15	May 12, 1868	Battle Creek, MI
7	16	May 18, 1869	Battle Creek, MI
8	22	March 15, 1870	Battle Creek, MI
9	17	February 7, 1871	Battle Creek, MI
10	14	December 29, 1871	Battle Creek, MI
11	18	March 11, 1873	Battle Creek, MI
12	21	November 14, 1873	Battle Creek, MI
13	19	August 10, 1874	Battle Creek, MI
14	18	August 15, 1875	Battle Creek, MI
1st Special Session	15	March 31, 1876	Battle Creek MI
15	16	September 19, 1876	Lansing, MI
2nd Special Session	16	November 12, 1876	Battle Creek, MI
16	20	September 20, 1877	Lansing, MI
3rd Special Session	22	March 1, 1878	Battle Creek MI
17	39	October 4, 1878	Battle Creek, MI
4th Special Session	29	April 17, 1879	Battle Creek, MI
18	39	November 7, 1879	Battle Creek, MI
5th Special Session	28	March 11, 1880	Battle Creek, MI
19	38	October 6, 1880	Battle Creek, MI
20	41	December 1, 1881	Battle Creek, MI
21	47	December 7, 1882	Rome, NY

(cont.)

Session	Delegates	Opening Date	Place
22	65	November 8, 1883	Battle Creek, MI
23	67	October 30, 1884	Battle Creek, MI
24	70	November 18, 1885	Battle Creek, MI
25	71	November 18, 1886	Battle Creek, MI
26	70	November 13, 1887	Oakland, CA
27	91	October 17, 1888	Minneapolis, MN
28	109	October 18, 1889	Battle Creek, MI

(The 28th session voted to hold biennial sessions.)

Session	Delegates	Opening Date	Place
29	125	March 5, 1891	Battle Creek, MI
30	130	February 17, 1893	Battle Creek, MI
31	150	February 15, 1895	Battle Creek, MI
32	140	February 19, 1897	College View, NE
33	149	February 15, 1899	South Lancaster, MA
34	268	April 2, 1901	Battle Creek, MI
35	139	March 27, 1903	Oakland, CA
36	197	May 11, 1905	Washington, D.C.

(The 36th session voted to hold quadrennial sessions.)

Session	Delegates	Opening Date	Place
37	328	May 13, 1909	Washington, D.C.
38	372	May 15, 1913	Washington, D.C.
39	443	March 29, 1918	San Francisco, CA
40	581	May 11, 1922	San Francisco, CA
41	577	May 27, 1926	Milwaukee, WI
42	577	May 28, 1930	San Francisco, CA
43	671	May 26, 1936	San Francisco, CA
44	619	May 26, 1941	San Francisco, CA
45	828	June 5, 1946	Washington, D.C.
46	943	July 10, 1950	San Francisco, CA

(cont.)

Session	Delegates	Opening Date	Place
47	1,109	May 24, 1954	San Francisco, CA
48	1,160	June 19, 1958	Cleveland, Ohio
49	1,314	July 26, 1962	San Francisco, CA
50	1,495	June 16, 1966	Detroit, MI
51	1,782	June 11, 1970	Atlantic City, NJ

(The 51st session voted to hold quinquennial sessions.)

Session	Delegates	Opening Date	Place
52	1,756	July 10, 1975	Vienna, Austria
53	1,925	April 16, 1980	Dallas, TX
54	2,044	June 27, 1985	New Orleans, LA
55	2,239	July 5, 1990	Indianapolis, IN
56	2,321	June 29, 1995	Utrecht, Netherlands
57	1,844	June 29, 2000	Toronto, Canada
58	1,903	June 29, 2005	St. Louis, MO
59	2,244	June 23, 2010	Atlanta, GA

Chapter Seven

Islands, NAD, Retirement

"About the only thing that comes to us without effort is old age."
Gloria Pitzer

"I was visiting some of our interesting island missions in the northeast of New Guinea," said Nathaniel Wilson when he was president of the Australasian Division, "We were traveling in one of our sturdy little 45 foot mission ships. We have over 20 of these fine little seaworthy diesel powered ships in our mission fleet which is the finest operated by any mission organization in the world.

"The endless darkness of the night sky settled peacefully over the Coral Sea, the six missionaries and two dozen or so Australians in our ship. We had boarded the ship *M.V. Leleman* which would soon set out for the island of New Britain where the Coral Sea Union was to meet in session.

"The night air was perfumed with the scents of the sea. 'Don't be afraid,' called the captain of the little mission boat. 'We won't take the short dangerous course tonight, but will go by another route that is perfectly safe.'

"But in spite of his encouragement, some of the passengers felt uneasy. We knew that the waters were infested with sharks and full of hidden reefs. One mistake by the man at the helm might land us on a coral reef where the sea would quickly pound our little boat to match sticks. We didn't want to be shipwrecked at night—among the sharks!

"I was traveling with Pastors A. V. Olson and E. E. Cossentine from the General Conference headquarters and three of our Australian missionaries of which one was the captain of our vessel. We had spent some days visiting our believers on some of those islands where every inhabitant is a Seventh-day Adventist and where the most remarkable transformations have taken place in the lives and habits of these people.

"Darkness was setting over the water as we came on board to sail across the Coral Sea to Rabaul, on the island of New Britain, not too far from Australia. Before the missionaries taught the natives of the islands the gospel most of them were wild savages and cannibals. When they caught a man from an enemy tribe, they would kill him, roast him, and eat him. I am told that some of the missionaries ended up in some of their pots.

"About 30 of us were on board that fateful night. We were tired, for we had tramped since early morning from village to village on an island visiting our members. Some of us felt nervous and uneasy about going to bed because we knew that we had a very treacherous sea around us. Much of the Coral Sea has hidden shoals and dangerous coral reefs. If a boat strikes these, it means disaster.

"So when the captain assured us all would be well, we went to bed and fell into a deep sleep. Everything went well, and we were enjoying the calm and peace of the ocean voyage until at 4:40 that Tuesday morning our ship plowed into a coral reef. Someone let out a blood curdling cry of alarm.

"The electric lights went out with the first crash. Pastor Cossentine was thrown from the top bunk, where he spent the night, across the cabin, and suffered a rather serious leg injury. We were all thrown about rather freely. Furniture was smashed, food and water supplies were destroyed, and our bags floated around in the salt water that poured in through the windows.

Highly Committed

"In the pitch darkness we felt the waves which were breaking at a height of about 25 feet beating against our little ship. Our ship and all its cargo, including suitcases and bags, were swamped with seawater. We greatly marveled at the strength of the ship in not breaking up as the result of the pounding from the waves on the reef. Surely God kept his hand over us otherwise the outcome of the whole experience could very easily have been most tragic.

"The only thing we could see was the white, hissing breakers as they roared toward us. Again and again the waves would catch the boat, pitch it toward the heavens, and throw it with great fury against the rocks—first one side and then the other. One moment the vessel would be lifted high on the crest of a new wave, and then dropped with a thud on the hard coral. For 10 or 15 minutes it seemed quite probable that not only the ship would be lost but all the lives of those onboard. It was a most terrifying experience.

"Nobody spoke. But nobody cried out. All on board knew that unless God worked a miracle our frail vessel would be broken into splinters and our bodies given to food for the sharks. Those were tense and terrible moments. Silently we were all praying to the One who stilled the waves of Galilee, to save us. God heard those prayers.

"As each succeeding breaker bore down upon us with the roar of a demon, it pushed our boat a little farther in onto the reef. After about fifteen minutes of this fearful punishment, we were beyond the reach of the breakers.

"'Try the radio,' someone said. 'Send out an SOS call.'

"The radio operator tried to send a message, but the radio refused to work. It was broken.

"God had protected us so far. We got out and looked around. Our beloved ship was battered and bruised, lying in shallow water, with the copper lining ripped from its side. To our great relief, the planks were still sound; there was no leak, and the machinery was in working order.

"We were hundreds of miles from our destination, marooned on a coral reef. There was some food aboard, but there were 30 of us to eat. How long would it last?

"It was soon evident that it would be a difficult and long process getting the ship into deep water again. With the receding of the tide and the opportunity to study the situation a little bit it was decided to try to slowly work the ship over the reef to the quiet waters on the other side. The brethren immediately started to work in waist deep water, preparing to be ready to throw the ship off of the reef when the next high tide was due in a couple of week's time.

"These first days after we were cast on the reef were both interesting and unpleasant. We discovered that we were almost completely surrounded by islands and reefs.

"There was a small coral island inhabited by probably 50 very primitive natives about 2 miles away from the place where our ship was on the reef. Toward evening of the first day several of us took the water soaked suitcases and bags to the little island in our rowing boat. The bags were unpacked, and between tropical downpours we dried the cameras, clothing, and other personal effects.

"It was all a rather difficult experience and we very much disliked treating our General Conference visitors in this way but conditions were entirely beyond our control. It was very hot and steamy, as it always is the case in these tropical places, and often we were drenched with either sea or rainwater.

"Hours pass. Then a Chinese man in a little open boat spied us. Seeing our plight, he promised to come back later. Early in the morning while it was yet dark—48 hours after the accident he arrived with his little motorboat and for a reasonable fee took three of us the nine-hour ride to Kavieng. We had hoped to arrive in time to catch a plane that afternoon for Rabaul; instead we arrived just in time to see the plane leave! In the whole town there was no hotel and no restaurant. Having had almost nothing to eat or drink for more than 56 hours, we were raving hungry. Finally we found a little store where we bought bread, fruit, and some canned goods, and sat down in the storekeeper's dirty kitchen and ate with gusto. No meal ever tasted better. 'A hungry stomach makes a good cook,' they say. A telegram was immediately sent to Rabaul and in 26 hours the flagship of our Coral Sea mission fleet, the *M. V. Batuna*, had traveled the 200 miles and was on hand at the reef to give help.

"The following afternoon a plane arrived and took us to our destination. How thankful we were to our heavenly Father for having brought us through alive.

"It took the salvage crew two weeks to get our boat off the reef. They had to blast a channel through the rocks before they could float the ship again in the open sea. All the passengers were saved and were unharmed."[85] This was not the first experience of this kind in the Australasian Division, which is made up of hundreds of inhabited islands. Some of the larger and more important of these islands could be reached by plane, but most could only be reached by the fleet of ships owned by the division.

Isaiah 11:11 predicts, "It shall come to pass in that day, that the Lord shall set his hand again the second time to recover the remnant of his people, which shall be left, from Assyria, and from Egypt, and from Pathros, and from Cush, and from Elam, and from Shinar, and from Hamath, and from the *islands of the sea.*"

Australasian Division

The mission field of the Australasian Inter-Union was made up entirely of islands, and the prophet of God, writing many centuries ago, very clearly indicated that when God would do His final work, a portion of His remnant people would come from the islands of the sea. At first the entire territory was but one union with the headquarters office in the city of Wahroonga, one of Sydney, Australia's most attractive suburbs. As the work grew and more members were added over the extended thousands of miles, it became physically impossible for one union to administer this large territory.

The problem was submitted to the General Conference for counsel, and the field was divided into four unions: The Trans-Commonwealth Union Conference with headquarters in Melbourne, Australia; the Trans-Tasman Union Conference with headquarters in Sydney, Australia; the Coral Sea Union Mission with headquarters in Lae, New Guinea; and the Central Pacific Union Mission with headquarters in Suva, Fiji.

These four unions functioned the same as a division in other parts of the world and were recognized to be a division. Later the name was changed from Australasian Inter-Union to the Australasian Division. The new organizational plan brought great strength and blessings to the division, and instead of having union leaders headquartered thousands of miles away, the leaders were brought close to the action. The leaders were able to become personally acquainted with the conditions and needs of their field and to give closer supervision to their employees. Thirteen million people were spread out over thousands of miles of land and sea. Many inhabited islands had only a village or two. In some instances a whole group of islands may have had only a few thousand souls. It was necessary for the division office to maintain the fleet of mission ships mentioned in the opening story of this chapter.

The division had a fine fleet of more than twenty sturdy little ships for their missionaries to use. Without the mission boats, the work among the islands could never be accomplished. When the weather was good, the sea calm, and the distance short so that they could sail in the daytime, this was both a safe and pleasant way to travel, though slow; but when distances were long and storms arose while they were sailing through reef-strewn seas, it was dangerous. The workers who sailed the seas were often in danger. Some lost their lives. Some of the delegates who attended one union session in Suva, Fiji, traveled 1,800 miles in their mission ship. It required courage and a spirit of real consecration and devotion to labor as missionaries on and among many of those islands of the South Pacific.

Highly Committed

Nathaniel Wilson was selected for his ninth position of leadership as president of the Australasian Inter-Union at the Autumn Council of the world headquarters in 1948 after serving two years as president of the North American Division. This large collection of islands was his new territory. Nathaniel always seemed to be present when new organization and church structures were formed. His counsel was a blessing.

Nathaneil and Hannah and the two youngest boys, Bruce and Donald, left Takoma Park and sailed from New York for Alexandria on July 26, 1949, on the *S. S. Excalibur*. They made a brief visit to Cairo, Egypt, to visit Neal and Elinor and their family before continuing on to Poona, India, for a visit with Clarice and Ivor and their family. Clarice had finished her nursing degree at Loma Linda in 1944 before coming home to Lincoln, Nebraska, where she and Ivor were married on December 26, 1944. The couple went to Campion Academy where Ivor was dean of boys for one year. In 1945 they left for Vincent Hill School and College as missionaries—Ivor as a teacher and Clarice as a school nurse.

Once Nathaniel assumed his role as president, he tackled many new and exciting projects and challenges. Of special interest, the health food work was growing in the Australasian Division with the opening of a dozen factories, several wholesale houses, some vegetarian restaurants, and numerous retail shops. The factories operated twenty-four hours a day and could not supply the demand for their products. The largest factory was the one on the grounds of Avondale College, which enabled a large number of the students to earn all or part of their school expenses. It was called the Sanitarium Health Food Company. It began as a very small food factory in Melbourne in 1897, its first product being a dry breakfast food—granola. This factory was soon moved to Cooranbong. A reconverted sawmill constituted the first factory building at the new school site. This small store grew into the dozen factories operating, with a new one to be erected on the grounds of the college in New Zealand.

Nearly 3,000,000 customers were served in the previous year in the retail shops and cafés. These customers were not buying largely of the major items manufactured by the factories, but rather of fruit, nuts, legumes, and specialty foods. The regular products of the factories, the ready-to-eat cereals, were found in every grocery store in the country. The Sanitarium Health Food Company was the largest company of its kind in Australia.

Mrs. White gave a number of health talks at the first camp meeting held in Australia, and this was responsible for the growth of this work. The leaders of the health food work in Australia were brought together in a convention to consider matters of importance on how to increase the development of this work. N. C. Wilson was the chair of all the meetings.

Nathaniel and his family had been a great supporter of the health message in their ministry, and they believed in her counsel "the work of health reform is the Lord's means for lessening suffering in our world and for purifying His church…. Keep the work of health reform to the front is the message I am instructed to bear."[86]

In Indonesia

In 1951 Elder Wilson received his tenth call to a position of leadership—the Indonesian Union. The family left Sydney by plane for Brisbane; from there they went by boat to Djakarta, Indonesia, where they arrived late in August of 1951. The two youngest children had to finish their education, and Hannah saw that this was done although Nathaniel chipped in when he could. He taught Donald one class of Bible on the boat.

Nathaniel Wilson tells one story about how the Advent message was on the move in Indonesia.

"In East Java wonderful things are happening. In one section five adjoining villages have grouped together and have asked for a series of meetings. There are from four to five hundred people attending the meetings. Many Bibles have been sold to these people who before have never so much as seen a Bible. The brethren are confident of a good harvest from these five villages.

"In the small but thickly populated island off the coast of Celebes, God is doing wonderful things for us.

A young man, Brother Taroba, from the island of Talaud, accepted the Advent message while working in Java. He felt he must return to his own people living on the small home island and share with them his wonderful discovery of the Advent truth. His reception at home was far from satisfactory. His father was a wicked man and a leader in idol worship. He made it very clear that he could not accept or have anything to do with his son's newfound faith.

"After some days of discussion the father proclaimed the superiority of his gods by declaring that his idols could not be burned. The son knew that due to the nature of the wood from which the idols were made it would be difficult to burn them. However, after repeated ridicule he accepted the challenge. A time was appointed for the demonstration, and nearly all the village people were in attendance.

"When the people were assembled and quiet, our young brother stepped forward and announced his joy in being on the home island with his own people, but he also explained the difficulty of the task before him in attempting to burn the idols made of such indestructible wood. Then he clearly stated his entire dependence upon the God of heaven, whose child he was.

"An earnest prayer for help and blessing was offered. Then a small fire was built, and the idols were placed one by one in the fire, and to the surprise of those assembled, all the idols were consumed. Not only were the idols consumed, but the fire spread in the dry grass, and soon the large jungle trees which constituted a grove for idol worship were also burned up. The people were utterly astonished and afraid. They felt that either our young brother would be struck dead by God or otherwise they themselves would meet a terrible fate.

"So they waited and waited, but the God of heaven takes care of His children. Nothing happened to the young man. This incident made such a deep impression upon Brother Taroba's family and others that they began to study the truth. Faithfully the young man guided his people and showed them how wonderful it is to belong to God's chosen people. Certainly God works in a wonderful way. As a result of this young man's faithfulness and his ardent prayers, his father, mother, brother, sisters, and a blind uncle have accepted the truth and are now members of God's remnant church. Brother Taroba is conducting a public effort in this village at the urgent request of the villagers.

"God is at work to gather out His children from the eighty million people of Indonesia. This is God's hour for advance in this island field. We are already engaged in the final assault on the enemy's strongholds."[87]

Home Again

After their five years of mission service in the islands was completed, the family headed home to the States. Much time was spent trying to complete the children's education. Hannah and the two boys headed to Pacific Union College for Donald to complete twelfth grade and for Bruce to graduate from college on June 5, 1955.

While there, Nathaniel Wilson received a call to the Georgia-Cumberland Conference to be pastor of the Greeneville, Tennessee, district. He wrote the following in a letter dated May 1, 1955, that was sent to his friends to alert them of his new address:[88]

"To our dear friends at home and abroad: We have wanted to write you now for many weeks but have hardly known just what to write or what address to give. Now that our plans are clear we hasten this word on to you and with it we send you our warmest and best greetings.

"You will see from our address at the top of this letter that we are now assigned to serve in eastern Tennessee. Elder G. R. Nash, a very good friend for many years, is president of the Georgia-Cumberland Conference, and it is good to be in his field and be associated with him once more in service.

"The Greenville district has three churches, the largest one being where the hospital is located. We like this country very much. Eastern Tennessee is beautiful and productive, and the people are friendly and nice. Our members here are wonderful—so loyal and active.

Highly Committed

"And now this little personal word. If you ever come this way in your travels be sure to stop to see us. Your stopping will cheer our hearts, and we will try to be helpful to you. We do enjoy our friends, and you are in that wonderful group. Greenville is on the main line of the Southern Railway between Washington and Chattanooga. It is also on the main highway between these centers—Washington to the central South. So please remember the Wilsons send you a very sincere invitation to stop to see us.

"We are happy and of good courage. God has been good to give us this pleasant and challenging place in which to serve Him. We thank our God for His love and mercy and for the many blessings we enjoy."

He affixed a second page about Hannah and each of the children. Then on one of the typed letters he added this handwritten addendum, dated May 11:

"To our good friends the Bradleys: I'm glad to be here—this is indeed a grand place. Only I wish Mrs. Wilson were here—which now won't be long. Dr. Coolidge has done a grand work for God here in this part of Tennessee. And please remember us here when you are along this way. I'm going to PUC for graduation in early June and to get Mrs. Wilson and Donald—we won't be back until late June so we won't see you at camp meeting—for that I am sorry."

Pastoring must have agreed with him because news stories started appearing in the *Southern Tidings* about the Greenville district. One article mentioned the revival meeting that Glen and Ethel Coon held with Nathaniel Wilson. "Twelve precious souls were buried with their Lord in the sacred rite. Two were received into the church on profession of faith... Elder Wilson knows by heart every adult and child in his churches. The pastoral interest he takes in the flock makes the non-Adventists desire to take their stand for the Lord and affiliate themselves with the Advent Movement.... There are many interested in the community, and we believe another baptismal class is in the making. Our fellowship with Elder and Mrs. Wilson, their faithful associates and the fine personnel of the Takoma Sanitarium and Hospital will long be remembered and cherished."[89]

Another article a few months later mentions "Brother and Sister Morgan and their three daughters were baptized. These dear people first learned of our work about 14 years ago through the medical ministry of Dr. L. E. Coolidge and his associates at the Takoma Hospital."[90] Elder Wilson took a picture with the family of five who were baptized. Other stories mentioned his speaking at Southern Missionary College and at a graduation service at Takoma Hospital and Sanitarium Training School.

The Kentucky-Tennessee Conference appealed to Nathaniel Wilson to join their conference. In 1957 the Wilsons left for Nashville where Nathaniel was called to pastor the Fatherland Street Church. After that he spent a few months in Covington, Kentucky, caring for two churches and serving as the chair of the Madison College Board.

It's interesting to note that Nathaniel Wilson had come full circle. He had started his ministry as a Bible teacher at Madison College, and now he was called to be chair of the board of Madison College.

A little later he wrote, "In the flood-distressed conditions in eastern Kentucky we here have seen the need of doing something to help our own people, and others too. When President Eisenhower proclaimed that section of territory a disaster area, we felt we should get busy.... Last Monday we appealed to our church people and to the public generally over the local radio and in the press for clothing for the Barbersville, Kentucky, area ... We understand the condition of our own people and others there is tragic, and our hearts have gone out to them in Christian love and helpfulness.

"Our church folk here, and the public in general have responded in a wonderful way. At one o'clock today Brother Everett Coolidge left for Barbersville Kentucky, with a well-loaded truck of clothing, mattresses, and general articles for both young and old in that flood-disaster community. There were approximately 1,600 separate articles of clothing alone, besides blankets, sheets, and mattresses. The truck used for the trip was furnished by local business men."[91] A picture of the flood relief supplies and the leaders who had helped collect the donations was included with the article.

It didn't take the pastors and laypeople long to see that they had a great counselor, hard worker, and productive leader in N. C. Wilson. After pastoring the Fatherland Street Church and the Covington, Kentucky, churches, Nathaniel was called to be the president of the Georgia-Cumberland Conference, and the family moved to Atlanta, Georgia. Donald was enrolled at Southern Missionary College at that time, and he graduated in June 1959. He then attended the seminary in Washington, D.C., where he worked on his master's degree in theology, which he finally received from Andrews University in 1962.

One of the greatest blessings that came to the Georgia-Cumberland Conference during Nathaniel Wilson's presidency was the Operation Dixie Crusade, which encouraged and assisted local pastors to conduct evangelistic efforts in their own districts. Heretofore, the pastors had waited for the conference evangelist to do the evangelizing. "Every activity of the church must center in soul winning. Each department of the conference and church has but one goal and objective, and that is bringing people to God's truth." Many of the efforts were conducted under tents. His watch cry, as always, was "evangelize! Evangelize!"[92]

Nathaniel Wilson had always been a strong Ingatherer. He promoted Ingathering with zest in his conference. Members were happy and thrilled to be members of the N. C. Wilson Club, which recognized those who raised large Ingathering sums. Senior members had a goal of $100; junior members a goal of $50; and primary members a goal of $25.

Hurlbutt Farm Again

One interesting development that brought Nathaniel Wilson back to his roots was his connection once again with the Hurlbutt Farm. For many years the Georgia-Cumberland Conference had desired to start an academy for its youth. Various plans had been proposed, but none had been acceptable. At a special conference session held during camp meeting on Sunday, June 5, 1959, led by the man who knew quite a bit about the farm at Reeves, Georgia, the executive committee was empowered to work out the details and arrange for the development and purchase of 600 acres from The Layman Foundation for a new academy.

William George Wilson and his wife, Edith, had gone to the Hurlbutt Farm when Grandma Hurlbutt had appealed to them for help. William George had worked and died there. Newlyweds Nathaniel and Hannah had spent the first months of their marriage there. And now N. C. Wilson was making plans to use the property for training and developing Adventist youth. Georgia-Cumberland Academy stands on the Hurlbutt property today.

Shortly thereafter, in 1960, the executive committee of the Michigan Conference invited Nathaniel Wilson to be its president. It would be his twelfth and final position of presidency in church leadership. Hannah and Nathaniel moved to Lansing, Michigan, on January 20, 1960 and served there until November 1966. Michigan was the oldest Seventh-day Adventist conference, and it was at Battle Creek that the General Conference of Seventh-day Adventists had been organized in 1863. So many of the important buildings and institutions of the church were in the Michigan Conference—Battle Creek Sanitarium and church, Andrews University theological seminary, Pioneer Memorial Church, and many other places of interest. It was a challenging assignment.

Scores of churches and school buildings were built and dedicated under his leadership in Michigan. He was the principal speaker for these important occasions. One of the highlights of his administration was the biennial session and the centennial camp meeting. "One hundred years ago in the city of Battle Creek, the Michigan Conference was organized. It was the first local conference organization in Seventh-day Adventist

Highly Committed

history. There were 18 churches in the conference with a total membership of less than a thousand. Two years later, when the General Conference was organized, with headquarters in Battle Creek, there were six local conferences, representing less than 4,000 members in all the world. Today the Michigan Conference has a membership of nearly 16,000, and our world membership is approaching 1,250,000.

"It seems fitting that the regular biennial session of the Michigan Conference could be held during its centennial year, in the very city where the conference came into existence....

"The unanimous vote to re-elect N. C. Wilson as president [and the entire office departmental workers and staff] ... speaks effectively and eloquently of the ability and devotion of the workers and the wonderful spirit of unity that prevails in the Michigan Conference."[93]

"The largest crowds in the history of the Michigan Conference thronged the annual camp meeting in Grand Ledge on the closing day, Home-coming Sabbath, August 12 [1961], and gave the largest offerings ever taken in Michigan–$120,000 for evangelism.

"Prevalent throughout the ten-day encampment was the Centennial theme. Members were reminded of the heritage of the pioneers whose zeal and dedication led to the founding of the conference in Battle Creek in 1861. The interest in the proposed $100,000 offering for evangelism was at a high pitch even before the meetings began, and it increased in intensity until the closing Sabbath. An accurate count was impossible, but there is no doubt that this was the largest attendance ever. Educated estimates place the total at 15,000....

"One of the high points of the afternoon program was a trophy march. All who had been baptized since the previous camp meeting sat in a special section and then marched across the stage. Many were interviewed and they told how God had blessed them in their search for truth....

"In planning for the observance of the Centennial N.C. Wilson called for a dedication to evangelism, and pastors and laymen rallied to the call.... Probably no one spoke more forcefully or made a greater impact on the audience then did Paul Harvey, newscaster on the A.B.C. Network. He spoke on Wednesday night. Earlier in the day, broadcasting from Battle Creek, he had told his nationwide audience of the beginnings of Adventism in Battle Creek and the contributions made by Ellen G. White."[94]

Baptismal records in the Michigan Conference during the centennial year shattered all previous records. Another noticeable achievement was attained in the Ingathering campaign, the largest amount raised ever in Michigan and in any conference in North America. The Michigan Conference was number one in the world in Ingathering in 1963, surpassing their goal of $300,000. No other conference in the world had ever received that much money in a single year. At the workers meeting, the 140 workers pledged themselves, by the help of the Lord, to surpass all previous records in soul winning. The true spirit of teamwork and desire to be involved in evangelism was evident.

The Michigan conference also led the entire world field in deliveries of literature by their literature evangelists during 1962. The 1962 General Conference session, once again in San Francisco, California, saw father and son, Nathaniel C. Wilson and Neal C. Wilson, as delegates.

Nathaniel C. Wilson knew how to meet and greet dignitaries from around the world. He invited the governor to come to camp meeting. Michigan Governor George Romney addressed more than 8,000 Adventists at the Michigan camp meeting in August of 1964. In his address the governor gave warm praise to the Seventh-day Adventist Church for its high principles and standards, and he stated that our nation as a whole needed a revival of moral standards if it was going to survive.

Two years later on September 5, 1966, more than 80,000 people, among them congressional leaders, business leaders, and medical official, turned out to celebrate the 100th anniversary of Battle Creek Sanitarium and to see President and Mrs. Lyndon Johnson. At the centennial anniversary ceremonies, it was revealed that Mrs. Johnson had visited the medical institution when she was 11 years old. As a memento she was presented with the original hospital admittance card sealed in plastic. She responded with a gracious speech, praising the spirit of service evidenced in the hospital. Just before President Johnson addressed the audience, N. C. Wilson, chair of the Battle Creek Sanitarium board, presented the chief executive with a medallion, especially prepared to commemorate the 100th anniversary of the health center and his visit.

If the dignitaries couldn't come to him, Nathaniel went to them. "Susan Coon, of Lansing, Michigan, recently presented *A Century of Miracles* to S. E. Imoke, minister of education in eastern Nigeria. The gift was a token of appreciation from N. C. Wilson, Michigan Conference president, for the many kindnesses the Nigerian official has shown the denominational educational system in his area. The presentation took place at the Lansing airport as Imoke left for his own country following his visit to Michigan State University. Susan, who has lived more than half of her eight years in West Africa, is the daughter of Elder and Mrs. Roger Coon, formerly missionaries to Nigeria."[95]

1966 GC Session

The 1966 General Conference Session was held in Nathaniel Wilson's territory in Detroit, Michigan. The church's very first session of the General Conference was held in the Michigan Conference in Battle Creek, Michigan, and now 103 years later it was being held again in the state of Michigan. With the union president J. D. Smith, Nathaniel C. Wilson greeted the assembled delegates. It was the fiftieth quadrennial session of the world conference. Detroit's Cobo Hall was one of the very finest convention facilities anywhere in the nation. This session was the thirtieth of the regular sessions of the General Conference held in Michigan with most of them in Battle Creek. Two were held in Lansing. Besides these, five special sessions were held in the state.

Again George Romney, the governor of Michigan, addressed the General Conference session. He had been invited by his friend Nathaniel Wilson. On Thursday night after the offering, George Romney entered, flanked by Elders Neal Wilson, new president of the North American Division; R. R. Figuhr, retiring president of the general conference; R. H. Pierson, president of the General Conference; and Nathaniel C. Wilson, president of the Michigan conference. "The Governor delivered a stirring speech, interrupted again and again by prolonged applause. He emphasized his concern about the evident decadence of the American society, and set forth personal Christianity as necessary to reverse this trend and change the sinful nature of man. At the close of the speech, Elder Figuhr responded to the Governor's words. This was followed by the presentation to the Governor of the ten-volume set of the *Seventh-day Adventist Bible Commentary* reference series"[96] by Nathaniel C. Wilson.

Nathaniel continued to reach out to the community. He saw an opportunity in shoes. "About a year ago a Michigan shoe manufacturer gave 12,000 pairs of shoes to the Adventist Church for welfare work. These were sent to Korea when that country was hard hit by typhoons and floods. Later, company policy changed.

"During the summer W. M. Buckman, lay activities director of the Michigan Conference made a courtesy call on this company to express appreciation for former favors and to leave the book *A Century of Miracles*. Two months later word came that in spite of existing policies the manufacturers were again making surplus shoes available for our welfare work. The conference van picked up from their warehouse 12,000 pairs of shoes in first-class condition, worth $50,000, with additional supplies promised for the future."[97]

On November 2, 1966, Nathaniel C. Wilson tendered his resignation to the Michigan Conference Committee, after serving nearly seven years in Michigan. He had served the church faithfully for more than forty-eight years all over the world. At age 69 he was ready to leave not only Michigan but leadership and administration. He indicated that he was ready for "semi-retirement."

Highly Committed

Nathaniel and Hannah moved to Healdsburg, California, but instead of taking it easy, he became the pastor of the Healdsburg church, serving in that capacity until June 1969. Once again he was returning to his roots. His father had been baptized and served as head elder in the church at Healdsburg after hearing Mrs. White, and now his son was returning to be the Healdsburg pastor. The *Pacific Union Recorder* details a number of baptisms conducted while he was there. He was especially successful among the young people. One picture shows him with a group of fourteen newly baptized members, another picture shows him with four newly baptized members, and later another with two newly baptized members. Another announcement details plans he made to build a new church and how the members were engaged in a fund-raising campaign.[98]

Nathaniel and Hannah moved to Grand Terrace, California, three miles from Loma Linda in June 1969 where Nathaniel was appointed pastor of the Sunnymead Church. The church was about thirteen miles south of Grand Terrace near March Air Force Base. He went back twice for a few months after his pastoral service terminated to fill the spot until a new pastor arrived.

While pastoring at the Sunnymead Church he hosted the second two-week period of a one-month field school of evangelism. He was called back to the Central Union as one of the special guests when the union opened its new office. The former conference office had no place for meetings except in the president's office, which no longer could accommodate even the union executive committee. The new office had five meeting rooms. Each one of the rooms was named after a former president of the Central Union, so one was named after Nathaniel C. Wilson.

Traveling in Retirement

Nathaniel was still willing to travel across country for a good cause. He had always been interested in making the church more acceptable to Jewish Christians. "Under the direction of Elder C. H. Lauda, secretary of the North American Missions Committee, and with participating speakers Elder Neal Wilson, General Conference vice president for North America ... as well as Elder N. C. Wilson senior the first Jewish retreat was conducted at Camp Berkshire [New York] during the weekend of September 8–10."[99] The purpose was to bring together Adventist Jews and others anxious for the salvation of their Hebrew brethren. An accompanying picture showed three generations of Wilson leaders dedicated to the Master's cause: Neal, Ted, and Nathaniel.

Nathaniel also became the president of the Southern Asian Division reunion group, which met regularly at Loma Linda University. "Bring your favorite Indian food and your own table service," the announcement said.[100] There was usually good fellowship, a special speaker, and a wonderful program.

The Wilson children arranged for Nathaniel and Hannah to celebrate their fiftieth wedding anniversary in the clubhouse at the Grand Terrace condominium where they lived. It was a very nice affair and something they would always remember.

Hannah and Nathaniel celebrated their sixtieth wedding anniversary in Washington, D.C at the home of their son Neal and daughter Ruth. All five children and their companions were there as well as many of the grandchildren and great-grandchildren.

The highlight of 1980 was the General Conference session in Dallas, Texas, which was held April 17–26. They were privileged to attend with their son Neal who was now the General Conference president. At the session it was a real privilege to live next door to Ruth and Bill and just across the hall from Neal and Elinor and Ted and Nancy and Emilie. This was the only time that a father of a General Conference president had been at a General Conference session while his son was serving as president.

Hannah continued to be the glue that held the ever-expanding family together, and her great joy was to stay in touch with her extended family by letters, cards, and telephone calls. She had a birthday book that included the names of her immediate family, her eleven sisters and brothers, her nieces and nephews and their children, along with many friends. As her eyesight began to fail, she reluctantly gave up writing to the family. A note from one niece said, "You are such busy folks and still you have never forgotten me on my birthday or Christmas. You'll never know how much this means to me." A granddaughter wrote, "Grandma, you are always so thoughtful remembering every birthday,–coming to see me in my dorm room,–always praying for us,–real assurance that I am loved."

In later years she took up the art of quilting. Hannah spent many, many hours creating beautiful color combinations in the quilts. Her children, grandchildren, great-grandchildren, and many others are reminded of her love and patience as they keep warm under one of her quilts. A granddaughter once wrote, "I enjoy snuggling under my quilts, and as I make the beds I think of the loving hands that made those quilts."

In retirement the pen that had sent letters around the world continued to put words to paper. Nathaniel took opportunity to write many letters to encourage and show appreciation to workers across the country. He often wrote to the *Adventist Review*. "Just a little message of cheer and encouragement. I feel you brethren are doing a great work for God in your preparation of the *Review* from week to week. The *Review* is better with every passing year–and I have been reading it now for more than 60 years. N. C. Wilson, Colton, California."[101]

Another letter went all the way to Australia to the Stewarts, a pastor and former coworker.

"What a pleasure it was to receive your final letter of March 24 and to know you are both well and of good courage. What a joy it would be to visit you today at 46 Browns Road. Yes, I well remember just where that is. The news you sent along is very fine, but we always expect good news from Australia–what a lovely place and what lovely people–especially those of the household of faith.

"We keep well and happy here. Following my resignation five years ago as president of the old mother conference [Michigan] we served as pastor of a small [150 member] church in northern California, and now for two years a church near Loma Linda–we are only three minutes from Loma Linda–but now I've resigned as pastor here for it seems to me when a man is nearly 75 it's about time for such a move.

"We see the Australasian brethren at times–those here in Loma Linda and those at the General Conference office.

"I have the satisfaction of knowing that on two of the past General Conference nominating committees I had a large part in electing those fine men from Sydney to the General Conference staff–and indeed they are fine men–Australia is full of capable and dedicated men.

"May God bless Mrs. Stewart and you–and the other friends there. Our Christian love and best wishes to you both. The N. C. Wilsons."[102]

Advancing age and declining health brought many changes and losses to this couple that had devoted their lives to the church. They had to leave their family home for a nursing home. Hannah began to lose her sight and hearing and suffered under the isolation it brought, but she never lost faith in God's promises. She faithfully watched over her beloved husband as his health failed. She hardly left his side because she felt she might be needed. On December 1, 1992, after 73 years of marriage and many years of service to the church, Nathaniel Carter Wilson closed his eyes in sleep. Hannah would continue to live for more than two years afterwards, passing away on March 18, 1995.

Nathaniel Carter Wilson had honored the pledge he took as a teenager when his father passed away. He had stayed committed to God, his church, his family, and his beliefs. Hannah Myrtle Wallin Wilson had honored the pledge of love that she took at their marriage–to honor, love, and cherish in sickness, in health, in good and bad times, till death do us part. She had traveled with her husband all around the world. She had given of her best to her husband, her family, and to her heavenly Father.

Highly Committed

Together they had experienced the joys of seeing so many faithful believers join the church and follow Jesus. Together they had been blessed by seeing many of the plans that they had crafted enacted around the world and put into operation. There should be many stars in their crowns in heaven.

All of their children graduated from college with the degree needed for their profession. Neal and Donald earned their theological degrees; Donald going on to earn his doctoral degree, and Neal being awarded a doctoral degree. Bruce earned his medical degree, specializing in neural ophthalmology. Ruth and Clarice earned their nursing degrees. Clarice's husband held a doctorate, and Ruth married a minister and administrator who served in the highest ranks of the church. All of them attended Pacific Union College for some period of time.

It is almost unbelievable the amount of travel and movement that came into this family's life in order to stay committed to the calls that were extended to them. They always responded favorably to a call from the brethren of the church. The dizzying pace of life never diminished even in retirement.

Nathaniel Carter Wilson is remembered as a grand old man—a wonderful counselor; generous, kind Christian gentleman; and a good pastoral administrator. Standing at 6 foot 2 inches, some say 6 foot 3 inches when he stood up tall, he towered above most men. Serving in eighteen positions of outstanding leadership for fifty-three years of service, he also surpassed and stood above most men in his dedication to the church.

His name was often mentioned in the nominating committees as the next president of the Seventh-day Adventist Church. It is said that he missed the appointment as president by only a few votes in the 1954 General Conference session in San Francisco.

But his son and grandson would have that honor.

The article "My Favorite Text" appeared in the *Review and Herald* on July 27, 1961, and was written by N. C. Wilson when he was president of the Michigan Conference.

"Nevertheless the foundation of God standeth sure." 2 Timothy 2:19.

"The apostle Paul was keenly aware of the transient nature of temporal things. All about him he had seen evidences of the instability of man's natural heart and of the affairs of nations. Some even in the church had been moved about by various unsavory influences and winds of doctrine. However, in his own heart he was certain of one sure and unfailing foundation, and that was the revelation of God to His people. It must have been a great tower of strength to the apostle to know that God's revealed will in His Word was something solid and immovable. He might be persecuted, his fondest hopes might be dashed to pieces, he might be homeless and alone, deserted by his friends and even by some of his brethren, but he had the abiding assurance that there is a God who is faithful and unchanging.

"In our world today we need the assurance that the foundation of God stands sure and fixed. If Paul needed this assurance in his day, we need it even more. Indeed, we have more reason to be assured of the eternal nature of God's revelation in His Word than did God's people of ages past. A great flood of evidence as to the surety of the foundation has come to us in these latter days that God's people in earlier times did not have. In our present day, so definitely marked by uncertainty and failure of those institutions long considered dependable, it is wonderful to know that the great pillars of our Christian faith are eternally secure because they have been given to us by our God who is "the same yesterday, and to day, and for ever" (Heb. 13:8).

Islands, NAD, Retirement

Service Record for Nathaniel Carter Wilson

1. Bible Teacher–Madison College, Madison, Tennessee, 1922–1925
2. President (Superintendent)–Bechuanaland Mission, Africa, 1925
3. President (Superintendent)–Northern Rhodesia Mission Field, Lusaka, Africa, 1925–1927
4. President–South East African Union, Blantyre, Nyasaland (Malawi), 1927–1929
5. President–African Division, Capetown, South Africa, 1929–1930
6. President–South African Union, Bloemfontein, South Africa, 1930–1934
7. President–Southern Asia Division, Poona, India, 1935–1941
8. President–Central Union, Lincoln, Nebraska, 1942–1946
9. President–North American Division, Washington, D.C., 1946–1948
10. President–Australasian Division, Wahroonga, Australia, 1948–1951
11. President–Indonesian Union, Jakarta, Far Eastern Division, 1951–1954
12. Pastor–Greeneville, Tennessee, District, 1955–1957
13. Pastor–Fatherland Street Church, Covington, Kentucky, Churches, 1957–1958
14. Chair of the Board–Madison College, 1957–1958
15. President–Georgia-Cumberland Conference, Atlanta, Georgia, 1958–1959
16. President–Michigan Conference, Lansing, Michigan, 1960–1966
17. Retired–1966
18. Pastor–Healdsburg Church, Healdsburg, California, 1966–1969
19. Pastor–Sunnymead Church, Sunnymead, California, 1969–1975

Highly Committed

A set of books was presented to Governor Romney by N. C. Wilson at the conclusion of his address at the Grand Ledge camp meeting.

President Johnson walked the several hundred feet from his car to the speaker's platform so that he could shake the hundreds of hands extended to him over the fences.

N.C. Wilson has a last-minute conference with Michigan Governor George Romney prior to the governor's speech at the Michigan camp meeting. J.D. Smith and R.R. Figuhr are at right

Elder N.C. Wilson, president of the Michigan Conference, presented President Johnson with a medallion commemorating his visit to the Battle Creek Sanitarium on its 100th birthday.

Islands, NAD, Retirement

Joseph Bates (left), a pioneer in the Adventist Movement, was the first president of the Michigan Conference. Nathaniel C. Wilson, pictured here during his term as the president of the Michigan Conference from 1960–1966.

President Lyndon B. Johnson and Mrs. Johnson greet the onlookers.

In the receiving line at the airport Michigan president N.C. Wilson shakes hands with United States president Lyndon B. Johnson while the young daughter of Administrator Louis Gordon, Jan Alyce, presents the First Lady with a bouquet of flowers

Chapter Eight

Neal Wilson: The Early Years

"Experience is never the ground of our trust, it is the gateway to the One Whom we trust."
Oswald Chambers

At the time they dedicated their lives to work for the Adventist Church, Nathaniel and Hannah Wilson committed to the Adventist "movement." Moving would be a characteristic of their marriage. Each one of their five children was born in a different city and three in different overseas countries. Neal and his younger sister Clarice were both born in California.

Hannah and Nathaniel left California on the train the night of their marriage, October 1, 1919, bound for the Hurlbutt Farm in Reeves, Georgia. Their stay there was short-lived. After staying with Grandma Hurlbutt in Georgia for a few months, they took a train back to California in May of 1920 to visit Nathaniel's aging mother, Isabella, in Lodi. Nathaniel wanted to help his mother who was battling cancer and reconnect with Walter Scott, his youngest brother, who was also sick.

Hannah took the long train ride back to California, even in her last months of pregnancy, in stride. Shortly after they arrived in Lodi, Neal Clayton Wilson was born on July 5, 1920, at Buchanan's Hospital. The young couple stayed on the farm at Lockford with Isabella until Neal was a year old, and then they moved closer to Lodi Academy. In March 1922 Isabella and the couple moved to Stockton where Clarice was born on June 7, 1922. Their births brought great joy to Grandmother Isabella who would pass away the very next year.

When Nathaniel was appointed by the General Conference to be the Bible teacher at Madison College, the young couple decided to make the trip from California back south to Tennessee by car. Hannah tells the story in her notes.

"We traveled by car, and it took us one whole month. There were no motels in that area in those days, so we took care of our own food and sleeping accommodations. One evening we had gotten nicely settled in what we thought was a quiet spot when all of a sudden we realized that we were surrounded by cattle; it was a pasture.

"We encountered many hardships on that trip; bridges out and no warning, and we had to drive across dry river beds; rain for a whole week and a leaky top on our car. To top it all off we broke the spring in our car and Nat wired in a block of wood, but going through a dip in the road the wood slipped and caught our steering gear and we had no control of the car and it ran down a five-foot embankment and we had a broken wheel. It was on the Mexican border and getting dark and raining. Nat fortunately caught a ride with someone into the small town of Toya, Texas, where we were able to get help. I felt rather afraid staying there alone with Neal who was two and Clarice only four months until Nat returned several hours later. We stayed in Toya three days before the car was ready to go. Nat had to wire his mother for money.

"Later we lost all of our clothes (Nat's and mine) in going through one of the river beds, where I had to stand on some of the small saplings. Fortunately we did not lose the children's clothes. You see our suitcases were tied on the running board and we did not notice that they were lost for some time, too late to go back and look for them. It was another week before we reached Madison. One evening in the desert we ran off the corduroy road into the sand and had to wait until someone came along with a rope and were able to pull us back on the road."[103]

Neal Wilson: The Early Years

They finally reached Madison, Tennessee, and Nathaniel began his work as the Bible teacher. Neal and Clarice had a normal family life on the farm at Madison. Then in 1925 they left with their parents for Africa. Neal was nearly five, Clarice, two, and Ruth was born shortly after they arrived in Africa. Their mother Hannah was their first and only teacher for their early years. Little Neal and his younger sisters were homeschooled by their mother in Lusaka and Blantyre. Hannah was a strict disciplinarian and saw to it that the children kept their heads in the books, yet she allowed them enough time to play outdoors and experiment with nature.

When Nathaniel was called to fill in for Elder Branson as the South African Division president, they moved to Cape Town in 1929 where for a short time Neal and Clarice attended their first formal school at Claremont Union College, which would later become Helderberg College, the first Adventist college in Africa. The college had a separately housed primary school and a separately housed high school, each having its own principal.

Later when they moved to Bloemfontein where Nathaniel was the president of the South African Union, Neal attended an

Neal shows the joy of experiencing his first snow and first pair of boots.

all boys' school. Grey College was not really a college but a high quality public school with grades one to twelve that was founded in 1855. Sir George Grey, the governor of the Cape Colony, made a large donation for the establishment of the school that is still operating today and is renowned for its outstanding sports teams. Its motto was and still is "Grey College has always been on the forefront of developing young gentleman for life."

In 1904 Grey College actually became a college and started offering a full bachelor's degree program. Shortly thereafter it separated from the lower grades and became Grey University College (GUC); today it is known as the University of the Free State. Grey College had a separate headmaster for the primary school and a separate one for the high school. It was renowned for a special handshake.

Neal probably developed an interest in sports while at Grey College from 1930–1934. The Grey College Primary Bloemfontein (GCPB) Internet promotional page says, "Grey College is known for its sporting excellence. On and off the field, our boys have proven themselves to be great team players, sportsmen with great sportsmanship and young men with a winning attitude - all core values of our school. They play with passion, under the guidance of some world-class coaches, who not only teach them the game, but also send them home with life skills. There are opportunities for every learner at GCPB to find a niche among the plethora of sporting activities. We encourage everyone to be involved in at least one of these activities. It is of importance to all well balanced young Grey gentleman."

Clarice attended the adjacent all girls' school called Eunice Girls School for a short time and then the little Adventist school before the Wilsons left for furlough. Eunice Girls School was also a high quality school founded in 1875 by the Reformed Dutch Church. The name Eunice is a biblical reference to the mother of Timothy in the New Testament and a Greek word meaning "happy victory." Corina Piercey, Clarice's little school friend, wrote an account of their time together in Bloemfontein.

"Whenever the Wilsons received a parcel from America with a gift of clothing, whatever Clarice outgrew

Highly Committed

came down to me; what I outgrew went down to her sister Ruth and I remember what a beautiful organza dress Ruth passed on down to my sister Wretha. What we received, we also shared in the same way. The Wilson children were all taller than we were, and for good reason. In church service, when their father and mine [Elder E. D. Hanson] stood on the platform together, Elder Wilson was so tall next to my dad; you should have seen them trying to share a hymn book.

"During that time, the little church school was started in Bloemfontein. And what a wonderful little school it was. There was no separate building. We met in the Junior Sabbath School room, where Miss Anna Ficker was our teacher. There were perhaps twenty-five children in the school, ranging from grade one to eight. By that time, Neal was already in high school at Grey College, but Clarice and I were in church school. As I look at the little snapshot still in my album, I count at least seven of us, including Clarice and me, who eventually went into the Lord's work in various parts of the world. There may have been more.

"The Wilson family had a profound influence on me as a child. They lived very simply, as did we all during the depression, but they were always hospitable, kind and loving."[104]

Just before the family left Bloemfontein, South Africa, to go on furlough, Bruce Wilson was born on March 16, 1934. The Wilsons sailed from Cape Town, Africa, for home by German freighter on June 2, 1934, via Hamburg. After spending two weeks in Hamburg, the family left for the United States by another boat and arrived in New York in August. They traveled west by car, stopping a short time in a little town called Nevada, Iowa, to help with Ingathering. Nathaniel could always be counted on to help raise money. They arrived at their final destination, Lodi, California, in November 1934 and secured a house where they lived for a few months. Baby Bruce had the whooping cough and was getting worse, so they took him to St. Helena Hospital for medical treatment. Hannah and Ruth stayed in a cottage with Bruce so that they could be near the hospital. Nathaniel spent most of the remaining two months of their furlough at Lodi so that Neal and Clarice could attend Lodi Academy for the 1934–35 school year.

The 1935–36 *Lodi Bulletin* shows both of them as members of the 1934–35 class. Although only for a short time, Neal would follow in the footsteps of his father and uncles by attending their alma mater, Lodi Academy. Everyone was concerned about Bruce's health as their furlough ended and the date of their departure for India drew near. It was only by God's grace and mercy that Bruce recovered in time for them to leave for their appointment to India. In April of 1935 they drove by car to Portland, Oregon, where they boarded a Pacific Island fruit boat, which had been used for the islands of the south but had been converted to a passenger ship. It was not really fit for travel in the north, having windows instead of portholes, which gave them a rough ride when they encountered stormy weather on the way to Japan.

When the family left the United States on April 23, 1935, bound for India, Neal was 14, Clarice was 12, and Ruth was 9. When they arrived in Poona in late May, Neal and Clarice had an Indian tutor for a few months. Ruth was taught at home by her mother. The last Wilson boy was born in Poona, India, January 9, 1938, and was named Donald Wallin Wilson.

Neal was coming into full manhood and found sports to be his new interest. He devoted every spare moment to this challenging activity. He became involved in track and field, polo, soccer, mountaineering, swimming, and other sports–sports that had been introduced to him at Grey College in South Africa. He soon found that he excelled in sports. His shelves and walls were decorated with medals, ribbons, trophies, cups, and pictures reminding him of his athletic ability. The 15-year-old lanky youth really felt proud when he won a national title in the regional sport of badminton in the Western Indian Championship.

"I had pictured myself really cast in a sport's world. I was enamored with that type of life. It's intoxicating, you know, to hear people clapping for you, cheering your efforts."

And then something happened that made him really think about his future—he was struck with infantile paralysis (polio). For weeks he drifted in and out of a high fever and delirium. The doctors gave him up for dead.

"Pastor Wilson, your son Neal has very little chance for recovery or even survival. Call the church and pray that he will survive, which we don't think he will. But if he does survive, he will probably have some kind of physical disorder or mental disability," the doctors said.

"I heard the verdict of the physicians that I wouldn't last for more than a few days at the most, and probably that would be best because even if I did survive I would be mentally impaired or physically disabled. My sports career seemed to be over. I was just 15 and my life was over! I thought about my future and I made a covenant with the Lord in the dark of that sickroom. 'Lord,' Neal said, 'If I ever get out of this bed, I'm going to do something other than wait for the sound of those applauding my sports achievements. I'll learn to do something for human beings that has a more enduring, a more lasting nature.'

"Almost instantly I felt my strength returning. Almost instantly I knew I had been cured. I got out of that bed in India and I knew I had a new direction for my life."[105]

Boyhood Commitment

God calls in mysterious ways. God called Moses from a burning bush. Isaiah was called in a vision. Nehemiah was called through distressing news. Jeremiah was called from his mother's womb, and Paul was called dramatically on the road to Damascus. A 15-year-old boy who was deathly sick with infantile paralysis heard a call in a doctor's grim prognosis. "I committed myself to God by faith, and God has blessed my commitment," said Neal Wilson.

His mother applied hot and cold packs to his legs for several weeks until his full strength returned. Even in later life, his family said that his left leg was weaker than the other. But he had tremendous strength even in the weaker leg. Sports were no longer the consuming passion of his life. He wanted to do things that would help prepare him for serving others. At his baptism in 1935, he gave his heart fully to Christ and the church.

Neal and Clarice attended Vincent Hill School and College from March 1936 until the end of the school year in November. (They were on the British system, and the school year started in March and ended in November.) Vincent Hill School and College was a coeducational Adventist boarding school on the senior high school level, with a basic American/British curriculum.

William Johnsson, who was a teacher there in the 1960s, gives this wonderful description of the place. "Situated on the first ridge of the Himalayas at 6,500 feet, the school was above the malaria line. It was at the end of the town of Mussoorie, a long, sprawling, up-and-down settlement that featured several high-class schools and attracted many tourists during the hot summer months. It was a grand, wild location.... Access to Vincent Hill School was by train, bus, and foot—train from Delhi to Dehra Dun, at the foot of the mountains; bus on the long, winding switchback road to Mussoorie; then by foot up the road to the top of Vincent Hill and down to the school several hundred feet below. The school owned no motorized vehicles. There was no accessible road to the school.

"The school had been cut from the rock. Everything was up or down. In the center was a large flat area holding the administration building, girls' dorm, cafeteria, and a play area. Up and down from the center were small cuts for staff housing. At the very bottom, on another large cut, was the boys' dormitory.... The school had a reputation for academic excellence. One year the average IQ tested at 117."[106]

The student enrollment of about 100 was made up mainly of children of the missionaries and workers scattered across India, Asia, Canada, the United States, and Australia who had made significant financial contributions toward the founding of the school. It had gone through several name and site changes before the Wilson family arrived, and at the time they were there, it offered grades one through twelve and two years of college. For students who wanted it, the high school curriculum prepared them for the Cambridge Senior School Leaving Certificate. Neal enrolled in his final two years of high school and then did his first two years of college.

Adventists do not operate the school today. "At the end of 1969 ... the school was closed and the property sold ... owing to the fact that the government's policy on granting entry visas restricted the entry of qualified personnel who might serve as teachers ... Therefore, the Southern Asia Division voted to join with the Far Eastern Division to operate Far Eastern Academy in Singapore and to send children of missionary parents there."[107]

Neal still wasn't quite sure what his future would be. His father and some others were encouraging him to take courses in commerce and business. In a letter to Elder E. D. Dick at the General Conference, he writes in his own handwriting, "Following your suggestion as well as that of my father, I started the year in school by taking a commercial course, however I did not continue long at this for it seemed that I simply was not destined to be a stenographer. However I kept up with my bookkeeping.... When Bro. Nelson came up at the end of the year to audit, he was interested in my desire to learn bookkeeping, and since Bro. Pein Gyi was going to Burma, he asked me to work in the Division office as bookkeeper until I left for America—needless to say I was delighted at the opportunity. I have now been working for some four months and have learned a lot—for the past six weeks I have been working as accountant and cashier in the Publishing House, as Bro. Nelson wanted me to get an idea of 'cash-accounting' which I feel I have a fair knowledge of now. I am really thankful that Bro. Nelson has taken this interest in me, and I feel that I have benefited one hundred percent in being able to handle real accounts; and also in having the responsibility of 'cash' on my hands, I hope I have proved worthy of the wonderful chance that has been afforded me."[108]

He had the opportunity to honor Vincent Hill School with his athletic ability. "A number of other schools were located in that area, but because this school was the smallest and served only vegetarian food in its dining room, it was the subject of ridicule.

"'The other schools would challenge us in all kinds of sports,' reflected Neal, 'but we always had to decline because of school policy. They said it was because we were afraid of them.'

"There came a time when a few students grew tired of the ridicule. The area schools held an annual competitive run to a mountain about twenty miles away that required crossing huge gorges spanned by rope bridges and scrambling steep mountainsides. The Vincent Hill students were again forbidden to compete.

"Three students, however, decided that they would enter the contest to demonstrate to all who criticized and taunted them that there was an 'Adventist advantage.' When the race had ended, Neal was at least a quarter of a mile ahead of the nearest competitor. And the two others from Vincent Hill School took the third- and fourth-place positions. 'After that,' said Neal, 'there was never any question about the 'grass eaters' and the Adventist advantage.'"[109]

Vincent Hill School and College agreed with Neal. He was chosen as president of his junior college senior class, and he looked forward to graduation. The class members spent a great deal of time on speeches and plans for graduation, which took place Saturday night, November 25, 1939.[110] He gave the president's address and sang in a mixed quartet. Clarice gave the farewell address. Neal's grades were excellent. He was among those who averaged above 90 percent for the fifth period of 1939.[111] He also played the trumpet and trombone in the school orchestra and took a course in the fundamentals of hymnology. He indicated that he personally owned his trumpet and trombone.

"Commencement exercises of 1939 were marked by simplicity and dignity which will long be remembered by the members of the class as well as by the students, teachers, and friends who were present. Pastor J. C. H. Collett had charge of the Consecration Service on Friday evening, and Pastor N. [Nathaniel] C. Wilson delivered a timely message from the book of Esther in his Baccalaureate sermon on Sabbath. The class night program contained well-prepared speeches and music numbers given by the members of the class. The words of the motto, 'Honourably and Courageously,' and the words of the aim, 'To Finish the Task,' were beautifully shown in the decorations of Royal Blue and Tangerine."[112] Neal graduated from the junior college and Clarice from the high school. The two graduation services were combined.

Having had a pleasant year in bookkeeping at Vincent High School and College, when he graduated Neal secured jobs working as an accountant and bookkeeper in the Treasury Department of the Southern Asia Division office for one year, and then he became the acting treasurer at the Oriental Watchman Press, the publishing house for the division.[113]

PUC

The Wilson family left India in 1940, and Neal and Clarice enrolled in Pacific Union College.

The two years that Neal spent at PUC finishing his bachelor's degree were busy ones. In addition to his classes, he served as a staff member of the school newspaper and participated in and led out in the *Campus Chronicle* subscription campaign. "Under the leadership of Elton Wallace the *Campus Chronicle* campaign opened at the chapel hour Monday, the 15th, to continue to October 15. The goal is '1941 subscriptions for 1941.' The students are divided into two bands those whose names begin with the letters A to J being led by Leonard Hare and Doreen Ingle, and those from K to Z by Neal Wilson and Iva Munson."[114]

While studying theology, Neal got a job as assistant to the cashier and a server at neighboring St. Helena Sanitarium, which proved to be a special blessing. An attractive young lady by the name of Elinor Neumann from Chicago admired the tall, thin college boy who served salads in the sanitarium dining room, and she was pleased when he started stopping by the San store where she worked.

This attractive young lady and her family had a very interesting history, Neal found out afterwards. Her mother, Theresa Neumann had immigrated to America around 1912 with the millions of European immigrants that entered the port city of New York at that time.

Her Austrian name was Theresa Werderich, and she earned her living as a seamstress. Her passage to America touched on one of the best-known stories of the twentieth century. Hoping for a better life and traveling alone, Theresa booked a single bed in the steerage class of a British vessel. Most immigrants traveled "steerage" or what was really third class in the lowest deck of the boat without windows, fresh air, or creature comforts. She knew the trip meant days aboard an overcrowded ship, possibly in hazardous weather. The substandard food and sanitation conditions compounded the misery.

When she attempted to board the British vessel she had booked, she was told that the ship was already full. Disappointed and alone and determined not to return to Austria, she managed to secure a ticket for the New World aboard a steam freighter. After a brief delay, she set sail in the wake of the vessel she should have traveled on—the *RMS Titanic*. "I can imagine the staggering sense of relief she must have felt a few days later when her boat pulled some 20 *Titanic* survivors out of the frigid Atlantic.

"I can also imagine the sense of fear and isolation she must have felt upon arrival in America. Not only was she without family or friends, but she did not speak more than a smattering of English and had little means of supporting herself. She had grown up in Welgerdorf near the Black Forest of Austria. It was a mountainous region of quaint villages and ancient castles. What did she feel as she set foot on the brash and often brutal sidewalks of New York City for the first time? Though the known facts of Theresa Werderich's life are few, she must have been a woman of considerable courage to embark upon the journey she did."[115]

Theresa continued her travels until she reached Chicago, and there she met Joseph Neumann, a Catholic

Highly Committed

barber from Budapest, Hungary. They met by chance at a community dance. Theresa was happy to meet another German-speaker in the tough city of Chicago. In a short while they were married. Theresa discovered all too quickly that Joseph drank heavily and was prone to violence when he drank. To this new family were born four children: Sue, Elinor, Joe, and Richard.

When Elder W. B. Ochs, a Seventh-day Adventist evangelist, arrived in Chicago and pitched his tent not far from the Neumann home, Theresa began attending the German-speaking meetings regularly. Joseph was definitely displeased at her interest in this strange religion, and when she got baptized on September 15, 1917 by Jacob H. Miller and started attending the Northside German SDA Church, he was upset. When she was ordered by sincere church members to remove her wedding band, Joseph was furious.

Joseph "had been drinking and was in a foul mood. An argument broke out about Theresa's conversion and the wedding band in particular. Voices were raised, and there was cursing. The tenant houses in their immigrant ghetto were narrowly separated, and the walls were paper thin. The neighbors no doubt heard everything, if they weren't preoccupied with their own disputes. Joseph grew increasingly enraged. Finally, in a fit of anger, he seized a large fish that was frying in the skillet and hurled it violently at Theresa. She ducked, and the fish smashed into the wall, leaving a large stain of brown fish grease. Theresa fled.

"The stain, however, remained. And Theresa did not remove it. Like the scarlet letters Puritan divines sewed to the garments of moral offenders to perpetually remind them of their sins, that greasy fish mark remained on the wall for years—a silent but powerful reminder to Joseph of the shame of his abusive act."[116]

Theresa worked at a number of jobs at the same time, including stretching curtains and seamstress work. She wanted her two daughters to get a Christian education, and she began supplementing her meager income by making flowers out of crushed crepe paper, which the girls then sold on the streets. With this money Sue and Elinor enrolled in Broadview Adventist Academy in La Grange, Illinois, where Sue graduated in 1935 and Elinor in 1937. Two years later Theresa died at the young age of 44 from a blood clot while Elinor was in college.

The youngest brother, Richard, was a little boy when his mother died, and his sisters tried their best to care for him. "Uncle Dick was about fifteen years younger than Aunt Elinor. Grandma Neumann died when Uncle Dick was three, and it became my mother [Sue Neumann Miklos] and Aunt Elinor's responsibility to take care of Uncle Dick in part because Grandpa Neumann was not an Adventist, and he also drank too much. Eldine Dunbar [a youth leader in the General Conference] and his wife Ivanette took Uncle Dick into their home and hearts and raised him as their son, Richard Dunbar. He later became a physician."[117]

The Neumann girls then enrolled at Emmanuel Missionary College (EMC) in Michigan (Andrews University today). "My mother went to St. Helena, California, from EMC to take nursing. I don't recall too much of the details why except that she went out because she was 'dating' someone that went to PUC, but that friendship remained just that. Aunt Elinor was still at EMC, at least for the first year that my mother was in nursing school.... I suspect that Aunt Elinor went out to join my mom after Grandma had died. She wasn't interested in nursing, but Aunt Elinor did work in the cafeteria at St. Helena."[118] And that's how Elinor Neumann happened to be at St. Helena where she met Neal Wilson while he was studying at PUC.

Neal took part in his first evangelistic series during his senior year. "Two evangelistic efforts are being conducted by members of the field evangelism class, in Vallejo and St. Helena, under the direction of the instructor, Elder Fred B. Jensen.

"The Prophetic Dome tabernacle designed by Elder French last year has been moved to East 14th street near the highway, in Vallejo, where every Sunday and Friday night Hugh Campbell, Neal Wilson, Lincoln

Levison, and Demetra Lewis preach.

"At St. Helena Harold Hare and Ejler Jensen are holding meetings. A good interest is being developed. Already at both places some are showing definite interest in the messages that are being presented."[119]

Neal often gave inspiring mission talks about India and Africa for Sabbath School with good results. Elder Robert H. Pierson tells the story of how "work has almost been finished on two *pakha* stone church buildings in the ... Tinnevelly District ... made possible through a special donation sent from America by a man who happened to listen to Neal Wilson give as a Sabbath school missions story the origin and needs of the work ... Impressed with the needs of the place, the man handed in a cheque to cover the cost of a neat building in this village."[120]

W. I. Smith, president of Pacific Union College, evaluated a group of students, including graduating senior Neal, in a letter that he sent out to the conference presidents. "At this time I am writing to you concerning several members of the senior class and of the professional classes in whom you may be interested ...

"Neal Wilson, 21, 6' ½", 150 pounds, health good. SDA membership at Lodi. Major: religion; minors: speech and history. Extra-curricular: S. S. Superintendent, Treasurer senior class, M. V. associate leader, S. S. Secretary, Master Comrade leader, speech editor and Chapel editor of *Chronicle,* activities editor *Diogenes Lantern,* prayer band leader, etc. Manual skills: accounting, one-year bookkeeping division office (Southern Asia); one-year bookkeeper and cashier Vincent Hill School, India; one-year assistant cashier St. Helena Sanitarium; printing; electricity. Desires: 1.ministry; 2.teaching; 3.accounting.

"Neal has a pleasing personality, capable, public speaker. Is not certain that he should take up work this year, though his father, N. C. Wilson, feels that it would be best for him to do so. He himself would be glad to continue another year though he is getting his degree this year."[121]

Graduation and Marriage

The year 1942 was a momentous time for Neal. He graduated on May 17, 1942, from Pacific Union College with a bachelor's degree in religion with minors in history and speech. At first it seemed as if he was going South to continue his ministry. The *Southern Tidings* announced a bit prematurely: "We are happy to announce that Georgia-Cumberland is getting one of the two special internes that are being given to this Union Conference. Brother N. C. Wilson, who is just graduating from Pacific Union College, has been selected to fill this place. Brother Wilson's father was President of the Southern Asia Division and at the last General Conference was elected as President of the Southern African Division. We are very glad to get this special intern and are happy to get this promising young man."[122] Apparently the call never materialized, and there is no record of him ever going to the Georgia-Cumberland Conference.

But another response was received from Elder E. H. Oswald, president of the Wyoming Mission, requesting Neal to fill out the two-page "Ministerial Internship Application for the First Year." Neal filled it out and returned it. The first part required a response from the college, and it came back quickly. "The faculty of Pacific Union College heartily recommends Neal C. Wilson for acceptance as a ministerial intern, signed by W. I. Smith, President of Pacific Union College." Then the form was forwarded to and voted on by the Wyoming Missions Committee and signed by E. H. Oswald, the president, for Neal to begin an internship on June 1, 1942, at a salary of $18.00 per week. The form was also signed by his father, Nathaniel C. Wilson, with approval from the Central Union Conference Committee. (The Wyoming Mission was a part of the Central Union Conference where Nathaniel C. Wilson was president.) Now he had his first job in the profession he had been training for.

Of course, the biggest event of the year was his marriage to Elinor Neumann on July 19, 1942. The marriage started out humbly. "Elinor had $300 to her name and paid for the wedding. Neal had $300 and bought a car—and that was enough to begin life together."[123]

Highly Committed

The newlywed couple drove to Sheridan, Wyoming, and Neal went right to work in the Wyoming field in a summer evangelistic effort. "Elder and Mrs. R. J. Thomas and Mr. Neal C. Wilson, a graduate of Pacific Union College, son of Elder N. C. Wilson, president of the Central Union Conference, are to conduct a public effort in a hall at Sheridan."[124]

Four days after their marriage a letter dated July 23, 1942, arrived asking them to consider leaving their work in Wyoming and going into mission service. It asked them to fill out the questionnaires required for mission service.

Muslims

"Dear brother Wilson: At the time of the Spring Meeting of the General Conference Committee earnest consideration was given to the necessity of having missionary families under appointment and securing such preparation as is available here in the homeland for work in various parts of the world field when this present conflict [World War II] ceases or when the Lord otherwise indicates that the way is open for missionaries to be sent forward once more. One section of the world field which received particular attention at that time was the Near East, consisting of several important Muslim countries. The work for these Muslim people constitutes one of the greatest challenges confronting this denomination at the present time. We have done practically nothing in the way of evangelistic work among the Muslim people of North Africa and the Near East.

"The General Conference has decided that ten families should be immediately placed under appointment and definitely earmarked for work in the Muslim lands in the Near East with the understanding that arrangements would be made for these missionary appointees to study the language of the field and other subjects here in this country in preparation for the time when they can go forward to those mission fields. It is understood that it may be a year or two or possibly longer before the Lord opens up the way for missionaries to go to these fields once more. The plan is, however, for these missionaries to be supported by the General Conference and continue in their language study and other preparation until the situation changes and transportation can be secured for them.

"Your name has been suggested to us as one who is interested in the mission field and we are wondering if you would be favorably inclined toward mission service among the Muslim people of the Near East. I am enclosing herewith questionnaire forms to be filled in by you and your wife. In answering these questions you will indicate whether or not you are interested in being appointed to foreign mission work and you will also give us information that we desire to have for our records. We shall be glad for you to fill in these forms and return them to us immediately, indicating the degree of your interest so that we may be able to give definite study to your appointment if the way seems clear. May God guide you and your wife as you give consideration to this matter and may He lead you to decide in harmony with His will."[125]

Three weeks later Elder Michael received an airmail letter from Sheridan, Wyoming, from Neal Wilson and his wife. It contained the completed questionnaires and the response that they were favorably inclined to prepare for mission service in the Near East. Neal indicated in his long handwritten letter that he would like to remain in his present field for at least two more months.

"My dear Elder Michael, I must take the opportunity of thanking you for the air mail letter which arrived some two weeks ago containing the questionnaires to be filled in and returned. I appreciate the kind words conveyed to me in the letter and can assure you that it was indeed a pleasure to hear from you, even though in the capacity of a business letter.

"As you can well imagine, both my wife and I have given the preliminary call earnest and prayerful consideration. Knowing me as you do, you can imagine my surprise over this invitation to return and work for people that I know considerable about. Well do you know, too, that nothing would give me more joy and satisfaction than serving in a foreign field—even though I can well appreciate the almost super human obstacles in encountering Islam.

"Now just a note as to my present status! Since June 1, I have been here in Wyoming. To begin with I participated in the Uplift campaign—then I took a few days off to get married, following which I have been busy on preparations and work in the effort. I am associated with Elder R. J. Thomas, who is a jolly fine fellow, and we get along very well. We have a song leader and musician to look after that end of things so we have a nice set-up. We are holding our meetings in the second largest theater in town which we were most fortunate to secure at a reasonable sum. I preach twice a week and then there is the pastoral work to be done—we have three churches so that means three or four sermons a week for that end of things. Last Friday night we had a record crowd in the theater when I spoke on India. At the present rate of our offerings we should be able to be self-supporting—having collected a little over $100 last week, which incidentally was our first week.

"Besides this I am on the air five days a week—over KWYO at 9:15–9:30 AM. As you can readily understand I generally get no more than about five hours sleep a night and for a dreamy Indian—it is quite a grind. Fortunately I got used to this programme in school last year when I was carrying a very heavy load of extracurricular duties, plus 18 hours schoolwork each semester and about 45 hours of work a week as assistant cashier at the St. Helena Sanitarium—but don't worry, the flag is still flying high. Now to return to the subject from which I so suddenly deviated. My programme over the air which I have named 'Whispers of Hope' is bringing very gratifying results.

"Many people write to the station and to me asking me to continue—and according to the station officials they say it is the best religious broadcast in this part of the country—in fact they [the manager and owner] offered me a job as assistant manager and news commentator at the tidy sum of $225 a month. These last few remarks are not in self exaltation by any means, but merely to give you an idea of my experiences which I thought you would be interested in. 'I am all-out for evangelism, and those who know me feel that evangelism is my place.'

"Such is my situation! I do not feel that the mission fields have been given their just measure as far as talent and ability goes, and therefore as much as I enjoy my work I shall be most happy to prepare for foreign service if you folks feel to suggest that—there is one request I have, though, and that is that I be allowed to remain here for at least two months longer. Of course, I don't know what you had in mind but if you thought to start me in language study, even though I might be six weeks late for school, I feel that my present experience would more than compensate. So whatever you folks decide will be heartily received by me; if you can just take this one request into consideration. I shall be most happy to hear as soon as things become somewhat known, as to just what I might count on; be it either positive or negative!

"Will you be kind enough to convey my warmest and most sincere greetings to Mrs. Michael and the Campbells. Then you might mention to Darren that I would cherish a short visit with him, were it possible, and ask him to accept my wishes for tons of luck in school otherwise!

"I shall 'pull the curtain' for this time, trusting that this finds you enjoying much of heaven's blessing. May the Lord bless you in your heavy duties and responsibility. With warm personal regards, I am, your sincere friend, Neal."[126]

Neal had tasted evangelism several times now, and it had definitely influenced and inspired him. He had forgotten bookkeeping and commerce. He was making $18 a week ($72 a month) as an intern—the offer of $225 a month as a broadcast speaker on a radio station, something that he was learning to enjoy, must have been tempting.

Neal was not aware of it at the time, but during his senior year in college the leaders of the church in

Highly Committed

Washington were concerned about the effect of World War II on the growth of the church overseas. Many governments were sending expatriates home and weren't allowing Americans to enter their borders. In many countries the mission program had almost come to a standstill. General Conference President W. H. Branson spoke of the situation several times at the Spring Council and at the General Conference Committees. A plan of action was developed so that missionaries would be trained on home soil and be ready to go as soon as conditions changed.

We will follow the action of some of these committees in trying to get missionaries ready for service throughout the world and especially in difficult areas.

"W. H. Branson stressed the need of keeping alive the mission spirit, especially in the hearts of our young people during this war period. It is naturally discouraging to those who are looking forward to foreign mission service to see missionaries being returned instead of being sent out. Our work in the mission fields is not yet done. We must prepare our young men and young women to serve in these foreign lands as soon as the way opens.... T. J. Michael spoke of the challenge of the Mohammadan fields, where our work has but scarcely begun. E. D. Dick said we should work out some practical way whereby we can save our young people for foreign work, and prepare them for this service.

"VOTED: that the chair appoint a committee to study the question of the maintenance of the missions spirit during the war emergency, and the saving of our youth to service in this cause."[127]

The Mission Spirit

Two days later the committee of eleven that was appointed to give study to this question presented its report and there was more discussion on the topic. A statement was prepared and it was agreed that this statement should be further edited and presented to the leaders in Washington for final adoption. Their main concern at this point was how to promote the concept.

"W. H. Branson spoke of the need of very definite endeavor being made during the present war period to keep the missionary spirit alive in the hearts of our people. He suggested that the men going to the camp meetings make it part of their program to acquaint the people with what is being done in the mission fields at the present time, and with plans in mind for carrying on the work even in the midst of difficulties. He suggested also that men returning from visits to overseas fields write articles for the *Review and Herald* and the union papers, reporting on the work in the fields visited, and that in every way possible endeavor be made to inspire our people with the thought that we are to 'carry on' even to the end."[128]

The committee discovered that the renowned Hartford Seminary in Connecticut had an interdenominational center called the Kennedy School of Missions which had a focus on training missionaries to cooperate with people of other faiths. It offered studies in Middle East cultures, Islamic history, and languages like Hebrew and Arabic. The committee felt it could send some mature families there to study.

"In harmony with a recommendation from the committee that is studying the question of maintaining the missions spirit in this wartime, and preparing for a forward move into the mission fields when opportunity offers, it was

"Voted, that five families be placed under appointment, and authorized to attend the Kennedy School of Missions in Hartford, Connecticut, with a view to making specific preparation for work among the Muslims if and when the war ends; The Appointees Committee being asked to make recommendation of the five families for appointment by this Committee."[129]

They made a further report, which was adopted as follows:

"We recommend, That during the period of the war emergency, when we have had to withdraw a number of our missionaries from the overseas fields, we plan to use a number of these missionaries in translation work, translating some of our literature into the languages of these fields, the expense of carrying on this work to

be charged to the respective division budgets. To this end we would suggest the following: ... That contact be made with N. C. [Nathaniel] Wilson in an endeavor to work out an arrangement for translation work in the Urdu or one of the other Indian languages to be done at Union College."[130]

As the committee continued their study, they formulated a plan to send students to our own Adventist colleges and to put ministerial interns into the program.

"5. That the General Conference Committee in Washington be requested to give study to, and, if found practical, put into effect a Missionary Appointees' Internship Plan by which selected young people may be placed under definite appointment to certain fields, to study language and make other specific preparations for service in overseas fields.

"6. That arrangements be made for the teaching of mission field languages at our various colleges in North America, so that as they complete their education our young people may have their hearts and minds turn definitely toward the mission fields and they may thus have opportunity of learning the language and making other necessary preparation for going overseas when the Lord opens the way for them to do so.

"7. That at these colleges where the mission field languages are being taught, translation work in the same languages be also undertaken, so that an abundant supply of literature may be available for use in the fields concerned when the present restrictions are removed. It is suggested that returned missionaries, and in some cases, national workers, can be employed for this language teaching and literature translation work."[131]

"Families for Muslim Work--Language Study:

"Under the plan previously outlined for the appointment of ten families for Muslim work, and for giving these families a preliminary training for their work through a period of language study, the arrangement was for five of the families to be located in Hartford, Connecticut, to attend the Kennedy School of Missions for the study of the Turkish and Persian languages, while the other five families would come to Takoma Park, to attend classes in the Arabic to be given at the Theological Seminary. In view of the limitations as regards housing accommodations in Hartford, the fact that the first year of language work at Hartford would be in the Arabic, since all workers for Muslim fields should have a knowledge of that language, and taking other factors into consideration also, it has seemed wise to revise the original plan somewhat. It was therefore

"Voted, that arrangements be made for the five families under appointment for Muslim work, who were to have attended this Kennedy School of Missions in Hartford, to come to Takoma Park instead, to join the other five families in the study of Arabic at the Theological Seminary."[132]

"Neal Wilson--Muslim Work:

"Voted, to place Neal Wilson under appointment for mission work among the Muslims, requesting the Central Union and the Wyoming Mission to release him in time to enroll for special training at the beginning of the coming school year."[133]

Another letter from Washington to Neal C. Wilson arrived in Sheridan, Wyoming.

"My dear Neal: Who would have thought that I would be writing to you so early after you have entered upon your work, placing before you a call to foreign mission service?

"I believe Brother Michael has raised with you the question of your attitude concerning a call to service in the Muslim work, with the understanding that you would come to Washington with your wife and enter upon the study of the Arabic language and other subjects in preparation for service in the Near East. If, after a year of study here, world conditions do not permit you to go forward to the field, there is a possibility that you enter upon further study at the Kennedy School of Missions in Hartford, Connecticut. However, this

Highly Committed

plan of study at Hartford has not been finalized.

"Now Neal, the General Conference Committee at a meeting held this morning voted to extend a call to you, and I am writing to inform you of this and to express the hope that you can be released and come forward without undue delay. The instruction in the Arabic language will begin here in Washington at the Theological Seminary on the 15th of September [1942], and it will be highly desirable if you could be here at that time. I see a note on your questionnaire that you would like to complete your present effort and radio program. While appreciating your desire to do this, yet at the same time you might suffer greater loss in not being here at the beginning of the school year if you remain by your work there, than you would if you have to leave your work early and arrive at the opening of school.

"I trust that you will find it in your heart to respond to this call, and be here by the 15th of September, or a few days earlier to get settled where the matter of accommodation is concerned.

"It is the General Conference policy that all missionary appointees undergo a complete physical examination, and we prefer that these be taken care of at one of our Sanitariums. If this is not possible, however, we would want you to go to a good Seventh-day Adventist doctor there at Lincoln. I am sending you herewith two blanks, one for you and one for Mrs. Wilson. If you will have these examinations taken care of immediately and have the reports returned to us immediately the doctor completes the examination, it will be greatly appreciated. The General Conference, of course, will take care of the expense in connection with the examination and all statements should be sent here.

"Trusting that we will hear from you within the very near future, I am sincerely yours."[134]

Paternal Consent

General Conference Secretary E. D. Dick felt that he had to inform Nathaniel Wilson of the General Conference Committee vote that day inviting his son to prepare for work with Muslims by studying Arabic. He sent a letter to Nathaniel C. Wilson immediately.

"My dear friend Wilson: It is hard for me to try to write this letter which I have before me, because I know that it will bring to you both joy and possibly a degree of disappointment, but I have no alternative and so I will come straight to business.

"You are acquainted with the plan for us to have up to ten young couples placed under appointment for service in the Near East. They will come to Washington to study the Arabic language, along with other subjects as well, while the Seminary is in session, but primarily to study the Arabic language the first year. If the war should continue and no transportation facilities are open by the end of the year's study, it is barely possible that they might be sent on to the Kennedy School of Missions for further study, but as to this we have not yet made any final decision.

"As the brethren have given study to the appointment of the young couples, we have been drawn to Neal's name and action was taken by the General Conference Committee this morning calling Neal to this work. We quite appreciate the fact that Neal is young and just starting upon his work, and argument might be made that it would be highly desirable if he had a wider experience in the work in this country before preparing for mission service. The brethren feel that there is no risk so far as Neal's ability is concerned and that for him to be placed under call now and to enter upon the work as a life work would be to his very definite advantage, rather than to postpone the call even though a wider experience here might be thought best.

"I am therefore writing, Brother Wilson, to place with you a call for Neal and highly realizing that this call will bring to you some disappointment through changing Neal's work to a place where you may seldom see him, yet we believe that Neal has ability and promise which is recognized in this call, and we hope that he will find it in his heart to favorably respond.

"The letter of call has been sent to Brother Oswald with the request that he place it in Neal's hands.

"With best wishes to you, Mrs. Wilson and the children, I am your brother in Christ."[135]

Nathaniel Wilson, in turn, sent a letter to Washington.

"Dear Brother Michael: I greatly appreciate the interest that you have taken in Neal during recent weeks. He has greatly appreciated your letters. Neal will be here with us for a day or two over the weekend and then will be going on through to start his Arabic language study in Washington. I was up to see Neal and Elinor a few days ago and they felt, or at least Neal felt quite clear that they should prepare for work in the Mission Field. Elinor stood with him on this too, but of course she is not quite as closely in touch with the problem as Neal is. In other words, Neal feels quite a desire to go back to those lands where he has grown up.

"I was certainly much interested in Neal's radio program. I heard two of his broadcasts. It is remarkable what some of these young fellows can do. He has a great sheaf of letters of appreciation from people in Southern Montana and Northern Wyoming. He has greatly enjoyed his work there. Really he has every opportunity there that any young man could expect.

"You know, Brother Michael, how much Mrs. Wilson and I appreciate your interest in our boy and his wife. May I just make this one observation or suggestion? We do hope that when Neal gets to Washington that someone with good judgment and a warm heart will be able to give them just a few minutes for counsel and help. I know that you are very busy and have many things to do, but if you can just give Neal a word of counsel, it will be greatly appreciated by him and certainly by Mrs. Wilson and me.

"I have particularly in mind the question of the place where they will live. Naturally, Neal has not had a lot of experience in this sort of thing. If someone can give him a little direction and make a suggestion or two as to where a suitable place can be found, it will be most helpful. Of course Neal will be only too anxious to have any suggestions from you. He has great faith and confidence in you and we are happy that this is the case. Probably he and you will be working together some day in a mission field and if that is the case, I hope that you will also take me along into the partnership."[136]

At the same time they were wooing the Wilsons, they were also trying to persuade Pastor George D. Keough to become a part of the teaching process. Pastor Keough entered the ministry in 1905 in the South England Conference. Although an Irishman, when he was invited to Egypt in 1908 he left his native Irish soil and worked for twenty-one years in Egypt. From 1929 until 1937 he served as a Bible teacher at Newbold College, but he returned to the Arabic union in 1937 where he worked until 1952. The General Conference took an action on this leader.

"George Keough--Arabic Teaching and Translation Work:

"Voted, that we inform George Keough, superintendent of the Arabic Union, of our plan for the preparation of missionaries for work in Arabic fields when the way opens for work to be resumed in those fields, and that he be invited when he evacuates from the Near East in harmony with instructions sent him from this Committee, to come to Washington to take charge of the Arabic teaching and translation work that is to be carried on at the Theological Seminary."[137]

The ten students had another teacher, Kahlil Ibrahim, a native of Iraq. Keough was expected to join Ibrahim in teaching and translation and in other instructional work.

The Spirit of Missions Committee also promoted and fostered the study of languages in the Adventist colleges as a part of the preparation of young people for service in the mission fields. At Union College students studied Urdu and Russian; at Pacific Union College, Mandarin and Chinese; at Walla Walla College, Chinese and Malay; at Madison College, Japanese; and at Emmanuel Missionary College, French.

Highly Committed

Keough told the story of how difficult it was with the various languages in Egypt. "Our Sabbath meetings are always conducted in three tongues. I speak first in English, and while the sentence is being translated into the Armenian or Turkish—according to the people present—I say it again in Arabic. It is quite difficult sometimes, especially when the Turkish translator does not get the meaning and it has to be explained to him again. The people are inclined to lose the thread of the subject on account of the periods between each sentence."[138]

Along with teaching and learning languages, time would be spent translating literature into that same language. The advantages of the program were many. First, they would not be caught unprepared when the day arrived for renewing and greatly expanding the work in the mission fields. Second, it would enable the missionary to begin their work the day they stepped ashore in a foreign land and contacted the users of the language they had studied.

Third, the plan kept a particular mission field definitely in the perspective of young people and younger workers from one to three or four years before they entered upon their chosen work. Fourth, it was of great spiritual value to a young person to dedicate themselves early on to the service of God in a definite and concrete way, shaping all plans with reference to a chosen objective. In the first trial year of the program approximately eighty students enrolled in the undergraduate plan and twenty appointees—students in the post-college project.

President Nathaniel C. Wilson came to terms with the fact that he would be losing his son and daughter-in-law to mission service. He would have preferred that they live and work in his territory, but he was glad to see them follow in the path he had taken as a youth as is demonstrated in a personal letter to his friend Dr. Vollmer.

"I very much appreciate your remarks regarding my son Neal and also Elinor. We feel thankful that Neal has such a good wife. They have accepted a call to attend the Theological Seminary in Washington and study Arabic, preparatory to serving in Muslim lands. This has been quite a concern to us of late. But Neal and Elinor have felt quite clear in accepting the call. Neal has only been in Wyoming a couple of months. He has been working with a very fine young man at Sheridan. They are now in the midst of a good-sized effort in the little city of about 12,000 people. Already ten or a dozen have come along and are now attending the regular Sabbath services of the church. This, of course, is very encouraging. Then Neal has been on the air four times a week with a little program called 'Whispers of Hope.' I was in Sheridan a short time ago and heard two of his broadcasts and was really surprised at what some of these young fellows can do.

"He was trained by Charles Weniger at Pacific Union College and made pretty good use of the opportunity he had. My own personal judgment was that it might have been better had they stayed in Sheridan for another year or two to get a training that a young man should get while he is still young, but they prayed earnestly about it and they feel that they should accept the General Conference call. Both Brethren Dick and Michael have known Neal ever since he was a little boy. Their letters have pretty strongly influenced him. Some of the other brethren, like Elder Branson, however, were not very glad regarding the matter. In fact, I think they were not very favorable.

"But I suppose we need to move forward in faith. Neal, of course, is foreign minded, having really grown up in Africa and India. I think Elinor and Neal will find the study of Arabic a pretty good handful. They will be with us over the weekend and will go on to Washington. I am taking the opportunity of mentioning to Elinor and Neal the remarks in your letter and they will be happy to know that you have remembered them in this way."[139]

After Neal and Elinor were settled in Washington, Elder T. J. Michael penned a few paragraphs to let Neal's parents know that the couple had found a good place to live.

"Sometime ago I received your letter of September 8 and since I have seen you since receiving that letter there is hardly any call for me to respond to it.

"I have pleasure in writing, however, to report that Neal and Elinor are here and we are extremely happy to have them in our midst. They spent most of Sabbath with us and we very much enjoyed their company. I have done the little that I could to assist Neal in finding suitable accommodation. It has been impossible to do as much as I would have liked to have done for we have been extremely busy with preparations for the Autumn Council during the past few days.

"Neal came in to see me a few minutes ago, however, to report that he and Elinor had at last found an apartment with which they were very well satisfied. The people in whose home they will be living are good people. The husband is a worker at the Review and Herald and the wife works here in the General Conference office. I know the house, but I have not actually seen the apartment which Neal and Elinor will occupy. Neal assures me, however, that it is by far the best of all the places they have inspected during the past few days and from his description we would have no reason for thinking that they would not be very comfortable in that accommodation. I have sought to counsel and guide Neal in this matter as I would my own boy, because that is just what I would desire you to do if the situation were reverse.

"Elinor has naturally experienced a little homesickness, but the fact that they have their accommodation problem settled and that the apartment is such a nice one, has gone a long way toward cheering her up. She seems to be a very fine young lady and we like her very much. We believe that she will make Neal a good companion. We are delighted to have them here and my wife and I only regret that we cannot have them living in our home. We were as excited in welcoming Neal as though he had been Darren. You may be sure we shall do everything within our power while Neal and Elinor are here to help and counsel them should they be in need of such help. We shall keep as closely in touch with them as possible."[140]

Cleveland Effort

Just before going overseas, Neal got an opportunity to participate in an evangelistic effort conducted by one of the great evangelists of the Adventist Church. He and Elinor took their Arabic books and materials and traveled to Cleveland, Ohio. Neal writes about the Cleveland evangelistic effort conducted by Roy Allan Anderson. "It had been said that the people of Cleveland, Ohio, would not attend religious meetings week after week. The meeting started September 12 in a huge Masonic Temple. Owing to transportation difficulties and Cleveland's gigantic war program, it is difficult for the people living in this large metropolitan area to travel long distances to attend meetings during the week."[141]

W. A. Scharffenberg, temperance secretary of the General Conference, and a fine sixty-voice choir combined with enthusiastic prophetic preaching saw the crowd increase daily. It was a valuable school of instruction on how to do public evangelism, and working with these experts, Neal learned many soul-winning techniques.

J. Robert Spangler, who later became the director of the Ministerial Association, was also a young preacher who participated in that effort. "We were taught the value of a soul. He [R. A. Anderson] was a leader in breaking out of Adventism's circumscribed philosophy which seemed to make us think we were neither in the world nor of the world. We learned that Christ had other sheep not of our fold," said Spangler.[142] It was a good learning experience for Neal Wilson, and he and Elder Anderson became close friends.

Elder Roger Altman continued to contact them while in Cleveland to obtain pictures and fill out application forms for their visas. Altman also contacted the War Rationing Board in their behalf to secure a kerosene cook stove and four extra shoe ration stamps "since supplies are quite inadequate" where they are going.[143]

The complications caused by the war were clearing up, and the candidates were progressing rapidly. The committee decided to send the three couples who were making the most progress on to their overseas posts.

"Voted, to begin negotiations at once looking toward sending three of the couples who are studying

Highly Committed

Arabic at the Theological Seminary forward to the field by the end of this year, suggesting as the three couples to go, Mr. and Mrs. Stanley Johnson, Mr. and Mrs. Alger John, and Mr. and Mrs. Neal Wilson."[144]

It was felt that these three could get a better start in their overseas posts if they were ordained. A committee decided to examine all ten of the candidates and make plans to ordain all ten of them at the same time if deemed appropriate.

"Ordination of Missionary Appointees:

"Inasmuch as there is prospect of the early departure of a number of the young men who are under appointment to the Arabic field, and in view of the desirability of their being ordained before going, it was

"Voted, that the officers be asked to appoint a committee to examine the following young men, in harmony with the denominational policy, and to arrange for their ordination if ordination should be indicated." The ten men were named: Neal C. Wilson, Sherman McCormick, Stanley Johnson, T. J. Jenkins, Charles C. Crider, Alger F. Johns, A. Gordon Zytkoskee, A. C. McKee, Benjamin J. Mondics, and Lester Pratt."[145]

After interviewing and questioning the candidates, the committee found them all worthy of ordination and recommended that they be granted ministerial credentials.

"Credentials and Licenses:

"Voted, That ministerial credentials for the year 1944 be granted to the following workers, who were ordained to the gospel ministry on Sabbath, February 26: the same ten young men were named."[146]

The *Review and Herald* carried the story of their ordination service which was conducted by the president of the General Conference himself and his ordination sermon was printed in the *Review and Herald*.

"A very unusual service was conducted in Columbia Hall of Washington Missionary College on Sabbath afternoon, February 26, when ten workers were ordained to the gospel ministry. Rarely are so many ordained at one time, and there were other factors that made the occasion an unusual one indeed. Elder McElhany preached the sermon, and readers of the *Review* are to share this stirring message with a large congregation who heard it in person. Nine of the ten who were ordained were young men who, with their wives, have been studying the Arabic language in preparation for missionary service in the Muslim lands of the Middle East. Elder George Keough has been their chief teacher and leader in this work of preparation. It was fitting, therefore, that the ordination prayer should be offered by Elder Keough. A. W. Cormack gave the charge, and the welcome into the fellowship of the advent ministry was expressed by T. J. Michael."[147]

A list of the young men who were ordained followed, which included this comment: "Neal C. Wilson has spent most of his life in Africa and India, and, with his wife, has accepted a call to preach the advent message to the Muslims....

"It was appropriate that this ordination service should have been held in Columbia Hall, for four of the candidates for ordination have been students of Washington Missionary College. It is also of great interest to note, in this group of missionaries being set apart for the ministry of this denomination, that all the senior colleges in North America were represented.

"May God grant that this consecrated group of young workers, who themselves are following the example of thousands who have gone before them, will themselves inspire by their example, a multitude more of the graduates of our colleges to turn their hearts and their footsteps toward the desperately needy mission lands of earth."[148]

Neal and Elinor Wilson boarded a Portuguese steamer in Philadelphia and sailed for Alexandria, Egypt, the next day—Sunday, February 27, 1944.

Neal Wilson: The Early Years

The field evangelism team at Pacific Union College in 1942. As a senior, this was Neal's first evangelistic crusade. Neal Wilson is standing second from the left.

With a religion major and double minors (speech and history) Neal still had time to be treasurer of his senior class, M. V. associate leader, Sabbath School superintendent and Secretary, Master Comrade leader, and many other leadership positions.

Neal showed good writing skills at college and helped with the school paper and yearbook. He was speech editor and Chapel editor of the Chronicle, and activities editor of the Diogenes Lantern.

Chapter Nine

In the Land of the Pharaohs

"Who knows whether you have come to the kingdom for such a time as this?" Esther 4:14, NKJV.

Neal and Elinor Wilson arrived in Alexandria, Egypt, in June of 1944. The trip had been long and tiresome, but they were the first in the Arabic class to reach a Muslim country. They took a cab from the airport to the union office. Ernest L. Branson and his staff were truly surprised to see them ahead of schedule—they expected them to arrive a month later.

Branson, the union president, immediately cabled Washington that they had arrived. He then arranged for them to get a good look at Alexandria, the second largest city in Egypt. Alexandria, "the pearl of the Mediterranean," was founded by Alexander the Great in 331 BC. The new arrivals were fascinated by this great seaport city, which had boasted Pharos, the legendary lighthouse that was one of the seven wonders of the ancient world.

After checking to see if their personal effects had arrived, and since they were so close, they arranged to visit Jerusalem, the holy land, and the surrounding area, which was one of Neal's dreams. When they returned Elder Branson offered to drive them to Cairo where they would live, a trip of about 125 miles. After his car left the bustle of the city, the road narrowed down and stretched out like a long ribbon ahead of them.

They squinted to protect their eyes from the glare of the hot sun as they tried to drink in the seemingly endless and enormous scenery of the "land of the Pharaohs." They marveled over the acres of endless sand, dotted with palm trees, pyramids, and Egyptians strolling around in traditional dress.

Ernest Branson, president but now their capable chauffeur, was born in 1906 and was the son of W. H. Branson who had been a General Conference president. Ernest Branson had followed in his father's footsteps and had also become a minister and distinguished administrator in the Adventist Church. After serving as a pastor and evangelist in Southern New England and in Missouri, he was elected president of the Missouri Conference. In 1938 he became superintendent of the Egyptian Mission and then superintendent of the Middle East Union Mission in 1942.[149] His father, W. H. Branson, had been the first president of the newly formed African Division in 1920 when Nathaniel Wilson had arrived in Africa. Just as the father, W. H. Branson, had mentored the young Nathaniel Carter Wilson in Africa, the son, Ernest Branson, would mentor the young Neal C. Wilson in Egypt. The two men, Ernest Lloyd Branson and Neal C. Wilson, came to respect each other. The two men worked well together in Egypt. When Branson left Egypt in 1950, Neal Wilson became superintendent of the union in his place.

As they drove toward Cairo, the noonday sun hung high in the Arabian sky. A caravan of camels lumbered slowly by, each beast mounted by a lone rider. A cool breeze lightly fanned the desert sand and gently ruffled the head cloths that covered the rider's heads.

They passed the three Giza Pyramids, the Sphinx, and some modern buildings sitting in close proximity. "We have only about 450 baptized members in all of Egypt," Branson informed them as he maneuvered the car around a roadside snake charmer that had tourists standing around. "As far as education facilities, we operate six village schools and three church schools. The work among the Muslims here is slow, very slow. Let me give

In the Land of the Pharaohs

you a quick overview of how the work began here in Egypt." He pumped his brakes to allow a hand-pushed cart to pass in front of him.

"On a warm Sunday afternoon in June 1882 three Adventists living in Alexandria, one from Ireland and two from Southern Europe, were murdered in a cruel way. They had been to the harbor to distribute tracts and gospel literature to the sailors of the many ships that were docked there, and on their way home they were attacked by an infuriated mob of fanatics. They were beaten to the ground with clubs and finally died after being stabbed many times with daggers and bayonets—more than 200 others lost their lives in the same way that day.

"The plan was to massacre all Christian foreigners, not just Adventists, but somehow it did not work out as the instigators had hoped. This is the earliest record we have of any Adventist believers in Egypt." Branson cleared his throat as he continued his story. "This sad incident was a great discouragement to the little group of Adventist believers, and for many years nothing was done to spread the work beyond the faithful few in Alexandria.

"Before World War II, because of political difficulties, all this territory was administered from Washington, D.C., with my father as president. Just recently all these mission fields were formed into the Middle East Union Mission administered from Alexandria, with me, your humble servant, as the director.

"Cairo is the 'Paris of the Middle East.' You'll love it. Lots of huge government buildings downtown. Lots of shops but very little in them because of the war, and everything is verrry expensive. But you'll live in Heliopolis, a suburb of Cairo. We have an apartment building there that houses all of our pastors, teachers, and workers together. We don't get much rainfall here. Water comes from the Nile. Egypt really is the gift of the Nile. Lots of oil here, too." They passed some bicycles loaded with baskets. Branson slowed down a bit.

"The Middle East is an attempt at mingling three great religions: Christianity, Judaism, and Islam, with Islam being the great winner. The word 'Arab' is applied to Muslims, Jews, and Christians who speak the Arabic language and identify themselves with the Arab way of life. Almost everyone speaks Arabic.

"Egypt is just now getting involved in World War II, and is talking about joining the United Nations and starting the 'Arab League.'

"Egypt is a country of everyday piety. You'll wake up tomorrow to the sound of morning prayers blasting over loudspeakers. But you are, no doubt, used to that, Neal, since you've lived in Muslim countries before. It's very difficult to convert someone directly from the Muslim faith. Most of the converts come from the old Orthodox Christian churches—the Coptic Church in Egypt, the Marionite Church in Lebanon, the Assyrian and Babylonian churches in Iraq, and the Greek Armenian churches scattered throughout those countries."

When they finally arrived at Heliopolis, they had shared many thoughts, ideas, and experiences. They settled into their new apartment and found out later that a letter had been sent to Elinor's father in Chicago to give him an account of their travels and let her family know about their arrival. It was sent from Elder T. J. Michael, and it read, "I have just sent you a telegram passing on to you the information that Neal and Elinor have safely arrived at their destination and are locating in Cairo. This word has just reached us by cable from the union leaders at Alexandria. We are extremely happy and relieved to know that they have finished their long and arduous journey.

"Neal and Elinor apparently made a wise choice when they decided to go overland from Angola. The other couples went around by steamer and as far as we know they have not yet reached Lourenco Marques in Portuguese East Africa. At least we have received no report from anyone to that effect. If that is the case it will be several weeks yet before they will reach their destination in the Middle East.

Highly Committed

"It has taken Neal and Elinor three months from the time they left Philadelphia to reach Cairo. Their journey has surely been long enough, but there is some comfort in knowing that their journey has been shorter than that of the Johns and Johnson families. Without a doubt Neal's background of experience in Africa, plus his initiative and persistent spirit, have made possible for him and Elinor a degree of progress which might not have been practicable for less experienced folks.

"I know that it will be a great joy and relief to you to know that they have at last reached the place where they can settle down to make their valuable contribution to the finishing of the work in the Moslem lands of the Middle East."[150]

Egypt

In a few weeks Neal returned to Alexandria to check on their belongings. Having just turned 24 years of age, the mature Neal didn't like any loose ends, and he needed to finalize on their cargo. While there he sent an informative letter back to headquarters updating the leaders in Washington on their progress and how they were settling in and getting adjusted. He was happy to be pastoring a church and was making plans for future evangelism.

"At last we have arrived in the 'land flowing with milk and honey'—sorry to say there is hardly any of either to be had; nevertheless we are both thankful and happy to be here. We had a pleasant trip from Portugal down to Africa, and then through and over Africa. The plane trip from Stanleyville saved us a tremendous amount of time.

"We visited a good many of our folks in Africa and cheered and encouraged them—it seemed that our coming was like a refreshing zephyr; it was nice to be so warmly welcomed. Of course the grand climax came when we walked in on Elders Branson and Krick—they about fell over; as we were about a month ahead of the arrival date we had wired them. We were not allowed to telegraph plane arrival dates ...

"Then Elder Branson is a first-class leader. He and I have many ideas in common, we see eye to eye and really make a team. It is a saving thing that he can go over to the Fall Council and really lay the problems before you brethren—there are some gigantic issues out here ...

"Prepare to receive him with warm hearts for he really has his hands full and needs plenty of cooperation from the officers there ... The field is ripe and I firmly believe that God is about to make Himself manifest here—a glorious day is in view and we are full of hope and courage; you know me, we are going to push ahead and do our best.

"The brethren have shown a great deal of confidence in me—they have put me in as the acting Superintendent of Egypt. This is a big task, and I feel humble, yet confident in the Lord as I face the work there. I am going to start a good strong English effort there in Heliopolis about the first of November. I plan to run a parallel English-Arabic effort down in the city of Cairo ... I will run about four meetings a week in each place.

"I have a pretty good assistant [national] Yusef Berbarry, and I want to swing him into an active programme ... Elder Branson has made an excellent start in establishing the two churches in Cairo, and now it is up to us to develop things and keep on increasing. It will take much of God's blessing, but He has promised that—remember us in prayer, won't you?

"If all goes well, I want to hold a series in Alexandria next spring and summer. I hope we can have another American worker by then ... One of the crying needs of Egypt is a good doctor with some sort of medical establishment so that the government may be more favorably impressed and more readily recognize our charitable organization ... I know it may be a year or two, but we must definitely begin some sort of plan very soon ...

"We are here in Jerusalem, but expect to leave in about 10 days for Cairo—Elinor will be so happy to get settled for a while. It is very interesting in Palestine, and I have learned much, as well as getting a wonderfully clear perspective of the Scriptures. It would be a boost for all our leading evangelists to spend from 6 to 12 months in our field; and could we use them during their stay!! I have met with all our believers here in Palestine and am going to Trans-Jordan over next weekend to see our people there and encourage them. We need a good effort here in Jerusalem.

"Our freight from the US arrived a few days ago but what a tragedy. I went up to Haifa to look over things, and found that two of our boxes were missing—as well as one of Johnsons', Johns' are all there—and then two of our boxes are absolutely empty, so apparently somebody helped themselves on the way. I did not have the lists with me but fear somehow our dishes, sewing machine and shoes are gone—Elinor is sick about it, but we will make out okay, just one of those things, you know?

"Some of the boxes were pretty badly battered up. I found Johnson's baseball glove all by itself over in one corner, having been swept up from the hold of the ship. Brother Cole did not have our things secured with iron bands. This should not happen again; I am not really provoked but a wee put out—but it is all in the 'game' so why worry? We do not have a bill of lading, neither an insurance policy on these things. The tragedy is we cannot replace the lost things here even at ten times the price. I'll write my further findings later—I am going up there the beginning of next week when I return from Trans-Jordan and make a thorough check ...

"Please pass along my evangelistic plans to Elder Anderson—tell him the flags are flying and we are forging ahead ... Tell the remaining 'Arab' class members to keep their chins up; we are counting on them and I'm praying for their speedily joining hands with the rest of us—we need everyone we can get and then some.

"Many people here send greetings to Elder Keough and so do we."[151]

A Hospitable Home

Neal and Elinor moved into their little apartment in Heliopolis, and Elinor made it into a comfortable and hospitable home. Every Sabbath and special occasion saw church members and friends seated at their dinner table. One soldier never forgot the warmth of their home and was able to remember some thirty-five years later the special Sabbaths in the Wilson home. "I had two years of very close association with the Wilsons while serving with the Royal Australian Air Force (RAAF) in Egypt. Their home was ever open to Adventists, men and women, from all parts of the Allied world, up to twenty-two sitting at their table for a meal on Sabbath. They were a great couple."[152]

Gordon and Evelyn Zytkoskee were among the ten students in the Arabic class in Washington who shortly followed the Wilsons to Egypt. Zytkoskee became the pastor of the church in Cairo and later a church administrator. At the time of this writing Gordon had passed away but Evelyn was still living in California, and she reminisced about the time they spent together. "While we were in class in Washington, Neal and I loved to study and learn Arabic, but Gordon and Elinor were not too interested in the language, so they got along real fine together. While Neal and I were laboring over the Arabic lessons, Gordon and Elinor would be shopping in town.

"When we got to Egypt, we lived several floors above the Wilsons in the apartment building. We always had something to borrow or get from each other, and the steps would wear us out so Gordon and Neal rigged up a rope and pulley with a box outside our windows, and we could send up a cup of sugar, laundry, or an iron or something else that we needed. That contraption worked real well and proved to be a real blessing to us.

"The school was on the roof of the church, and Elinor and I were on the teaching staff. It was not a large school, but it was very good and well-respected and many of the non-Adventists wanted to attend the school."[153]

Dr. Richard Lesher and his wife, Veda, served in the Middle East Union at about the same time as the Wilsons. Dr. Lesher later became the president of Andrews University and served at the General Conference as a vice president. The first time he met Elinor Wilson was while she was visiting Beirut, Lebanon, for a meeting with Neal.

Highly Committed

She had brought a number of empty suitcases with her that she intended to fill to take back with her. "Beirut had just about anything you could want at that time. It was just like America. She had bought a great deal of supplies to take back to Egypt, which was suffering from the war, and she was having trouble closing her suitcase. She didn't want to leave anything behind, so we crammed and stuffed things until we finally got those suitcases to close."[154]

Although he was called to Egypt to be a pastor and evangelist, when the leaders saw Neal's enthusiasm and zeal for the work, he was appointed superintendent of the Egyptian Mission very quickly in addition to his other responsibilities. Early in 1945 Neal had an overwhelming conviction to start a school that would train Egyptian young people to prepare for ministry. A faithful Armenian brother in Cairo dedicated his life savings to this project. Further blessings came when a special appropriation from the General Conference and "a gift from abroad" by an anonymous donor gave him sufficient funds to begin looking for a suitable place to locate the new school.

The money was insufficient to purchase a building that already existed or to buy improved land. The price of land in the Nile Valley ranged between 200 to 600 Egyptian pounds ($800 to $2,400) for an acre. The money they had was enough to purchase about thirty acres of cheap land, but that left nothing for the construction of buildings. So they began to look for unimproved land, but most of the unimproved land in Egypt was along the edge of the desert.

Seila

The search committee looked and looked. Finally they came to Seila, an oasis in Faiyoum about seventy- miles southwest of Cairo. This oasis was about thirty-five miles in diameter and was separated from the main valley of the Nile by about twenty-five miles of desert. It was considered a fertile section of Egypt and was noted for its lovely fruits and vegetables.

The seventy acres was surrounded by beautiful green fields and palm trees; but because this land was four to fifteen feet higher than the other land around, it had never been improved. There was no way to lift the water from the canal onto the land.

It rarely rains in Upper Egypt—everything is very dry. Life was dependent entirely on water from the mighty Nile. In fact, the whole province of Faiyoum was watered by a huge canal called the "Joseph River," which was believed to have been built by Joseph himself.

One of the many branches of this Joseph canal formed the eastern boundary of the property. On the west there was a rather deep valley; to the south the main railway line joined the provincial capital city of Faiyoum with Cairo; and on the north there was another small canal.

Besides these natural boundaries there were several other big advantages. On one corner of the property was the district police station, which gave them a calming sense of security, and the district post office, and close by was the railway station and the telegraph office. And because it was higher than the surrounding properties, it was more healthful and enjoyable with a cooling breeze that came off the green, water-soaked grain fields.

In November 1946 the foundation was laid for the administration building, and the school started with twenty-five young men who lived in tents for about six months. Then thirty young boys moved into the administration building, and some of the teachers lived in the partially completed dormitory. The rest of the teachers lived in the city and traveled twenty-five miles each day to and from the school. It was a difficult situation, but God blessed.

Thanks to a ten-inch pump that lifted gallons of water from the canal and poured it on the thirsty land, the desert began blossoming like a rose. Two thousand orange and lemon trees were planted along with hundreds of mango, guava, apricot, olive, pomegranate, and palm trees, as well as a variety of vegetables.

But the villagers did not like the Adventist Church and the school that had been built. One Sabbath morning the young men were quietly getting ready for breakfast when one of them happened to look across the fields in the direction of the nearest village, and soon every boy in the school was on the alert. "Here come the villagers; stop these men; protect the Lord's land," shouted the students "as they armed themselves with sticks, knives, hoes, stones and anything they could get their hands on.

"These boys meant every word they said, and fully intended to defend the school property against the angry villagers. Had it not been that the officer and several of his men from the district police outpost, came galloping up on their horses in response to their appeal for aid, the story might have had quite a different ending. These nearly one hundred armed villagers had been provoked by several unfortunate incidents, and now having been incited and urged on by their fanatical religious leaders they had decided to drive [the students] from the place and destroy the school."[155] These same people later became their friends and supporters instead of enemies. Neal Wilson tells the story of how this happened.

"One dark night a few weeks ago a raging fire broke out in their village about a mile north of our school. The villagers tried their best to put it out; but, the fire fanned on by a strong wind and the people were overcome with fear and panic, it seemed that nothing could be done to stop the hungry flames from devouring the whole village. People were beginning to flee and in their fright they were fighting with one another—a scene of dispair [*sic*] and confusion!

"To this inferno came Principal Robert Rowe, some of the teachers, and our boys. After a desperate hour of methodical and brave battling, the blaze was well under control and finally put out, with the loss of only six huts. Since this experience the villagers cannot praise our boys enough, and their praise has been heard all over the province and has even reached the ears of the Governor.

"These students saved the villagers from the flames of veritable destruction, but soon they will be out rescuing perishing souls from the fire of sin. They will go forth to battle the fear and panic and confusion that Satan is bringing into the hearts of men. Armed with the word of God, strengthened in prayer and led by the Sweet Spirit of Heaven, they will advance throughout this land of Egypt bringing hope and courage and causing men and women everywhere to be in readiness for the soon-coming of our Lord and Savior."[156]

Gift From Abroad

The following letter from Neal's father seems to suggest that the "gift from abroad" to the training school from the donor who wanted to remain anonymous was from their longtime friend and supporter Elder W. H. Anderson.

"Dear Brother Anderson: I have wanted to write you a little note regarding a letter recently received from Neal. He has written a very interesting and fine letter concerning the work out there, and he asked me to pass on a few items of interest ... Quoting just a sentence or two from Neal's letter—'Also I am going to send the pictures to Elder W. H. Anderson. He was a 'heaven-sent' in making possible our new school at Fayoum. I was there last week and we arranged for the official opening, to which the governor is coming and the vice-governor; also many other fine government officials as well as lawyers, doctors and noble citizens in abundance. I wish Elder Anderson could be there for the opening of our school at Fayoum.'

"I wanted you to have that word from Neal. He has certainly not forgotten you and greatly appreciates your fine help ... Sincerely your brother, N. C. Wilson, Vice President, North American Division."[157]

This Egypt Training School (later named the Nile Union Academy and the Adventist Theological Institute of Egypt) was moved in 1954 to Gabal el-Asfar near Heliopolis. When in the mid-1950s government curriculum requirements caused the church to close most of its schools, this school, along with the Heliopolis Adventist School, remained open.[158]

The Egyptian government, attracted by the character of the educational work being done at the training school, requested that Seventh-day Adventists help in the care of the underprivileged village children. In response, Neal was able to start a little orphanage in the suburbs of Cairo in 1946. Typical of the reaction of these homeless children is the testimony of one little girl: "My father is dead. Mother was very poor and had to beg food for us in the village where we lived. I ate only bread and salt. When I came here I thought I was in heaven."[159]

"There is a spacious garden surrounding this Mercy Home. Here 22 little children between the ages of 4–8 years are tenderly cared for by Mrs. E. Kruger, a trained nurse; a fine young man who is the teacher, and a young lady helper. These boys and girls are brands actually plucked from the fire. Before they came to the orphanage they had nothing but rags for clothes, they were infected with all sorts of internal and external diseases, they had no proper home and they either begged for or stole their food. I wish you could see them now.

"What a wonderful change has been brought in their little lives! If you could step into their worship period just before they go to bed and hear their sincere prayers and their sweet childish voices blended in singing 'Jesus loves me', you would find your eyes beginning to moisten and a lump creeping into your throat.... I feel certain that your doubts will be dispelled by this little incident just reported by Pastor Gordon Zytkoskee, who is in charge of our work in the Cairo area. He says that not many days ago the older boys at the Orphanage called a secret meeting of all the children. They did not know, however, that Mrs. Kruger was watching them through a window. One little fellow was the chairman and he got up and asked for silence. Then he said, 'We must be good because Jesus is coming soon. We must use kind words and speak the truth. When we play we must not fight, when we study we must be quiet, when we eat we must be polite. Don't you see?' he urged 'we must be good all the time because Jesus is coming soon and we all want to be together when He takes His people to Heaven.' The meeting was dismissed, and as Mrs. Kruger turned away all the toil and trouble of caring for these dear children seemed very much worthwhile."[160]

Nearly every child suffered from trachoma, a dreaded eye infection, and some had several other diseases. Some told of stealing and lying; others were beggars; some of these young children could be seen squatting on the edge of a filthy sidewalk smoking cigarette butts picked from the gutters, their clothing hanging in shredded rags and tatters; but all had one terrible thing in common, perpetual hunger. It was thrilling news to report that now these same children were healthy in body and happy at heart with their medical needs taken care of and the addition of nourishing food, clean clothing, new Bibles, schooling, and a knowledge of Jesus as their friend.

Despite all odds, the Mercy Home, as the orphanage was called, was rebuilt in 1963 and its capacity doubled! The biblical philosophy that Christ taught for every Christian to suffer the little children to come was being accomplished.

An article in *The Advent Review and Sabbath Herald* voiced the hope that the orphanage would remove prejudice against the church and make friends. "Of recent years our mission work in Egypt has had to contend more and more with government restrictions. We are sure that an orphanage which N. C. Wilson is establishing just outside Cairo will do much to break down prejudice and create friends for the mission among the official class. Sister Kruger, who previously had done excellent work as a private nurse and midwife, will be in charge of the home. Pray for this work."[161]

The seventh-day Sabbath made some of the government officials suspicious of the Adventist Church. These officials thought Adventists were connected with the Zionists (supporters of a Jewish state). Neal Wilson felt it was necessary to make a statement concerning the relationship of Adventist beliefs to the Jewish faith.

So he wrote and printed a booklet in Arabic titled *Return of the Jews*, which was a Bible study on the return of the Jews to Jerusalem. Neal stated in this little tract that the Jews are no longer the people of God, and that the only way a Jew can be saved is to accept Jesus Christ as his or her personal Savior, just the same as everyone else is saved, Arabs, Aryans, and all others.[162]

He sent copies of this leaflet to the office of the Arab League, and to his pleasant surprise, they responded enthusiastically by ordering 500 copies! Furthermore, the chief of the sheiks was greatly impressed and some of the prejudice against the Adventist Church seemed to be removed.

"A number of the Arabic newspapers in Cairo have been publishing excerpts from our literature on Daniel, and the pamphlet on the Palestine question which Pastor Wilson has written."[163]

Big Baptism

Alger Johns, the Bible teacher at the Adventist College of Beirut, Lebanon, tells how excited the college was to baptize nineteen students and Neal Wilson's part in that baptism.

"Sabbath, May 19 [1945] was a red-letter day for the Adventist college of Beyrouth, Lebanon. If you had visited us then, you would have seen unusual activity. Almost all the students and faculty crowded into three large buses, and soon were on the way down the sides of the mountain, along the narrow, winding road.

"We were leaving from the mountain hotel which had been the temporary location of the college, and soon we arrived at our church in Beyrouth. As the students rode along, their joyful hearts and voices joined in singing our familiar gospel hymns. Sometimes the words were in English, and sometimes they were in Arabic. Why should this day be joyful? It was the day of the baptism for the college....

"Most of them were from non-Adventist homes and environment. Their acceptance of this message is largely a result of the soul-winning agency of our schools, both the college here and our secondary schools in their home countries. When they come to the college, every endeavor is made to provide for them an environment which is in harmony with the Holy Scriptures. Every student takes one or more classes in Bible every day.

"In addition to this, we were privileged to have N. C. Wilson, Jr., of Cairo, conduct the autumn Week of Prayer. At this time many made their definite decision to accept their Saviour, and a baptismal class was formed....

"This baptism is one of the largest, if not the largest, which our people have ever held in the Middle East.... Such a step as this was not easy for many of our young people to take. More than half of these nineteen face the opposition of home and family. Some face trials and bitter persecution. Since school is over, and they have returned to their homes, we know of at least one such instance. The parents of one of the students have burned her Bible and forcibly detained her from attending church services. They have also burned her passport, so that she might not be able to return to school here next year."[164]

Neal Wilson was still excited about evangelism. He conducted Bible studies and a series of evangelistic efforts in Cairo, Assuit, Heliopolis, and many other places. He wanted all the pastors and workers to know how to win souls through evangelism. Later that same summer of 1945 with H. G. Rutherford of Palestine, Neal organized a six-week evangelistic council. Workers came from some of the Muslim countries of the world: Iran, Iraq, Syria, Palestine, and Egypt. Study and practical work as well as methods of evangelism were taught. They went over personal evangelism and Bible doctrines. The most important feature of the council was the practice effort, which was held for the people of Beit Mery, the surrounding village. Every night three of the young men attending the council were given the opportunity to preach and practice what they had learned in class. As many as 250 people attended every night. At the close of the four-week meetings, there were more than 100 names of persons asking for free literature. They invited W. H. Anderson, the friend of the Wilson family and veteran missionary of Africa who had inspired his father to come as a guest for three weeks. Elder Anderson presented daily devotional studies and stories about African missions.[165]

While in Egypt Wilson was "locally famous for scaling the outside of one of the Giza pyramids in record time. You'd have to see those pyramids to appreciate the full scope of that accomplishment. Although in the

Highly Committed

distance the pyramids appear to be perfectly smooth, the rough blocks of which they are made are so large and uneven that climbing one is not a project I would want to undertake."[166]

The first camp meeting in Egypt was held September 10–18, 1948, at the Fayoum Training School. The services were held in a tabernacle of canvas stretched over a wooden framework. This canopy was decorated on the inside with bright colored designs stitched to the canvas in intricate Egyptian patterns.

The school provided sleeping quarters for those in attendance. Food was prepared in the school kitchen. The total attendance of 150 taxed the facility of the school, but little or no sickness was reported, and the Christian fellowship more than made up for minor inconveniences. The daily program began with the morning devotional at 7 o'clock and ended seven meetings later with the silent signal at 9:30 at night.

Neal Wilson was in charge of the overall planning for the meetings, and in the first sermon on Friday night, he presented the motto "greater and more effectual evangelism" as a theme for the entire camp meeting. Elinor assisted with the music.

Several of the local and provincial police officials visited the campgrounds and furnished three policemen to guard the camp at night.[167]

There were great difficulties, but the work was moving forward. "At the recent union meetings Elder Neal C. Wilson gave an interesting report of the progress of the Advent Message in Egypt. He pointed out some of the difficulties confronting the work. There was the difficulty of traveling and holding workers' meetings because of the necessity of having an identity card [or] passport at all times. There were financial difficulties because Egypt had withdrawn from the sterling area. There was the political unrest due to U. N. O.'s decision in favour of partition in Palestine and Egypt's close connection with the Arab League.

"A spirit of nationalism made foreign work very difficult, and, although our work may be organized on a national basis, the Moslem government is very much opposed to Christian work. Then the cholera plague made visiting impossible. Thirty to thirty-five thousand people died from this epidemic according to official figures, though there is reason to believe that the actual figures are even greater. Elder Wilson expressed gratitude to the General Conference for sending out anti-cholera vaccine, and stated that none of our members had been affected by the cholera in any of the areas.... It is impossible in this brief summary to include all that Elder Wilson reported, but it is gratifying that our work in Egypt is progressing in spite of opposition and apparently God is turning obstacles into stepping-stones to success."[168]

Neal and Elinor had been married for nearly eight years when they discovered that Elinor was expecting their first child. Since Elinor was pregnant, they requested their furlough. It was granted beginning April 1, 1950.[169]

Neal's sister, Ruth Murrill, was teaching nursing at Washington Sanitarium and Hospital, so it was decided that the "San" would be the best place for the delivery. Ruth and her husband, Bill, drove to New York to meet the expectant parents who arrived by boat. "Elinor had the baby almost as soon as they arrived from Egypt on May 10, 1950," said Ruth.

Neal had started out in Egypt as a pastor and evangelist, but the church leaders quickly saw fit to place the leadership of the entire Egypt Mission Field on his capable shoulders. While he was on furlough, they split the division into two unions and voted him president of the Nile Union, which included Egypt but also several other difficult and unentered countries such as Sudan, Libya, Saudi Arabia, and Aden.[170]

Their furlough ended too soon, and the Wilsons sailed from New York for Alexandria, Egypt, on December 10, 1950, on the S. S. *Alcoa Planter* with a new son, "Ted" Norman Clair (N. C.) Wilson, and a new responsibility, president of the Nile Union.[171] Their second child, Shirley Jean, was born in Cairo on January 24, 1953.

In the Land of the Pharaohs

The political situation in Egypt became quite uncertain again during the 1950s. Prime Minister Nasser was facing internal strife and had nationalized the Suez Canal. "There were blackouts almost every night," said Evelyn Zytkoskee. "We had to put black covers over the windows because there were bomb threats." At one point Elinor and the children had to abandon Cairo and go to Lebanon for the safety of the family. While in Beirut they had to go to Italy for a few weeks until the situation became calmer.

Ted and Shirley were put into the Italian Union School in Florence for a short time where B. B. Beach was principal. "I first met the Wilson family in Italy, and we have been friends ever since," said Bert B. Beach, who is now retired but for many years served as director of Public Affairs and Religious Liberty at the General Conference.

Military Conflict

There seemed to be some type of military conflict going on all the time, yet the work had to move forward and the citizens had to be warned of the imminent coming of Christ. The leaders continued to preach and evangelize in spite of the political situation. Wadie Farag gives a little picture of the effect of war on the advancement of the gospel. "During the recent military action in Egypt we lifted our eyes to heaven and pleaded for mercy. Love, kindness, tenderness, compassion, reason, peace, and life were the keen desire of our heavy hearts. The terrors of war around us offered us everything but what we longed to have!

"Do you really know war? Not if you haven't been in one. Reading about war in the papers is altogether different from experiencing it.... God was a sure shelter to us in the time of storm. For several days the brutalities of war were all around us. A number were killed one Sabbath about a mile from where we were worshiping. The terrifying sounds of fearful explosions drowned out the voice of Neal C. Wilson as he was preaching. The church building was shaken and the shrapnel of the explosives tore the branches of the trees and dropped them on our place of worship. The dreadful sounds of the gigantic weapons of war set up about thirty feet from the church drowned the voices of singing and prayer."[172]

Sometimes the family had to leave Egypt. We have several accounts of their return after a hasty departure. "Due to the lifting of travel restrictions in certain parts of the Middle East, it has been possible for those who were evacuated to Beirut to return to their respective homes. On April 17 Mrs. Neal C. Wilson and children left for their home in Cairo."[173]

Middle Eastern Division President George Appel related one of Neal Wilson's preaching experiences to associate General Conference Secretary W. P. Bradley.[174]

"One of the very interesting items that we have had recently is that of the large evangelistic campaigns which started throughout the division in September and will run through to the end of the year. Wherever it is possible to hold evangelistic efforts, there is a very deep interest in the Third Angel's Message. I attended one of the meetings in Alexandria, Egypt, last Sunday night and found a fine group of intelligent people deeply interested in the truth. They are planning to call December 29 [1951] 'Victory Day' in their efforts in the Nile Union, when they expect that there will be between 80 and 100 ready for baptism. That truly is a new day for the Middle East. We expect, so far as we can tell now, that the total baptisms from these very, very difficult lands will be 225, which is far in excess of any previous year in the history of our work. A goal has been set for 1952 for 500 baptisms.

"One night after Brother Wilson had finished his sermon in one of the efforts in Egypt, two men were waiting for him, and told him that they would like to see him for a few moments. After shaking hands with those who had attended the meeting, he sat down for a few moments with these two men. They told him that they had been sent by the government especially to investigate what was being carried on there in the effort, with a definite plan of closing it down, and they said they came there with the full expectation of notifying him that that was the last meeting.

Highly Committed

"However, during the meeting the Spirit of God so impressed their hearts by what they heard that they said that they were more than pleased with the message that he had given, and felt that such messages should be given to the people throughout the whole nation, and that in place of closing down the effort they were going back and give a favorable report to the government of the activities of our workers in that field. Truly it is a wonderful factor when with the situation as it is men's hearts are impressed with this message to the place where from opposition they turn to be favorable to the proclamation of the sacred truths."

The Voice of Prophecy, newly launched by Pastor George Keough and headquartered in Cairo, was penetrating into the ranks of the various religions of the East. It had grown in just a few years to where they were sending out more than 500 lessons a day. Many who could be reached in no other way were listening to it and enrolling in the Bible Correspondence School. Among those were Muslims, Jews, Catholics, adherents of the ancient Christian sects, and devil worshipers (Yezidis). One young man, a worshipper of Lucifer, enrolled in the course. "Only five of these people, so far as we know, have ever become Christians. We wondered what his reaction would be to Lesson No. 6, 'The Origin and Destiny of Satan.' To our great joy he wrote, 'I am now convinced that Jesus Christ is the only Saviour, and I want to be baptized into the Seventh-day Adventist Church.' He also sent in the names of fifteen devil worshipers to be enrolled in the correspondence course."[175]

Neal Wilson credits The Voice of Prophecy as being one of the ingredients in producing the largest ever baptism in Egypt. "On June 13 we had simultaneous baptisms throughout Egypt, when this rite was administered to 76. This does not sound like a large number, but it is by far the largest number ever baptized on a single day in the history of our work in the Middle East. This brings our total baptized thus far in 1953 to more than 150. We are beginning to reap a very rich harvest from the seed that has been sown through our Voice of Prophecy work here in this field. About 30 have been baptized now as a direct result of this work, which began in Egypt two years ago."[176]

Neal enjoyed meeting government officials and was at his best when he was in their company. "The Assiut Intermediate School on June 21 presented a school program which was attended by over five hundred persons. We were happy that Pastor Neal C. Wilson, President of the Nile Union Mission, could be present as well as many of the leading dignitaries of Upper Egypt. These included the General of the Southern Egyptian Army, the Governor of Assiut, the Chief Inspector of the Educational Zone and others."[177]

Neal also used the right arm of the gospel, the Adventist health and temperance message, to make friends for the church, especially among civic leaders, and take the message into new areas.

"On April 9 the Governor of Alexandria and many Army, Navy, and civic personalities viewed the temperance film *One in 20,000*. Elder Neal C. Wilson was the chairman of this *Temperance Rally* at the Municipal Stadium First Aid Hall."[178]

Feeling a need to open the work in the huge country of Sudan, he used temperance again to knock down prejudice and prepare the soil.

"Just recently we were able to hold two large public meetings on temperance subjects, when a total audience of 1,200 people heard the lectures conducted by Elder Wilson. Everyone present knew that the Adventist people don't drink or smoke, or eat swine's flesh. This impressed the hearts of all Moslems to respect and encourage us in every way possible. Many officials and personalities attended and were well pleased. We hope that these efforts and the visits made by Elder Wilson and me [Farris B. Bishai] to the prime minister and other government officials will prove a definite turning point in our work in the Sudan, so that we can increase our workers and establish our work along the lines of spiritual, educational, and medical aspects."[179]

Wilson recounts how he followed up to open the work in Khartoum, Sudan.

In the Land of the Pharaohs

"At midnight on January 12, 1953, I boarded an airplane in Cairo and traveled south to Khartoum, where I was to meet Hilmy Barbawy and Brother and Sister Ferris Bishai and their baby son. This couple were to pioneer our work in the Sudan. They had preceded me by several days, having traveled by train and river boat. This they did in order to take along their belongings, something they could not have done had they traveled by plane.

"When I arrived we immediately began to search for a desirable place to establish our work. We wanted a presentable building, with a nice yard, close to good communications, and in the center of a good residential area. We did not know at the time we began looking for such a place how scarce such places are in Khartoum. At the end of the first day we were almost disheartened, feeling that we would not be able to find a center that would measure up to the dignity of our message. Just then the unusual happened. Someone told us about a building that had been vacated a few days prior by a certain club.

"Early the next morning we went to see this place, and found out that it met our requirements perfectly. And we were overjoyed when we found that the rent was very reasonable."[180]

Twenty Year Wait

Wilson went on to explain that others wanted the building and the wealthy businessman was not too interested in renting it to Adventists. That evening they had an earnest season of prayer together and asked the Lord to bless them when they went to see the owner again the next day. "As we approached his office he met us at the door on his way out to meet an appointment. Realizing that we had come again to talk over the matter of renting his building, he was not at all anxious to take any time with us. However, we began to tell him about our worldwide work and the very specific message that we have for the nations today, and this seemed to grip his attention. He invited us into his office, where we spent more than two hours explaining our message and our work to him. We walked out of his office with a contract in our pocket and with a sincere prayer of thanks in our hearts."[181]

As soon as the neighborhood learned that Adventists were in the community, the priests and pastors of other denominations started to warn their people to harden their hearts against our doctrines. While the building was being renovated, they tried to find another place to rent to hold public meetings on Sunday nights, but none was available. And then a miracle happened!

"Early Sunday morning I [Neal Wilson] was informed that a gentleman was in the lobby of the hotel wanting to see me. I discovered that he was a godly man about eighty three years old, and he was a master carpenter working with the Sudan Government. He told me that he had built a little church many years ago, but that he had never found those whom he thought were honestly and truly presenting God's truth to the world. For this reason this church had not been used—but for one exception. Each day at five o'clock he went alone to this little church and spent an hour in quiet meditation and prayer. For twenty years he had been waiting and praying for God to send someone with a message for these tremendous times in which we are living.

"I told the elderly man that the message that Seventh-day Adventists have is the same as that of John the Baptist, the voice of one crying in the wilderness of these modern days, 'Prepare ye the way of the Lord.' He hastened to assure me that this was the very message that he wanted to be given in his little church. He thereupon offered to let the workers here use this church whenever they wished. We had a very encouraging meeting that evening, and once again we realized that God is moving upon the hearts of men and women in every part of the earth ..."[182]

Wilson was quick to give praise to those who were involved in the work in Sudan.

"... Much of the credit for opening up the hitherto closed doors of the Sudan must be attributed to Brother Hilmy Berbawy, our Union Home Missionary and Publishing Secretary. In June of 1952, he made a trip to

Highly Committed

the Sudan, and at that time he sold a large number of books as well as taking several hundred subscriptions for our Arabic paper 'The Hope.' Besides this splendid work he enrolled some 600 new students in the Voice of Prophecy Correspondence Course. While doing this he made a host of very valuable and devoted friends. These contacts have been of tremendous help to us in getting things started in the Sudan. God has been wonderfully good to us, and for this we give Him thanks."[183]

He shared with Elder Roenfelt at the General Conference his desire to open the work in Aden. "As we enter 1954, our confidence in God's promises is unshaken. We know that what He has promised He is more than able to accomplish. Our workers are of good courage, and we look forward to the greatest victories and developments during 1954 that we have ever witnessed.

"Enclosed you will find a short report which I presented to the Division Committee a few weeks ago in Beirut. This, along with the report on Aden, will help you to grasp in some measure the providences of God on behalf of His people and His work in our field. You will be cheered, I am sure, when you know that we have made definite provision for Pastor and Mrs. O. K. Anderson and Pastor Chafic Srour and his family to open up the work in Aden towards the latter part of the summer of 1954. We hope by that time also to be in Libya with our initial medical work. Our new Union office building is now being occupied, and we find it very comfortable and convenient. A few days ago, we ourselves moved from the place where we had been living, and are now almost settled in one of the two lovely apartments that have been provided on the top floor of our new headquarters building ... The first of February, we plan to start construction on a portion of our administration building on the new training school property 10 miles out of Heliopolis. You can see that 1954 promises to be a busy and unusual year for us in the Nile Union.

"God has given us good health, and we have so much for which to be thankful. Teddy is just over three and a half years old. He is a strong, happy and active little fellow, and naturally is a great joy to us. Our little girl, Shirley, is almost a year old, and we think she becomes sweeter and more charming every day ..."[184]

At the bottom of the page he added these words, "Nile Union Motto: Souls-Our Goal, More in 'fifty-four.'"

Elder Neal C. Wilson, in the company of Chafic Srour and Ormond K. Anderson, on the morning of Sunday, April 3, 1954, "finally heard the official call 'All aboard,' at 8:45 A.M., and we hurried to take our places ... To our surprise we found that the plane was a DC-3 transport; we hope you never have to ride on such. The remainder of the trip over high mountains and plains, including two short stops, landed us at the port of Djibouti. About noon we took off for Aden, and after a couple of hours' flight across the Red Sea we landed at our destination. Right glad we were to get out of those uncomfortable, unsprung metal seats of that trusted, old transport.

"After the cool invigorating air of Addis at 9,000 feet, now we found ourselves down at sea level on a spot where 'Old Sol' shows no mercy, and soon we were in a lather of sweat. *The New World Encyclopedia* declares that, 'Aden is one of the hottest cities in the world.' We don't disbelieve this testimony, for during our sojourn of eight days in that city and environs, we took three cold showers per day and spent every possible hour under whirling fans....

"Some may think that as this area is under administration of the British, the gospel would be given free course. This is not the case, for while British administration has always favored the calls of Christian mission endeavor, in lands where the great majority of the people are strictly Moslem in faith, the administration in no wise desires that we make the usual enthusiastic public evangelistic approach, but rather that we begin quietly, accentuating health, educational, and temperance and welfare work.... We look forward to the day when Aden will have our own church, school, and medical units operating."[185]

In the Land of the Pharaohs

The *Middle East Messenger* lets us know that Neal suffered some type of illness in 1955. "After a severe illness Elder Wilson is back on the job again. His many friends wish him a speedy recovery and added strength and vigor."[186] We don't know what illness he suffered from, but it did not stop him for long from advancing the work.

He worked hard on getting the work started in the United Arab Republic, but the results did not come until after he left. "The Seventh-day Adventist organization in the Southern Region of the United Arab Republic has been officially recognized by the government as a national religious denomination. This recognition gives our work a status equal to that of any other Christian group. The drive to obtain recognition began in 1957. After a period of waiting for final denominational clearance denominational recognition was obtained in April 1960. Pastor Neal C. Wilson and Brother Ramsis Mina initiated the drive for recognition and Pastors A. G. Zytkoskee and Hilal Dose carried it through to victory. In many respects this recognition is a miracle of God's grace in behalf of His remnant church."[187]

Libya

Elder Wilson was quite concerned about opening the work in Libya. Libya was twice the size of Egypt in area but the population of Egypt was about seventeen times larger than that of Libya. Nine tenths of Libya was desert. In 1953 Neal and Gordon Zytkoskee visited there to do a survey of the needs and conditions. Libya is mentioned in Mark 15:21 where we read: "And they compel one Simon *a Cyrenian*, who passed by, coming out of the country, the father of Alexander and Rufus, to bear his [Christ's] cross." Cyrenaica is the province in Libya in which Benghazi is situated.

The survey team discovered that 75 percent of the population throughout the kingdom lived in rural areas and there were very few Libyan nationals who had been trained as doctors, lawyers, engineers, teachers, and other professions. Malnutrition was very prevalent among the lower classes and accounted for very high birth and infant mortality rates. Pulmonary tuberculosis was a great curse there. Thousands of its victims were denied adequate treatment because of the lack of a hospital or medical facilities. Ignorance of the laws of health rendered many of the people physically incapable of doing the necessary daily labor. In conversing with the minister of health and the director of medical services, they came to the conclusion that the church could render valuable and practical service by opening a modern up-to-date clinic.

His Majesty King Idris was most gracious in receiving the group, and he assured them of his wholehearted support of such a program. In his desire to see this project succeed, he went as far as to ask the church to select a piece of property in any of the cities of Cyrenaica, and he promised to personally see to it that the government made it available for the beginning of such an institution. Another fine gesture on the part of the Libyan government was the kind promise that the church would not need to pay custom duty on any materials or equipment brought into the country for medical or welfare purposes. They felt that it might be possible to repair some of the war-damaged buildings and open a small but well-equipped and efficient clinic.

Dr. and Mrs. Roy S. Cornell of Pasco, Washington, learned about the project and, upon selling his splendid practice and home, Dr. Cornell and his wife and two sons accepted the call to Libya. After working for nearly two years to get the building in shape and find the required staff, the hospital opened.

The Advent Review and Sabbath Herald carried the story. "Ceremonies opening the Adventist hospital in Benghazi, Libya, on May 21 [1956] marked another milestone of progress in entering one more of the few countries of the Middle East in which our work has hitherto not been established....

"The weather was ideal for the opening festivities. Hundreds of friends, leading government officials, other dignitaries, businessmen, consular representatives, and others gathered in the street, which had been cordoned off by the police for the occasion. The large military band, which had been sent especially for this occasion, played a number of selections while the crowd gathered.

"Neal C. Wilson, president of the Nile Union, led out in the opening exercises by making mention of the splendid cooperation of His Majesty the King, the Minister of Health, and other leading government officials, without whose cooperation this medical center would not have been possible....

"After this, Roy S. Cornell, M.D., who with his family and associates has worked untiringly for more than a year to make this institution a reality, expressed his heartfelt gratitude for the splendid cooperation of all, and the hope that the staff would be able to contribute inestimably to the relief of suffering and to the health and well-being of that city and country....

"After the cutting of the ribbon, which officially opened the institution, the guests were conducted through the building in guided tours and were served refreshments."[188]

Takoma Hospital Gift

Neal C. Wilson sent a thank-you letter to Takoma Hospital, which was published in the *Southern Tidings*. Nathaniel C. Wilson, Neal's father and former foreign missionary, was now pastor of the Greenville, Tennessee, district in which the Takoma Hospital, an institution of the Southern Union, was located.

"I want to express our sincere appreciation and thanks for the gift that the Takoma Hospital has made available to us. It is not an easy matter to begin medical work in a foreign country with limited appropriations and finance. But God has wonderfully led in the establishing of our medical work in Libya and we have seen His divine hand at work in every move being made in this new country.

"Ours is the only religious organization which has been given permission to carry on any type of work in Libya. We have been received very cordially by the king, ministers of the cabinet, and directors of departments. Dr. Cornell is now in Benghazi and, while the building that we plan to use is being remodelled to accommodate 25 beds, he is acting as the chief surgeon in the government hospital. The former chief surgeon was a highly qualified Englishman, but unfortunately he was an alcoholic and the government found it necessary to dismiss him. Dr. Cornell's willingness to help in this institution will be the means of bringing a knowledge of this message to many in that country.

"We were in great perplexity to know how to get the equipment we needed in order to open this little institution, and just at the time we were having a real struggle to decide what to eliminate we received the word that there was a possibility of a gift of this X-ray machine that you were making available to some mission hospital. We prayed about the matter and asked that if it was the Lord's will He would work it out so that this equipment might be sent to Benghazi. We are so happy that you brethren have been led to decide in favor of our new institution."[189]

Neal focused his efforts on opening the work in new areas and getting better places of worship in all the major cities. In 1954 he wrote a passionate letter to the treasurer of the General Conference making a persuasive case for establishing an evangelistic center in Cairo and imploring him for special financial assistance for this center that he envisioned. He sent carbon copies to the president and many other leaders at headquarters.

"Dear Elder Torrey, I am writing this appeal from Minia where I have been spending some time, with several of our men, in searching for a more suitable place of worship than we now have. As you know only too well, it is most difficult to find neat, spacious, quiet, and centralized places of worship for rental in cities. It is even more difficult to find places suitable for evangelism in acceptable areas of those cities where we can present this message in an attractive hall and in an arresting manner, so as to appeal to the wealthy, educated, cultured, and better class as well as to all other groups.

"It is a lamentable fact that up to the present we have been contented with some little room in an obscure and poor section of the city. I have been persistently trying to find better and more suitable halls and places of worship, and the Lord has been wonderfully good in helping us, and in a number of the provincial capitals we have now rented places that are in keeping with the dignified and exalted message that we must bear to the world.

"In many of these places the work has never risen above the class of people that we have catered to and provided for. It is now costing us more in rent etc. than hithertofore; but the compensation of getting the Advent Message before the leaders of the country as well as higher classes far outweighs the cost.

"As you approach this Fall Council, I know full well that many pressing, urgent, and apparently imperative requests have been placed before you.

"Among the requests for special appropriations already in your hands, you will find one from the Nile Union for the Cairo City Evangelistic Center. As a result of the liberal and much appreciated "Special" of last year, along with some funds that were on hand, we have been able to purchase one of the most desirable and centrally located sites in Cairo, not far from the main railway station and at one of the main pivots of Cairo's transportation system. On the enclosed summary you will see more clearly what funds were available, how they were spent, and what is needed in order to carry through to finality this splendid project.

"Cairo is a city of over 3 million inhabitants—the largest city in the Middle East, and on the continent of Africa. Cairo is also the leading city of culture, education, commerce, and politics in the Middle East. Besides this it is the home of the Al Azhar University, the highest place of learning and culture in the Islamic world, and the nerve center of all Islamic propaganda and missionary endeavors. We must have a representative center in this great metropolis, and crossroads of the world, in which to present a full and coordinated program of evangelism in all of its various phases.

"While it seems true that at the present moment the government is outwardly friendly and somewhat lenient toward such projects, it must not be overlooked that there is a very strong undercurrent of fanaticism which might break loose at any time. If this should happen, it would then be well-nigh impossible to build an evangelistic center such as we have in mind for Cairo. Then too, there is a proposal to build a beautiful new mosque in the 'Bab-El Hadid' square just opposite to the main railway station of Cairo. If this is built before we build, it will rule us out, because the law requires that any church constructed be at least 150–200 meters distance from the nearest mosque. All this adds up to but one conclusion—What we do not do now we may never be able to do; at least in this, particularly desirable, locality. Hence this fervent appeal that we endeavor to take advantage of the opportunity that now presents itself.

"We confidently believe that God had led in every phase of this project thus far; and the securing of permits and other official documents has, in some cases, been almost a miracle. These permits are valid for only one year from the time of issue, and unless something is started on the project before the expiration of such a permit, it is impossible to predict with any degree of accuracy as to whether the permit will be renewed. If the Lord impresses you brethren to answer this appeal after reading this letter, and after prayerful counsel together, then we shall feel that the Lord's hand is in this matter, and that we should arise and build immediately. If because of the urgent and worthy appeals from other countries, and if because of a lack of sufficient funds, this request cannot be met, then we shall also feel that somehow the Lord in His great wisdom and love is planning in some other way for this proclamation of the Advent Message in this great metropolitan area.

"I hope that you brethren do not feel that I am unduly urging this matter, but at the same time I do hope that you have sensed that I am exceedingly concerned and in earnest over this vital and strategic project..."[190]

Attached to the letter was a plan for the first floor and auditorium of the new proposed center, two apartments above the auditorium, expected income from the sale of the materials in demolishing the present

Highly Committed

building on the property, and the monies pledged by the Cairo church. The total request for completion of the new Cairo Evangelistic Center was $39,480.

At the Autumn Council, the General Conference surprised Neal with a very fine special appropriation toward the new Cairo Evangelistic Center, and with an additional amount that the Middle East Division appropriated, they were ready to get their building permit.

"Neal C. Wilson, president of the Nile Union Mission, told a thrilling story of how we obtained a permit for the erection of buildings and the establishment of a mission center in the most centrally located square of the important city of Cairo, the nerve center for the propagation of the Islamic faith. For three years we held title to the land by purchase, but no permit for building could be secured. Brother Wilson sought the aid of the minister of the interior and of the governor of Cairo, who immediately made telephone calls to the director general. This official ordered engineers and architects out of bed at 11:30 P.M. to study our application. They were impressed that the Adventists must be important people if they could secure the favor of the governor.

"As Brother Wilson was leaving for this conference, the Feasts of the Ramadan, the annual month of fasting, was to begin. Fifty-five signatures were needed to give approval to the application. It seemed an insurmountable task to accomplish in one day. But the eye of the Lord who never slumbers nor sleeps watched over this project in this ancient city of the Nile. Brother Ramses Mina, union treasurer, began his rounds of the government offices. Ten minutes before the offices closed he emerged with the last signature. A present-day miracle had been accomplished. The permit was granted, and as we sit here at this forty-eighth session of the General Conference, construction is under way. We marveled when great centers of our work were established in London and New York, but as we think of this wonderful providence in a Mohammedan stronghold, we are moved to exclaim, 'What hath God wrought!'"[191]

About the end of 1959 the Cairo Evangelistic Center was opened. A few years later it faced a great crisis, as related by D. L. Chappell when he visited Cairo. "... shortness of time permitted me to visit only the Cairo Evangelistic Center at Ramses Square. I learned that a year or so ago, the members had a day of prayer and fasting in behalf of the Center building, which had been slated for demolition by the City Planning Board, so as to make room for a large park by the statue of Ramses II. For no known reason, the committee changed its plans, and settled for a smaller park, leaving the Adventist Center standing–after all the unsightly buildings formerly surrounding it had been torn down!

"I had the privilege of meeting six of the forty-seven fine-looking people who were baptized at the Center in 1965."[192]

On November 26, 1958, the General Conference Committee voted to authorize the permanent return of Neal C. Wilson from the Nile Union upon his request and in harmony with the recommendation of the Middle East Division.[193]

Neal and Elinor in 1953 with young Ted and Shirley.

The Wilson men: From left, Donald, Bruce, Nathaniel, and Neal.

Chapter Ten

Leadership in North America

"My son, observe the postage stamp! Its usefulness depends upon its ability to stick to one thing until it gets there." Henry Wheeler Shaw

Lights burned late in the Heliopolis Church on Tuesday evening, April 8, 1958. Usually the church stood dark and silent on a Tuesday night after prayer meeting, but tonight was different. The Wilson family had decided it was time to bring their fourteen years of service in the Middle East to a close. It had been good. It had been exciting. Their work in the Muslim countries had produced growth and results. The Wilsons had arrived as a couple, but they were leaving as a family. Ted and Shirley were a big part of their lives now. They had come as strangers but were leaving as friends—dear friends. They had come as novices but were leaving as serious church leaders.

The farewell party that convened after prayer meeting drew people who had come to love and respect Neal and Elinor over the years. There was food and speeches, music and festivities. But there was sadness in the hearts of most, because they knew they might never see these dear ones again. The final farewell prayer was offered, and the church stood dark and silent once more. The Wilsons went home to finish packing.

Several of the workers and members went to the port to bid the Wilsons farewell when they left Alexandria harbor on April 19, 1958, bound for the States.[194]

Neal was scheduled to attend the Institutes of Scientific Studies for Prevention of Alcoholism in Washington, D.C., from July 21 to August 1958.[195] While there the family visited the world headquarters and friends.

After also taking time to visit family, Neal and Elinor headed to San José, California. Neal had received a call from the Central California Conference to lead the Religious Liberty, Medical, Radio and TV, and Public Relations departments. "We are happy to announce his arrival in the Central California Conference, and we welcome him and Mrs. Wilson and their two lovely children. May God bless their work in this field," said D. E. Venden, president of the conference.[196]

When Neal received a letter from Washington about the call, he let them know he was already on the job. He sent them a note. "Dear Elder Dunn: Your letter concerning our call to the Central California Conference reached me a few days ago, and although we are already happily located in San Jose perhaps I should write this letter of official acceptance of this call.

"There were many other contacts that we had and a number of other openings that we could have fit into, but I believe that a few years of experience here in Central California will be of benefit. We shall endeavor to do whatever we can to promote and develop the departments which have been assigned."[197]

One of the programs that Neal Wilson promoted in his new responsibility was the cancer prevention study of the American Cancer Society (ACS). The leaders in the ACS project believed they could compare the health practices and habits of Seventh-day Adventists with others in California and find out which habits prevented cancer. This important comparative data was requested from a questionnaire that they wanted every Adventist over the age of 30 to complete. "We believe," he wrote to the members in a joint article with

President D. E. Venden, "that the facts furnished by California Seventh-day Adventists as a block will be testimony to the world that those who follow God's plan of life are more healthy and more happy.

"The spirit of Christianity is to give of *one's self.* So often we are willing to give money, or a little time to help in some worthy cause or community project—but seldom do we really give anything of ourselves. By providing this information, you will be doing something much more concrete toward combating cancer than would be the case if merely providing money for research. Give a little of yourself, won't you?"[198] This study was the beginning of a number of studies on Adventists that would validate the fact that they are some of the healthiest people in the world.

In that same issue Neal made an appeal for the support of the *Faith for Today* telecast. "While in Sacramento recently, I visited with an assistant in the Attorney General's office regarding a matter pertaining to our work. During the course of our conversation, we referred to the *Faith for Today* telecast. This fine gentleman told me that he watched the telecast nearly every week. He expressed deep, and I believe genuine, appreciation for the spiritual blessing he had received. Then he said, 'The only trouble is, when I travel sometimes, I can't seem to get *Faith for Today* in the city where I am. Why don't you expand your coverage so that everyone can gain the inspiration of this program?' I had to tell him there was just one main hindrance, a lack of finance."[199] And then Wilson went on to appeal for an offering of $200,000 that would be just sixty-two cents per member. Neal Wilson continued the art of meeting important people and promoting church programs.

When you're doing a good job, word travels fast. The Columbia Union, headquartered in Takoma Park, Maryland, placed a call for the young pastor to come east to do the same work. Neal Wilson was now 39 years old and took up his new work on February 1, 1960. He was to be the new secretary for the Religious Liberty and Medical departments as well as for the Association of Self-Supporting Institutions (ASI) for the Columbia Union under the leadership of President L. E. Lenheim. Neal's son, Ted, was now 9 ½ years old and Shirley was 7 years old.

"The new Religious Liberty Secretary," voiced the union paper, "comes to us with a rich background of experience in pastoral, mission, executive, and departmental experience. Within a short time he will be visiting churches throughout the Columbia Union Conference territory and becoming acquainted with the many problems in the religious liberty field."[200]

And visit churches he did. We have record of him visiting all the conferences and many churches in the union promoting *Liberty* magazine and the cause of religious liberty. He also gave temperance talks, traveled to New York to work on the narration of a script for an Australasian Division film, and promoted special offerings.

In 1959, before Wilson came to the Columbia Union, church leaders were dialoging with Mr. and Mrs. Eugene W. Kettering about the donation of a 100-bed hospital in Dayton, Ohio, in honor of Mr. Kettering's father, Charles Kettering, the famed scientist, inventor, engineer, and industrialist who had died some months earlier. The Adventist leaders had met with the Kettering family several times and with the Dayton community to see if they could indeed accept the gift.

On Sunday, November 8, 1959, a group of prominent citizens of Dayton traveled to Hinsdale Sanitarium and Hospital in Illinois to observe a typical Seventh-day Adventist medical institution in operation. "They commented on the excellence of the plant, its equipment, and its maintenance, but the thing which impressed them most was the fact that they saw a staff of dedicated people, and it was of the people and their obvious devotion to high ideals of service about which they talked the most during the course of their visit."[201] These leaders pledged another million and a half dollars (which they exceeded) for an additional 100 beds. This was matched

Highly Committed

by the Ketterings to bring the total bed capacity to 300. On Friday, November 13 at the Biltmore Hotel in Dayton, Ohio, a formal presentation took place transferring the ownership and operation of the hospital to the Columbia Union Conference. At the event the only son of the late inventor made the following public statement:

"The proposal for a new hospital in Dayton was prompted by two considerations. One was a desire to create something in Dayton which would serve as a memorial to my father.... Mrs. Kettering and I have had considerable contact with the Seventh-day Adventist hospital in Hinsdale which some of you visited last Sunday. We have seen the important service this hospital provides for the community and the effective manner in which it is operated by the Seventh-day Adventists. We are extremely happy that the administration of our hospital will be in skilled hands. We know from first-hand experience at Hinsdale what Adventists can do as operators of hospitals and schools of nursing. They are skilled. They are broad in their understanding of community problems."[202]

The Dayton newspapers covered the hospital story and printed pictures of the mayor of Dayton presenting the key to the city of Kettering, Ohio, to George B. Nelson who would be the administrator of the new hospital. When Neal joined the Columbia Union as the medical secretary, he also continued to report on Kettering Hospital to keep the membership informed about the progress of the project. "On Thursday evening, April 27 [1961], a special community meeting was held in the auditorium of the Fairmont High School in Kettering, Ohio. This function was especially planned for the citizens of the Dayton-Oakwood-Kettering area as an information meeting regarding the new hospital.... Construction is expected to get underway July 1, 1961, and we hope the doors will open in 1963."[203] When the first board of trustees for the new medical institution was elected, Neal C. Wilson, the medical secretary of the Columbia Union, was included as one of the 13 members.

Columbia Union President

Don Roth, former associate secretary of the General Conference and a worker in the Columbia Union, tells the story of how Neal Wilson was called to and eventually elected as president of the Columbia Union. "We had called Neal to the Columbia Union because he was the only person that we could find who would fit the description of the person we were looking for. My first contact with Neal Wilson was when I was a member of the staff at Columbia Union Conference in 1954.

"I started working in Pennsylvania, and they asked me to go to the union as the editor of the *Columbia Union Visitor*. They wanted somebody who had PR, RL, Medical, Radio and TV and overseas experience. Neal was one of the few people in the entire church who qualified with everything they needed. He was doing just about that in Southern California. After about two years in the Columbia Union, Elder Lewis E. Lenheim, who was the union president, resigned in 1963. The GC had their candidate, Elder Scriven, a long-time president of the North Pacific Union Conference who needed a change, and the GC was supporting him. Nobody in the Columbia Union knew him well.

"Elder R. R. Figuhr, president of the GC, and Elder William B. Ochs, president of the NAD, were presiding at the nominating committee meeting. It became apparent that support for Neal Wilson grew among his fellow workers in the union. When the nominating committee met, a list of more than a dozen names was put on the board, and Neal Wilson's name was among them. Speeches were made highlighting the accomplishments of each name on the board. The GC visitors recounted all the good traits of leadership of their candidate. After the first ballot was counted, Neal Wilson had twenty-three, the largest number of votes, followed with a scattering of votes for Marvin Loewen, Don Hunter, T. E. Unruh, and one or two others of the local conference presidents. Their candidate Scriven had four.

"They were visibly upset and decided that they needed to visit with Elder Wilson. Elder R. R. Figuhr called for a recess and met privately with Elder Wilson for more than two hours. It was evident that he tried to get Neal to withdraw his name from the list. Neal refused to withdraw his name. Neal liked leadership and leadership positions, and he was beginning to see that leadership was his gift. He wanted the position. After all, they said, Elder Wilson had never before served as a local conference president in North America, and in those days one received appointment as a Union Conference president only after serving on the local conference level.

"He had been president over the Egypt Mission and the Nile Union, but that didn't count with these leaders who wanted to follow the North American protocol. We reconvened to prepare to cast another vote. They gave more speeches in favor of their candidate, hoping that would swing him into a more favorable position and then proceeded to cast ballots again.

"The final vote was still heavily for Elder Wilson. He got three or four *more* votes than before and their candidate got *fewer* than before. The chairman could not do anything else but declare Elder Neal Wilson as the new president of the Columbia Union Conference."[204]

In "A Message from Your Union Conference President" Neal expressed his willingness to serve the union. "It is a privilege to greet each of the 41,000 members in the Columbia Union Conference. I only wish that it were possible to express in a personal way my great desire that you might prosper spiritually, even as the Lord has prospered you physically and materially.

"Mrs. Wilson and I have enjoyed our association with many of you over the past two and a half years. Teddy, who is 12, and Shirley, who is nine, also have become strong supporters of the Columbia Union Conference and its schools and youth programs. As a family we hope to be an example in conversation, in love and dedication, in courage and faith.... We seek your understanding, your loyalty, your fellowship, and your prayers."[205]

"Two major items which confronted the new executive upon taking office was construction plans for two major projects in the Union—the new school of nursing at Kettering Memorial Hospital in Dayton, Ohio, and the new addition to Halcyon Hall of Columbia Union College. He also headed the delegation from this Union to the General Conference session."[206]

Building the School of Nursing at Kettering Hospital meant that the union had to raise nearly a million dollars, and the Halcyon Hall addition was also a big financial challenge. The new president quickly found support for these projects and was cheered to find that a surprise expansion plan for the hospital came when the family of O. Lee Harrison, long-time personal friend and professional associate of Charles Kettering, presented a gift of $900,000 which was matched by the Ketterings for the purpose of adding a fifth floor and an additional 100 beds, bringing the total bed capacity to 400. The $13 million gift was dedicated in a series of services from February 14–16, 1964, with Dr. Edward R. Annis, president of the American and World Medical Associations, as the principle speaker at the formal dedication. General Conference President R. R. Figuhr served as the consecration speaker, and Neal Wilson, now chair of the Kettering Board, spoke on Sabbath.

In concluding his article about Kettering, Neal wrote, "The weekend religious services highlighted the spiritual significance of one more Adventist hospital, whose chief asset must ever be an ability to bring healing not only to the body but also to the mind and spirit. Programs have been developed at the hospital to maintain on a high level the principles and standards of the denomination. A new church has been organized.... And so there opens a bright new chapter in our worldwide medical work."[207]

Around this time the Civil Rights Movement was in full swing across the country, especially in the Southern states, as the author, DeWitt Williams, recounts. "I was born in Philadelphia, Pennsylvania. In 1957, I left Philadelphia bound for Huntsville, Alabama, to attend Oakwood College. For the first time in my life I was

Highly Committed

surrounded by all of the realities of segregation. Entrances of buildings were marked 'white only' and 'colored only.' For the first time in my life, I had to face the fact that I couldn't eat in most restaurants and go every place I wanted just because of my color.

"What surprised me the most is that this evil was in the Adventist Church. On one occasion we went to the local white church in Huntsville, Central Adventist Church, to hear the choir from Southern Missionary College. They had been advertising throughout the city and obviously wanted visitors to hear this outstanding choir. Not suspecting that Adventist Christians would hold to the same rules, some Oakwoodites came and sat in the main church auditorium. We were new to Huntsville and loved music. We were surprised when the master of ceremony, after praying for God's blessings on the service, said that the program would not continue until the 'boys from Oakwood' went to the back of the church or up in the balcony. After we complied, the program began.

"In 1962, my senior year, Martin Luther King spoke at Oakwood College. Our gym was the largest auditorium around at that time, and the black citizens of Huntsville asked if we would host the event there. What an event! The gym was packed to capacity and then some! I will never forget his speech and the hope he inspired in me, in us all, as young black students.

"I was the president of the United Student Movement and was one of the leaders on campus. The Sabbath School lesson that quarter was on the brotherhood of humankind. For thirteen weeks Adventists all over the world studied about the unity of the human race. Inspired by the message of Martin Luther King and hoping that the lessons would have had some positive effect, a group of young theology students (Henry Wright, Ron Lindsay, Willie Lee, Benito Hodge), including myself, decided to visit the Central Adventist Church for Sabbath School about six weeks into the quarter.

"We drove to the church, entered, and each went to a different class. About ten minutes after sitting down a dignified lady came to my pew and beckoned with her finger for me to come and follow her. She said she wanted me to go to the pastor's study, and she pointed me to where I should go. When I got there several of the fellows were already there, and very shortly the whole group from Oakwood was standing there. She began, 'I'm the pastor's wife, but my husband isn't here today. However, there is one of our union leaders here, and he will be here in a minute to talk to you.'

"To make a long story short, the leader from the union (Elder Oscar Heinrich, I found out later) told us that we had to leave the church immediately. We argued with him for about ten minutes, and finally he said that if we didn't leave right then he would call the police. We decided that if there had been no change in the hearts and thinking of these church members who had been studying those wonderful lessons we would leave. As we were about to get in the car, I will always remember the church member who ran over to the car and began to apologize. He was holding a boy about two years old in his arms, and he began to cry, loudly. In between sobs he managed to get out a few words, 'Please forgive us. Please forgive us. We are not all like that here. Please forgive us.' We drove out of the parking lot with this Christian gentleman standing there weeping, his tears ran down his face and dropped onto that little boy in his arms.

"The nation was struggling with the civil rights question in 1962. Segregation up north was not as flagrant and visible, but it certainly was there, and in most of the churches, including the Adventist Church. Martin Luther King said that the most segregated hour in America was the 11 o'clock hour on Sunday morning. In the Adventist Church it happened a day earlier on Sabbath morning."

Neal Wilson, as president of the Columbia Union, was quick to see that the problem of racial segregation existed in his territory, too. And he determined to fight it and make a change. He knew it would cost him some friends and some votes, but he knew it was an evil he couldn't allow to continue.

Leadership in North America

Elder Theodore Carcich, vice president of the General Conference for North America at the time, was also trying to bring about change. He sent out a letter to all the unions requesting that they set up Human Relations Committees to begin discussing this issue. He followed it up with another letter asking if the committee had been set up and if it had produced any change.

Neal Wilson replied that the Columbia Union had established a Human Relations Committee and that it had been rather active in a number of workshops that had been planned throughout the union. "The group is made up of all the conference presidents, several from the union conference, and several additional members. Enclosed you will find the names of our committee members." He himself was the chairperson, and there were fourteen other members. In his final paragraph he said that there was every indication that a different spirit existed in most of the churches than was the case a few years ago.[208]

Church officers from throughout the Columbia Union Conference were invited to attend a daylong study session on human relations. Three sites were chosen: the Takoma Park Church, Blue Mountain Academy, and Columbus Junior Academy. The attendance was excellent. Neal Wilson and Charles D. Brooks were at each of these meetings. "Elder H. D. Singleton, Secretary of the Regional Department of the General Conference presented a paper at the meetings on 'The History of Segregation in the United States.'… The discussions were open and frank and covered every phase of human relations. There was no bitterness or rancor in the freely expressed thoughts of those present."[209]

After becoming vice president of the General Conference for North America Neal Wilson became even more active in this area. "On January 13 [1970] a broadly representative company of approximately 100 Seventh-day Adventist laymen, ministers, educators, medical workers, businessmen, administrators, and writers, largely from the Regional conferences, met in Washington under the chairmanship of Neal C. Wilson, vice president of the General Conference for North America, to discuss and plan for the work of the church as it relates to the black people of North America."[210]

Regional Conferences

To the vast majority of the members of the regional conferences (a term used to designate the black membership of the church), Elder Neal C. Wilson was just a name. But as he became more active in the area of diversity, he became well-known in this community. He made it a point to make extended visits to the regional conferences. "From December 12th through the 16th Elder Wilson, accompanied by his son, Ted, and Elder R. L. Woodfork, president of the South Atlantic Conference, toured the South Atlantic Conference from Raleigh, North Carolina, to Miami, Florida…. Elder Wilson and his son enjoyed real southern hospitality in the modest homes of their 'brothers and sisters' as they partook of the traditional soul food in the form of black-eyed peas, collard greens and corn bread….

"Elder Wilson stated that he appreciated the five days in the South Atlantic Conference and that he and his son will place this experience among their most treasured memories."[211]

Neal often traveled with his son to different churches, and he left opportunities for a time called "Issues and Answers" on Sabbath so that he could discuss in depth the position of the church on race relations.

Many of the black leaders felt that full participation in the current structure of the church would never happen in the United States, and they recommended the creation of black unions. The General Conference President's Executive Advisory Committee (PREXAD) was set up to bring greater unity between the black and white members and to strengthen the growing black work. "One solution proposed to help the black work was the formation of two Regional (black) unions, with the present Regional conferences placed under their jurisdiction. In August, 1976, exploration of the desirability of this organizational change commenced. About 12 major position papers, as well as responses, statistical reports, and other materials, were prepared by individuals and committees for study. PREXAD listened to both proponents and opponents of black unions.

"After much prayer and careful deliberation, taking into account the spiritual benefit to the entire church, the committee decided that formation of black unions would not be judicious or wise. But PREXAD was not just rejecting one solution—it was recommending other ways that it deemed more effective in meeting the true goals of the church and that would give more promise of pulling together the membership in North America and provide greater support for evangelism of blacks and whites.

"In taking this positive action, PREXAD recognizes that there has been, and in many areas still is, a failure on the part of the church to accord ethnic groups true partnership, to incorporate them fully into the existing decision-making structure, and to establish a truly integrated church community."[212]

Elder Charles D. Brooks was called to the union office by Neal Wilson during this period, and he saw firsthand Neal's commitment to cultural diversity and equality.

C. D. Brooks' Story

"I remember the first time I set my eyes on Neal Wilson. I was pastoring the Glenville church in Cleveland, Ohio, around 1960. The union wanted my church to host a large officers' meeting. A group of men from the Columbia Union staff would present at the general sessions and some at departmental breakout sessions.

"When they broke out into these smaller groups, I decided to float from group to group and observe to make sure that everything was going well. I couldn't help but notice that the union men appeared rather uncomfortable and apprehensive about being around so many black people and in a black community, despite our friendliness and hospitality.

"When the closing prayer was offered and the meeting ended, those union men were gone as quick as a flash. They seemed anxious to get back to their 'safe' hotels and out of this 'threatening' environment. I walked down the halls of my church, smiling to myself at what I had just witnessed. I turned the corner going toward my office. The doors of the main auditorium were still open. Suddenly, I saw this tall white gentleman sitting on the piano bench talking casually to a group of about ten 'colored' delegates. I walked over to the door and listened quietly. This tall man was not talking about departmental work. In fact, he was not talking about the church. He was just having a good conversation about life with his brothers and sisters. It was so impressive and refreshing.

"'Who is that?' I queried. 'That's Neal C. Wilson, Religious Liberty and Medical Secretary of the Union.' I didn't see him for a while after that experience in Glenville. He soon became president of the Columbia Union.

"Soon afterwards I became one of the delegates to the union session where we would elect officers. Elder Carcich was chairing the nominating committee, and Neal Wilson, the secretary of the committee, sat next to him. This was my first time serving on the committee, and I was one of three African Americans besides the eighteen whites on the committee. We were in the throes of the Civil Rights Movement. The lay activities director had already announced his retirement, and I nominated Don Simons, a black pastor, to fill this vacancy. I noticed a very interesting thing developing. We took time to introduce all of the candidates, and Don Simons got very good recommendations. He was well-known, very articulate, and very knowledgeable.

"We took straw votes by secret ballots and would drop off a name or two until we got down to the two highest vote getters. One was a Caucasian and the other was Don Simons. On the final vote Don Simons got three votes the other man got eighteen. I was okay with it. We prayed. One of the important leaders from the committee and our union got up immediately without being asked to lecture the 'colored brothers' about the democratic process. I didn't know then that the way to get the chairman's attention was to move about and raise your hand, and he would recognize you and write your name down. While he was talking I stood up right beside him. I was full. When he finished the chairman, had no choice but to call on me.

"I said, 'Mr. Chairman, we resent being lectured on the subject of the democratic process. I pastor the largest black church in this union. We use the democratic process every year in selecting officers in our church. I use it in board meetings. The other man over here is president of a conference. He's thoroughly acquainted with the democratic process, and the third one of us is an entrepreneur and knows all about the democratic process. We have a problem in this church and this union, and it is not going to be solved by a lecture. Somebody has to decide what is right in this church and then do it. I don't really blame you for selecting your man. I want you to notice that Don Simons got three votes. Would you like to know who voted for him? I don't blame you for voting for the other man because you know him. Some of you went to school with him. Why wouldn't you vote for him? That is the proof that this problem will never be solved by the democratic process.'

"Elder Carcich said to me, 'Elder Wilson is the new president, and he is going to do something about that.' I should've kept my mouth shut, but I added this line as I took my seat. 'We will watch carefully to see what he does.' At that time I didn't know him very well. I remembered that day after the workers' meeting in my church when he stayed by and chatted with the leaders sitting on that piano bench.

"A few weeks later I got a very kind letter from Elder Wilson inviting me to join the Columbia Union staff as the general field secretary. I declined. The Lord called me and made it specifically clear what He wanted me to do. And I was happy doing it. I was never ambitious to take anything else. I would be the first black worker to be a regular officer of the Columbia Union. My father-in-law, Elder Wagner, was on the union committee, but he was in charge of the regional work.

"I wrote back a letter letting him know that I was humbled by this offer, but it was not what God wanted me to do. A few days later I received a second letter from Elder Wilson. It essentially said the same thing. And I wrote a second letter akin to the first, and I must say I was greatly and sincerely humbled.

"We were called to Pine Forge to pitch camp for camp meeting. It's awfully hard and hot work, but we enjoyed it because of the fellowship. A car drove down across the field where I was working, and one of our conference workers got out and said, 'Pastor Brooks, you have a long distance call, and you may use that telephone right there.' It was Elder Neal Wilson. He had written twice and now he was calling. Just anybody wouldn't have done this. This is what made him unique in this area of human relations. He saw a need, and he wanted to take care of it. We talked, and he tried to persuade me, and I let him know again that I didn't fit. Finally he said, 'I'm asking you to come down to Takoma Park.' I said that it would be a futile trip. He said 'Are you trying to tell me to look for someone else?' I said, 'Sir, I suppose that's what I'm doing.' He said 'All right if you won't come to see me, I'm coming to see you.' That's extraordinary. I don't know anybody else on earth who would have done that.

"I thought he might be up on the weekend. The next day when we went to dinner somebody came and said, 'Two men are here to see you.' There at the table was Elder N. C. Wilson and another pastor. I walked over, apologized as I stood afar off and explained that I was sweaty from pitching tents. He said, 'We know what you're doing. Just get your dinner and come and join us.' And I did.

"Then he began all over again, appealing to me to join the union. The other pastor with him started telling me the financial advantages of working at the union—you'll get more per diem, you'll get more for this expense and that expense. I kindly stopped him and said, 'Pastor, we don't need coddling. That's not what our decision has been all about.' I continued, 'Gentlemen, I am going to tell you something that will probably surprise you. From the time I first heard from you my wife and I hadn't even prayed about this. But when you called me in the field, Mr. President, I hung up and dialed Cleveland, Ohio, immediately. My wife and I went into a long discussion. I said, 'Honey, at least we ought to pray about it.' We started praying right there on the phone in the hot

Highly Committed

sun. We prayed again by appointment that night, earnestly, and the next morning and God gave me clarity as to what I should do, and I have never regretted it one iota.'

"Before Neal wrote to me, he told his union conference committee that I was his choice, and there were several conference presidents who objected. When he mentioned my name, the room exploded. 'What! Isn't that the young man that got up and said so-and-so at the nominating committee?' 'Yes.' 'You want him?' Elder Wilson said, 'Yes, what kind of man do you think we need? A yes man who just nods his head in agreement with everything? I will welcome different views and strong defenses. That's the kind of man we need.' And he prevailed in that room until they voted to invite me.

"It was the beginning of an experience that I wouldn't trade for anything else on this earth. You have to remember that we were in those awful civil rights struggles. This was daily news. But the Lord blessed me and taught me how to be plainspoken without being mean-spirited. We became friends quickly, and we loved each other.

"As soon as I came to Washington, my first assignment was to be the keynote speaker at three human relations workshops. One of them was over in Bethlehem, Pennsylvania, one was in this area, and one was in the western part of this union. They wanted me to give the same message each time because we were talking to different groups. There were about 3,000 people gathered. This was a mixed group about evenly divided, 50 percent black and 50 percent white. And of course you have a new generation of black preachers. I'm not trying to take anything away from those upon whose shoulders we stood. I know the strain, the power and yet the love of these older men. We would go to meetings and actually be neglected and mistreated and go home and tell our members all the wonderful positive things but never mentioned those bad things. We didn't want to inflame anybody. That's how delicate things were. Elder Wilson was determined to do something about it.

"Elder Wilson didn't tell me what to say. He left that to me. I was able to talk clearly and cleanly without anger, and I saw emotional responses from Caucasians who were present. Some women came to me weeping. They didn't say anything. They just took my hand and they would say, 'We didn't know. We didn't understand.' Others were a little more belligerent and would ask, 'What do you folk want?'

"Neal Wilson and I traveled together many times. It was always the same when you were with him. You didn't wonder. You felt that you were respected. And I wasn't ultrasensitive about this anyway. Elder Wilson was the consummate, the epitome, of fairness and equity. He and I would be driving along in a car heading for a meeting and he would say, 'If you can't stay, I don't stay. If you can't eat, I don't eat.' He lived by that and he himself was as clear and as plain. Our problem today still exists. I call it a leadership problem. Leaders are chosen to correct this.

"There was one field that sent out the word that the new colored man Brooks will not come to this conference. Neal Wilson called that president in and made it clear that there wasn't a corner in his union that Brooks could not go and will not go. Make your peace with that. I had several camp meeting appointments that summer. At one of them, a huge camp meeting, Elder Wilson and I were to be there together. On Thursday night I was to speak at the youth pavilion, and Elder Wilson was to speak in the main pavilion. I arrived, took a shower, and went out to speak to the young adults. Friday night we were to exchange places. He would speak to the young adults, and I would speak in the main pavilion.

"On Friday night when I walked out on stage at the main pavilion, I was surprised to see Elder Wilson. He sat down and appeared to be really burdened. I wondered, 'Why is he here when he has to speak at the same hour to the young adults. It's a walk of two or three blocks to get there.' Finally he stood up to introduce me.

"He told the people that he had to go and speak in the other pavilion, and their services had already begun.

When he finished a pastor came up and played instrumental music for the meditation before I was to speak. Elder Wilson came and stood behind my chair in the presence of thousands and began to massage my shoulders, and he said, "CD, this crowd needs to hear the gospel." He left when I stood up to preach.

"I spoke again in the main pavilion Sabbath morning. We had a good time there, and we returned to the union office. Monday morning my phone rang, 'CD, can you come to my office?' I went down, and Neal said, 'I want to tell you now what I couldn't tell you until now. This was the conference where I had made it clear that there was no corner of this union where you would be excluded. Not only that but when I arrived there were over 100 people sitting in the school library waiting on me. The person in charge wanted to know if I had run out of white men up there. 'We can't understand why you insist that this black fella come down here and preach to us.'

"Neal said, 'I have to preach myself in about half an hour; we just got off the road. But I never run from a discussion when it's truthfully and honorably conducted, so let's have a meeting, but please let's do it Sunday, not tonight [Thursday]. Now that I have agreed to meet with you and honor your request, I have a request for you.' They said, 'That seems reasonable, what is it?' 'I want you to go and hear him preach. Don't stay away from the meetings.' And that showed the difference in his attitude Thursday night and Friday night.

"Elder Wilson called me to his office to tell me this. He said on Sabbath he would be walking through that crowd from one place to another and time and time again folks would come up to him and say, 'Elder, we don't need to have a meeting.' And that settled that. And I give God the glory. And those people became my friends. I got so many invitations from that conference and from all over. My first appointment after I came out of my office was Blue Mountain Academy. I was invited there so many times that people accused me of being on the staff.

"I have a funny one I want to tell you. The same conference invited me back two years later. I had five sermons to preach in two days. I had just preached two sermons, and it was very hot. I had the afternoon in front of me so I went to my room. I had a room right on the campgrounds. The air conditioner was on. I pulled off my shirt and tie, fell across the bed with my trousers on, and just relaxed. I could hear the things that the people were saying as they were passing by. I'm hearing compliments.

"All of a sudden I heard the voice of an old person as clear as a bell. 'Listen, y'all can go where y'all want, but I ain't going nowhere but to hear this nigger one more time.' So I jumped up and went out. I honestly was not peeved. As soon as I stepped out of the door, she was right there. And she saw me. And she said, with love in her voice, 'Oh, we've enjoyed you. You know one thing, I was going to get my hair done, but I'm not going to get it done until you leave here.' I told that to a white congregation some time later, and you could feel the tension until I smiled. It was no big problem. These are things that we overcome. She probably didn't even know that this word was offensive to my people.

"One thing we did as a Columbia Union family was to have a pizza party. Infrequently, but we all looked forward to it. Ledo's pizza. All you could eat. We would order a pizza and a great big bowl of salad and dressing. Then we'd just have a good time socializing in the union office.

"One evening Elder Wilson came down, and he had a couple with him. We had begun eating, but he got our attention, and he introduced this couple and said that he was going to be publishing director of the union. We all applauded, and we were glad to meet and welcome him. The next day he was supposed to meet with Elder Wilson, and he didn't show up. Elder Wilson became worried and checked and found out that he didn't spend the night like he was supposed to. Elder Wilson kept trying and finally the phone rang in the union office, and it was this gentleman, and he spoke to Elder Wilson and said something to this effect, 'We were all

Highly Committed

right until we got to the pizza social and saw this black family, and my wife said she couldn't take it, so we left. I'm sorry.' And you know what Neal said? 'You did exactly what you should have done! If you feel that way you have no place here with us.'

"We've made a lot of progress. The man responsible was Neal Wilson. We had an official human relations committee set up by the union. I and another pastor were cochairmen. I noticed a trend. When we were into what were considered important considerations, I would sit up there with him. When I was chairman, he would sit up with me. And I would look out and see divided attention. All the blacks, about half of the 3,000 maybe, would be earnestly clinging to every word, nodding their heads and listening prayerfully, hoping that we would make some progress. A lot of my Caucasian friends were chatting or reading the *Review and Herald.* I was worried that we didn't have their attention, so I decided that during my time I would get their attention. I said to them, 'I think there's something we need to clarify. Ellen White didn't write volume 9 of the *Testimonies.*'

"I immediately had their attention. And after I enjoyed it for a moment, I said, 'She wrote everything in it. But the racist projections that you like to point us toward and give the sacred gift responsibility for is not the responsibility of the gift of prophecy or the messenger but of the compilers and editors who dragged things out of context to say with divine authority what they felt in their hearts. It's wrong. It's sinful. It's dishonest. I have the burden to prove that. I quote, "Coloreds should not seek to be equal with whites." That's enough to drive folk out of the church if they knew it was there. But one day I had a terrific experience. I heard that statement in context. I would like to read it to you again. "Coloreds should not seek to be equal with whites, because whites are not their example. Jesus is their model."'"

"Later on, in working with several laymen, especially Mylas Martin, an action was taken to reprint portions of *Testimonies* volume 9 and *Southern Work* and get these words circulated abundantly. Neal Wilson and the Columbia Union took the lead in this. [See action taken at the end of the chapter.]

"We had the privilege of living close to the Wilsons. A builder constructed eighteen townhouses in Burtonsville called Pitcairn Place. When we lived in Pitcairn, we were a tight group. We loved each other. Elder Wilson, Elder Pierson, Elder Holbrook, all eighteen families. We had the house on the end. The Wilsons lived across the street from us. The thing that I loved was the regular social get-togethers. In the springtime we had a big strawberry feast. Later on in the summer we would have a corn roasting festival. They were just wonderful occasions. Christmastime, Thanksgiving, and on other special days we got together. We enjoyed it tremendously.

"If it snowed and you knew that somebody was traveling overseas, you didn't wait to be asked; you shoveled your own snow and then you would shovel his. The others joined in, and it didn't take us long. We would shovel six or seven at a time since many of the men traveled. We got the idea of protecting one another. Since that whole street was occupied by Adventists and there were trees on both sides, if some miscreant had an idea to do some wrong, he could have a field day because nobody was there on Sabbaths. We began to assign one person to stay home from church and this person would walk around and would be visible. It was a wonderful place to live." This extended testimony from Elder C. D. Brooks, a leader who worked closely with Neal C. Wilson, shows the progress the church made in the area of race relations under Wilson's leadership.

As Wilson worked to unite the union under his leadership, the 50th General Conference session came around. The year was 1966, and Seventh-day Adventists from around the world converged on Detroit, Michigan, which is approximately 100 miles from Battle Creek where the pioneers of the Advent movement held the very first General Conference session 103 years before.

There were now 1,578,000 Seventh-day Adventists scattered throughout 14,650 churches in nearly 200 countries of the world. The first order of business was to select a world president since R. R. Figuhr, who had served in the top post of the church for twelve years, was retiring. It did not take the nominating committee long to present the name of the new president. On Friday afternoon the delegates ratified the nomination of Robert H. Pierson, who had been president of the Trans-Africa Division.

It was not until the seventh business meeting on Monday, June 20, 1966, that the rest of the report of the nominating committee was heard and voted on. Neal C. Wilson had been elected vice president of the General Conference for North America, replacing Theodore Carcich. "As the Vice-President of the General Conference in charge of the North American Division, he will oversee the activities of 24,000 church workers, 3,300 churches, 1,134 schools, and 38 church-operated hospitals."[213]

Sketch of Neal Wilson

Knowing that many people in the Adventist Church were not acquainted with Neal Wilson, the new leader of North America, Miriam Wood gave this little sketch of him. "First of all, he's the kind of man who can be known to persons of all ages as 'Neal' without his losing one whit of authority, leadership, or dignity. He has self-confidence—fortunately, since a leader who doesn't possess this quality isn't worth his salt. But he doesn't have the kind of towering ego that makes disagreeing with him a hazardous undertaking. In spite of the fact that I've had some brisk disagreements with him through these many years, our friendship is still intact. No matter what the provocation, no matter how long the hours of debate may continue in council sessions, no matter what fragrant discourtesy he may encounter, Elder Wilson never seems to become heated or strident.

"Physically, he has the lean, spare build of a greyhound, though he is no mean trencherman at mealtime. However, he can go an entire day (and possibly longer, though I don't know for sure) without food with no diminishing of energy or mental power if a tight schedule demands this. His body seems to adjust itself to whatever instruction he gives it. His health is unsurpassed, a blessing that sometimes brings a feeling of near envy to those of us less fortunate in this area. For instance, once when he saw me taking an aspirin and commented on this, I asked him what he took for headaches. Taken aback, he replied in surprise, 'I've never had a headache.'

"Moreover he can and does function at top efficiency on five hours' sleep at night, though I have heard him say that it is 'nice' to have six hours. Throughout our years of acquaintance I have never seen him look or act sleepy, no matter how late the hour. I wish I knew his secret." [214]

George Romney, the governor of Michigan, addressed that General Conference session. He had been invited by his friend Nathaniel C. Wilson. On Thursday night after the offering, George Romney entered, flanked by Neal Wilson, new president of the North American Division; R. R. Figuhr, retiring president of the General Conference; R. H. Pierson, new president of the General Conference; and Nathaniel C. Wilson, president of the Michigan Conference.

The governor delivered a stirring speech, interrupted again and again by prolonged applause. Romney emphasized concern about the evident decadence of American society, and he set forth personal Christianity as necessary to reverse this trend and change the sinful nature of man. At the close of the speech, Figuhr responded to the governor's words. This was followed by the presentation of the 10-volume set of the *Seventh-day Adventist Bible Commentary* reference series to the governor by Nathaniel C. Wilson.

Arriving back in Takoma Park, North American leader Neal Wilson later made a statement on the Christian Radio Network and on WGTS–FM. "I take up my new responsibilities with the knowledge that one by himself can do little. I cherish the support and cooperation of the nearly 400,000 Adventist Church members in North America as well as the many friends of the church.... We must seek every possible way to exalt the name and the delivering power of the gospel of the Lord Jesus Christ. This is the time when the church must diligently strive for true brotherhood regardless of color or race. To this end we are unitedly committed."[215]

Highly Committed

Nathaniel C. Wilson, his father and current president of the Michigan conference and the host of the 50th General Conference session, had been elected to the same post at the General Conference session exactly twenty years earlier in 1946. Neal was following in his father's footsteps, and he was elected to the post in his father's territory! Nathaniel C. Wilson was in his very last official post of service and would retire from church service in Michigan. Neal C. Wilson would go on to serve thirteen years as vice president of North America and eleven years as president of the General Conference.

North American Division Presidents
(before 1979 they were called vice presidents)

G. A. Irwin	1909–1911	L. K. Dickson	1945–1946
W. T. Knox	1911–1913	**Nathaniel C. Wilson**	**1946–1948**
I. H. Evans	1913–1918	W. B. Ochs	1948–1962
E. E. Andross	1918–1922	Theodore Carcich	1962–1966
J. E. Fulton	1922	**Neal C. Wilson**	**1966–1979**
O. Montgomery	1922–1926	C. E. Bradford	1979–1990
J. L. McElhany	1926–1932	A. C. McClure	1990–2000
W. H. Branson	1932–1936	Don Schneider	2000–2010
M. N. Campbell	1936–1939	Dan Jackson	2010–
W. G. Turner	1940–1945		

The North American Division comprises nine union conferences, which are in turn composed of fifty-eight conferences.

After consultation with the sixteen world vice presidents of the Seventh-day Adventist Church, General Conference President Neal C. Wilson issued the following public statement on June 27, 1985, regarding racism:

"One of the odious evils of our day is racism, the belief or practice that views or treats certain racial groups as inferior and therefore justifiably the object of domination, discrimination, and segregation.

"While the sin of racism is an age-old phenomenon based on ignorance, fear, estrangement, and false pride, some of its ugliest manifestations have taken place in our time. Racism and irrational prejudices operate in a vicious circle. Racism is among the worst of ingrained prejudices that characterize sinful human beings. Its consequences are generally more devastating because racism easily becomes permanently institutionalized and legalized and in its extreme manifestations can lead to systematic persecution and even genocide.

"The Seventh-day Adventist Church deplores all forms of racism, including the political policy of apartheid with its enforced segregation and legalized discrimination.

(cont.)

"Seventh-day Adventists want to be faithful to the reconciling ministry assigned to the Christian church. As a worldwide community of faith, the Seventh-day Adventist Church wishes to witness to and exhibit in her own ranks the unity and love that transcend racial differences and overcome past alienation between races.

"Scripture plainly teaches that every person was created in the image of God, who 'made of one blood all nations of men for to dwell on all the face of the earth' (Acts 17:26). Racial discrimination is an offense against our fellow human beings, who were created in God's image. In Christ 'there is neither Jew nor Greek' (Gal. 3:28). Therefore, racism is really a heresy and in essence a form of idolatry, for it limits the fatherhood of God by denying the brotherhood of all mankind and by exalting the superiority of one's own race.

"The standard for Seventh-day Adventist Christians is acknowledged in the church's Bible-based Fundamental Belief No. 13, 'Unity in the Body of Christ.' Here it is pointed out: 'In Christ we are a new creation; distinctions of race, culture, learning, and nationality, and differences between high and low, rich and poor, male and female, must not be divisive among us. We are all equal in Christ, who by one Spirit has bonded us into one fellowship with Him and with one another; we are to serve and be served without partiality or reservation.'

"Any other approach destroys the heart of the Christian gospel."[216]

Neal Wilson made racial integration a priority, says Charles D. Brooks (back row, right). Here Wilson stands with the leaders of the Columbia Union and the Allegheny East Conference.

Chapter Eleven

World Church President

"Only a life lived in the service to others is worth living." Albert Einstein

A deep silence hung over the assembled delegates, Review and Herald employees and General Conference staff gathered for a joint worship at the Annual Council of the General Conference. It was Monday, October 16, 1978, and Pastor J. Robert Spangler had just delivered a challenging message for the morning devotional. As the meeting closed, those assembled were about to leave when Pastor and Mrs. Robert H. Pierson moved quickly to the microphone. Pastor Pierson asked all present to remain a little longer and lightheartedly quipped, "Don't be afraid, my wife and I are not going to sing."

The audience chuckled but knew something important was about to happen. The packed Takoma Park Church waited in hushed anticipation as Pierson gave his surprise and shocking announcement.

"There come times in our experience when we have to make decisions that we would prefer not to make—decisions that cut deep into one's heart and that have far-reaching effects. Last Sabbath morning before we went to Sabbath school, after much prayer and agonizing, Mrs. Pierson and I made such a decision.

"Eight years of service in emerging, exploding Africa with all of its pressures and perplexities, and 12-and-one-half years of happy, but problem- and stress-filled, years in Washington have taken their toll. Our physicians tell us we must shift our burdens to younger shoulders. We had hoped we could complete our term of service in 1980 at Dallas, but apparently the Lord has other plans for us and for the church. In harmony with medical counsel we plan to leave Washington for a few weeks' rest and then retire January 3, 1979. We are sorry not to be able to fill some appointments we had looked forward to filling, but arrangements will be made to care for these.

"As soon as we understood what the future held, I spoke with Elder Franz and Elder Emmerson. Last evening I had the vice-presidents of the General Conference and the division presidents with me, and I conveyed to them the decision of the doctors. This morning I spoke with our General Conference officers and conveyed to them our decision. I have asked Elders Nigri, Franz, and Emmerson to work out the constitutional issues involved in the election of the new president before this Annual Council ends. For a few weeks there will be a president and a president-elect, but my brethren see no problem in this. Today PREXAD [President's Executive Advisory Group] and the division presidents will meet to work out final details in this transfer of office, and all of you will be kept informed. We know the Lord's hand will be over His work and the events of the next few days as plans are laid for a great surge forward in God's work during 1979.

"It's harvest time, brethren, and it's 1,000 [baptisms]-a-day time.

"This has not been an easy decision for Mrs. Pierson and me to make. We love our work. We love the Advent workers and members around the world. Every one of you is precious to us. I want to express my deepest appreciation to all of you—world leaders and General Conference office staff alike—for all that you have done to make 12-and-a-half wonderful years for Mrs. Pierson and me here in Washington and around the world where we have traveled. You have been an inspiration and an encouragement to both of us.

"This is not goodbye this morning—not *hasta mañana, au revoir, dosvadonia*, nor *sayonara*. We will be with you for a few more weeks. In the meantime, let us go right ahead with our work as usual. There is yet much to be done at this Annual Council. We have no time to lose. We have a work to finish, a work of preparation to be effected in every life in preparation for the return of our Lord—in our day! Yes, brethren and sisters, it *must* be in our day!

"My pen, my voice, as long as God gives me strength, will be dedicated to this one all-consuming passion! We solicit an interest in your prayers, and may God bless and keep every one of you."[217]

Few had known that during the past year Elder Pierson had been subject to transient ischemic attacks (TIAs) when under heavy pressure, which seemed to be most of the time. During the attacks numbness would develop on his left side. His doctors warned that unless he was relieved of his heavy responsibilities, the risk of a stroke was high.

Following Pierson's announcement that he would resign, PREXAD plus the presidents of the world divisions met to study procedures for electing a president when Pierson would retire on January 3, 1979 (his birthday). A subcommittee was set up to recommend the special nominating committee to be made up of representatives from all the world divisions. Once selected, the sixty-six-member nominating committee met at 10:00 a.m. the following day, Tuesday, and voted Cree Sandefur, president of the Pacific Union, as chair and Calvin Rock, president of Oakwood College, as secretary. Prayerfully and carefully, the committee worked until 12:15 p.m.

Sandefur spoke about the unity that prevailed in the meeting. "Nine names were submitted as candidates. Because of age, three were deleted on request of the candidates. The remaining six were thoroughly discussed. On the first vote, taken by secret ballot, 61 out of the 64 votes cast favored Neal C. Wilson. The vote was made unanimous and the nomination was taken to the entire council at 3:00 p.m." C. B. Rock, secretary of the committee, read the report to the entire assembled delegation.

"VOTED, to elect Neal C. Wilson to serve as President of the General Conference."

As soon as the report of the special nominating committee had been approved, Robert H. Pierson ushered in Neal C. Wilson and his wife, Elinor. They were warmly received and given a huge standing ovation.[218] Neal Wilson moved to the speaker's desk and began his acceptance speech.

"If my face looks drained of color, it is because I realize something of the sacredness of the vote that has just been taken. You heard Elder Sandefur [chairman of the nominating committee] describe the atmosphere that existed in the special nominating committee; you heard him speak of five earnest public prayers that were offered at various points during the committee's work; you heard him describe the unity that existed; and I can only tell you that all this places an overwhelming feeling of responsibility on my wife, Elinor, and on me.

"It isn't often I feel my heart palpitating, but when I realize that the church has spoken in this way, there is only one response I can give. If I could have found a good reason to decline I would have done it; I would have liked to be one of those who stood and asked that their names be withdrawn from the board. [A reference to the fact that during the nominating committee several leaders who were of retirement age asked that their names be erased from the blackboard.] But I also realized that God has allowed some of us to spend years working with our current president, Elder Pierson. God has allowed some of us to have a varied background of experience, some of it outside of North America.

"Personally, because half of my life has been spent outside of my home country, I feel very much a part of the whole family. As a lad of four and a half years I went with my parents to Central Africa. There, digging my toes into African soil and joining my little African friends in typical boyhood activities, I established my early roots, gathering culture, language, and information. From there I went to South Africa, and later to India, where it was my privilege to become acquainted with a new culture and to acquire new insights. Several of you in the congregation here this afternoon were with me in India as boyhood friends and schoolmates or as leaders in God's work in India at the time.

Highly Committed

"It was at that time that I first met Elder and Mrs. Robert Pierson. They had come to Southern Asia, where my father was the division president. They brought into the work a dynamism that captivated my young heart (I was 17 or 18 at the time). I had the privilege of living in their home for some weeks. From that time on Elder Pierson has been to me a tutor and an example, one whom I have greatly admired and respected. Later our lives were thrown together in service, including the past 12 years here in Washington. Many times Elder Pierson and I have knelt together in prayer. As he has put his hand on my shoulder, together we have asked the Lord to show us the way through, and it's marvelous how God opens the way when we give Him a chance.

"I spent almost 15 years in the Middle East, another cultural area, and found my service there an unusually helpful education for a young worker.

"I will ever remain thankful to my mother, who from my earliest days guided me in the study of the Scriptures and the writings of Ellen White. She led me to believe firmly and to trust implicitly the counsel God has given to this church through His special messenger, Ellen White. In some of the difficult situations the church has faced in the past few years it has been a joy and comfort to know her guiding influence.

"I feel deeply grateful for the team here in the General Conference. I feel thankful for our division leaders, whom I know personally and whom I trust and in whom I have great confidence.

"And while I pray for light, I pray also the larger prayer for love for God and man—God's people throughout the length and breadth of the earth. It's harvest time, and we need to gather those who do not yet know they ought to belong to God's family and to get them ready for the coming of the Lord.

"I claim the blessing of Asher this afternoon: 'As thy days, so shall thy strength be' (Deut. 33:25). I believe this is God's promise not only to Asher but to each one who looks to Him for guidance and help.

"Now let me summarize the way Elinor and I feel today as we bask in your love demonstrated to us in your standing ovation as we came before you this afternoon. We feel as did Solomon when he was asked to be king over the great nation of Israel. Ellen White says of him at that time, 'Solomon was never so rich or so wise or so truly great as when he confessed, "I am but a little child: I know not how to go out or come in." Those who today occupy positions of trust should seek to learn the lesson taught by Solomon's prayer. The higher the position a man occupies, the greater the responsibility that he has to bear, the wider will be the influence that he exerts and the greater his need of dependence on God. Ever should he remember that with the call to work comes the call to walk circumspectly before his fellow men. He is to stand before God in the attitude of a learner. Position does not give holiness of character. It is by honoring God and obeying His commands that a man is made truly great.'—*Prophets and Kings,* pp. 30, 31.

"That's the challenge for each one of us. In this harvest time I earnestly solicit your prayers that God may enable me to carry the responsibilities involved in leading His remnant people."[219]

When Neal and Elinor sat down, Elder Pierson took the podium again to respond to Neal's speech and welcome the newly elected president.

"This afternoon I am not sure whether I should congratulate Brother Wilson or offer him my condolences. Instead of either, I am going to wish him God's blessing and assure him that he is going to be frequently in our prayers. I'm sure that, as we have listened to Brother Wilson and have noted the various places he has lived, we can see that the Lord was preparing him for his present leadership role. To me the fact that he has lived in four divisions and is acquainted with Africa, Asia, the Middle East, and North America is an important consideration, and I'm sure that the Lord had His hand over the nominating committee as they made their decision.

"As Brother Wilson has said, it has been my happy privilege to know him for many years. I appreciate particularly the 12 and a half years that I have served with him here in the General Conference. I have observed the way the Lord has blessed him as he has faced North America's many problems. The memories that I cherish the most are those of the times that we have knelt in prayer and together have spoken to the Lord about the problems we were unable to solve in our finite wisdom.

"Brother Wilson, I have just one word of counsel for you this afternoon. When problems come to you in the days ahead, may your first reaction always be that expressed in Zedekiah's appeal to Jeremiah, 'Is there any word from the Lord?' (Jer. 37:17). You will need always to be sure that it is God who is leading, not expediency or mere human rationalization. Find in the Eternal your strength, your wisdom, your guidance, and your help.

"I know that there are great days ahead of this church. I hope, however, that they will not be prolonged. I hope we'll not be having many more General Conference sessions. Somehow, under the guidance and blessing of God, may the work speedily be finished so we can go home. God bless you, Neal. We love you and believe in you, and all the best to you.

"Sister Wilson, we want to tell you that our prayers are going to be with you. It's not easy to be the wife of the General Conference president. My wife can tell you that. There will be many times when you'll have to be lonely, but there are compensations, too. I want you to know that our prayers are going to be with you as they are with Neal, and may God bless you."[220]

After speaking these words of welcome to Neal and Elinor, Elder Pierson had prayer.

The Lord Isn't Here Yet

Elder Spangler recounted the story of how he visited with Elder Pierson, now the ex-president, the day after his resignation. "Tuesday morning, October 17, I spent about 30 minutes with Pastor Robert H. Pierson, president of the General Conference, discussing plans for *Ministry's* President's Page. The president's announcement of retirement in January, 1979, had come as a shock to everyone the day before.... The knowledge that in a few weeks this man, who had given his life to the church, would be retiring created an atmosphere of sadness.... As we sat together for those few precious moments, I tried to think of something encouraging to share with him. 'Brother Pearson,' I stated, 'the Lord has greatly blessed your leadership.'

"'The advance of the work during your tenure of service has been nothing short of remarkable.' I sincerely meant what I said for since 1966 church membership has doubled, until by the end of 1978 it stands at well over 3 million. There was a pause of silence. He looked at me, not with a smile, nor with the expected pleased expression of one who has just received a great complement, but rather with the look of perplexity. His lips quivered, his eyes filled with tears, and his voice broke as he said, 'But the Lord isn't here yet, Bob, and anything short of that is not success.'"[221]

This same passion for Christ to return by finishing the work became a hallmark of Neal Wilson's presidency. The burden laid on him by his presidential predecessor and his father seeped into his soul. On the first day of his presidency, he was confronted with the challenge of the cities. "As I landed at La Guardia Airport in New York City on the morning of January 4, I thought to myself, In no better way can I spend my 'first day' as president of the General Conference than in concentrating on the challenge of the great metropolitan centers of the world and the promises of our Lord regarding work in the cities.

"At five-fifteen that morning my radio alarm clock had awakened me to a new day, the first day in my new position. The weather outside was bitingly cold (about 12 °F., or -11 °C.). Several General Conference leaders had joined me that morning as we boarded the eight-o'clock air shuttle from Washington, D.C., to New York City. As members of the New York Metro Ministries board, we were fulfilling a promise, made last September, to attend the winter meeting of this unique organization....

"When on earth, our Lord spoke with feeling and concern about the cities.... The cities are rife with violence, crime, sickness, noise, environmental pollution, wicked entertainment, labor problems, and loss of individual

Highly Committed

identity on the part of their inhabitants. In the overcrowded cities are multitudes living in poverty and wretchedness, while in the same territory are those who live luxuriously, piling up colossal fortunes, and spending their money on self-gratification and soul-debasing vices. Demon-possessed men and women engage in heart-sickening violence resulting in brutal, fiendish destruction of human life. The corruption that prevails is beyond the power of human pen to describe. The cities of today are fast becoming like Sodom and Gomorrah of Bible times...

"We must go forward in faith to restore the broken relationships between the human family and God, and among the members of the human family. What we do we must do quickly!"[222]

A few months later Neal Wilson shared with the church a letter he received from his 82-year-old father. "Something over a year ago after Elder Pierson visited us here at our house, I started a letter, jointly to him and you. However, that letter was never completed, but I now feel I must share with you some of my thinking about the one great burden of our hearts—the completion of the task committed to the Adventist Church.... I fear, however, that this burden has not been shared as generally as should have been the case." In the article Neal wrote, "My father points out that it seems ... that the fires of evangelism in the local church burn rather low much of the time."

His father continued, "In my mind, the vital issue is to get the General Conference plans and burden to the local pastor. The burden of the General Conference seems to get sidetracked somewhere. The local conference and church are most vital, and the burden of change and revival must reach them with warmth and concern. I regret to state that from my observation the church pastors hear and feel very little of the heartbeat of the General Conference....

"What I have written, Neal, demonstrates the heavy burden on my heart ... Things have just been too good and easy—money is plentiful, life generally has been rather comfortable, conditions have produced luke-warmness! It may be that God will find it necessary to use unfavorable world conditions to awaken and energize His people, resulting in a mighty movement and the completion of the task ... Love, as always, Dad."[223]

On January 8, 1979, 58-year-old Neal and his wife, Elinor, were honored in a special program called "Saluting President and Mrs. Neal C. Wilson." Since the presidential election took place at an Annual Council and not at one of the General Conference sessions, the officers felt that some distinct program should actually take place to "officially" install him in office. The officers, departmental leaders, local pastors, and friends met on the 10th floor of the General Conference building. The short service started at 5:30 p.m. after work had finished. Typed at the top of the program were the words "...The Lord thy God is with thee withersoever thou goest" (Joshua 1:9). After the invocation and blessing by Elder Emmerson, food was served. A. J. Patzer served as the emcee, calling on several to give tributes to the new leader. Mrs. G. Ralph Thompson sang "Bless Our Church" to the tune of "Bless This House."

Bless Our Church

Bless our church, O Lord, we pray
Make it safe by night and day
Make each member strong and true,
And each conference and union too.
Bless each home and family
Let Thy peace be full and free
Bless these folk who strive to win
Ever open to joy and love.

Bless our leader with his plans
Keep them safe in Thy dear hands.
Bless each institution bright
Letting in God's heavenly light.

Bless the youth who attend therein
Keep them pure and free from sin
Bless us all that we may be
Fit, O Lord, to dwell with thee
Bless our church that one day we
May dwell, O Lord, with Thee.

The self-styled poet laureate of the church, Adlai Esteb, penned a poem especially for Neal Wilson. In his absence Elder C. D. Henri presented it.

One of our great American Poets wrote:
"Lives of great men all remind us
We should make our lives sublime,
And, departing, leave behind us,
Footprints on the sands of time."

Elder Pierson as our leader,
Left his footprints sharp and clear.
Elder Wilson, his succeeder,
Now will be our honored seer!

He has been a man of vision,
He's been tested in the fires!
He's a leader with a mission,
With the courage God requires!

He has been a missionary,
Half his life he's spent abroad.
"VISION" but not "visionary,"
But a "WORKER" for His God!

We now welcome you as leader,
And, our heartfelt tribute bring,
May you be strong "like a cedar,"
Made strong by our Lord and King!

Highly Committed

As you guide the church to heaven,
May His Spirit God impart;
With the "present truth" as leaven,
Fill each happy, holy heart!

We invoke God's richest blessing,
Grant you wisdom, peace, and power,
And, when problems are distressing,
Guide you through each trying hour!

You have kept in step with Moses
Since you lived beside the Nile.
Life is not a bed of roses,
But rewards come after while!

Elder Henri humbly acknowledged that he didn't usually read or write poems but under the inspiration of the occasion he had come up with two special verses.

Blessings on you, Neal and Elinor
Make your footprints sharp and clear.
We will follow as you lead us.
Christ before you never fear.

Armageddon's day draws nearer,
Problems great will multiply,
But the promised Holy Spirit
Power and wisdom will supply.[224]

Soon the entire Adventist community knew what North America knew—Neal Wilson was an outstanding leader and a great committee chair. "Neal Wilson ... relished committees—and the Adventist Church runs on committees. Wilson's mastery of the agenda at the councils of the church became legendary. He studied and prepared for every item, becoming thoroughly versed in the pros and cons, options, nuances, concerns, anxieties. If a major matter came up for consideration, Wilson always took the chair ...

"When Wilson was in the chair, the committee did not break. You had to make your own arrangements to get a drink or visit the restroom. Wilson wouldn't budge all morning, all afternoon, or through a long night session. Committee members humorously remarked to one another that he was like a camel."[225]

His skill as a chairperson, his high standards and high principles became renowned among Adventist leaders. In 1980 at the General Conference session held in Dallas, Texas, he had no trouble at all being reelected to the presidency. The year and a half he had served as president of the world church gave ample evidence of his dedication and skill as leader of the church. He was reelected in record time.

"It seems that the nominating committee was so unanimous in their support for Elder Wilson that it reached its decision almost immediately. At the end of the treasurer's and secretary's reports, the microphone was given to the nominating committee chairman, H. H. Schmidt, who turned it over to the committee secretary, J. G. Smoot—and the minute he mentioned Elder Wilson as the nominee there was a movement in the audience as the assembled delegates rose to their feet in a spontaneous outbreak of love and approval. W. J. Hackett, session chairman, said he would take that response in lieu of a vote and declared Elder Wilson elected. It was a touching scene as Elder Hackett called up Mrs. Wilson to share this sacred moment with her husband. The next to express their love and support were his parents, Elder and Mrs. N. C. Wilson, veterans of the Lord's work in many areas. Then son Ted, and his wife, Nancy—who carried up little Emilie. Catching sight of the new General Conference president, she called out—as any 21-month-old child might—'Grandpa!' which had to be rewarded with a grandfatherly kiss, to everyone's delight. It was a moment long to be remembered."[226]

Four generations of Wilson's stood on the platform at a General Conference session! The past, the present, and the future! Herbert Douglass, writing about the events of that day, penned these lines, "Never before has it happened, but before our eyes something beautiful was unfolding. Elder Neal C. Wilson, president of the General Conference, is the first son of an Adventist minister to be elected to that office, and to authenticate that fact, Elder N. C. Wilson, Sr., stood by his side and offered the morning prayer. When that seasoned voice, still clear, warm, specific, took the world church in his arms and presented it to God, the hall was hushed. When we heard, 'I pray for my son ...' the roll of low Amens sounded like a distant waterfall."[227]

At the 1985 General Conference session in New Orleans, Louisiana, Neal Wilson was again reelected to the highest office of the church. "... the chairman and secretary of the Nominating Committee, Richard Lesher and Calvin Rock, have just come onto the platform. Everyone feels a stir of excitement. Dr. Rock announces the selection of Neal C. Wilson to continue as president of the world church. Applause breaks out. Alf Lohne, chairman of the meeting, acknowledges the endorsement of the applause, but 'just for the record' asks for a show of hands, and the election becomes unanimous."[228] Once again four generations of Wilsons stood on the platform. The chair also presented Elder and Mrs. Robert Pierson, former General Conference president. They were given a big round of applause when the members saw them and learned that Elder Pierson's health had improved.

The pace of the presidency in the twentieth century with its modern means of travel and communications was exhausting and seemed to accelerate. Everyone wanted a visit from the chief executive of the church. In his first year as president, he visited all of the world divisions.[229] If Neal Wilson had not had unusual physical strength, the duties and expectancies might have worn him down as it had his predecessor.

Ten years into his presidency, William Johnsson describes one trip (similar to scores of trips he took each year) in Africa that lasted for five weeks. "Accompanied by his wife, Elinor, Elder Wilson arrived August 29 [1988] at the Kotoka International Airport, Ghana, welcomed by a crowd of more than 2,000. The government of Ghana received the Wilsons as state guests ...

"Wilson's visit to Ghana commemorated the centenary of the founding of the Seventh-day Adventist Church in that country.... During the 10-day itinerary, the Wilsons dedicated churches, were paraded through the streets of Kumasi with police motorcade, were received by the traditional rulers (Ashanti), spoke to a Sabbath audience of more than 20,000.

"The Wilsons next flew west for a week of 'vacation.' Elder Wilson grew up in Africa: later he and Elinor served as missionaries in Egypt for 15 years. For more than 50 years Wilson had dreamed of one day climbing Mount Kilimanjaro, 19,340 feet, the highest point on the continent of Africa. On September 12 he set out to realize that dream....

"At 68 Elder Wilson is one of the oldest people to scale Mount Kilimanjaro [see details in chapter 14].

Highly Committed

"After descending the mountain September 16, Wilson preached the following day to a Sabbath congregation of thousands in Arusha, Tanzania. The service concluded with the baptism of more than 500. Sunday he met with the vice president of Tanzania and later formally opened Health Expo and the LaVerne Tucker evangelistic crusade in Arusha.

"Kampala, Uganda, was the next stop on the Wilsons' precouncil itinerary. They were met at the airport by the head of government, prime minister Dr. Samson Kisekka. Dr. Kisekka, a Seventh-day Adventist, devoted his entire weekend to the Wilson visit. On Sabbath, Wilson preached to a packed congregation of about 8,000 and Sunday was taken by police motorcade for the one-and-one-half-hour meeting with Uganda's chief of state, President Y. Musevni.

"Four days before the opening of the Annual Council, the Wilsons flew to Addis Ababa for a weekend of meetings with enthusiastic Adventist believers.

"And after Nairobi the Wilson road is wending still further in Africa. Instead of returning to Washington, D.C., at the conclusion of the council, the Wilsons will spend 10 days with members in places less frequently visited—on the islands of Madagascar, Mauritius, Réunion, and the Seychelles."[230]

And then he gave the keynote address at the opening of the Nairobi Annual Council on October 4 and proceeded to chair that meeting, which lasted several days.

While Neal traveled around the globe, the rest and relaxation prescribed by his doctors was good for former president Robert Pierson and helped to extend his life another decade. As his strength returned, he accepted preaching appointments and other pastoral assignments. He turned 78 on January 3, 1989. Just before that birthday he and his wife, Dollis, accepted an invitation to serve as interim pastor of the Kailua Church on the island of Oahu in Hawaii. They were only a few weeks into their two-month assignment when Elder Pierson suffered a massive heart attack.

He had been awakened early Sabbath morning, January 21, by discomfort in his chest and left arm. A physician friend and houseguest was summoned. Pierson told the physician that there was no great pain. The physician insisted that he go to the emergency room of the nearby Castle Medical Center anyway. Before he would leave for the hospital Elder Pierson was observed kneeling in prayer. He collapsed there and could not be resuscitated. His funeral service was conducted in Hendersonville, North Carolina, on January 26, 1989.

More than 1,000 Seventh-day Adventists from near and far gathered to pay tribute to the former General Conference president who had so many times called the church to revival and reformation. He had been born in Brooklyn, Iowa, in 1911 and had begun his ministry in Decatur, Georgia, in 1933. Although he began as a pastor, he spent most of his 46 years of ministry as a church administrator in India, Jamaica, Trinidad, Tennessee, Texas, and Zimbabwe. Nearly thirty books flowed from his pen and hundreds of magazine articles. Neal C. Wilson spoke at the funeral.

"'Rather than calling this a funeral service, this is one of praise and remembrance,' said General Conference president Neal C. Wilson in a short homily. He drew strength from Jesus' words at the raising of Lazarus—'I am the resurrection, and the life: he that believeth in me, though he were dead, yet shall he live: and whosoever liveth and believeth in me shall never die. Believeth thou this?' (John 11:25, 26)—and from other passages of confidence in God's power to bring His sleeping saints back to life.

"Elder Wilson related Robert Pierson's impact on him personally: when he was 16, Elder Pierson conducted a Week of Prayer at Vincent Hill School in India, where Wilson was a student. 'Today I feel somewhat alone,' said Wilson. 'No one really knows and can sympathize with the burdens of this office except someone who has borne them.'"[231]

Thursday, July 5, 1990, was an important day for Neal Wilson. It was his 70th birthday. It was also important because as president of the world church he had to give the keynote address to the delegates assembled in the Hoosier Dome for the fifty-fifth session of the General Conference of Seventh-day Adventists. It was also important because as the incumbent president he had to be reelected here to serve for the next five-year term of service. No one foresaw any problems with his reelection. Wilson's health was good. His mind was sharp, and his leadership was still dynamic. It was a very good day.

That evening after his keynote address, he met with the 224 members of the nominating committee to help them select its chair. Eventually Robert Folkenberg, president of the Carolina Conference and a good friend of the Wilson family, was selected for this task, and Benjamin Reeves, president of Oakwood College, was chosen as the secretary.

Nominating Committee Surprise

On Friday morning the nominating committee met early, and the floor opened for nominations. Twelve names were quickly put on the board (the names and ages of the men were as follows: Neal Wilson, 70; George Brown, 66; Jan Paulsen, 55; G. Ralph Thompson, 61; Robert Kloosterhuis, 57; Cyril Miller, 62; Calvin Rock, 60; Ken Mittleider, 61; Walter Scragg, 64; Ottis Edwards, 61; Joao Wolff, 60; and Bekele Heye, 53).

The floor was then opened for discussion on these names, and the next hour and a half was taken up by speeches praising the leadership of Neal Wilson, mostly from Europe, Africa, and Russia. In his analysis of the event Ronald Graybill mentions that the impact of the many speeches in favor of Neal Wilson was weakened because the only microphone in the room was on the chairperson's table. Many of the delegates in the large room could not hear or had to strain to hear all the praise for Wilson. When the microphones were finally brought in for the delegates, the tone of the speeches was beginning to change.[232]

Tom Mostert, president of the largest union in North America, stood up and, after acknowledging Wilson's many gifts and outstanding service, stated that Wilson had been president of the North American Division for twelve years and president of the General Conference for another twelve years. If he were to be reelected that would mean that North America would be under the strong influence of one man for approximately thirty years. Twenty-four years was long enough. Once the door was open others lined up at the microphones to call for change and point out the merits of George Brown, Inter-American Division president.

"The influence of that first clear call for change may have been further enhanced by the fact that it was followed immediately by a break in the proceedings, during which the delegates were asked to nominate choices for vice-chairman and an associate secretary for the committee.... Was that break in the action fateful? No one will ever know what might have happened had the committee rushed to a vote on the president before the break. The break gave the delegates a chance to mingle more freely with one another and to share their thoughts."[233]

Southeastern California Conference President Stephen Gifford felt that the youth were disenfranchised and believed the church's leadership was too aged and "stereotyped." It was time to give the church a fresh breeze of optimism and use Wilson as a goodwill ambassador for the church, not as General Conference president.[234]

The first ballot was taken around noon. After kneeling in prayer the delegates rose to vote. The two top vote getters were Neal Wilson with 76 votes and George Brown with 75; the rest of the votes were divided among the other nominees. After more discussion the third and final ballot was taken, which resulted in 130 votes for George Brown and only 81 for Neal Wilson. Most of the committee sat in shock, first, because the incumbent president had not been returned and, second, because for the first time in the history of the church they had nominated a non-Caucasian to run the church. George Brown had been born in the Dominican Republic to an Antiguan father and Dominican mother (and his wife was from Suriname).

Highly Committed

Folkenberg and Reeves found it their lot to break the news to Wilson. Then George Brown was informed that he was now the newly nominated president of the General Conference. Stunned by the news, Elder Brown consulted with his family and several close advisers and requested time to pray about the matter. Several of the committee members tried to persuade him that he should accept, but the more they talked the more he felt that he should not accept the responsibility. He was only four years younger than Neal Wilson, and at age 66, he did not believe he could see the task through to completion in one five-year term. He was not at all sure his health would allow him to go two terms. He made his way to the committee room and regretfully told the chair that he must decline the invitation.

The nomination committee convened once again. A new list of names was put on the board. Finally Charles E. Dudley, president of the South Central Conference in the Southern Union, nominated 49-year-old Robert Folkenberg, who was chair of the nominating committee. Now it was Folkenberg's turn to be shocked. When he left the room at about 4:15 in the afternoon so that the committee could discuss his name as well as the others, he really didn't expect his name to go any further. The delegates on the main floor were anxious to hear the report from the nominating committee before the meeting closed and the Sabbath hours began. The delegates were told to sing "In a Little While We're Going Home" and a few other songs.

Folkenberg was literally speechless when he was told that he was the newly nominated president. He asked for time to speak with his wife, and in forty-five minutes he returned to a standing ovation where he said, humbly, to the committee members, "I hope you folks know what you're doing."

By now the report had been read to the entire session. Many people were shocked that Neal Wilson had not been reelected, and other asked, "Who is Robert Folkenberg?" Elder Wilson was called on to make a statement, and he stood before the delegates and said, "My fellow delegates, brothers and sisters, as of noon today it was quite apparent to me that the Nominating Committee wanted to make a change. Anyone who allows himself to be nominated for an elected position in this church should understand and have no regrets when the process that elected him may decide, using the same process, to elect someone else. This is the test and measure of an individual who allows himself or herself to be elected....

"It was my privilege last evening to look into the faces of the majority of the Nominating Committee. I know a great many of those individuals. I believe in them.... So Elinor and I have remained very calm and peaceful, undisturbed.... We have done our best, and what we have done we have done in genuineness.... My appeal to you this evening is to give the one who has been suggested by the Nominating Committee our strong, prayerful, undivided support. And I tell you that he's going to need it....

"I praise the Lord tonight that even though we may have made some mistakes, there have been many victories in this church....

"Elinor and I will sleep peacefully tonight. There are no regrets on our part. Rest assured that we do not feel rejected at all....

"Please, tonight do the right thing and let us start the Sabbath in unity and with rejoicing."[235]

Bill Johnsson, former editor of the *Adventist Review*, commented on the election: "The process is brutal: president today, voted out of office tomorrow. I wish we Adventists could come up with a more compassionate way of electing our leaders; however, I do not have a plan to suggest. My heart went out to Elder Neal C. Wilson. He did not just pack up and leave. He had to stay on, chairing the session through sensitive items, keeping the business moving along, although he was now a 'lame duck.' He deserved better—much better."[236]

For now, Robert Folkenberg would step into the shoes of Neal Wilson.

Some of the outstanding accomplishments during Neal C. Wilson's presidency are as follows:

"**Doctrine:** Wilson presided over the first major restudy of Adventist beliefs in nearly 50 years, culminating in the adoption of the 27 fundamental beliefs at the Dallas General Conference session in 1980....

"**Minorities:** During his 16 years as General Conference vice president for North America, Wilson put himself on the line in favor of the full participation of Blacks in the life and work of the church. As president of the world church he continued to press for a community of equality and justice.

"**Church growth:** 'It's harvest-time,' he declared as he assumed the mantle of the GC presidency. Growth became the watchword of the next 12 years ...

"**Crises:** Wilson confronted a series of major problems—challenges to Adventist understanding of prophecy and the heavenly sanctuary, and to Ellen White's writings; and financial crises in the Davenport investments and the bankruptcy of Harris Pine Mills....

"**The media:** [He was always at ease in front of a radio microphone or television camera. He could quickly respond to any question.] Wilson was quick to grasp the potential of the mass media for propagating the Adventist faith. Under his direction the church established the far-reaching short-wave radio outreach on Guam, and embarked on a similar scheme for Italy.

"**Structures and organization:** The Wilson presidency spelled out the role and function of the General Conference and its divisions, cleared the way for full division status for North America ... Likewise he led in restructuring the church in Africa, Europe, and Southern Asia.

"**Scholars:** ... He fostered research, high tech medicine ... and input from experts in the church's decision-making.

"**Women's roles:** ... Wilson encouraged a greater role for women in the work of the church, opening doors for women to serve in gospel ministry and as local church elders.

"**Global Strategy:** Always looking ahead, Elder Wilson has pointed the way for the nineties—a global strategy for global mission....

"He is as much at home in Africa, India, or South America as in the United States. He represented the church with dignity and grace as he met heads of state. He is wise with the wisdom that comes from loving people as people.

"And, in one of the final actions of his presidency, the General Conference session voted in a new division July 5 [1990]—the Soviet Union!"[237]

Highly Committed

After announcing his retirement, Robert H. Pierson counsels the newly elected General Conference president Neal Wilson and his wife.

Two administrators consult together: Neal Wilson with his successor, Robert S. Folkenberg, Sr.

World Church President

As General Conference president Neal Wilson visited more than 170 countries. He stands here with his treasurer, Lance Butler, in Rwanda with several African leaders. On the far left is DeWitt S. Williams, who, at that time was president of the Central African Union which included the countries of Rwanda and Burundi.

Mrs. Celia Conley and Pastor J. B. Conley visit together at the North Fitzroy church during the Australian Centenary commemoration (1985). Pastor Conley, then eighty-six, served as an evangelist in India while Neal Wilson was a student there and was a factor in Wilson's conversion.

Highly Committed

As the Wilsons bow in prayer, Elder Pierson asks God's guidance as they prepare for their new duties as president of the General Conference.

Neal Wilson receiving his honorary Doctor of Divinity in 1976 at Andrews University.

With a warm embrace Elder Pierson congratulates Elder Wilson on his new job.

Role Models: Neal Wilson stands with his son Ted N. C. Wilson, then ministerial secretary of the Africa--Indian Ocean Division. The three Wilson ministers, father, son and grandson, are the only Adventist family of three generations known to have been officers and members of the General Conference Committee which cares for the business of the world church between quinquennial sessions, with each having been president of a world division of the church and these two as world church president.

World Church President

"It's not easy to be the wife of the General Conference president," retiring president Elder Pierson warns Elinor Wilson.

Neal and Elinor Wilson enjoy the 54th World General Conference Parade of Nations in New Orleans after being reelected; granddaughter Catherine sits with them.

Neal Wilson with a large group of clergy listening to President Ronald Reagan speak. Picture courtesy of Pacific Press Publishing Association.

A large crowd listens to Neal Wilson at the Dallas Brooks Hall in Melbourne, Australia during their Centenary Year 1985.

Chapter Twelve

The Final Years

"To me old age is 15 years older than I am." Bernard M. Baruch

Neal Wilson was swept into the office of president of the world church abruptly at the sudden resignation of Robert Pierson, and now he had been ushered out of office equally abruptly. It probably never crossed his mind as he flew into Indianapolis that he would not lead the church for another five years, or more. Although 70 years of age, he was still in remarkable physical health, and everyone knew his sharp mental acumen.

To discover that his own division, the North American Division, had led the charge on his departure must have been a bitter pill for him to swallow. Even while giving his sincere and generous concession remarks and congratulation on Friday night to his successor, he must have felt a great deal of sadness and maybe a modicum of bitterness on being forced to leave the office to which he had devoted all of his energies for the last dozen years. He loved leadership and administration. Giving up his first love must have been very difficult.

"But Wilson refused to allow bitterness to consume him or stint his usefulness. He donned the mantle of elder statesman, giving counsel to Elder Folkenberg and later Elder Paulsen, keeping open the door of the little office that he retained at church headquarters. All who sought his wise advice were made to feel welcome."[238]

He requested and was granted his official retirement benefits the next year. The action read, "Recommended, to grant North American Division Retirement Plan benefits to Neal C. Wilson following 51.08 years of service effective February 1, 1991."[239]

This action was followed by a vote of appreciation.

"Voted, to express deep and grateful appreciation to Neal C. Wilson, recent President of the General Conference, for his 51.08 years of unstinting and dedicated service to the Seventh-day Adventist Church....

"Various committee members expressed gratitude for Wilson's leadership and his influence in their personal lives. Wilson is appreciated for his strong spiritual emphasis, keen intellect, interpersonal skills, committee leadership, formidable memory, and immediate grasp of a situation or problem. His broad understanding of the world field and its needs, the use of his God-given speaking skills, and his open and fair approach to examining issues and problems have brought strength to the Church. He has given strong promotion to and shown great interest in evangelism by his leadership in The Thousand Days of Reaping, Harvest 90, and Global Mission as well as his personal example in holding evangelistic meetings. His unshakable belief in the authority of the Scriptures, the relevancy and authenticity of the Spirit of Prophecy, the need of the Holy Spirit, and the Seventh-day Adventist Church as it nears Christ's soon second coming ...

"Wilson will continue to serve the Church in retirement since he has been asked to serve as the general administrative consultant in nurturing the USSR Division of the General Conference of Seventh-day Adventists working closely with the General Conference President and the President of the division to ensure the fullest possible support. He will also take special assignments as requested by the General Conference President. He continues to be a member of the General Conference Committee, as do all former General Conference Presidents. He will continue to serve on a variety of denominational boards including Adventist World Radio,

The Final Years

Geoscience Research Institute, Home Study International, Loma Linda University, and as a lifelong member of the Ellen G. White Estate Board."[240]

Interestingly, Ted N. C. Wilson served as the secretary of the General Conference Committee meeting when this action was taken.

Subsequent General Conference Committee minutes show actions voting him to visit the Euro-Asia and the East Africa Divisions to participate in their year-end meetings, and a visit to the Inter-American Division and the Euro-Africa Division. It was difficult to plan a retirement event for a man who was constantly on the move.

An "Appreciation Day" was finally arranged between travels to be held at the world headquarters to celebrate "Pastor and Mrs. Neal C. Wilson for Their Many Years of Ministry to the Seventh-day Adventist Church" on Monday, October 28, 1991. The festive day started at 8:00 a.m. with worship in the chapel. President Robert S. Folkenberg set the tone of the meeting with a welcome and introduction, which was followed by special musical numbers and a devotional by J. R. Spangler.

The midday reception in the atrium began at 11:30, and the 800 or so employees of the building lined up to shake hands, give hugs and kisses, and extend their appreciation to a couple who had become friends as well as their leader. Treasurer Don Gilbert presented a tribute book, and Secretary G. Ralph Thompson read letters and citations, and George Rice and Ezra David made additional presentations. There were lots of good food and plenty of music. Then there was the "short" response from the retiring president.

The tribute dinner at 7:00 p.m. was by special invitation, but it culminated the day's activities. Myrna Tetz ends her book with an account of that dinner: "A Neal C. Wilson appreciation banquet took place with Gary Patterson as host. After giving several biblical models of world travelers with an all-encompassing mission, such as Paul, Silas, Luke, and Mark, Patterson told how 'the church family had gathered to hear the good news, rejoicing with their leaders in successful missionary journeys.' Then he added, 'But more than this, they came to give their offerings. Such is our model tonight. We have shared in the joy of the gifts God has given to NCW. And we have shared our own gifts as an honor to him and to our Savior.'"[241]

The Honorable Constance A. Morella presented a tribute to Elder Neal C. Wilson before Congress, which is recorded in the *Congressional Record* of the 102nd Congress on Tuesday, October 22, 1991.

"Mrs. Morella. Mr. Speaker, I wish to congratulate an extraordinary constituent, Elder Neal C. Wilson, who was world president of the General Conference of Seventh-day Adventists for the past 12 years. On October 28, the Seventh-day Adventists will honor Elder Wilson for his more than 50 years of service to the church.

"Elder Wilson demonstrates qualities that improve the world for all peoples. He has always shown compassion, love, and respect for all races and religions. His dedication and devotion are an inspiration to everyone with whom he comes in contact. He brought the church's message and services to humble homes as well as to palaces. His global vision has been responsible for his being instrumental in the development of the church and its preparatory schools, colleges, universities. He has helped millions of people around the world in times of famine, natural disasters, and wars....

"Elder Wilson's personal accomplishments are also extraordinary. He can converse in eight languages and has visited more than one half the countries where Adventists have medical, educational, evangelical, or publishing work. He has climbed some of the highest peaks in the world, including Mount Kilimanjaro, and he belongs to a family in which three generations have been ministers in the church.

"I offer my best wishes to Elder Wilson and his family, who reside in Burtonsville, Maryland. I thank him for his munificent spirit and selfless devotion to improving the lives of others. And I thank him for his friendship. I congratulate him, for he is a beacon of light for us all to follow."[242]

Highly Committed

Elder Folkenberg arranged for Neal Wilson to have an office on the first floor at the General Conference, and he was given very substantive assignments at home and abroad for the next two years. "The new president wisely chose to give Elder Wilson the task of fostering the growth of ... the growing work in the Soviet Union ... and a businessman, [the] former second secretary of the Soviet embassy in Havana, Cuba, was giving them some trouble.

"Neal arranged to invite this man to the United States in the company of the prefect [mayor] of the Kremlin area, in the heart of Moscow, the prefect of the southwestern area of the city, where the university was located, along with a newly rich Seventh-day Adventist businessman, for a two-week visit that included the largest Adventist hospital in Orlando, Florida, as well as the van ministry in New York. Elder Kulakov's married daughter, a student at Southern Adventist University in Tennessee, was the translator; and I [Charles Taylor] was chosen, as Neal's former assistant, to host the group in New York, Washington, and Orlando.

"Playing on the special interests of problem people, surrounding them with positive and powerful partners, succeeded!"[243]

Goodwill Ambassador

Neal was present at George Vandeman's retirement in 1992. In October 1994 he was a featured speaker when more than 1,000 seniors converged on Andrews University. We have record of him attending the 1995, 2000, and 2005 General Conference sessions as a delegate where he made speeches from the floor. He attended various camp meetings and youth rallies across the country and accepted various speaking appointments here and there. He often traveled to Loma Linda where his mother and father had retired. In addition, he was still a member of the Loma Linda University Board. In 1997 he was present and featured at the PUC alumni weekend.

The year 2000 was an exceptionally busy year for him. In May he acted as a goodwill ambassador when Sir James Carlisle, the Governor-General of Antigua and Barbuda, visited Washington Adventist Hospital. Later he spoke at Sligo by the Sea in Ocean City, Maryland, a summer feature of the Sligo Church in Takoma Park.

And when the Historic Adventist Village in Battle Creek, Michigan, opened on June 24, 2000, Neal was in attendance. "'Ladies and Gentleman, this is a day we should never forget; the spirit of Battle Creek is still alive!' proclaimed Neal Wilson ...

"An estimated 1,500 people from many countries and several states attended the historic occasion as the church's heritage was highlighted in this new nurture and evangelistic endeavor. An official ribbon cutting ceremony followed remarks by state, civic, and church officials.

"Excited guests eagerly toured the Village. Walking from site to site, visitors were able to learn about the dedication and zeal animating many of the early church pioneers....

"Visitors to the one-room schoolhouse heard the story of the first official Adventist church school from volunteer guides.

"In the James and Ellen White house, visitors were able to tour the upstairs bedroom where in 1858 Ellen White wrote the first edition of *The Great Controversy.*"[244]

At the fifty-seventh General Conference session in Toronto, Canada, in 2000, North American Division President Al McClure, who was chairing the tenth business meeting, opened the morning session with these words, "I want to welcome you this morning; I'm glad to see that so many are involved in the business sessions as well as the devotional periods.

"As we begin this morning I would like to take time to remind you that there are some very important days that we have been celebrating. Sabbath, July 1, was Canada Day, a special day for the nation in which we find ourselves, the great nation of Canada.

"Yesterday was United States Independence Day, July 4, and a lot is made of that in that nation.

The Final Years

"Today is another very special day. You may not be aware of that. I am not sure that it is a national holiday anywhere that is of particular importance this morning, but it is a special day to a very important figure in the Seventh-day Adventist Church. Today is the birthday of Elder Neal Wilson, and it is a very special birthday, his eightieth. Elder, would you please stand?"

At this news the delegates loudly and enthusiastically sang "Happy Birthday" to Elder Wilson.

McClure continued, "A remarkable man, one whom we all love and who has served this church for most of those 80 years. His father was a leader in the church; Elder and Mrs. Wilson have served the church in many capacities internationally, as well as being our General Conference president. So, Elder, we want to wish you the very best of birthdays and many, many more."[245]

Yes, Dad?

On a lighter note, the heavier "legal" meetings were balanced by moments when Ted Wilson, newly elected vice president and chair of a session, acknowledged a question from his father with the phrase, "Yes, Dad?" To which his father responded, "Brother Chairman, my dear son."

Neal Wilson had always been a champion of the health and temperance principles of the Adventist Church. He lived these principles and promoted them. He supported the Health and Temperance Department and was responsible in part for meeting the challenge of alcohol and other drugs that were beckoning to the youth of the church in the eighties.

It was through his support that the Institute of Alcoholism and Drug Dependency of Andrews University was set up. When he heard the survey of drug use in the Adventist Church he quickly set up the Commission on Chemical Dependency and the Church. He was a supporter of Adventist Youth to Youth, the church's response to addressing the problems of chemical dependency. One of his last speeches on the floor of the General Conference expressed his concern about this issue and this department.

Name Change

A proposal had been brought to the floor to change the name of the Department of Health and Temperance to the Health Ministry Department. Neal Wilson went quickly to the microphone and explained his concern.

"Brother Chairman, I think a little further explanation ought to be given to this assembly of leaders on this particular item. It is almost like pulling down the flag. Seventh-day Adventists have been known worldwide for their strong emphasis on temperance. The word 'temperance' is not an easy word to translate into some other languages. In fact, in the world we live in today, 'temperance' may not be a highly accepted word. My concern is that we do not ever become ashamed to speak about the matter of temperance, including alcohol, tobacco, and drug dependency. In fact, temperance is needed more in the world today than it has ever been needed.

"And let me tell you, it is needed in the Seventh-day Adventist Church. My concern is, Brother Chairman, that we are not lowering the flag, diluting the emphasis that we are going to be giving. Many health experts today never think about temperance as we think about it, and they may feel that we have just now melted into the atmosphere of the world, which is a little more acceptable. I would simply like to have some statement made to this group that in spite of the change of the name there will be no de-emphasis—in fact, it may increase our emphasis. I understand the background of it, but many will sort of feel that we have lost one of those great characteristics that identified us worldwide these many years. That is my appeal, Brother Chairman."[246]

Dr. Allan Handysides, the director of the department, gave his viewpoint. "I am very appreciative of the words that we heard from Elder Neal Wilson. I think the history of the Health and Temperance Department is one of which we can all be proud, especially when we think of the work that has been done throughout the world in the name of temperance. I think we can be very proud of that history.

"Sometimes words do change in meaning. There is a very prominent Adventist family who changed their name because of the change in meanings given to their name. The work of the Adventist Health Ministry Department is to minister to the whole person, and we cannot minister to the whole person, especially in the presence of the enormous deluge of substance abuse that we see. The very fabric of society is being torn apart by alcoholism and drug dependency. I would like to see our department give redoubled effort to work against the abusive substances that are so prevalent in society.

"Friends, we need to establish national branches of the International Commission for the Prevention of Alcoholism, so that we can generate enthusiasm in the churches. My plea is that the nations here represented take upon themselves the burden of working together with us so we can make Health and Temperance our focus. I am pleased that we have the word 'ministry' in our name change.

"It is unfortunate that the world is using and has usurped the use of the word 'temperance.' To the world it does not mean what it means to us. We mean 'abstinence,' and I pray that that message is taught to our young people in ever-strengthening tones. I would give you the pledge that those of us who are promoting health want to see ourselves as ministers to the needs of the world and to the church."[247]

Thomas Neslund rose to add his thoughts. "Many of us have been involved in health and temperance work for a long time. Nearly 30 years of my life has been spent in this type of activity. Since the merger of the Health and Temperance Department at the General Conference, it has been a cumbersome effort to make the two united and work together. There have been strides made, obviously. But I think by this name change we have finally found a home for temperance. At least now we have something not as an add-on but as a part of a ministry that is a part of the church. The world—specifically, the alcohol industry—has stolen a march on us in terms of the moderation concept. As I travel worldwide for the ICPA as their executive director, I find that the word 'abstinence' works much better than the word 'temperance.' And from that I can talk about self-control, which is really one of the gifts of the Holy Spirit."[248]

Dr. Albert Whiting, a former director of the department, requested time to speak. "I fully support this action. I'd like to give a little background to it. We had a meeting several years ago of all division health and temperance directors, and all except one voted in favor of this change, realizing that it was needed because the word 'temperance' is translated all over the world as 'moderation.' This church does not accept moderation when it comes to drugs and alcohol. The word 'ministry' implies organization. It implies service and is very appropriate. I plead for you to support this recommendation."[249]

The vote was taken, and it was "*Voted*, To change the name of the Health and Temperance Department to the Health Ministries Department"[250] with the blessings of Neal Wilson.

Neal Wilson continued to be invited to special events within the church and the country. "When President Bill Clinton and Prime Minister of India unveiled the new Mahatma Gandhi statue in Washington D.C., former General Conference president Neal C. Wilson and his wife were among the invited guests.

"While [his father, Nathaniel, served] as president of the Southern Asia Division, Wilson met with Gandhi on [two] different occasions ... Gandhi, who influenced Martin Luther King Jr., is best known for advocating non-violent means of achieving freedom. 'My formative years were deeply enriched by living in India,' Wilson says. 'I was deeply impressed by this great personality.'"[251]

In 2004 Neal, father, and Ted, son, had the opportunity of conducting a public evangelistic meeting in Northern Ireland, their ancestral home. "Many of the meetings were held at the City Hotel, a few hundred yards from the docks where Wilson's great-grandparents departed for a new life in America."[252]

The Final Years

"My grandfather, seeking a new life, sailed from this river, the Foyle, to the United States at the time of the potato famine," Neal Wilson told the people in Londonderry, Northern Ireland. "We have returned to our roots to tell again the wondrous love of our Lord Jesus Christ."

The three week series titled "The Revelation of Hope" began on Sunday, May 16, at two locations in Londonderry: the YMCA, Drumahoe, and the City Hotel, Waterside.

"Joining the father-and-son team were Dr. Peter Landless, associate director of the health ministries for the world church, who presented a nightly series of health lectures, and youth volunteers from Australia, Sweden, Finland, and Switzerland…"[253]

"Attendance at the series 'was measured not by hundreds, but in tens' of people, And while attendance was consistent, years of religious factionalism have engendered some resistance on the part of the general public, he said. Only one person was baptized at the end of the series; another professed a desire for baptism and several others may be baptized in the near future."[254]

Several of the people who attended the meetings were led back to the Bible by the Holy Spirit, no longer letting tradition dictate their beliefs. Ted Wilson described one attendee, Margaret, as an example: "Margaret hardly missed a night. She was drinking it in and always taking notes." But he added that even though she was obviously affected by the truth, he knew it would take time for her to "work it out within her own personal circumstances."

The Wilsons found the experience to be rejuvenating. "'There is a much greater visibility for the Adventist Church [in Northern Ireland] because of this lecture series,' [Ted] Wilson said.

"Wilson, and his father … were each given civic plaques by Mayor Shaun Gallagher, an event featured in the local newspaper."[255]

Last GC Session

The 2005 General Conference Session showed a picture with the caption "The four who've come to more. Searching for those who have attended the most General Conference sessions, including the current session, the *Adventist Review* found the following four contenders: (from left) Neal C. Wilson, former president of the General Conference, has been present at the last 15 consecutive GC sessions; his first was in 1941. Kenneth H. Wood, chair of the Ellen G. White Estate board of trustees and former editor of the *Adventist Review*, has attended 14 GC sessions. He was a young boy when he went to his first in 1926. Bert B. Beach, director for Interchurch Relations of the General Conference Public Affairs and Religious Liberty Department, is credited with being present at 14 consecutive sessions. He and his wife, Eliane, spent their honeymoon at the 1954 session. Roscoe S. Lowry, former president of the Southern Asia Division, has attended 10. Wilson voiced his hopes for the 58th General Conference session: 'Somehow this session needs to help hold the church together in these times of great fragmentation, and help the members become better prepared to fulfill God's mission and be ready for the Lord's great appointment for His second coming.'"[256]

The fifty-eighth General Conference session in Saint Louis in 2005 would be Elder Wilson's last General Conference session. His health would not permit him to attend the fifty-ninth session in Atlanta, Georgia, where his son would be elected president of the world church.

The steps of the 85-year-old church statesman were beginning to slow a bit. He was willing to keep going, but he noticed that things were changing a bit for his dear wife. Elinor needed more care and attention. She forgot things more easily and seemed to have a difficult time getting through the day. He spoke with Ted and Nancy, and they said that they had noticed a difference in her, too. Elinor had been physically frail for a number of years.

After discussing the situation, it was decided to put Elinor in Elternhaus, a nearby assisted living facility. Elder Wilson visited her every day.

Highly Committed

Two years before Elder Wilson passed away Bob Nixon, former General Conference communication director and legal counsel, posted a message on the Internet requesting friends to send the Wilsons greetings through Christmas cards. Here is his message:

"Last year from time to time I noticed Elder Wilson driving his silver Mercury Marquis on Highland Road, near our home. One day the thought crossed my mind that he might be driving to Elternhaus, the assisted living center just around the corner in Dayton, Maryland, to see his beloved Elinor.

"'Yes,' son Ted replied when I asked. 'He drives from their home to Elternhaus every day to spend much of the day with Mother, who is suffering from dementia.'

"And then after some months, I realized I hadn't seen Elder Wilson's Mercury in our neighborhood. Ted advised that his father also was now staying at Elternhaus—established more than 20 years ago by Don and Diane Crane as a country home for seniors. So one morning I stopped for a visit.

"'What are you doing here, Bob?' Elder Wilson asked, as I entered the common room. He seemed ready for my unannounced visit—with vested dark-blue suit and white shirt and tie.

"'I've come to visit you, Elder Wilson.'

"He nodded, took my hand in his, and patted it

"'Thank you,' he said.

"Then we chatted. Yes, he stays at Elternhaus now, to be with Elinor. Ted—a general vice president of the General Conference—visits several times a week when he's not traveling—and also Nancy [Ted's wife] and sometimes grandchildren. Nancy's mother, Mary Lou Vollmer, also is a resident at Elternhaus, so it is truly a 'family' home.

"Elder Wilson spends most of his time with Elinor—or reading his Bible, taking a short walk outside in good weather, or watching Adventist television programming. Although suffering from some eyesight challenges, he is learning to cope by using some medical recommendations so he can keep reading the Bible and the Sabbath School Adult Bible Study Guide in large print.

"On subsequent visits I found a less formal Elder Wilson—suited still, but without vest or tie.

"'Going to sit in on the Spring Meeting at the General Conference this year?' I once queried.

"'No, Bob,' he smiled. 'I've been to more than my share of meetings. They'll do fine without me. I'll stay right here with Elinor.' He did make an appearance at the recent Annual Council for one morning, according to Ted. Elder Wilson is still quite interested in the progress of the world church but views it from a more permanent perspective since he no longer travels. He is so happy for the promise of the soon coming of our Lord, Jesus Christ ... Elder and Mrs. Wilson, both 89, don't surf the Internet."

Nixon then requested in his message that friends send Christmas cards to Neal and Elinor at Elternhaus. During his career Wilson visited more than 170 countries and met with heads of state and other officials. He also received keys to a number of cities as well as international certificates of appreciation and recognition. But now he was content to give up travel and be at "home" with his wife.

Nancy's mother came to live at Elternhaus after falling and breaking her hip in November 2008. Up until that time she had lived on her own in the retirement home that she and her husband, Dr. Donald Vollmer, had built in 1983 when Dr. Vollmer retired from his medical practice. The home was located in Andrews, North Carolina, near their son, Dr. Jim Vollmer. Their other children were out of the country at the time of their retirement: Pastor Don Vollmer was serving as a missionary in Ireland and their daughter, Nancy, was with Ted in Africa and later in Russia. Sadly, three years after retiring, in 1987, Dr. Vollmer suffered a cerebral hemorrhage and passed away. Nancy's mother, Mary Lou Vollmer, lived twenty-three years longer than her dear husband.

Mary Lou lived at Elternhause for fourteen months before passing away. Her daughter Nancy Wilson informed me that on February 5, 2009, "she had a small infarct in her brain stem and had a hard time swallowing. We had a huge snowstorm here in Maryland. My brother drove up as soon as the snow stopped, put her in the car and took her back down to her home [in Andrews, North Carolina, to die]. They arrived on Friday morning, and she passed away on Sunday morning. She was 90.

"She was very musical. She painted. She could write poetry. Her head was full of poetry. Two weeks before she died I was reading Thanatopsis to her by William Cullen Bryant. I just picked up the book and started reading, not realizing that it was all about death. I stopped near the end of the poem, and she finished it for me.

"Mother was very pragmatic, and she hated the way the whole funeral business was managed. I think most of us feel that way. They play on your emotions when you're so vulnerable. She said, 'I just want a pine box. I don't want anything else. Just put me in the ground the day I die.' Every Friday night my brother and his wife and this other fellow and his wife who was an attorney in Andrews would come for Friday night dinner, and one Friday night they started talking about the whole funeral business, and mother said, 'I just want a box. I just want a pine box.'

"Tim was a skilled craftsman, and he said, 'Mary Lou, I'll make you a box.' So he came out and took measurements for her and made a box for her like the old Western coffins. She even got in it to make sure she fit. My mother was a hoot. She had an incredible sense of humor up until the day she died. Quick witted.

"She had the coffin made, kept it stored, and that Sunday morning when she died, February 14, 2010, Valentine's Day, the hospice nurse came and said, 'Do you want me to take care of her?' We said, 'No.' My brother got a bag of cedar chips, and we put a blanket in there and gently put her in there.

"She used to say a thing of beauty is a joy forever. She loved nature and was a natural gardener. She couldn't take a walk without picking up little flowers or pretty leaves in the fall. She loved dried leaves. We found all these dried leaves in books on the bookshelves, so my daughters put one in each hand and sprinkled them on her.

"It was a very meaningful service. The closest friends and neighbors came, and Ted and my brothers dug the grave. It was up in the mountains. My brother built a fire so we could stay warm. It snowed all weekend and that afternoon we buried mother. Then we had a wonderful memorial service the next weekend."

The Last Years
Ted tells the story of his parents in their advancing age. "Mom was in Elternhaus for about four years, and Dad was there for about two years. The last years were challenging years. My mother's lack of cognitive ability was a challenge. She couldn't remember much. She couldn't interact easily. But she was always pleasant and happy generally. Dad found it increasingly challenging to take care of her so he said that it was time for us to find a good place, and fortunately we were able to get a good place at the Elternhaus. They treated her wonderfully and my dad as well. I can't say enough good things about Don and Diane Crane and their staff who are members of our church.

"The last couple of years were kind of tough because the ability to relate started fading and you just go and visit and sometimes the best thing you could do was to be there and you just give them a kiss and a hug and whatever. I remember the last time I was there my mother didn't recognize me at all. That was the case for the last two or three years.

"My mother was always pleasant and nice. She might've thought I was her father or somebody related. She might have these little occasions of bright openings. I remember the last time she really recognized me was about six months before she died. She came around the corner in her wheelchair, and she looked up at me and she said 'Ted!' That's all she said.

Highly Committed

"I remember toward the end it was too difficult to talk to Dad about anything substantive. This was very odd because Dad was the master of speaking with a very knowledgeable understanding about most anything he wanted to talk about. He was in my opinion an incredibly brilliant person. But after a while it was very hard to talk to him about much of anything specific. I remember going in and just singing with him. It was very touching. He just joined in. He knew the words. And it just brought tears to my eyes. He would mouth the words and try to sing. I would read the Bible to him and tried to encourage him.

"We're not completely sure that he knew I became president of the General Conference. It was explained fully to him a number of times, but I don't know if he ever understood that. I think the real thing that he appreciated most was that I was just there with him. He would make some kind of acknowledging remarks. I don't know if it really fully sank in.

"It was kind of interesting because when I came to the General Conference office I found different things that were here which are things from his era. His initials. Pictures on the wall. This was his office for about a year and a half. He moved here from the old building. Here's a calendar from 1989. I leave it there because it's kind of a connection with him. In the end he just kind of faded away. And mom the same thing. It was sad. Mom died when she was 91, and Dad died when he was 90. Mom was six months older than dad."

Memorial Service

The sun set for good on the life of Neal Clayton Wilson on December 14, 2010. The memorial service was held a month later in the General Conference auditorium in Silver Spring, Maryland, on January 19, 2011, at 2:00 p.m. The beautiful and touching two and one half hour service was filled with music and laughter, tears and reflections, preaching and speeches. It was a fitting tribute to a life well-lived.

Orville Parchment, the platform coordinator and special assistant to the president, opened the service. "We are here today to celebrate the memorable life of an outstanding leader of the Seventh-day Adventist Church, Elder Neal Clayton Wilson. On behalf of the family I welcome you. Not only those of us seated here in the General Conference auditorium but also those who are joining us via the church channel on Hope television and also the Internet." He then introduced Ted Wilson.

"Thank you, Pastor Parchment and thank you to each of you for being here," Ted began. "... It is fitting that we hold the service here today in this auditorium, for this is the building where dad spent a number of years working after it was built and of course he helped to plan and execute the construction of this building. Dad died on Tuesday, December 14 last month. We buried him two days later on Thursday, December 16, in a quiet family-oriented graveside service while the snow was falling. It was a very touching time. The children and grandchildren were able to provide their version of how they reacted and connected with my father in a very personal way.

"Today we have planned a very simple service to give God the glory for His power over death and His soon second coming." Ted then introduced the participants in the service. Scripture was by the grandchildren; words of biblical hope was by C. D. Brooks and George Rice; prayers were by Robb Long, his pastor, and Calvin B. Rock; collegial tributes were given by G. Ralph Thompson, Jan Paulsen, Charles E. Bradford, Ambassador Joseph Verner Reed, Francis W. Wernick, Robert S. Folkenberg, William Johnsson, and Kenneth Mittleider; music was presented by Sherilyn Gibbs, William Fagal, and Karla Rivera; and a video tribute was shown. There is not enough space to include all of the tributes, but the following are a few.

C. D. Brooks, former Breath of Life telecast founder and speaker and personal friend, gave a homily and tribute.

"Elder Neal C. Wilson invited me to come to work with him in the Columbia Union. I became aware that God had chosen him to address a major concern in the remnant church, and when I came to work with him,

The Final Years

I discovered one of the most extraordinary men I had ever met. Truly I call him a great man, and I've done it around the world, and his humanity validates that idea of a great man.

"The Bible says that the Sabbath is a sign that God is our God, Ezekiel 20:12, 20. Oh, we love that one. We love that one when we do evangelism. We want the world to know that's what we believe but there's another one. In the book of John 13:35 the Bible says 'by this shall all men know that you are my disciples if you have love one toward another.' That's God's other sign, and we were coming up short.

"So God called Neal Wilson to lead out in changing the very course of the church and establishing a corrective that cannot be forgotten. He was fearless in duty, exemplary in conduct, consistent in his witness and during a very critical time in this country's history—the civil rights revolution. Our wonderful church seemed unconcerned, willing to be the tail and not the head. "Elder Wilson showed us Jesus Christ. It had to start with him that way. You can't be a phony and fool us all. You have to be for real. He told us a simple truth. Our message, especially our message, is to go to every nation, kindred, tongue, tribe, and people. I learned as I worked with him that our problem was not so much hatred as misunderstanding. We didn't know each other. And when we got to know each other better things got better. He brought us together by the Holy Spirit's power. Neal Wilson stood as a tower of righteousness in a desert of despair, and he brought hope to our hearts, especially to those disadvantaged peoples amongst us. And now he sleeps and somebody remembered his idea, his consuming idea, summed up in one word, hope."

From the video presentation, Rosa Banks, secretariat, gave her tribute. "He was the one that opened the church's eyes to the need to use the greatest force that we have in terms of numbers, women were more in number than any other group. I think this will be his greatest legacy because the church is now aware that women have talents, too, and they are using them every place possible."

Former General Conference president, Jan Paulsen said, "My close working relationship with Elder Wilson was developed during the years when I served as division president in Europe, and he was General Conference president. I think I speak for many division presidents who served at that time, some are here now. He was extremely supportive of his division presidents. He trusted them. He let them get on with their business. I suppose that the distance may have helped. But he was always very, very supportive of his division presidents. We were his eyes, his ears, his instruments in the various distant parts of the world. And I have often thanked God for the strong support that I felt that Elder Wilson gave to us.

"One day I had a telephone call from Elder Wilson. He said, 'I have just received an invitation from Russia to attend a peace conference in the Kremlin. I wonder whether you would like to join me.' What do you suppose? Sure, I was very happy to do that. So we went to Moscow, an extraordinary, unforgettable experience there in the Kremlin itself in the halls of the people in this atheistic environment where the walls and ceilings are painted with images of scenes of the Bible, of Creation week. It was an amazing experience to walk through those halls and to see those things.

"I was impressed by the way Elder Wilson, with grace and dignity, was able to relate to people who obviously did not share our faith. They were politicians. They were atheists. They were primarily driven by motives and goals, which were very alien from those which we held as a church. But he was very skilled and very diplomatic in dealing with and relating to these leaders in those circumstances.

"I still remember us in between session at that peace conference, in a more informal setting, meeting with even members of the Politburo. He was able to communicate the values that we as a church exist for and are engaged in. And he brought out the best so that our church could be seen in its best light. With Elder Wilson I was able to visit heads of states and leaders of government in several countries in Europe. I was with him as he

Highly Committed

visited leaders of other churches, bishops of other churches and again the openness with which he sought to relate to people and show respect for the assignments that they carried.

"It taught me something very important in this stage of my own leadership. The importance of finding out how you can relate in a non-hostile manner with people who were very different from ourselves who may not have the most positive view of you or our church and yet for us to be able to be understood by them in that context and relate to them and communicate the values which we hold sacred and for them to understand and see us as a church which is good for society and good for the world in which we live. Elder Wilson showed me the extreme value of moving around among people, among leaders with strength, clarity, and dignity, and I thank God for the example that he gave me."

Ambassador Joseph Verner Reed, United Nations Under-Secretary-General and Special Advisor to Secretary-General Ban Ki Moon, said, "...Mimi, my wife of 51 years, and I are proud and humbled to be at this service. Elder Wilson was a remarkable man. We consider Elder Wilson to have been a friend.... I came to know Elder Wilson some 20 years ago. We met at the Parliament of Man, United Nations in New York. Thanks to Elder Wilson's introduction to the distinguished Dr. James Slater and Loma Linda University I undertook treatment for cancer at the proton service center. It was the vision of Elder Wilson that he took the lead from Dr. Slater to establish the proton therapy center. It was a bold stroke to create the center. Thousands, 15,000, have benefited from the proton therapy treatment, and now there are many proton centers in the United States and the world.

"Subsequently, Mimi undertook treatments two times at Loma Linda. On our first visit, our very first visit, Elder Wilson was at the front door of the hospital to welcome us. He supervised every aspect of our treatments. Mimi and I salute Elder Wilson's legacy. Elder Wilson will forever be missed and will live in our hearts forever. May God bless Elder Wilson in his eternal life in heaven as his presence blessed so many of us on earth. Dr. Wilson and friends, be well, be safe, be happy."

Former world president Robert S. Folkenberg shared his thoughts. "Inevitably everyone makes their way through life guided largely, if unconsciously, by their worldview. Modern society largely excludes God and His will and instead considers personal opinion and self-interests as ultimately authoritative. In stark contrast is the life of Elder Neal C. Wilson. He was among those who not only lived life to the fullest but valued God's revelation of his own character of his own sense of values above all else.

"He enjoyed a zest for life that would take the whole afternoon if that's the picture that we were focusing on exclusively. I saw one small taste of that zest, a fearful view of that zest. On a visit to Victoria Falls I found a position on the bank where I could look down that gorge, and the roar was deafening and the smoke of that cascade was so awesome you could see it 50 to 100 miles away when you were flying when you approached it. But Neal would not be satisfied. I was positioned so I could get extraordinary pictures of Victoria Falls. For me that was adequate. Not for Neal Wilson.

"I stood back there with my mouth hanging open. He did not tiptoe gently to the edge of the stream. He took a careful look at how far it was across to the first branch of water, and he jumped, and the falls were right there. He did not tiptoe. He did not wade. He jumped, and then he backed up to the edge of that rock, and he jumped close to the next one and to the third one, out to the big rock that hung out over the edge. And he stood over the edge as that rock divided the primary amount of the waters coming down that Zambezi, and he stood there. It was not sufficient to see the falls. He wanted to taste them. He looked down into what I have no other way of describing except as a watery inferno, and he stood there quietly meditating, savoring the experience. Such was his zest.

The Final Years

"The Folkenberg and the Wilson family paths crossed long before this. It was his father, Elder N. C. Wilson, that called Anita and me into the ministry back in the Michigan Conference. We served in the Columbia Union with Elder Roger Holly of the Columbia Union, and then after some time in the Columbia Union in evangelism, we were called to Panama. And then on Christmas Eve 1965, he participated in my ordination. And the next morning Anita and I began the 10,000-mile drive across the United States and all the way down to Panama.

"I was impressed by Elder Wilson long before I had any idea of all of the pressure he had to endure there at the headquarters. I was impressed that he did not want to lead by proclamation, by cajoling, but by example. He didn't just encourage evangelism; he did it. He took the time from his daily pressures that are unbelievable and went to Panama, and he preached a full evangelistic campaign. It was a joy to be there as part of his team, but it was the biggest encouragement to listen to him, listen to him come alive, and listen to the passion with which he preached the message that was the focus of his ministry. That was his hot button, and it was hot. He did an extraordinary job.

"In contrast, I remember when we went to the Inter-American Division, and we had a retreat over on the west coast of Florida, and Elder Wilson, recently elected to the General Conference presidency, came to the division retreat. My son, tall, skinny, lanky, full of energy, and full of vim and vigor, was commenting around the dinner table with Elder Wilson on the other side of the table about how well it had gone for him that morning as he took somebody and wiped them out playing tennis. I think that was just a little too much for Neal Wilson to handle.

"To see the cock sureness of this young lanky fellow, and he said, 'I'll take you on.' The next morning found a very humbled son after Elder Wilson sort of cleaned up the court and brought Bob back down to some size. He left some wonderful memories until this day.

"Now most of you are aware of his diplomatic skills and the role he played in the development of the Soviet Union, of the seminary, of the publishing house. But what you may not be as aware of is what he did before that made that possible. You may not realize that after the 1917 revolution the Seventh-day Adventist Church for various and sundry political reasons tended to fragment all across that vast country and things and ideas and concepts tended to cluster these churches into small groups so when you look at the Seventh-day Adventist Church across the Soviet Union from 1917 until the mid-80s, the latter part of the 80s, the Adventist Church in Russia was fragmented into at least seven or eight separate groups. Without the Adventist Church becoming unified, there was no platform upon which to build the relationships between the church and the government.

"The work that he did with Elders Kulakov and Zhukaluk, presidents in Russia and in the Ukraine, working carefully, patiently, lovingly, tenderly together to bring about a unification just below the surface. It was there and people could see it happening. There were some tensions and some good times, but when it was all done, there was a Seventh-day Adventist Church that could approach the government of the Soviet Union and that was the platform upon which he was able to stand, and God opened the doors to the leadership in a remarkable way. All of that would have been impossible if it hadn't been for his quiet, invisible diplomacy to bring the Adventist leadership of that country, to bring them all together so they could stand as one before God and before the leadership of that country. Most people are not aware of it, but it was one of the high contributions that he made to the Seventh-day Adventist Church.

"Knowing his passion for souls, he took advantage when the Loma Linda Foods was sold, remember that? And he brought a recommendation to the Annual Council that the proceeds of the sale of Loma Linda Foods would reside under the control of the General Conference executive committee and be used for evangelism. And it sat there not in everybody's mind and sight, but he never forgot it. I will never forget after an Annual

Highly Committed

Council in the Philippines, I think it was, he came back and started talking about global evangelism. And it was born from his vision of the financial proceeds of Loma Linda Foods and the mission that God had entrusted this movement, and he looked for ways to take those resources and apply them to mission and moved them into the realm of identifying every people group, every unentered territory around the world. That was the dream that was driving it. God used this man in a remarkable way.

"I am particularly grateful that when I was still wet behind the ears, having no idea of the magnitude of the task that had fallen my lot in 1990, knowing that I knew nothing of what was happening in Africa and India that this guy who had no need to travel anyplace else—he was tired of traveling—he was tired of being away from home—still accepted my invitation to go with me on a training trip to India, to Africa, so I could understand some of the currents that were extant in those areas. I thank God 'til this day for that unselfish leadership that he exemplified.

"I'm going to close with this. For the last year or more Elder and Mrs. Wilson and my mother have enjoyed the extraordinary care offered by Don and Diane Crane at Elternhaus in Dayton, Maryland. Regularly my brother and I visited there, and my sister came to meet with my mother a couple of months before Elder Wilson passed away. It's hard for me to talk about this. But I will never forget that Sabbath afternoon Elder Wilson was by himself sitting in the living room area. There may have been one or two other people in the room, and he was sitting there gazing at the floor just letting time go by. I came in and sat down and saw this man of God lonely and wondering what was happening. I don't know.

"I pulled up a chair and put my arm around the back of his shoulder, and I started reminiscing. It took a while to get his attention and his focus. Little by little his eyes opened up, and he started paying attention. We started telling stories about all the times I could recount that his ministry had touched my life. In a little while tears were streaming down his face and mine too. Two old men rejoicing in what God had done. One day we're going to finish that conversation. I can hardly wait!"

More Tributes

William G. Johnsson, former editor of the *Adventist Review*, added his remarks. "One other brief instant if I might. He was my boss. We got to know each other very well. I loved this man. He was very kind and very affirming to me. Very often we would get together in his office at lunchtime. He would bring along his brown bag of lunch, and I would bring my brown bag, and we would sit and talk for an hour. And sometimes he would offer me some of the items from his brown bag, and I likewise. It was just a pleasant and delightful time to be together. First name basis, always like that, with Neal. And with Ted. I like that very much.

"Here was a man who had a basic simplicity about him, simplicity in the way he dressed, in the car he drove, the way he lived. There were no airs about Neal Wilson. He was real. He was genuine. He loved the Lord, and he loved this church, and he gave his all to it. Of all the many, many things that impressed me, and there were so many, I would have to say it was his passion for justice and equality that I consider his greatest gift to this church. The poet Rupert Brooke said only the ashes of the just smell sweet and blossom in the dust. And so Elder Wilson's heritage to this church is vast and his crown is laid up for him."

Daughter Shirley Wilson Anderson, a professor at Walla Walla University, with the help of PowerPoint pictures on the screen recalled many attributes of her father.

"I have always had a wonderfully supportive big brother. So Ted is going to let me go first. I want to acknowledge some of his best qualities. I am a college professor, so I have to have some equipment here, some technology. I need to make sure it works. To Daddy. These are some of his best qualities that I remember.

"Loyalty. These are probably two of the most important men in my life, my father and my son [pictures of them on the screen]. My dad taught me loyalty. He taught my son loyalty. My son is the fourth grandchild and the first grandson. He held a special place in my dad's heart. He told my son something one day. He took him aside, and he said, 'You know, Jonathan, stay close to your mother. She really believes in you, and she'll be there for you for a long, long time. So don't forget about your mom.' And I appreciated that so much.

"Determination. Two and a half years ago my son Jonathan graduated from Walla Walla University. He had been accepted to medical school at Loma Linda University. We already knew it at that time. My dad was very proud of him at that time. It's hard to get into medical school and hard to get out of medical school. I'm planning on getting him out of medical school, but my dad was very supportive, and my dad had a long, close history with Loma Linda University.

"I want to share a little e-mail that was sent by Dr. Hadley, head of the medical school, where my son is now. Dr. Hadley said this about my dad, 'I am one of the thousands of people who your dad could remarkably remember their names, their role in the church, their families, and their most recent interactions. Clearly he was committed to not only the SDA Church but also to Loma Linda University. He will be remembered as one of the most important people in the spiritual growth of Loma Linda University.'

"Encouragement. That's another thing my dad did well. My dad always knew how to treat the women in his life. Those being my mother, myself, my sister-in-law, three granddaughters, and he always had special little cards that he would send to us. He was very faithful with that. And it was not just, 'love, dad,' but there was always a little special memory in there. He certainly was an encourager. For me during difficult times, during relationships, or marriage. He was always there. He always believed in me and was always there and was encouraging to me and that was so very important.

"I want to read you this little card. It's a little bit old. We were going through some old things and found this one. My parents would've been married sixty-eight years this year, and my mother was wonderfully supportive of him all through these years, and this must have started early. And this shows my dad caring and encouragement to this wonderful woman in his life. This must've been about 1950. It says, 'To the most wonderful wife and companion in all the world. Every passing day I thank God for you, sweetheart. Eight happy years with you, and by God's grace and help we'll be together forever.' I believe that will happen for them. He always brought flowers. Almost every week he gave her flowers. That was very nice as well.

"My dad was also an athlete. Before he became a minister, he wanted to be an athlete. He was wonderful in sports, and he was very talented. Until he had a life-changing experience medically in his life, he was going to be an athlete. That love of athletics and jumping from one rock to another at the waterfall as we heard before was passed down certainly to my son, Jonathan.

"Jonathan loves almost every single sport that there is out there. Just last weekend he climbed Mount Gregornio, I think it was, in California. He went up on snowshoes and came down on skis with friends and went mountain biking on Sunday, and so he continues that trend and history of sports and athleticism that my dad had. My dad was very encouraging with athletics with all of us. All of us I think enjoyed hiking, and you've heard about his Mount Kilimanjaro trip. And there were many others. And we all in our family have inherited that love of hiking and being outdoors in the fresh air.

"I always will remember dad with some kind of a little piece of grass or straw in his mouth, and he would be chewing on that and encouraging people to go forward with their hike. My cousin, one of my cousins, sent me a little notice and she said that's what I remember the most about him. Pushing my brother up the hill and my cousin, saying you can make it, you can make it. He was very strong and wonderful in the area of nature and hiking.

"My dad had a sweetness to him as well. He had a big heart. You see that heart-shaped balloon there. These are some children in our extended family here that were visiting and his big heart showed when he dealt with children and lots of different people from different points of view. That sweetness has been something that I remembered for a long time. I do want to mention as I was holding his hand and with him as he was passing away. As a nurse I kept feeling for his pulse because I knew that his heart was strong. You always hope that it will just never stop. He's athletic. He had a very good, strong heart. As I was sitting there with him, I began to feel that pulse getting a bit thready.

"I just hope for the future where we can be together, and we can go and sit on a wonderful big swing and enjoy watching the people go by, as you see there. He was a wonderful role model. One of my friends in this area who is a lawyer sent me a message saying, 'Your father's qualities are being passed down to you and to your brother. He will live through you and your grandchildren and the great-grandchildren.' So he's been a wonderful role model to all of us.

"Successful. He was a successful man, and he encouraged my son, Jonathan, who really regrets that he can't be here as one of the grandchildren. As I mentioned he's in medical school in internal medicine. Studying right now for his tests. They keep them pretty close and make them learn everything. So they can take care of all of us. He regrets that he cannot be here, but he really felt that his grandfather gave him a lot of lessons to help him know about success, how to get to success, how to love people, care about people, how to lead, how to take care of your finances, and how to take care of those who are in your family.

"My dear mother who survives my dad, and my dad was very devoted in caring for her, and my dear mother has survived him. She is such a wonderful, sweet person. If you go out to Dianne and Don Crane's place she may not remember your name. She will not be like my dad who would say your name, but she will smile at you. And that has been such a wonderful strength and she has been such a wonderful support to all of us in the family.

"My mother is a wonderful dear mother, and the last time I was there right after my dad died she was quite coherent and talking to me quite a bit. And one of the things that she said was 'Shirley, what we do now?' And the only thing I could think of to say besides hugging her and loving her is to look toward the mountains, look toward the skies, and look into God's face to turn our eyes toward Jesus. Look in his wonderful face and the things of earth will grow strangely dim in the light of His glory and grace. So please let us turn our eyes to the sky and look at where God is going to come back to take us to heaven so that we can all be together with Him— new, fresh, alive, healthy, well, and ready to love each other."

After Shirley finished her presentation, Ted got up and told her, "You can stay right there in case I need some advice." Shirley replied, "Happy to do it."

"We come to the close of this service, and I want to thank you for your patience and for reliving with us and with those who have spoken. Our precious mother is not here today, and we purposely decided not for her to be here. She is living in a happy state and most of the time living in her own world. But she's happy. One of these days soon she will be remade as all of us will. This Friday she will be 91. She is staying, as has already been mentioned, at the Elternhaus assisted-living facility and what a wonderful, beautiful place that is for Christian care.

"Our parents were wonderful parents, and Shirley and I were grateful to have grown up in that Christian home. But I wish to honor someone else in closing here who is another mother in Israel and a kind of a second mother. I have two or three kinds of people in my life who stay close and one is my aunt, my father's sister closest to him, Clarice Wilson Woodward. She's here today representing the Wilson family because now you are the matriarch. And we honor you for that.

"She represents two other living siblings, a precious Aunt Ruth Wilson Murrill whom many of you know and also an uncle of ours, Neal's brother, Dr. Bruce Wilson. The youngest brother Dr. Donald Wilson died a few years ago, so now the oldest and the youngest have died. We're very honored to have Donald Wilson's son, his youngest son, Andrew, here with us today. And what a blessing that is. I want to thank you Aunt Clarice for being here to represent the immediate family of Nathaniel and Hannah Wilson your parents, our grandparents. And thanks to her daughter Gwen for accompanying her. Your presence really means so much to all of us.

"You see soon Jesus will come, and the resurrection will take place, and I will see my father again. Dad was an ardent evangelist and a pastor. He was a very capable church administrator, a wonderful father and devoted husband, and he was one of my best friends. Many, many e-mails and letters have come. I thank you for those. How wonderful it is to believe in Christ and in the blessed hope.

"I have in my hands three Bibles. One, my grandfather's. The second one, my father's. The third one, mine. Three generations of preachers. Preachers who preached the love of Christ, Him crucified, risen, ministering in the holy place and soon to come back. Preaching the three angels' messages of Revelation 14. The power of reformation and revival through the power of the Holy Spirit is coming soon, and the great Second Advent, our hope, will be realized. This is Dad's legacy. This is our legacy. Let's keep preaching it not only as a tribute to my father but because it is God's truth and message for this hour. Maranatha."

Bill Fagal led the audience in the closing hymn. He said before starting, "And now we have the opportunity to sing together, not a *dolorous hymn* but a hymn of victory, 'When We All Get to Heaven.'" (Elder C. E. Bradford had related earlier that Mrs. White counseled that we should not sing dolorous hymns but hymns of hope and victory.) "We want to keep the vigor of the hymn going all the way through to the end of the verse, and when we get to the last stanza, we want even more of that vigor to come through."

Fifty-Three Years of Service

It was a wonderful memorial service commemorating the life of a great leader of the remnant church! It is interesting to note that Neal Wilson's fifty-three years of committed service (about two and a half more official years after his retirement and plenty more years of non-official service) were a duplicate of his father's service. One hundred and six years of service for Christ and the church between father and son! The three Wilson ministers, Nathaniel (father), Neal (son), and Ted (grandson), all served on the General Conference Committee, the denomination's highest decision-making body. Each of the Wilsons also served as officers of the General Conference, and each has been president of a division of the world church, and two became president of the world church—a unique circumstance in Adventist history!

A few weeks later after the *Review* reported on the life of Neal Wilson and his memorial service, a short letter appeared in the letters section of the *Review* written by a classmate telling how he remembered his schoolmate.

"Much has been said and written about the late Neal C. Wilson. Practically all these testimonials concerned his contribution to the church as president of the General Conference. I have seen nothing about his life before that.

"At Pacific Union College in 1943, Wilson and I were fellow students. All of us fellows lived in Grainger Hall, which was the only men's dorm at that time. All the rooms were equipped with a transom above the door, an opening about 36 inches by 20 inches with a hinged door, to furnish fresh air without opening the room's door.

"One day Bob Reiger locked himself out of his room. A group of his neighbors gathered around to help. If someone could just climb through the transom, they could open the door from the inside. But none of us were physically designed to do that.

"Then along came a tall, lanky fellow named Neal Wilson, who fit the bill; he looked about right to fit

Highly Committed

through the narrow opening. He agreed to help. So we pushed and shoved and lifted him up, and he managed to squirm through the transom and open the door. So even early in life, Neal Wilson showed signs of meeting the challenges of life and rising to the occasion."[257]

Neal Wilsons' life testified to the fact that he was capable of meeting the challenges of life and rising to the occasion.

Almost six months to the day, the morning of June 8, 2011, Elinor Esther Neumann Wilson, age 91, passed to her rest at the Elternhaus assisted-living facility. She had quietly supported and enthusiastically worked with her husband all over the world for sixty-eight years. Besides her own skills as a wonderful Christian teacher, she will be remembered as the only woman to be the wife of a General Conference president and the mother of a General Conference president. She was buried quietly next to her partner in life at the George Washington Cemetery in Adelphi, Maryland.

Neal Wilson sits with his wife at Christmas 2007, three years before his death.

The Final Years

Ambassador Joseph Verner Reed, United Nations Under-Secretary-General and Special Advisor to Secretary-General Ban Ki Moon poses with the Wilsons. He had just given remarks at the memorial service of his friend, Elder Neal C. Wilson.

An expectant fifth generation Wilson church leader, Emilie stands with her husband Pastor Kameron DeVasher in front of one of the churches he pastors in Michigan.

Chapter Thirteen

Ted N. C. Wilson: The Early Years

"A teacher affects eternity;(S)he can never tell where his (her) influence stops." Henry Adams

Elinor and Neal had been married for nearly eight years when Elinor discovered she was expecting their first child. Their Middle East friends "worried" about the young American couple because they didn't have children yet. A big family was considered an asset, so the local custom was to marry very young and have children very quickly. The Wilsons had been in Egypt close to six years and were eligible to go home, and since Elinor was pregnant, they requested their furlough. It was granted beginning April 1, 1950.

Neal's sister, Ruth Murrill, was teaching nursing at Washington Sanitarium and Hospital in Takoma Park, Maryland, and it was decided that the "San" would be the best place for the delivery. Ruth and her husband, Bill, drove to New York to meet the soon-to-be parents who arrived by boat. "Elinor had the baby almost as soon as they arrived here from Egypt. He was born May 10, 1950. He was a beautiful baby boy and was delivered without any complications by Dr. Emma Hughes who had brought many children into the world. It was late in the evening."

"They stayed with us for a while, and when Elinor was stronger, they arranged to go to Chicago to show him off to Elinor's family. When they came back, they stayed in the General Conference apartments, which were furnished with dishes and everything that they needed," Ruth said. "The apartments were around the corner from the General Conference headquarters in Takoma Park and not far from us."

Ruth continued, "There was quite a bit of discussion about the baby's name. Some thought he should be named after his father or his maternal grandfather, and that was discussed for some time. His paternal grandfather was Nathaniel Carter Wilson [N. C. Wilson], and his father was Neal Clayton Wilson [N. C. Wilson]. Since Neal was not named after his father but had the initials N. C. in his name, it was decided that this pattern should be followed. Norman Clair Wilson [N. C. Wilson] finally surfaced, and everyone was happy with this name except Elinor. My mother, Hannah Wilson, who had spent the last few years in Australia thought that the new baby boy was cute and cuddly just like a Koala bear. In Australia they called one of those cute little bears 'Teddy,' and my mother started calling him Teddy. The nickname stuck."

Elinor was her son's first teacher, and she read to Teddy at an early age at home. About three years later the Wilsons welcomed another member into the family–this time a baby girl. "I was born on January 24, 1953, in Cairo, Egypt," said sister Shirley. "Ted has been such a good brother to me except for one little incident right after I was born. I guess he couldn't figure out who I was and why I was getting so much attention so he came over and slapped me. After that, he made up for it and really looked after me. He used to call me 'Sister Baby.' He was the best brother any sister could have."

"I don't remember calling him Norman even once," continued Shirley. "I don't remember anybody else in the family calling him Norman. The family all called him Teddy, and as he got older we got a little more sophisticated and called him Ted in public."

Ted Wilson vividly remembers all his teachers and his early educational experience. Teachers were his heroes. His first grade teacher was Mrs. Olsen. The 1956 Suez crisis made a huge impact on his life. He had to leave Egypt and eventually go to Beirut. The British, French, and Israelis were bombing the airfields of Cairo and dropping flares at night. There were total blackouts. At night the Wilsons slept in the basement of the Nile Union headquarters on mattresses. When the flares came down, his mother would run upstairs and pack the suitcases because she could see from the flares, and then she would run back downstairs because the bombing began shortly thereafter. They were not bombing residential areas just the airfields. After his mother packed, the next day they all got into the car and headed out in an enormous convoy that went to Port Said with many other expatriates. There were hundreds of other people evacuating, not just Adventists.

When they got to Port Said, the sixth fleet was there to pick up all the Americans. Elder Neal Wilson decided to stay in Egypt during the whole Suez crisis. But all the other missionaries evacuated. The missionaries got on the ship and headed out into the Mediterranean as the British, French, and Israelis began bombing Port Said. The Wilsons hoped and prayed that "Dad" would be safe. On the troop carrier the sailors wanted to entertain all of the kids, so they took them into a big room and put a sheet up and showed a movie. The children remember that the neat thing about the movie was that you could see the picture on both sides of the sheet. It was a film about World War II with lots of war scenes. While they were watching the film, they heard all the bombing outside and the mothers said, "No, this is too much." They finally gathered the children and left the film. The evacuees went to Crete and transferred to another carrier. Finally they disembarked in Naples where the officers read the names of all the departing passengers.

Since they were calling the names alphabetically, the Wilsons were the last ones to be called. All the other Adventist missionaries had gone by then. They had forgotten the Wilsons completely and only later on did they ask, "Where are the Wilsons?" But Elinor and the kids were stuck in Naples. Neal had given Elinor some Italian lira, and she tried to use them, but the local people said, "No, no it's out-of-date money; you can't use that now." So they were totally stuck.

An American Red Cross lady had compassion on the party of three. Her husband was a high-ranking NATO officer there, and she was volunteering for the Red Cross. She took the Wilsons and mothered them, put them up in a hotel, and brought them some cornflakes, Baby Ruth candy bars, and Kleenex. It was cold in Italy, and it turned out that the Wilson family was better off with the American Red Cross lady than they would have been if they had stuck with the other missionaries. Finally the other missionaries found where the Wilsons were, and they regrouped.

They stayed in Florence for several weeks at the school where Bert Beach was principal. From there they flew to Beirut and were there for about five months or so until things subsided in Egypt. It ended up being a pretty exciting school year in Beirut where Ted began first grade! The children made many close friends during that time with the Keough family, the Osborn family, the Lesher family, the Zytkoskee family, and others.

The Suez crisis had quite an impact on the family because they were separated from their father. Neal would come to Beirut for a little while and visit and then go back to Cairo. He didn't want the local church members there to feel abandoned, so he stayed in Egypt. The governor of Cairo was a very close friend, and he sent at least one if not two detachments to protect him. The government set up machine guns on the Nile Union property to protect Neal Wilson who had several threats on his life. When the family rejoined him in Egypt, Ted took second grade through home study under his mother's tutelage.

The Egypt Mission operated a school on the roof of the church in Heliopolis. During earlier years Elinor had taught the lower grades, and Evelyn Zytkoskee taught the upper grades of the church school. It was not a large school, but it was very good and well-respected, and many non-Adventists wanted to attend.

Ted remembers coming home to the States from Egypt. "In 1958 we went back to the United States, and I had my eighth birthday on the boat. We went from Egypt to Italy by boat and purchased a little VW and toured Europe for a few weeks and left from Rotterdam on the *SS Rotterdam*. It was a wonderful experience for me as a little kid. After your initial experience of getting a little seasick, then you were fine. When you're in the back of the boat you see the waterway below and then it rises and comes up. It was fun." Little Ted fit his home studies around his travel and adventures.

"We were in India teaching," said Clarice Woodward, Neal's other sister, "and we didn't see the children until 1958 when they came back from Egypt on permanent return. They lived with us for about six months in Southern California. Neal was busy speaking at camp meetings and churches. Ted went to school for a short while at San Gabriel Union School [later San Gabriel Academy] which is a little east of Los Angeles with our children, Gwen and Cathy. We were overjoyed to have such a delightful young boy and his pretty little sister around us for a while. Shirley was not yet in school."

Early Schooling

Ted had Mrs. Lopez as his third grade teacher at San Gabriel. When Neal was hired by the Central California Conference, young Ted attended Campbell School with Miss Sackett as his teacher.

After that, when Neal was called to the Columbia Union, Ted attended the Sligo school in Takoma Park, Maryland, for the last part of his fourth grade year, and he finished his remaining elementary education at nearby John Nevins Andrews (JNA). The principal, Miriam Tymeson, exerted a strong influence on his life. The Tymesons had no children of their own but had a great burden for Seventh-day Adventist Christian education. She devoted her entire life to educating hundreds of young people and helping them catch a vision of what they could accomplish. Ted speaks highly of his fifth grade teacher, Mrs. Thelma Bird, his sixth grade teacher, Miss Bernice Pittman, and his seventh grade teacher, Mrs. Betty Miller Jauros. He had several teachers in the eighth grade, including Mrs. Barbara Vandulek, Mrs. Marie Spangler (wife of Elder Bob Spangler) and the principal, Mrs. Tymeson.

Victor Peeke, a real estate agent and businessman, recalls, "My father, Jewel Peeke, headed up a department at the General Conference, and our families went to some of the same functions together. My mother taught at JNA and was librarian also. I remember Mrs. Wilson teaching second grade. I remember Elder Neal Wilson coming to the school once to talk to Ted who was in the gym. At that age I thought everyone over 30 was old and feeble. Elder Wilson got on the high bar and started doing chin-ups. I couldn't believe how many he did. He just kept going on and on and on. He was very athletic and had great upper body strength. Our families spent a special day together at the Seattle World Fair. I believe we were at the General Conference session in San Francisco, the Cow Palace, and after that session, the grown-ups took time out to be with the family at the world's fair. Ted and I went our way for a few hours and then met up with the parents a little later on. It was a great time we shared together." Ted completed high school at neighboring Takoma Academy (TA).

Shirley said, "We were good students. I remember Mr. Ken Wilson my biology teacher at TA. He was not related to us, but we called him 'Uncle Willie.' I was the president of the biology club for one year and got to know him quite well. We went on a couple of caving trips [spelunking]. I think it was called the Biota Club. My dad helped me organize the trips. He liked to explore the caves with me. Dad and I spent the weekends dodging bats and looking for treasures. Ted liked to hike and climb mountains, so I don't remember him going with us. Ted was also the president of one of his classes, I believe, and we both sang in the chorale at TA. One year we went to sing in Zürich, Switzerland, at the Youth Congress. We had a good time at home for worship. I played the flute and violin, Ted played the clarinet, and my mother played the piano."

Dr. Ken Singleton, a black physician, remembers going to school at TA with Ted. "Ted was a good student, very conscientious. We thought even then that he would go into the ministry. He was the pastor of the senior class, and I was the treasurer. He had no hang-ups on race and didn't mind at all being my friend. I always felt that his family was a model Adventist family."

Ted Wilson describes his educational path after high school, "Most people don't know that I went to La Sierra College my first year of college. I had a fine experience out there. Jiggs Gallagher and I were going to go to Newbold College, but the American group of students that were there the year before were so rambunctious that Newbold made a decision that no freshman coming from outside could attend there. Then we had an idea to go to Norway. We wanted to go somewhere outside of Takoma Park. That didn't work out, and then we made plans to go to La Sierra College. About three weeks before it was time to go, Jiggs found out he couldn't go, so I said I'm going to go anyway. I only knew about three or four kids out there. I had a great year and got acquainted with a lot of students. Besides studying, I probably worked twenty-five hours a week at La Sierra in a factory called Ace Drill Bushing. They made bushings for factories. I also worked at the desk in the dorm."

Ted returned to Columbia Union College (CUC) for his second year. He was actually able to finish college about a year earlier than what he was supposed to because CUC was on a trimester program that allowed students to attend school year-round. He was scheduled to graduate in 1972 but graduated in 1971 because Joseph Gurubatham, the registrar, helped him arrange different available classes beyond the class load. He ended up with a bachelor of arts degree with a double major in religion and business administration. "Teachers and educational administrators who truly take a strong interest in helping students often make a life-long impression on those students. I cannot say enough good things about consecrated, faithful Seventh-day Adventist educators who love God, His truth, and their students," Ted said.

Contemplating a Business Career

As his father before him, Ted contemplated a business career for a short while. Victor Peeke mentions that he and Ted worked for a small brokerage firm called Sade and Company in downtown Washington, D.C., during the summer months after graduating from academy. They worked in the back office and were responsible for collecting checks from clients, logging them in, doing accounting, filing, running security bonds, messenger service, and miscellaneous tasks. "The lady in charge was bipolar and was very difficult to deal with. I think any aspirations that Ted may have had about business evaporated in this office. She would flare up constantly, but Ted was always steady and considerate in spite of her personality challenges," said Victor.

Ted was active in events beyond the classroom. *The Sligonian*, the school paper, tells of a visit of some CUC students to nearby church headquarters. "Five students took the floor of the North American Division meeting at the General Conference yesterday. Led by Ted Wilson they attempted to show the assembled church leaders the problems of youth in the Adventist church.

'We aimed to give a feeling of support from the youth to the denomination,' said Wilson. The sophomore religion major was joined by Roger Tatum, Jerome Davis, and Malcolm Russell, all seniors, and Dick Osborn, a 1969 graduate of CUC.

"Speaking first, Tatum told the group of the need to have a closer personal relationship between man and Christ. He emphasized the need to rediscover the zest of the early Advent movement. Davis, speaking on [behalf of the] Urban Service Corps, invited the delegates to visit the ghetto and the program and decide its appropriateness for themselves.

"Stressing the need to recapture the imagination of the youth, Russell advocated a broadening of church views on minor matters and more emphasis on bringing God to the young. Osborn ended the talks by accenting the fact that the youth will carry the gospel to the world, and that they need general guidelines rather than

Highly Committed

specific lists of complex rules.

"Elder Neal Wilson, Ted's father, chaired the Wednesday discussion and turned the platform over to the five students. Following their presentation, Elder R. H. Pierson, General Conference president, thanked the students for their spirit and asked them to supply the answers. Elder K. H. Emerson, General Conference treasurer, called for a vote of thanks to the students. The vote was without opposition."[258]

One year at Columbia Union College Ted served as the editor of the yearbook, *Golden Memories*, and the next year he was very much involved in directing the Friday evening vespers and working with the youth pastor at Sligo church, Bill Hayner. He ran for Student Association president one year. He decided to do that on the spur of the moment just before the election, so he didn't win.

Dr. Wendell Cheatham, a classmate and now a physician, comments about that election. "Ted was actually considered a favorite to win but he made a statement (I can't remember whether it was in a debate or in a stump speech) regarding the injustices and struggles that minority individuals, especially African Americans, were having, and this was in the years just after the assassination of Martin Luther King and Robert Kennedy. He was very bold in making that statement, and I was so impressed that I wrote a note to his dad saying how proud he should be of his son because he had really stuck his neck out to make that statement. Ted was perceptive and sympathetic to be aware of the inequities that existed. I knew it would cost him the election, and it did. But the African American students who were attending CUC appreciated so much his kind words of support."

Dr. Cheatham continued, "I remember when Ted was a young boy about 11 years old. My dad was the president of Allegheny Conference and had invited Neal Wilson to preach at Berea Temple in Baltimore. Elder Wilson came and brought his two children with him. He brought them up on the platform with him and asked them to say a few words. I remember Ted getting up and speaking about their experiences in Egypt and the Middle East. He told about his fondness for the Arabian horses, their beauty and their mannerisms and how he loved the people of that area. It was evident that Ted was destined to be a real leader. I admired his father for teaching him at such an early age to stand up and speak to large groups of people. My dad did not do that with his children. He felt that children should be seen but not heard. I could see even then that Ted was incorporating the mannerisms and confidence of his father into his speaking style."

Growing up in a minister's home and with his grandfather also being a minister, Ted obviously leaned in that direction. But his father didn't want him to be forced to take their life work. Ted talked about his future several times with his parents, and they considered something in the medical field, perhaps medicine or dentistry. He loved geography and some aspects of history. For a while his inclination was to go into architecture because he loved designing, renovation, and carpentry work. Architecture remains a hobby with him. In the future he would have the privilege of helping to design two division offices in Africa and Russia.

"Starting at an early age the Lord kept tugging at my heart. When I was 12 years old there were a series of special meetings at Takoma Park Church. Elder E. L. Minchen was the speaker, and of course he loved young people. On the last night of his series, he made a very special and specific call for young men to come to the front to be ministers, to preach Christ, and I responded to that call. I gave my heart fully to Jesus and determined to be of service to God and man. That was perhaps the most marked time I felt that God was calling me to go into the ministry. Following that commitment, on May 19, 1962, my dad baptized me at the Takoma Park Church. I went backwards and forwards as to what area of ministry I would pursue, but by the time I got to the latter part of academy, I was pretty much headed in the direction of the gospel ministry.

"While at CUC I had a wonderful job for two years as a student chaplain at Washington Adventist Hospital, which pretty much let me know what I must do with my life. That job gave me tremendous experience in working with people. I learned an awful lot about service. I was helping and praying for people who were going into surgery, into critical situations, mental health patients, people in detox and psych units. It helped me decide that I wanted to go into the gospel ministry. I had a set area of the hospital that I had to visit. It made me think deep and hard when I saw people dying.

"I had a somewhat funny but sobering experience one day. I went into a hospital room, and the lady looked like she was sleeping so I left my business card with my name on it on the bedside table and added the words, 'I hope you will be feeling better.' I came out of the room, and a nurse stopped me and asked, 'Did you go into that room?' I said, 'Yes.' She said, 'I think that lady is dead.' I went back into the room and quietly took my card back. But I kept wondering whether the lady was ready to die. Was she prepared to face eternity? Had she given her heart to Christ? Did she have a relationship with Jesus? It was a real ministry, that chaplaincy job."

Student Chaplain Responsibilities

There was a very strong Five-day Plan to Stop Smoking program at Washington Adventist Hospital. It was well-known throughout the Washington area. Chaplain A. C. Marple and Dr. Donald Mashburn led out in it. They made a tremendous team along with Mrs. D. A. Delafield, another chaplain there, and the team was a wonderful encouragement to Ted. Dr. Mashburn, a kind, nurturing pathologist at the hospital, even allowed the young student to come into an autopsy. Together these leaders at Washington Adventist Hospital helped him get a picture of how to interact with people who had challenging health issues.

Those experiences helped him to make up his mind about what he was going to do, and he applied to the seminary to prepare for his ministry. He applied to six or seven conferences to ask if they would sponsor him to the seminary. He got positive responses from a number of the conferences including Greater New York Conference. His father said, "All of these places that are offering to sponsor you are nice places, but if you really want a challenge go to Greater New York Conference. New York City is a great challenge." So at age 20, Ted Wilson finally knew for certain what he wanted to do and where he wanted to do it.

Ted began carrying in his Bible what would become one of his favorite Spirit of Prophecy statements. "My father sent it to me when I was a freshman, and I have treasured it ever since. It helped me face various challenges that came my way."

"'Consecrate yourself to God in the morning: make this your very first work. Let your prayer be, "Take me, O Lord, as wholly Thine. I lay all my plans at Thy feet. Use me today in Thy service. Abide with me, and let all my work be wrought in Thee"... Thus day by day you may be giving your life into the hands of God, and thus your life will be molded more and more after the life of Christ.'[259] I still have that statement in my Bible today."

The summer following graduation from CUC was packed. Ted enrolled in a conjoint program between Andrews University and Loma Linda University. The joint program required nine quarters at Andrews University that resulted in a master of divinity degree and then another two quarters at Loma Linda, ending with a master of science degree in public health. The summer of 1971 the Loma Linda program combined with Andrews University to provide health-oriented credits and a field school experience in San José, California. The field school was run by Dr. Wilbur Nelson, Elder Bruce Johnston, Dr. Leo Van Dolson, and Dr. Mervyn Hardinge. The Greater New York Conference agreed to sponsor him to both Andrews University and Loma Linda. "My dad had suggested that I join the conjoint master's program. Dad had a lot of influence on how I was to prepare my life for service," Ted said.

Before starting the program, Ted lived in New York for six weeks. He then attended the field school in California before going to the seminary.

"I went to New York and lived six or seven weeks in the New York Center on W. 46th Street. I was assigned to the 11th St. Church in Bohemian Greenwich Village under the direction of Bill Jackson a former Salvation

Highly Committed

Army officer who had become a Seventh-day Adventist and a very fine pastor. The church membership was small, but the facility was large. This was in the heyday of the hippies. Somebody suggested that we go down in the basement and look around.

"Earlier, when I sent out my graduation announcements, I had requested that my friends send me a check for New York City evangelism instead of a gift. I collected a fair amount of money, which I turned in to the conference, and it was sitting there when we were looking at this basement area. We found a passageway through the coal bins underneath the sidewalk, and it turned out to be a fantastic place for a 'coffeehouse' setting where you could talk with people about Christ in an informal setting with snacks and non-alcoholic and non-caffeine drinks. We talked to the church board. There were a couple of older members who were a little bit hesitant about it because we had to chop out some blocks of concrete to get access to the street. There was just a window there and we took out the blocks and put in the door and steps. There was a lot of carpet down in the basement, which we put over the dirt floor and then fixed up these coal bins with lights.

"It was the perfect place for a coffeehouse setting and the right atmosphere. Tony Romeo designed the sign that said 'The Catacombs.' Rick and Gwen Shorter and Lloyd Scharffenberg helped with the planning as members of the church. The young people of the Manhattan church worked together with the Adventist Collegiate Taskforce (ACT) to invite youth to consider Christ.

"There was quite a team that fixed it up. We put in tables, candles, and literature. Then we opened it, and I left that very night to go to Takoma Park to get ready for the field school of evangelism in California. We did a lot of work and the Lord blessed that outreach. I wasn't there to see all of the fruits of it. I helped get it started along with other people. I used the money from my graduation gifts to renovate the space. It was an exciting venture."

Don Hawley, public relations secretary for the Greater New York Conference, recalls a visit to the Catacombs. "To get to the Catacombs, one must travel to the Greenwich Village area and then to the Seventh-day Adventist church on West Eleventh Street. During the day the sidewalk in front of the church looks pretty much like any other sidewalk, but at about 9:00 p.m. a rather mysterious opening appears in the front wall of the church building, revealing a steep, narrow stairway with a sign, 'The Catacombs,' and another, 'Watch your head.'

"Expectedly I negotiated the stairway and followed a narrow tunnel back under the street itself. Suddenly I came into a long, narrow, low brick room with an arched ceiling formed out of soft, red brick. A number of niches in the walls and ceiling had been wired for light, and candles stuck into odd-shaped bottles flickered on two or three table-and-chair arrangements.

"The floor at one end of the chamber was covered with old carpeting and stuffed mats that invited anyone young enough, to sit down cross-legged. Colorful religious posters decorated the walls.

"In an adjoining room, actually in the basement of the church itself, several more sets of tables and chairs provided discussion centers. At the end of the room was a serving counter where visitors could order a vegetarian Sloppy Joe, popcorn, and a glass of punch. There was no charge, but a 'donation' jar stood at the end of the counter. A faint trace of incense hung in the air, and everything about the place seemed to say, 'Come in, sit down, let's visit.' But there is more involved than the physical aspects of the Catacombs. What really matters are the individuals who are reached for Christ.

"One would not be likely to find the Catacombs by chance, so advertising is in order. Hundreds of flyers are handed out each week, and earlier efforts in nearby Washington Square helped to prepare the way....

"One Friday night about ten or 12 of us went to Washington Square with our guitars to sing and witness.

We formed a loose circle near the fountain and began to sing gospel songs. Before long we had perhaps 150 people either singing with us or just listening. Many were older folk, and quite nicely dressed. While the singing was in progress, some of us visited with those in the crowd and passed out 'love' leaflets with the address of the Manhattan church. In each case, we gave our simple witness about what Christ had done for us.

"Sometimes as many as 100 people visit the Catacombs on a typical Saturday night. By 10:00 p.m. everything is in full swing with several animated discussions concerning Christ and His message in progress. A little later guitars appear, and our Adventist young people lead out in the spirited singing of gospel choruses. Everyone joins in.... More discussion and more music, and then a closing prayer circle, where all who wish may pray."[260]

Hawley mentions that he was told that on the first night they were planning to serve only lemonade as a drink. However, everyone kept asking for coffee, so they opened up some Loma Linda Breakfast Cup. The visitors thought it was organic coffee and thought it was great, thus giving it the name "coffeehouse."

The Catacombs

Another account tells how a visitor, after three visits to the Catacombs and after reading much of *The Great Controversy*, accepted Jesus and was ready for baptism. His wife, who was about to divorce him, saw how he had changed from a user of alcohol and other drugs to a stable Christian father and husband, and she decided that she and her two children would stay with him.

There was no fixed program at the Catacombs. Besides the music, it was "a quiet, peaceful place where people from the street gather to talk, to communicate with friends and God."[261]

Ted shares an experience as he prepared to leave for field school after the opening of the Catacombs that shows the relationship he had with his father. "I didn't own my first car until I had graduated from college. It was a little Opel Kadette. I put a little money in it, but my dad actually bought it for me. My parents usually had a car around that I could use, so I never lacked for any transportation. I remember a little incident I had, and this will show you the kind of relationship that parents can have with their children.

"That night after opening the Catacombs, I returned to Takoma Park. The car had been parked quite some time. You don't need a car in New York; you just park it. I had not looked at the car much, and I probably wasn't completely in tune with all its operations at that time. I'm better versed now. A red light on the dashboard kept coming on, and I didn't know what the problem was. It was at night driving home from New York, and I would've been home about one o'clock in the morning. I was going to drive to Washington, park the car, and then fly to the field school in California.

"I was driving along the New Jersey Turnpike, and it kept getting harder and harder to see. The headlights were getting dimmer and dimmer. All of a sudden the car started jerking and lurching. Fortunately I was able to get off the highway down near a Delaware exit, and I found a place where I could pull the car off the highway.

"I found out later that the alternator wasn't working and the battery wasn't charging. I didn't know what to do, and it was about two o'clock in the morning. I didn't have AAA. I found a telephone and called my dad. He had been sleeping. All he said was, 'Son, where are you?' And dad came to the rescue. He came in his car up to Delaware about four o'clock in the morning. When I went back to the car the policeman stopped and asked if I had a problem, and I told him that I had called my dad and the problem was solved.

"I went back and slept in my car until Dad came. We took the battery out, charged it up, and put it back in the car. By that time it was light. In the daytime you can drive with your battery for a long ways even if the alternator is not working. But at night time it just pulls the juice with the lights. So we got home. Little things like that made me appreciate my dad who was not too tired to come to the rescue as he always did. It actually turned out to be a wonderful experience. We got it fixed, and I went to the evangelistic field school. When I came back later, I drove up to Andrews in my little Opel Kadette with a new alternator."

After finishing field school in California, Ted returned to Takoma Park and drove to Andrews University. He secured a basement apartment in Berrien Springs that he shared with a young man who would later become the director of the General Conference Communication Department, Ray (Rajmund) Dabrowski. Two others shared the house. His second year he lived with Dr. Tom and Hazel Geraty. "They were very close friends from Egypt days. They had a spare bedroom, and I ate with them like family. It was a great experience."

During his first year at Andrews, he worked in the business office. "It wasn't difficult work, but it was interesting to work in the business area." During his second year, Ted secured a job at WAUS, Andrew University's 24-hour classical radio station (90.7 FM), where he worked as a student announcer. He was on an hour program called *Morning Magazine* that delivered religious news, inspirational thoughts, and music. "That was a very formative and learning opportunity for me. Every few Sabbaths I was in charge of doing the whole shift for broadcasting the Pioneer Memorial Church service. I had to get a third class radio license. It was a great experience, and I enjoyed it a lot. I got to choose a variety of music from their library. However, it was primarily classical. It was a job reserved for seminary students since they wanted somebody who could do pastoral things on the air.

"Every Friday night I was responsible for the on-air vesper service that announced the beginning of the Sabbath. I played beautiful background music as I said something like, 'The sun is setting on the Andrews campus. A beautiful transition is taking place. We now move into holy time.' And then I would give a vesper's thought. I would usually use the morning watch book written by Harry M. Tippett who used to be a very strong editor in the Adventist Church. It worked beautifully. I enjoyed working at the radio station. There were a number of seminarians who did this job."

His two years at Andrews went by quickly and he left for Loma Linda, California, to complete his master's degree in public health. On Sabbaths there he taught a Sabbath School class for young people at the University Church.

"I actually took three quarters at Loma Linda, more than I had planned to. I did a project for the School of Health, twelve television programs for a local cable television program on health. Dr. Kay Kuzma had a grant, and she needed these programs done so she asked me. I did that plus I had one more class to complete that quarter. It was good that I stayed the extra quarter, which was all in the Lord's plan, because that's when I met my future wife, Nancy."

After obtaining two graduate degrees, he was ready for his first job as a pastor. Elder Lloyd Reile had extended the call to the young intern to attend Andrews University, then Loma Linda University, and then take up his first official position in the Greater New York Conference. "Elder and Mrs. Lloyd Reile, the president and first lady of the conference, were so kind to me. I graduated from CUC in April of 1970, and I was still just 20 years old when I came to New York. They graciously advised and guided me during that summer and looked after me."

After Ted finished graduate school, the *Review* carried a small piece about his appointment as a pastor. "Ted Wilson, a graduate of the SDA Theological Seminary, Andrews University, and the School of Public Health at Loma Linda University, a ministerial intern, is pastoring Patchogue, Long Island, church."[262]

Patchogue was a small town on the south shore of Long Island, New York, named after the Native American Patchogue tribe, which once inhabited the area. Approximately 60 miles east of Manhattan, it utilized its natural riverfront, beach, and harbor to become a modern and largely self-contained community. Today the cozy white brick Adventist Church is well-known and respected in the community. At one time a small church school and a Spanish-speaking congregation met in the basement. Today the Spanish congregation has built its own edifice in another section of the town, and its membership is as large as the mother church.

When Ted arrived at Patchogue, the church was a very old, rundown building with an equally rundown house on the right-hand side of it. The young intern was to work under Nikolaus Satelmajer, the district pastor, who was primarily responsible for the Huntington Church. The two pastors worked together on different evangelistic projects and became well-acquainted.

There wasn't a church school when Ted first got there, but a number of members wanted a school. There had been a school before, but it had been disbanded for ten or more years. By God's grace there were about thirteen young people when he arrived there in July 1974, and by September, with a lot of prayer and planning, he had a teacher and enough students to open a school. "The Lord helped us, and we started the school. It was exciting. It continued the whole time I was there, grew larger for a period of time and only more recently was discontinued. Maybe it will start up again.

"The parsonage was next to the church, but it was in a rundown condition. I had the idea of renovating the parsonage, and when it was finished, I lived in part of it. On the lower level we had a Better Living Center. The Adventist Book Center of Greater New York gave us some books on consignment, and we opened a mini ABC there. We had books and packaged vegetarian food in one area, and in another area we had clothing and a community service center. I lived upstairs in a living room, a little bedroom, and a bathroom. There was a kitchen downstairs that I and other people could use. I painted the place and put scraps of carpeting down and furnished it with my parent's cast-off stuff. I wasn't married then so it was quite functional and worked really well."

Patchogue Evangelism

The church papers carried news of two of the activities conducted by the young pastor of the Patchogue Church. The first one spoke of his evangelistic meeting. "Four nights each week during the entire month of March [1975], Pastor [Ted] Norman C. Wilson of the Patchogue church conducted evangelistic meetings in the church.

"On the opening week end and the closing week end, the father of Pastor Wilson, Elder N. C. Wilson of the General Conference, did the preaching. Dr. J. Wayne McFarland, also of the General Conference, spoke to the group on the third week end of the meetings.

"Attendance was good throughout the entire program. At the conclusion ... several were baptized and fifteen others are considered to be definitely interested in becoming members of the family of Sabbath-keeping Adventists."[263]

The second one spoke of his collaboration in a drug seminar. "After months of planning, an Alcohol, Tobacco, and Drug Education Seminar was conducted in the Memorial Junior High School, Huntington Station, New York, March 11, 1975. Temperance director of the conference, P. J. Salhany, had worked closely with Huntington pastor, Nikolaus Satelmajer, and Patchogue pastor, Norman C. Wilson, to plan the program. High point of the morning came when Kenneth Butterfield, mayor of Huntington, came to say a few words to the assembly. The program consisted of films, discussions, and demonstrations. During the day a group of students from the school came in to form the audience for a classroom demonstration conducted by Pastor Nick Satelmajer. They were shown 'Smoking Sam' and the harmful effects of tobacco."[264]

At the 1970 General Conference session, a special offering was collected that amounted to $1 million. Many felt that the world church membership could have reached far beyond the million-dollar goal if they had been so challenged. So, rather than have a goal that in a sense could become restrictive, it was felt that members should be challenged at the General Conference session in Vienna in 1975 to give a personal faith objective of one week's income. This large offering would be for special needs around the world, but a large percentage

Highly Committed

would remain in the local conference for special projects.

Since there were very few Seventh-day Adventists on Long Island, one half of the Greater New York Conference's share of this "Adventure in Faith" offering, as it was called, was designated for Eastern Long Island evangelism. Pastors Satelmajer and Wilson were designated by the conference to promote the offering. The members gave generously when they saw what their offerings would accomplish in their conference. Not only did Ted help in promoting the offering, but he was instrumental in helping Pastor Satelmajer to establish one of the three new churches that came into existence because of this offering. Elder Neal Wilson helped organize all three of the churches on a single weekend.

"Sabbath, February 7, 1976, was a big day in the history of Greater New York. Three new churches were organized and requested membership in the conference sisterhood of churches.

"Dyckman: The organizations began on Friday night, February 6. Special guest speaker from the General Conference, Elder Neal C. Wilson; Conference officers ... plus friends and guests ... joined together for the organization of the Dyckman church ... The Dyckman church started as a result of the Adventure in Faith offering taken during 1975.... Elder Neal C. Wilson spoke to the congregation challenging them to be a true light in the northern Manhattan area.... Charter membership of the church is 93....

"Plimpton: Another Spanish evangelistic crusade resulted in the formation of a congregation ... in the Plimpton section of south Bronx.... By the fall of 1975, newly baptized members and those who came from other Adventist churches made a congregation of more than sixty ... The organization for the University Avenue church took place at 9:00 a.m. Sabbath, February 7.... Elder Neal C. Wilson presented a sermon and appeal for them to grow and witness in the community. The charter membership is 43....

"Riverhead: ...Under the leadership of district pastor Elder Nikolaus Satelmajer, assisted by Pastors Ted Wilson and Frieder Schmid, a congregation began to form in eastern Long Island.... The Riverhead church has been formed without a large city-wide effort ... Bible studies have been given. The health screening van has spent some time in the city.... After a fellowship luncheon, the service of organization got underway at 1:00 p.m. Many visitors from the Huntington and Patchogue churches were present....

"In the organization service Pastor Ted N. C. Wilson gave a history of the church. Pastor Frieder Schmid called for a vote on the official name.... Elder Neal C. Wilson presented a sermon of inspiration and encouragement to the congregation. The day had a special interest to Elder Wilson because his son, Ted, had been very active in establishing the new congregation. The charter membership is 25. Prospects are good for growth in the area. Three new churches in one day was cause for great rejoicing in the Greater New York Conference."[265]

Pastor Ted Wilson shares more about his pastoral days. "I pastored for about a year way out in this quiet village and was still single. It was a long ways from any Adventist center, and even though God was blessing me I sometimes got a bit discouraged and wondered whether I should do something else. I contacted my good friend and mentor Professor J. P. Laurence, principal of Takoma Academy in Takoma Park, Maryland. We were good friends, and he really helped me a lot when I attended TA.

"Professor Laurence said, 'Why don't you come down to Takoma Academy, and I will introduce you to some people at the University of Maryland, and you can get your doctorate there and teach here at TA.' So I drove down to Maryland. I went to the University of Maryland with him, and he introduced me to a lot of people. Professor Laurence was well-connected and involved with the Middle States Accrediting Association.

"Everything looked like it might work out for me to attend the University of Maryland and teach Bible classes at TA. And then all of a sudden the Lord impressed me that He called me to preach and I should stick with that. I called Professor Laurence and told him that I appreciated all of his help, but I thought the Lord was calling me to be a preacher and a pastor. I remembered so clearly the decision I made at twelve years of age when I went forward at the call of Elder Minchin and dedicated myself to be a preacher of the gospel. All of a sudden the Lord rewarded my decision and things just turned around. By the end of the summer I was married."

Ted Wilson tells how he met his life companion. "I first saw Nancy at a friend's wedding in 1970 in a church in Takoma Park. She was to me the prettiest lady in the wedding. I inquired and found out that she was already dating somebody, so I didn't go any further. Several years later, in 1974, I was in California attending the School of Public Health working on their conjoint program with the seminary at Andrews University. The last month before I was leaving, I had to visit the Loma Linda University hospital to take some tests. While there I met an older lady, struck up a conversation with her, and invited her to church.

"The next day I picked up the elderly lady and took her to the University Church. We selected a pew where Nancy and her grandmother, Mrs. Marion Vollmer, were sitting. My parents knew the Vollmer family quite well."

Meeting the First Lady

Nancy Wilson continues telling the story. "When I was at Loma Linda University my membership was in the Campus Hill Church. Pastor Bill Lehman was the pastor. He was a dynamic pastor, and the church was packed every Sabbath and Wednesday night for prayer meeting. That was my church, but Grandma and Grandpa always went to the University Church. On the Sabbath I met Ted, Grandpa was ill, so I took Grandma to the University Church. We walked in and sat down. Grandma and Grandpa knew the Wilsons, but I had never met any of them. Ted came in with a little old lady and sat down in the same pew where we were sitting. He leaned over and saw Grandma, smiled and they waved at each other. Grandma sat back, poked me in the side and said, 'You stick with me, and I will introduce you to Teddy Wilson after church.'

"And that's exactly what happened. After church we walked out into the foyer of the Loma Linda University Church, and Grandma introduced us. We talked together until we were the last ones to leave the foyer. He told me he was just finishing up his MSPH, had already graduated from the seminary, and would soon be on his way to Long Island to pastor. He had parked in the same parking lot that I had parked in which was behind the School of Dentistry. As we were walking back to our car, Grandma said, 'Do you think we should invite him to Sabbath dinner? Or would that be too much?'

"I thought about it quickly. I had two older brothers, and girls had made fools of themselves chasing them. I was determined never to do that. So I said, 'Grandma, I think that's a little too much. I just met him.' I never wanted to make the first move at all. We got in the car, and we were standing there still debating what to do, and he was at his car looking back at us, hoping that we would invite him to dinner. We decided it was too soon. We would wait for him to make the first move. So we didn't invite him.

"I found out later that he had this huge project to finish, and I didn't hear from him for at least two weeks. When he called he asked me to go out to lunch the next day. We went to Nena's, an authentic Mexican restaurant in San Bernardino, and that's how it all started."

Ted picks up the story. "I tried to call Nancy again but found out that she had gone to St. Helena Hospital to visit with her grandfather who had broken his hip and would be there for some time. I arranged to visit my Aunt Sue Miklos who lived very close to St. Helena, so I got a chance to see Nancy again before heading back East to pastor. We wrote for a while, and then we didn't. Independently of anything related to our relationship, Nancy decided to accept a call to work as a physical therapist at the Reading Rehabilitation Center in Pennsylvania.

"My cousin, Ivanette Miklos Osborn, whose husband was also working at the Reading Rehab Center in Pennsylvania, helped to get us back together. I had helped Ken and Ivanette get together, and now they were helping me. A few years prior to this, Ken Osborn was interested in meeting Ivanette Miklos, who was my mother's sister's daughter. I invited him to come to dinner one Sabbath and also invited Ivanette. On this particular Sabbath Pastor M. P. Kulakov was visiting the United States, and my father had invited him to come to eat at our house. That was 1970. From that interesting Sabbath together, Ivanette and Ken began dating and finally got married. So they wanted to return the favor.

"I was pastoring on Long Island, which was about four hours away from the Reading Rehabilitation Hospital where Nancy was working. Ivanette and Ken contacted me and asked me to come and visit them. They contacted Nancy to come and babysit for them that same evening. They told Nancy before they left that she might want to prepare herself because Ted Wilson might be coming by. I drove over to their house expecting to see them, and there was Nancy. What a pleasant surprise! To make a long story short, we finally started dating and got married not long after that on September 14, 1975. Nancy has been and is a wonderful spiritual support to me. The Lord has blessed our relationship."

The Vollmer Family

Nancy Vollmer had been born into a prominent Adventist family. Her mother, Mary Louise Evans Vollmer, was the daughter of an Adventist preacher and administrator. Elder Irving M. Evans had been a leader in publishing before becoming president of the Georgia-Cumberland Conference, Alabama-Mississippi Conference, and the Arkansas-Louisiana Conference. His brother, L. C. Evans, was also an Adventist minister. Her mother's sister, Dorothy Evans Ackerman, was a prominent musician with a powerful contralto voice. She taught music at Shenandoah Valley Academy, Columbia Union College, Atlantic Union College, Madison College, and finally Southern Missionary College. She was named professor of music emeritus by Southern Adventist University upon her retirement in 1980. Ackerman Hall, a recital auditorium, was named in her honor.

Nancy's father, Dr. Donald Henry Vollmer, was a physician and the son of Dr. Henry W. Vollmer. Her grandfather, Dr. Henry W. Vollmer, took medicine at Battle Creek under Dr. John Harvey Kellogg and became medical director of the Loma Linda Sanitarium and Hospital in 1918, and in 1924 he transferred to Glendale Hospital and Sanitarium. In 1926 he became director of St. Helena Sanitarium and Hospital, a position he held for fourteen years. In 1940 he became medical secretary of the Pacific Union Conference, a position he held until his retirement in 1952. His first wife, Rose, died at an early age, and he and his second wife, Marion, then worked with Dr. J. Wayne McFarland of the General Conference to conduct practical courses in healthful living and cookery based on the Spirit of Prophecy writings all across the United States. He practiced what he preached and died in 1981 just a few days short of his 100th birthday.

Nancy's father, Dr. Donald Vollmer, followed in his father's footsteps. He received his medical degree from the College of Medical Evangelists (Loma Linda University), and during World War II he served in the Army Medical Corps for four and a half years. When the war ended, he and the family returned to California where he began a residency in internal medicine. In 1949 he set up his practice of medicine in Asheville, North Carolina. He was a fellow of the American College of Physicians and in 1978 received the Outstanding Physician of the Year Award from the Buncombe County Medical Society.

"I was born at the White Memorial Hospital in Los Angeles shortly before Daddy finished his residency in internal medicine," Nancy said. "Years before when he graduated from medical school he came to the Washington San to intern. He had to sign a one-year contract that he would not date during that one-year internship. Things were a lot different then. That's when he met my mother who was taking nurses training there."

Nancy has two brothers. Older brother, Donald Evans Vollmer, is a retired pastor/evangelist who also served as a missionary to the Irish Mission. Don also inherited the family musical talent and was a member of the renowned Wedgewood Trio. Don lives in Loma Linda. Her other brother, Dr. James Merl Vollmer, is a prominent dentist in North Carolina. "Jim has lived in North Carolina since he graduated from Loma Linda in 1973. He's a real mountain man and loves those people, and they love him," Nancy commented. Surrounded by her own clan of preachers, physicians, and musicians, Nancy felt very comfortable around the Wilson family.

"I grew up in a home where Friday night was the best part of the whole week, something we looked forward to. I hear people talk about how their upbringing was legalistic. I never knew what they were talking about because for us the Sabbath was the most special day of the week, especially Friday night.

"By sundown the house was sparkling clean. The cooking was done; we always had special, but simple meals. My mother was a terrific gardener, and she had fresh flowers from the garden in the house all summer long. And those flowers were as much a part of Sabbath as a clean house and special food. Our house had a massive fireplace, and in the wintertime we would sit around the fireplace and watch the fire and have family worship together. Sabbath really was a wonderful day for us."

Nancy attended grade school in Ashville, North Carolina, and then Mount Pisgah Academy just outside of Asheville. She attended Atlantic Union College for one year before going to Southern Missionary College to finish her prerequisites for physical therapy. She then attended the School of Allied Health (School of Health Related Professions at that time) at Loma Linda University to become qualified as a physical therapist.

Marriage

About 400 guests attended their wedding in Asheville, North Carolina, at Nancy's home church. The reception was held in the home Nancy grew up in. Elders Neal Wilson and Nathaniel Wilson performed the wedding ceremony.

Ted recalls their first home. "After we got married of course we did not live in the small church parsonage but moved to another home. I found a nice little house for rent right next to the ocean. The only caveat was that we could only be there for nine months. It was the summer beach home of people who lived in New York. When winter was over we would have to give up the home. Nancy, of course, wanted to live in this lovely home by the beach, and we rented it for our very first nine months. We took pictures of where everything was in the house then packed away the people's items and put our own belongings in. When we left we put things back exactly as they had it when we got there, and they wanted us to rent again! It was a lovely cottage to start our marriage and to entertain our church young people. However, the timing worked out perfectly since at the end of those nine months, I was invited to join Metro Ministries. So we moved from Patchogue New York to Pearl River in Rockland County just north of New York City."

In 1952 the General Conference spring meeting allocated accumulated funds of the China Division for 1952, 1953, and 1954, which had been given by members all around the world, and because of the political situation could no longer be used in China, for the establishment of evangelistic centers in London, New York, and Chicago. In the heart of London, close to Piccadilly Circus, the British Union Conference used its portion of the funds and bought the New Gallery Centre in 1953.[266]

In the United States November 10, 1956, was a day of great rejoicing–a day which many felt was a fulfillment of the Spirit of Prophecy counsel and vision. Promoted as the Adventist lighthouse at Times Square, the New York Center was opened and consecrated on that day. The modern, six-story former hotel was purchased with the United States' share of the funds three years before. The building was renovated both inside and out. Three years of prayer, planning, and hard work had now come to fruition. Now it was ready to serve as a religious, educational, and cultural center to the diverse people groups who called New York City home. At the time, one out of every eleven Americans lived within twenty miles of the New York Center.[267]

World president R. R. Figuhr, officials from the General Conference, Ernest L. Branson, president of the

Highly Committed

Greater New York Conference, the official owners of the building, representatives of the National Council of Churches, and the Protestant Council of the city of New York were all there to celebrate this great event with Adventist believers. It brought new hope and courage to all who carried a burden for the unwarned millions of that great city. More than 100 years ago in 1901 Ellen G. White wrote of the work in New York: "Here let a center for God's work be made, and let all that is done be a symbol of the work the Lord desires to see done in the world."[268]

About 200 Protestant ministers attended a preview of *The Great Commandment*, a religious film shown during the opening week of the center. The main auditorium, which seated about 850 people, was equipped with a wide screen and a projection booth for showing religious films. The stage of the lower auditorium was equipped with a modern demonstration kitchen. The upper floors provided space for offices, chapels for small foreign-language congregations, classrooms for adult education, and rooms for teenage small groups. There were also nine apartments and twelve guest rooms for staff members and missionaries who might be passing through the city. The lower level also housed an Adventist Book Center.

The Atlantic Union as well as the Greater New York Conference participated in the planning of the building. It was usually called the New York Center, but often referred to as the New York Center for Evangelism. The anniversary issue of *The Advent Review and Sabbath Herald* under the heading "Highlights of Adventist History—1939 to 1975" listed five outstanding events for the year 1956. *It Is Written* telecast began that year, but the article also listed as a highlight the opening of the New York Center for Evangelism.

The first of a series of evangelistic lectures began the week after opening on November 18. Most of the union papers carried the story with this appeal: "If you have relatives or friends in the New York metropolitan area to whom you would like to have invitations sent, will you please fill in this form and mail it to Elder Joseph Barnes, director of the Center ... As soon as you do so, please join the staff in prayer fellowship that this beautiful new Adventist center will be used by God to draw to His truth hundreds of sincere people not previously contacted by the missionary efforts made in the city."[269]

The New York Center

It was hoped that the New York Center would offer an easily accessible location and necessary facilities for all kinds of interchurch activities such as rallies, dinners, institutes, etc., and unite the members in New York City in a closer fellowship of service. Sabbath church services were offered in English, Ukrainian, and Hungarian.

Twenty years later Neal Wilson commissioned Lowell Bock to chair a committee to study how to make the outreach ministry in New York more effective. The committee met several days at Camp Berkshire. From that meeting an interunion, interconference board was set up that coordinated *It Is Written* and *Faith For Today* and Voice of Prophecy telecasts; the Adventist Nurse Service Agency; a Spanish evangelistic team, which included a Spanish radio and TV program, "Ayer, Hoy, Manana"; an evangelistic team working primarily for the black population; and a wide variety of ministries and activities. Two unions, Atlantic and Columbia, and five conferences, Greater New York, Allegheny East, Northeastern, New Jersey, and Southern New England, worked together and representatives from these organizations made up the board.

The new expanded organization was called Metro Ministry, and three persons were appointed to grow the baby ministry. Eric Hon, veteran evangelist and health educator from Australia, was named the director. "I had been on that committee that met at Camp Berkshire and had been in the discussion and planning of the new ministry and was familiar with what was happening. A short time later while I was pastoring in New York I got a surprise call from Neal Wilson asking if I would be willing to work with Elder Hon as the associate director. I was excited about the new challenge and accepted," said Nikolaus Satelmajer.

Ted N. C. Wilson was also selected to be an assistant director. "... God [has] a marvelous design for New

York City. God promises that if the church will follow His formula for approaching the cities, it will set in motion a mighty movement. New York would become a symbol of what God wants to happen in every large city," wrote Neal Wilson.[270]

Hon outlined a thirteen-point plan of operation, among them: Teach and train church members in the whole-message concept leading into person-to-person ministry; use church facilities for the promotion of medical missionary work in the form of health evangelism and community services; establish vegetarian restaurants; establish outpost centers to fulfill the counsel in regard to homes for workers, a training school for young people, and sanitarium facilities; give strong support to literature evangelists and utilize them as front-line contacts; and conduct field training for students in evangelism and medical-missionary work.[271]

Later that year the three directors traveled to Annual Council at world headquarters and "gave visual and oral reports about the work of Metro Ministries, setting forth the challenge of evangelism in New York City."[272]

Some of the items they discussed were the leadership of June Croft and the Adventist Nursing Service Agency with its 600 home-help aides who gave loving care to people on all levels of society; a black evangelistic team under the leadership of Harold Brewer; a Spanish evangelistic team, which included Spanish radio and television directed by Jorge Grieve; and the programs of *It Is Written*, *Faith For Today*, and *The Voice of Prophecy*.

The center hoped to teach and train church members in person-to-person ministry; establish a vegetarian restaurant and health food shop; sponsor evangelistic teams; conduct health lectures and vegetarian cooking classes; engage in temperance outreach; offer training for young people; conduct field training for students in evangelism and medical missionary work; and offer other related urban evangelistic activities outlined in the Spirit of Prophecy.

Ellen G. White made clear that God had a marvelous design for New York City. God promised through His servant that if the church would follow His formula for approaching the cities, it would set in motion a mighty movement. Following the quote in *Evangelism*, New York would become a symbol of what God wanted to happen in every large city.

Health played a great part in the work of Metro Ministry. Metro Ministry was involved in Five-Day Plans to Stop Smoking, health fairs, cooking schools, and vegetarian seminars. Nik Satelmajer recounts how their booth was very popular and distributed thousands of *Life and Health* magazines and cookbooks to the 28,000 who attended a one-day event. "At least for one day Loma Linda Linketts outsold hot dogs at the New York Coliseum, a sports arena. Nearly 500 Linketts on slices of bread were sold at a booth sponsored by Metro Ministry at the first annual Diet and Nutrition Expo ... Owing to the popularity of the linketts ... the supply ran out at the height of the demand."[273]

Dr. Robert H. Dunn later joined the staff as medical director. Dr. Dunn made news when he was featured on WNYC, an AM and FM radios station with a public affairs/classical music format. During their special "Health Fair of the Air," Dr. Dunn was interviewed about Adventist philosophy and the practice of vegetarianism and preventive medicine. Andre Bernard, host and a devotee of natural living, asked Dunn probing questions such as: "Does a vegetarian diet supply sufficient amino acids, and why do Adventists choose to emphasize natural remedies instead of drug therapy?"

Dr. Dunn took advantage of the opportunity to promote the various programs offered by Metro Ministry, including their upcoming Five-Day Plan to Stop Smoking, vegetarian cooking schools, and stress control seminars.[274]

Satelmajer said that the Five-Day Plan to Stop Smoking made many friends for Metro Ministry. They were

Highly Committed

called on to conduct the program for the Long Island Railroad employees, several large banks, and investment companies. From there the ministry connected to many high-end business people, which resulted in lots of publicity.

Later, a Harvard graduate and former official in the New York City government joined the staff as city ministries coordinator. Luis E. Cadiz had been deputy commissioner of the department of correction and supervisor of the food service, laundry, and commissary, successfully managing a budget in excess of $10 million. Cadiz was responsible for planning urban vegetarian restaurant complexes as well as assisting in the establishment of rural reconditioning centers as outlined in the writings of Ellen G. White.[275]

Two years later Ted Wilson was appointed director of the center. "Ted N. C. Wilson has been elected director of Metro Ministry in New York City [October 1978]. He replaces Eric Hon, who has served as director for the past two years. Elder Hon, a denominational retiree, had requested a change so that he might serve the church with lesser responsibilities. The new director of Metro Ministry has served as assistant director for the past two years.

"An associate director of Metro Ministry, Nikolaus Satelmajer, [left November 1978] has accepted a call to be secretary-treasurer of the New York Conference, Syracuse, New York."[276]

While serving as assistant director of Metro Ministry, Pastor Ted Wilson was recommended for ordination. *The Atlantic Union Gleaner* gives the report of his ordination service, which was held on July 8, 1978, at the Greater New York Conference camp meeting. "The candidates for ordination during English camp were Jonathan K. Paulien, Trevor H. Fraser, Marco A. Valenca, and N. C. (Ted) Wilson who is director of Metro Ministry in New York City.

"A short biographical sketch of each candidate was read to the congregation by someone who has had a special influence on the life of the individual. Elder N.C. Wilson, president of the North American Division, gave the biography for his son and made an appeal to all the candidates to be faithful ministers. He also offered the ordination prayer."[277]

Dr. Trevor Fraser who was ordained at that Sabbath service is now a professor at Oakwood University in Huntsville, Alabama. "I still remember Elder Neal Wilson's remarks to us. He challenged us to a lifetime of faithful service to God and humanity. And I will never forget the words that he spoke to his son. Playing on the text in John 3, he publicly said to Ted, 'This is my beloved son in whom I am well pleased.' And you could see the joy, the love, and pride that he had in seeing his son being ordained to the gospel ministry to serve as he had served and as his grandfather before him had served."

Elder Kenneth Wood, editor of the *Adventist Review*, gave the sermon. Elder G. M. Kretschmar, the president of the conference, welcomed the men into the ministry and his wife, Juanita, gave a warm welcome to the wives of the newly ordained ministers. Each candidate was given opportunity for a short response where he recounted the leading of God in his life.

"It was quite evident that Nancy Wilson was expecting," said Dr. Jon Paulien and his wife, Pamela, who participated in the service that same day. "We didn't think she would make it out of the service because she looked like she was about to go into labor any minute. But somehow she made it through the service." Three days later Emilie Louise Wilson was born on July 11, 1978. Their second daughter, Elizabeth Esther Wilson, would be born two years later, November 23, 1980.

On several occasions study had been given to the effectiveness and practicality of the work of the New York Center. It was costing the Greater New York Conference approximately $100,000 to keep the center functioning each year. The large facility was often under used. Several committees, including a special blue ribbon committee, had recommended that the New York Center be disposed of if a reasonable offer was received.

A qualified appraisal of the facilities in New York was also made. As early as September 18, 1969, a sales-purchase contract was submitted and scrutinized by GC attorneys. A vote authorizing the Atlantic Union and the Greater New York Conference to sell the property and develop plans for the use of the money received from the sale was taken and recorded in the General Conference minutes.[278]

"Voted: to concur with the Atlantic Union and the Greater New York Conference on the sale of the New York Center for $2,500,000. Expenditure of the funds received from the sale shall be approved by the General Conference."[279] In the end, the Church of Scientology purchased the building, and it became one of their headquarters buildings.

Relocating

Because of the impending sale of the New York Center, the administrative offices and departments of Metropolitan Ministries were relocated to 144 Central Avenue, Pearl River, New York.

"'I feel God is using this move to scatter us so there can be more lights for Him in different parts of Metropolitan New York,' says Elder Ted Wilson, director.

"The move of the administrative offices to a quiet suburban area is based on the counsel of Ellen G. White in the book *Country Living* on page 28: 'The instruction is still being given, move out of the cities. Establish your sanitariums, your schools, and *offices* away from the centers of population.'"[280]

Elder Earl W. Amundson, new president of the Atlantic Union Conference, made a special trip to New York City where he spent the day with Ted Wilson. "Elder Ted Wilson, director of Metropolitan Ministries escorted Elder Amundson on a mini-tour of the city, taking him to a possible site for the proposed vegetarian restaurant Metropolitan Ministries is planning to establish and operate.

"After dining at a natural foods restaurant of the type and style planned by Metropolitan Ministries, Elder Amundson, along with local conference and Metropolitan Ministries leaders, was taken to a beautiful hilltop facility north of New York City which Metropolitan Ministries is considering as a location for the outpost center and health retreat....

"'It was delightful and a privilege to have the new vice chairman of our board spend an entire day in New York City and get a grassroots grasp of the problems we face in this metropolitan area. At the end of the day he expressed deep satisfaction for having been with us and said he would carefully analyze our plans and programs,' notes Elder Ted Wilson."[281]

After legal and other fees were taken out, the remaining $2,392,000 from the sale of the New York Center was put into a special fund held by the General Conference treasury to be allocated to the Atlantic Union and Northeastern and Greater New York conferences.[282]

Ted Wilson recently reflected on the work of the New York Center. "It was a sad time when they sold the New York Center. We didn't know it then but not long after that the property values increased exponentially. The neighborhood was cleaned up and it became an outstanding real estate area. It would have been better to keep the building but the problem was that there were no real activities that were filling the space. It was a decision that was made and we just had to move on.

"Actually we need many properties in the city. The original thought of the New York Center and of the London Gallery was to try to reach the cities. That was an admirable goal. But you cannot reach the entire city from one location. We need many different centers of influence as Mrs. White called for. It could have been a real anchor for the future in New York.

"Congregations are small in New York. We have some large ones but most of them are small. To try to maintain large buildings with the type of funding that was available just didn't seem proper. That was one of the reasons they sold the New York Center. But the Greater New York Conference purchased another building on W. 42nd St. where the ABC is now. It's probably one-third the size of the other building. It's right opposite the New York City library and very nice. The Hungarian church meets there and maybe one or two other congregations.

"The Metro Ministry was probably a mixed bag. It wasn't quite a failure, but it wasn't quite a success. It was an endeavor to try to put the Spirit of Prophecy plan for the cities, at least part of it, into effect but probably it could have been administratively better placed working through the conferences that were there, Northeastern Conference and Greater New York Conference, rather than working through a separate organization which created some feelings of uneasiness. The conferences said, 'It's not our organization.' Maybe that contributed to the challenge.

"But we're not giving up on New York. The General Conference, the North American Division, the Atlantic and Columbia unions, and the local conferences will be giving special emphasis to evangelizing metropolitan New York in the future. Years ago we tried to establish a vegetarian restaurant and have health lectures, but we didn't have the other component, an outpost center. Those things take money and personnel. The Lord may have had other plans. It's very interesting how things develop. The hand of the Lord moves in interesting ways. Metro Ministries was dissolved after I left. Certain appropriations and assistance were given to the conferences to help them with some of their projects. But when I left the organization ceased to exist.

"Certainly the church conducted some very successful evangelistic activities in New York in the past. But anytime you're trying to put into effect the plan that the Spirit of Prophecy has outlined, the devil doesn't like to see us succeed. We probably didn't always do it in the right way. However, the Lord has different ways of accomplishing things and that was one phase. We learned some precious lessons which will help us in the future."

Wilson later talked about his educational experiences in New York. "I went to New York University while I was doing all these other things. I never lived on NYU campus. They had programs set up for busy professional people. Many of the classes took place late in the afternoon and in the evenings. There was a program of religious education under the Department of Cultural Foundations. The man who was the head of that program, Dr. Lee Belford, and his associate, Dr. Norma Thompson, were very kind and considerate people. Dr. Belford was a member of the Episcopal Church and was from the South but had a very strong connection with Seventh-day Adventists. He knew a number of Adventists who either entered or would enter the doctoral program. Dr. Richard Lesher, Dr. Gaspar Colón, Dr. Leonard Barnes, and a number of others went through this program.

"Dr. Belford took a particular liking to Seventh-day Adventists because we tried to live according to certain principles. He found us fascinating, and he helped me greatly. It was a tailored program for professionals, for clergy and other religious educators. It was a very good experience for me. I learned a considerable amount, especially about how people relate in the world. Within the religious education community, I met professors and individuals who were very helpful and encouraging. They looked at Seventh-day Adventists as being something of a unique breed.

"I felt good about having finished my course work. And then I woke up some months later and realized that I really hadn't started working on my dissertation and that's the hardest part. I look back at that as being a good experience, a very tough experience in the sense that you finally get to the point where you have to use every ounce of self-discipline and organization to complete this dissertation. But that is a critical part of your training. I'm glad I went through it. It really was one of the most valuable components of the doctoral program.

"Dr. Belford suggested, 'Why don't you do something on Ellen White?' I offered the subject on exactly what I was doing in the city at Metropolitan Ministries. I felt the research would help us with our program. The Lord just worked things out, and it was accepted. I went through the proposal seminar and defended my proposal. The Lord guided in so many ways. I'm still a member of the American Public Health Organization, Phi Delta Kappa, and a Certified Health Education Specialist (CHES). For quite a period of time I was a member of the Religious Education Association."

An article was published in *The Atlantic Union Gleaner* in which Ted talked about his degrees. "'Having a degree in health as well as religion has given me an appreciation for the health aspect of evangelism, made me more competent in conducting health programs, and given me credibility when I deal with the public,' Wilson observes."[283]

The title of his dissertation was "A Study of Ellen G. White's Theory of Urban Religious Work as It Relates to Seventh-day Adventist Work in New York City." Once he submitted the dissertation he obtained a doctor of philosophy degree in 1981 from the School of Education, Health Nursing, and Art Professions of New York University.

On September 21, 1981, Pastor Ted N. C. Wilson, M.Div., MSPH, Ph.D., with Nancy and two little girls left New York City bound for Abidjan, Ivory Coast.[284]

Neal Clayton Wilson's Family

Neal Clayton WILSON (son of Nathaniel Carter Wilson and Hannah Wallin Wilson)

- Born: July 5, 1920, in Lodi, California
- Died: December 14, 2010, in Dayton, Maryland
- Married: **Elinor Neumann** on July 19, 1942, in Chicago, Illinois. Elinor was born on January 21, 1920, and died on June 8, 2011, in Dayton, Maryland. The couple had two children, Ted and Shirley.

Ted N. C. WILSON

- Born: May 10, 1950, in Takoma Park, Maryland
- Married: **Nancy Louise VOLLMER** on September 14, 1975, in Asheville, North Carolina. Nancy was born on August 13, 1948, in Los Angeles, California. The couple have three children, who are as follows:

Emilie Louise WILSON DeVasher

- Born: July 11, 1978
- Married: **Kameron DEVASHER** on August 10, 2008
- Child: **Henry Kameron DeVasher** was born on July 21, 2010

(cont.)

Elizabeth Esther WILSON Wright

- Born: November 23, 1980
- Married: **David WRIGHT** on July 6, 2003
- Children: **Lauren Emilie WRIGHT** was born on January 31, 2007; **Matthew David WRIGHT** was born on February 12, 2009; **Maryanne Elizabeth WRIGHT** was born on April 1, 2011.

Catherine Anne WILSON Renck

- Born: January 4, 1983
- Married: **Robert RENCK** on November 23, 2008
- Child: **Charlotte Rose RENCK** was born on September 6, 2010

Shirley Jean WILSON Anderson

- Born: January 24, 1953, in Cairo, Egypt
- Married: **John Edward ANDERSON** on July 29, 1973. John was born on March 23, 1953. They have the following child:

Jonathan ANDERSON

- Born: April 18, 1985

This cover article was first published in the fall 2010 issue of *Spectrum*.
It is reprinted with permission.

"Reflections on a Lifelong Friendship with the New GC President"

By Jiggs Gallagher

Let me introduce you to my best friend, Ted Wilson. I don't use the word "friend" lightly. Sociologists say that if we develop three to five strong friendships over the course of a lifetime, we're doing very well. Many of the people we call friends are more accurately acquaintances, colleagues at work, Facebook "friends," and the like. True friends are something else altogether.

Ted and I met in fifth grade at John Nevins Andrews School in Takoma Park after his family moved from California to Maryland when his father became a departmental director in the Columbia Union.

We became fast friends and shared the experience of growing up through high school at Takoma

(cont.)

Ted N. C. Wilson: The Early Years

Academy. Ted went off to La Sierra College for his freshmen year (I almost joined him there, but attended Columbia Union College.) Then he came back a year later, and we both graduated from CUC.

Our young lives in Takoma Park were blissful by today's standards. We talked of schoolwork, girls, music, politics, popular culture, possible careers, and yes, religion and theology. We were both among six or seven "youth evangelists" who spoke at the Takoma Park Church for an evening series in 1967; we were half of a male gospel quartet (Ted was baritone, I was bass) formed by Ted's mother. He was a positive person with a great sense of humor and a great deal of compassion for people—all people, Adventists and otherwise. I could see that from the beginning.

We did fun things like editing the 1970 CUC yearbook in a marathon three-day, day-and-night session. On New Year's Eve of 1970, we hopped a Trailways bus in downtown D.C. and rode to New York to be in the studio audience at Johnny Carson's live Tonight Show. We hiked from the Port Authority Bus Terminal across Times Square, which was already teeming with people, at 9 or 10 that night, and on to Rockefeller Center and the NBC studios. Then after the show, at 1 a.m., we walked back through the cold and the debris to the bus depot and slept on the 4-hour ride back to D.C.

Another adventure was returning his uncle's Porsche from Maryland to Loma Linda. His uncle was a physician who spent a year in the army in Vietnam in 1969-70, and he lent the car to Ted. After exams were over at CUC in April (literally, at 4 p.m.), we piled in the car and started driving west. By 5 a.m. we were at the arch in St. Louis, which we walked up to but obviously couldn't go in at that hour. A homeless man asked us for money, and Ted offered him a sandwich his mother had packed for us. When we had to get a mechanic's help in New Mexico, he witnessed to the man on the tow-truck ride. The man was visibly touched....

I remember talking with him on hot summer nights in front of my house about what we both wanted to do with our lives. At one point he was thinking about a career in Egyptology—archeology basically focused on ancient Egypt. Not surprising for a boy who called Cairo his home for the first eight years of his life.

God's ministry was never far from his heart, even as an academy and college student. And he was in a hurry! After finishing his double major in religion and business administration at CUC a year early, graduating in 1971, he attended the Theological Seminary at Andrews, receiving his M.Div. degree by 1973.

Not satisfied with this level of education, he set out for Loma Linda University and earned a master of science degree in public health. Then he settled into the ministry as pastor of a church in Patchogue, Long Island, NY. I visited him there once, when my life was in a bit of turmoil, for a weekend—just to get my head clear and my bearings straight. Ted had a way of doing that for people. He was still single at this time, and I remember on that Friday night a (single) lady (church member) showed up at his door with a casserole. He was very popular!

Ted married his lovely wife Nancy (*née* Vollmer), whom he met at Loma Linda when she was getting her degree in physical therapy. The couple located in suburban New York City, and Ted directed Metro Ministries there for several years while also getting his doctorate in religious education at New York University. They began a family which now includes three lovely and accomplished young ladies

(cont.)

(Emilie, Catherine and Elizabeth) and their husbands and children.

Most of his career has been spent overseas, beginning with service in Abidjan, Ivory Coast, during the 1980s. After a two-year stint in the General Conference Secretariat in Silver Spring, he headed the church's work in Russia (based in Moscow) after the fall of the Soviet Union. Returning again to the United States, Ted served as president of the Review and Herald Publishing Association in Hagerstown. He was elected a general vice president of the church in 2000 at the GC session in Toronto, and re-elected to the post in 2005.

All through this time, through various media and technology, we stayed in frequent touch, first through letters and phone calls, and later through e-mail. His work often took him to Loma Linda, and because I was living in Southern California by that time, we almost never failed to get together once a year or so for a meal, for church or even for a quick half-hour chat. He would often visit my ailing mother and have prayer with her. On her death in 2007, he cleared his morning calendar during Annual Council to conduct her service.

Our adult lives have taken us both in vastly different directions. I have not worked for the denomination since 1988. I'm probably what many people would call a liberal Adventist, whatever that means, and of course Ted is not. I eat meat, and he is a life-long vegetarian. I've been divorced and remarried—and, thankfully, he has not. I have a gay daughter who's legally married to a woman here in California.

However, none of those things matters between us. And he doesn't judge me for any of it. We don't argue about church politics because they couldn't divide the bond of friendship we share. His generous spirit and spiritually supportive personality continue to buoy me in my life's journey, as they have throughout my life.

Knowing him as I do, over his lifetime and mine, gives me a unique window into the soul of this man. I have been with him as a child, as a teen and as an adult, under pressure and during good times. I know his deep commitment to God and to the Church, and his burning zeal for taking the Adventist message to as many people as possible, as quickly as possible.

Ted knows the challenges, and he knows that he needs God's special guidance in taking up the duties of this job, as would any human being elected to such a pivotal position. Of course I wish him and his family well, and I would wish an extra dose of wisdom that could come his way for him to make good, far-sighted decisions during his term of office. I would wish for him always to see the big picture, to put the souls of the flock and of the wider world constantly before God.

Knowing him as I do, I know that would be his prayer as well.

Jiggs Gallagher is a grant writer for California State University, San Bernardino. He holds a master's degree in journalism from Columbia University.

Ted N. C. Wilson: The Early Years

Ted and Nancy with their grandparents at their wedding.

Ted and Nancy Wilson on their wedding day September 14, 1975.

Highly Committed

The happy couple after their wedding in Asheville North Carolina.

Ted Wilson at one and a half years old.

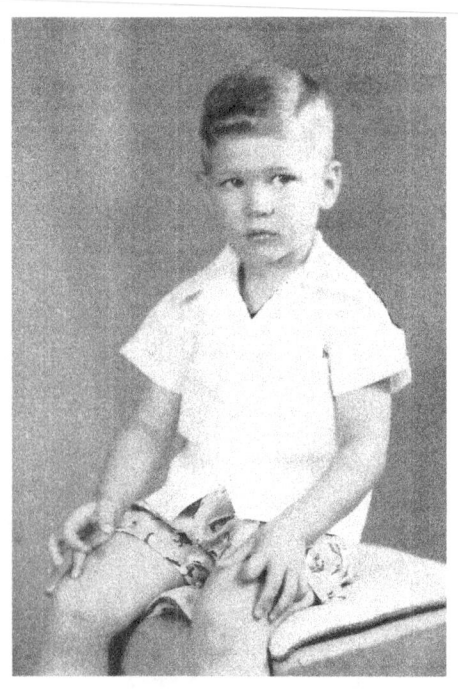

Ted Wilson at three years old.

Ted N. C. Wilson: The Early Years

Ted Wilson and Nancy Vollmer during their dating days in 1975.

Ted and Nancy in 1981 with three year old Emilie and two month old Elizabeth.

Elizabeth Wright with her son David.

Chapter Fourteen

Abidjan, Russia, and the Review

"Service is the rent we pay for being. It is the very purpose of life, and not something you do in your spare time." Marian Wright Edelman

Dallas, Texas, hosted the fifty-third General Conference session in April 1980. The first business session authorized the creation of a new African division. This new division would bring together thirty countries and islands, home to approximately 250 million people, the majority of whom were French-speaking. Officially named the Africa-Indian Ocean Division (AID), the church's newest division headquarters would be located in Abidjan, Ivory Coast (Cote d'Ivoire). Its new president, Robert J. Kloosterhuis, had served the church most recently as president of the Franco Haitian Union and was selected not only for his administrative skills but also for his ability to communicate in French.

Kloosterhuis reminisced on the staggering challenge that this new division presented: "The first AID executive committee meeting took place around the dining room table at the home of the Ivory Coast Mission president. Four members were present. The only office supplies available were some 'borrowed' blank sheets of paper on which to take notes. There were no letterheads, treasury forms, paper clips, or any other basic office necessities. Every detail, even simple decisions, had to be thought through, organized, and put into operation. It was truly beginning from scratch.

"Gradually additional personnel arrived. Organizational structure and policies took shape and form. Brick and mortar for office and homes was secured. From that humble beginning, AID grew and developed into its present organization."[285]

At first, AID operated out of a rented building, but later it purchased the residence and offices of the Indian ambassador who lived just a few feet away from the president of the country. "I began interviewing people to come to Abidjan to head up departments and be administrators."

In the process, Kloosterhuis interviewed Ted Wilson. "I secured Ted Wilson's bio and references and that of several other leaders to see if they had the qualifications for the jobs that were available. I had to go to Glacier View, Colorado, for an important meeting before flying back to Abidjan. I arranged to see Ted and Nancy at the airport in New York. Ruth and I met them there and interviewed them. They liked the idea of mission service in Africa, and we liked their outlook on life and their preparation."

Ted Wilson continues the story. "We had a couple of options while at Metro Ministries. One was to go to the Middle East as ministerial secretary for the Middle East Union. I was almost 98 percent sure that's what I wanted to do. I felt that was my destiny since that was my home. I needed to go back home and help the church there. Almost certainly we were going to go there, and then the civil war in Lebanon developed with all of its fury, and we realized that this was not the best place to go.

"So when this other opportunity arose and the new division was being organized in Africa, we agreed to meet with Elder Kloosterhuis at JFK Airport in New York. We talked for quite a while, and then he and his wife Ruth, who were in transit, took off for Africa. Nancy and I talked and prayed about it. It was a new division, and all the leaders, including myself, would be pioneers. When they extended an official call to us to what eventually became the director of ministerial, stewardship, and health and temperance, we accepted. It looked like something very interesting and extremely challenging. But we knew nothing about West Africa. I didn't even know where Abidjan was even though I enjoy geography.

"We soon learned very quickly about Abidjan and made some preliminary visits to different places in the U.S. in anticipation of our work. I remember going to Loma Linda to make some contacts for health aspects. I also went to Oakwood College and spent some time with Elder E. E. Cleveland, who had been a great evangelist and was a professor there, to get information and ideas since I was going to be ministerial secretary. He was extremely helpful. Quite tutorial. To sit and listen to Elder Cleveland was a great experience and helped me a lot. I also visited with Elder Eric Ward, the pastor of the Oakwood College Church. He was very encouraging and gave me some great ideas. I talked with Elder Bob Spangler who lived right next door to my family at Pitcairn Place. We were longtime family friends. Many people helped us in preparation.

"When we were finally ready to go after we had finished visiting our family elsewhere, we came to Washington. We were to fly from Washington National Airport to JFK in New York. My parents organized a little send-off. We were in the Washington airport only for a few hours. They invited some friends to help send us off right. We had a picnic and prayed together during our layover just before we got on the plane.

"We flew to Europe and then to Abidjan. At that time they didn't have the program to send missionaries to Collognes, France, to study French. The division made a decision to teach people French in the division. We were put at a big disadvantage arriving there in Abidjan and not being able to speak the language. I learned French, but it took a while. They set up some French classes at the division office, and we got a decent foundation.

"I wanted to learn more French, so I enrolled in the University of Abidjan and started taking classes there and was learning quite a bit. Then the school had a strike and that ended that experience. After that I came back to the States for a meeting, and I tacked on about two weeks of French study at the Berlitz Language School in Washington. That gave me a jumpstart. I spent eight hours a day with somebody who wouldn't speak one word of anything except French to me. I ate with this person and walked and talked with them, and we spoke French only.

"By the time the day was over I was just craving to speak to somebody in English. It really helped me. In Abidjan all the meetings were translated from English to French and from French to English, and I listened intensely in each meeting when they translated. I picked up a lot just listening to how they translated the words I didn't know, and I started using French more and more. Soon French became somewhat second nature to me.

"We had a marvelous time in Africa. I would come home from work and tell Nancy that I couldn't believe that they paid me to do this! We thoroughly enjoyed our work and our living conditions. We had a great time preparing materials for pastors, and we ran evangelistic meetings and did health promotion."

In a letter to Elder Bob Spangler, Ted let him know how much he was enjoying his experience in Africa and some of his plans for the future. "I am happy that you have kept up on our activities through my parents—it sure is great to have wonderful parents. We were glad to have my folks here recently and Nancy's mother is coming this Friday, so we don't have much time to be homesick. In fact, we feel quite at home here in Abidjan. We really like our work and lifestyle. I am REALLY enjoying my job and the exciting and challenging aspects of it....

"There are many projects that we have in the fire at the moment. Where shall I start?... This will be a first-hand report to my association superior!! I am enclosing a copy of our audio-visual project, which we have moved ahead on.... Yes, we are going to try to fulfill the hope of producing *Ministry* for our division using maybe 60-70% of your material and adding African material. We hope for about 8 issues the first year beginning

Highly Committed

with April or May of '83.... I'll be the main editor and of course we will list you men as the editors also.... We also want to produce a ministerial continuing education cassette club for ministers. It will be in French and English, and we will try to tie it into some type of educational upgrading."[286]

As ministerial association secretary, Ted encouraged his pastors to evangelize and set an example by holding some meetings himself. "I did an evangelistic meeting in Monrovia, Liberia, with Ron Wright and his wife, Equilla. They organized it very well, and we ended up with 666 baptisms. Quite an interesting number! It was an exciting thing, and they started a new church. I did another one with them in Bamenda, Cameroon, which was tough. It was in the English-speaking area of Cameroon and a somewhat neglected area."

Ted pushed hard for a surge in evangelism during the One Thousand Days of Reaping, which set a goal to baptize 1,000 new souls a day for 1,000 days beginning September 18, 1982, and ending June 15, 1985. This would add one million new members worldwide to the church, and Ted's zeal was infectious in AID. Elder Kloosterhuis shared this account of the evangelism and stewardship progress of his division in the *Review*.

"Division Ministerial and Stewardship Association secretary Ted N. C. Wilson, along with a galvanized leadership, marshaled the workers and laity into a dynamic, powerful unit under the banner of the One Thousand Days of Reaping. Recently while reviewing AID's evangelistic accomplishments, Elder Wilson commented: 'During the past quinquennium, approximately 263,000 new believers have been added to God's church through His power. The spirit and momentum of evangelism have accelerated dramatically in the past two and one-half years with the strong spiritual evangelistic program of the One Thousand Days of Reaping. This program has caught the imagination and enthusiasm of the members throughout the division. Laymen and pastors have united together. With the blessings of the Holy Spirit they have pushed the division growth rate to one of the highest of the world divisions. The Africa-Indian Ocean Division is throbbing with evangelistic activity and energy.

"Public evangelism is spreading like wildfire in Africa. Presentation of the gospel under a tent has gripped the public's attention and caught our leaders by surprise. It began in Monrovia, Liberia, in early 1983. There two public campaigns, one conducted by J. J. Rodriquez, a student from Oakwood College, and the other by Ted N. C. Wilson, together produced 1,275 baptisms. R. J. Wright, then West African Union Ministerial Association secretary, coordinated both efforts, with only eight months separating the two campaigns. Unprecedented large baptisms have taken place in Ghana, where laymen have seized the initiative and pushed baptisms to an all-time high.

"The same is taking place in the Zaire Union, where last year's total of baptisms was 21,730, a 46 percent gain over the previous year. The Rwanda Union's total baptisms for a recent four-year period was 62,057. Recently the Togo-Benin Mission, with a membership of 592, suddenly discovered itself confronted with an influx of 650 people requesting baptism following a series of meetings held by Frederic Durbant in Lomé, the capital of Togo. Unfortunately there are no church facilities to house them....

"Because of the heavy demand on finances for evangelism, the division has given much attention to the area of stewardship. A recent division-wide stewardship council resulted in a division committee decision to aim at 100 percent self-support by local fields and unions by 1995. Such an ambitious objective will require continued education of stewardship principles on the part of leadership. The use of tithe and offering envelopes as a means of systematizing the church members' orientation to stewardship is heavily promoted. The Family Planned Giving program is strongly encouraged.»[287]

In 1985 Wilson was elected secretary of the division, but he still promoted evangelism in AID and the Harvest '90 program. "Cameroon has the third-highest alcohol consumption per capita of any country in the world. After a campaign held in the mountainous city of Bamenda by assistant division secretary (now division secretary) Ted N. C. Wilson, at least a few Cameroonians exchanged their liquor for the new wine of the Holy Spirit.

"The campaign was held under a pavilion built in the middle of the local sports stadium. Materials from the pavilion will be used to build a new church on a mountainside overlooking Bamenda.

"Coordinated by Pastor Ron Wright and his wife, Aquilla [*sic*], the crusade doubled the membership of the church, which had been meeting in the local pastor's home. 'This new church will be like a light on the hill,' says Wilson....

"'The evangelistic thrust of this division during the One Thousand Days of Reaping was truly one of God's wonders,' says [division secretary G. S.] Valleray. 'As we continue to sow the gospel seed we expect to reap an even greater harvest as the latter rain falls during Harvest '90, the church's new five-year evangelistic program.'"[288]

The *Adventist Review* reported on his meeting in Zaire. "A month-long crusade conducted by Ted N. C. Wilson, Africa-Indian Ocean Division secretary, and David Saguan, Zaire Union Mission ministerial director, in Likasi, Zaire, resulted in 145 baptisms. Crusade workers are now working with more than 60 additional interests, Saguan reports."[289]

Meeting the President

Ted was quick to make friends in the local community and was invited to many events such as the annual reception of the president of the country. "The guest list for the recent annual reception of Felix Houphouet-Boigny, president of the Ivory Coast, for government, civic, and religious leaders included four Seventh-day Adventists. Representing the Ivory Coast Mission were president Michael Kra and secretary Paul Scalliet, and from the Africa-Indian Ocean Division were secretary Ted N. C. Wilson and ADRA/AID director Wallace Amundson.

"According to Wilson, a cordial rapport developed between the Adventist delegation and the Muslim leaders attending the reception."[290]

The *Adventist Review* reported on several seminars that Ted organized and participated in: three ministerial seminars held in the Central African Union and Zaire Union with Walter D. Blehm of the Pacific Union and Raoul Dederen of Andrews University, and the first leadership seminar to be conducted in the division with GC vice president Enoch Oliveira and W. L. Murrill, GC undertreasurer.[291]

Elder Kloosterhuis, first division president of AID, affirms that Ted Wilson had a knack for architectural projects, and it was his skills that brought about the modification of the new division office. "I gave Ted quite a bit of latitude to come up with a good plan. We purchased the former Indian embassy, office, and residence, and these three buildings had to be connected and modified for division use. The first four years we were in rented buildings. Our new division office was in an exclusive neighborhood just 300 yards from the president's home [of Ivory Coast]. I left in 1985, and they were still working on the modifications when I left. As leaders, we talked about the design and had a general outline of what should be done. Ted was happy to do the architectural planning and oversight of the work and had great skill in this area." The work was completed and the building was ready for occupation in mid-1987.

"On June 3 a rainbow of 32 flags of African nations greeted church and government officials who participated in dedication ceremonies for the new office complex of the fast-growing Africa-Indian Ocean Division (AID). The building stands in the embassy section of Abidjan, capital of the West African country of Côte d'Ivoire.

"The new offices were remodeled from three buildings—one a former embassy—bought in 1983. The unique architectural design results in an aesthetically beautiful, functional, and friendly building that combines

Highly Committed

dignity and style. As an especially attractive feature, the offices surround an open-air tropical garden.

"A distinguished Ivoirain statesman, former Foreign Minister M. Usher Assouan, and I [Neal Wilson, the General Conference president] officially opened the complex by cutting a ribbon of the Ivoirain national colors—emerald, orange, and ivory. The Honorable Mr. Assouan now serves as mayor of Cocody, the community in which the office is located.

"The ground floor of the new complex includes the chapel, treasury, and data processing. Formerly an Embassy ballroom, the chapel overlooks a green lawn, colorful shrubs, and stately coconut palms that border the grounds. The upper floor provides offices for the division's president, secretary, and departmental personnel, plus a library and a meeting room for the division executive committee.

"One wing houses the communication department and media center, with its computerized equipment for the division's bilingual (French and English) publications, audio-visual sections, darkroom, and production suite for the French-language Adventist World Radio-Africa programs, broadcast by shortwave from Radio Gabon—'Africa 1.'

"Division president Jacob J. Nortey formally welcomed participants, who were protected from a tropical downpour by a large blue tent....

"AID secretary Ted N. C. Wilson, outlined the division's history since the alignment of the church's African divisions in 1980....

"After the official dedication, guests toured the new facility. They received attractive literature celebrating the day and telling of the work of the church.

"Each visitor also received a ballpoint pen on which was engraved a reminder of the frequency and time of the one-hour daily shortwave radio broadcast from Radio Gabon. The division hopes to expand this evangelistic outreach by adding an English broadcast later in 1987 if Adventist World Radio can secure additional funding to reach this important segment of Africa's population."[292]

Although Ted was used to living overseas, Abidjan was the first overseas post that Nancy ever experienced. She adapted well to the challenge of overseas living and quickly became a real missionary. Ted bragged about her ability to adjust. "Those nine years were a very formative time in our lives. Our last daughter Catherine was born during the time we were there. Nancy flew back on the last PAN AM flight from Africa, and Catherine was born in Asheville, North Carolina. Nancy came back from the states when Catherine was three weeks old. It was a very formative place for us. We loved the country of Cote d'Ivoire and the people of West Africa."

Climbing Mt. Kilimanjaro

A few years later Ted was ready to tackle another big project—climbing Mount Kilimanjaro. Neal Wilson had spent twenty-five years in Africa—ten years as a boy and fifteen as a missionary in Egypt. He had climbed many mountains in Africa and had always entertained the hope of one day climbing Mount Kilimanjaro. But he never seemed to have the time or the opportunity. Ted, realizing that the 1988 Annual Council would be held in Nairobi, Kenya, saw an excellent opportunity for his father to realize this dream. Since he was the secretary of the division and already lived in Africa, he began to lay careful plans for his father and him to climb the 19,340-foot mountain just before the session. Mount Kilimanjaro, the highest point on the continent of Africa, was just south of the Annual Council meeting place and not far from Arusha, Tanzania.

From September 12 to 16, six Seventh-day Adventists, Neal and Ted, two laypeople, and two editors—William Johnsson and Delbert Baker—climbed the mountain hoping to succeed. Every year about 5,000 people came from around the world to climb to the summit. On average, one in four reached the top. But all six Adventists were successful. Neal Wilson reached the "top" at Gilman's Point (18,700 ft) and the other five made it to the very top at the far end of the ridge at Uhuru Point (19,340 ft).

Abidjan, Russia, and the Review

From the entrance of Mount Kilimanjaro National Park to the top and back the hikers traversed 63 miles. The trip was spread over parts of five days. They were accompanied by guides as required by the park service and porters to carry their gear and prepare food. The altitude causes many people to suffer nausea, headache, and coughing at about 14,000 feet. Altitude sickness can cause cerebral or preliminary edema, fluid buildup in the brain cavity or the lungs that can be fatal. The only remedy is to immediately descend to a lower altitude. Another challenge was the cold weather. When they left, the thermometer registered 23°F (-5°C) at the 17,000-foot mark and the wind was blowing. The air got much colder and the wind blew harder as they continued those last 2,000 feet.

On Thursday they woke up at 1:00 a.m. after a few hours of fitful sleep at that high altitude. They dressed, putting on layer after layer of clothing to ward off the cold. At 2:20 a.m. they were on the trail. Step after slow step they gradually ascended the switchbacks. After more than six hours on the trail, they finally saw the pole that marked the top. Just 80 feet more to go! On Friday morning they made the final leg of the descent. That evening as they sat around the table heaped with food all six wore T-shirts that read "I Have Climbed Mount Kilimanjaro in Tanzania." The next day, Sabbath, Elder Neal Wilson preached to a huge outdoor crowd in Arusha. He preached powerfully about Bible mountains he had visited—Mount Ararat, Mount Sinai, Mount Nebo, Golgotha, and he let his audience know that only two days ago he stood on the top of Mount Kilimanjaro.

"The team developed a marvelous sense of sharing together. We spent many hours on the trail; we ate, slept, worshiped together. We faced adversity and pain together. We laughed and we prayed together. So close did we come to one another that if any one of us had failed to reach the top, all would have felt the loss."[293]

"Although there was a general feeling of unity among the team, I was so impressed with the closeness of Neal Wilson and Ted Wilson, father and son, on this climb during those five days. At that time Neal Wilson was 68 years old, and the rugged terrain would challenge the physical and mental fortitude of even the youngest members of our team. There was some risk that the president was taking to make this climb. He might receive criticism if he were to hurt himself. So his son watched over him very carefully. But more than just the risk factor, Ted had such a loving regard for his father. They walked together, talked together like school chums, and stayed in the same hut. There was really a tender bond between them. They looked like the best of friends. I didn't know it then," says Bill Johnsson in a telephone interview, "but here was the current president and the future president of our church walking together."

Nineteen eighty-nine was an interesting year for the Adventist Church. After years of delay, the General Conference staff moved into a brand new $30 million world headquarters building in Silver Spring, Maryland. The official opening took place just before Annual Council convened so that world delegates could participate in the event. It was a festive occasion: Pathfinders in drill uniforms, beautiful music, speeches, honored guests, and prayers of thanksgiving.

Delegates from all over the world learned that church membership had passed the six million member mark. The Annual Council agenda included several items that had rarely been discussed in previous meetings. One was the controversial topic of the role of women and women's ordination. Although the council did not recommend their ordination to the gospel ministry, it did approve an action that allowed qualified women ministers the previously withheld privilege of baptizing and performing wedding ceremonies—a landmark step.

It also voted an action unthinkable a few years before—the formation of the church's eleventh world division—The Soviet Division. Glasnost and perestroika (openness and restructuring) were words that the American people had been hearing often in connection with the Soviet Union. Winston Churchill had famously described Russia as an enigma wrapped in a riddle and covered with a mystery. But these two words were making a big change in the USSR. After indoctrinating the people with Marxism for seventy years, closing churches, imprisoning many practicing Christians, and forbidding religious publication and education, the Soviet government had reversed its course.

Strong winds of long expected liberty were blowing. Many doors that had been closed to Christians were starting to open. Christians were getting more and more opportunities to witness and share their beliefs. During the two previous years the government not only abandoned all limitations on the construction of new church buildings but was actually returning those buildings that had been taken away in the past. Many who had suffered oppression and persecution saw prospects of freedom in the future. In the latter part of the 1980s, the church was given freedom to conduct the election of its leadership according to church working policy.

William G. Johnsson, editor of the *Adventist Review*, commented on the formation of the eleventh world division in his editorial. "The pace of developments in the Soviet Union boggles the mind. In only three years the Adventist Church has built a seminary and organized new union conferences, and now is on the verge of establishing a publishing house. Recently the same department responsible for jailing and exiling Adventist leader M. P. Kulakov invited him to organize a ministry for prisoners in the 800 jails across the nation.

"The 1989 council voted an action unthinkable a short while ago—the formation of a Soviet division of the world church (The General Conference session next year will formally take up the recommendation.)"[294]

Pastor Mikhail P. Kulakov was elected president of the new division, and appeals were made to different countries to join in and help spread the gospel there. Families in the United States responded and donated time and money to seize the opportunity to get the gospel into Russia. Garwin McNeilus and his wife donated more than $20 million to expand the campus of Zaoksky Theological Seminary, build churches, and support the work there.

Thousands of others made smaller sacrificial donations. Several conferences and unions in North America got involved. The North Pacific Union created a program called "Operation Bearhug," which sponsored members from its territory who wanted to go to Russia and become engaged in public evangelism, the building of churches, and the distribution of literature.

Following the presentation of the first full report from this area for seventy years, world delegates to the 1990 General Conference session in Indianapolis, Indiana, gave a standing ovation to the fifty-five members (thirty-six official delegates, three guests, and sixteen musicians) from the Soviet Division. It was a very historic and emotional moment. The action of the 1989 Annual Council to make the Soviet Division the eleventh division of the church had no problem being officially approved by the delegates.

Members who visited the new division and participated in an evangelistic crusade or distributed literature came back home inspired and encouraged to see how the Lord was blessing.

Elder J. R. Spangler put it this way, "Try to imagine your feelings if you found a gigantic building with 285 million people and all of the doors and windows have been closed for 70 years. Suddenly the doors and windows fly open and the precious people inside stretch out their hands and hearts for political, economic, and, above all, spiritual help.

"This graphic portrayal of the Union of Soviet Socialist Republic superpower is not overdrawn." And then Elder Spangler told readers about an evangelistic meeting he conducted in Moscow. "Without any financial aid from other sources, the Moscow church under the leadership of their pastor, Paul Kulakov, rented a lovely three-year-old 1,250-seat cultural palace. Leaders printed posters and sold tickets for two and four rubles each. This was the first evangelistic meeting I ever conducted where people bought tickets to attend. One leader said that if the meetings were free, the people would not consider them worth coming to. The plan worked. The meetings began Friday night, October 12, and by Sunday evening, October 14, the place was packed.

"The evangelistic budget included expenses of the Chamber Choir of Seventh-day Adventists, composed of musicians from across the nation. Some of the choir members took vacation time from work to participate in this public series.

"The weekend meetings in the Cathedral Center format were unusual. Our choir presented a 30-minute outstanding musical program, singing from an experience of oppression, persecution, and suffering. The harmony and beauty of the presentations made it difficult to keep the tears back. Following the music, translator Michael Kulakov, Jr., and I made a 45-minute presentation of the gospel and prophetic themes.

"A 30-minute intermission gave people time to purchase Bibles, religious books, and records. At times people almost fought over who would get a Bible! The program was concluded with more choir renditions and a 20-minute appeal.

"The response was overwhelming. The eagerness to learn more of God and His ways gave a sense of fulfillment to us. What a delight to preach to precious souls who are eager to hear the Word of the Lord."[295]

At the 1991 Annual Council the division was renamed. "The former USSR Division, which was newly organized and recognized at the 1990 General Conference session in Indianapolis, was re-named as the Euro-Asia Division [ESD] by the 1991 Annual Council that was held in Perth, Australia, in October.

"This change comes as a result of recent political events in the territories that had formerly comprised the USSR. The new name more accurately describes the geographical location of this division, rather than using the political terminologies of the past.

"Covering the large continent, which includes both East European and Asian territories the Euro-Asia Division serves a population of 300 million people and comprises the five unions that existed in the former USSR."[296]

Associate Secretary of GC

Ted and Nancy were still in Africa while all of this was happening in the Soviet Division. They returned to attend the General Conference session in 1990, and Ted was asked to be an associate secretary of the General Conference. He accepted and the family moved to Maryland. In this new position he was in charge of overseeing the Africa-Indian Ocean Division, the same division he had served in, as well as being the liaison with SUD, the Southern-Asian Division and EUD, the Euro-Africa Division. While he was serving in this post at the General Conference, he received a request to become the president of ESD, the Euro-Asia Division, the former Soviet Division.

They wrestled with the decision because they thought they were home for a while now that their three girls were approaching academy age. Finally, they decided to go because they felt the Lord was leading.

Arrangements were made for Nancy and Ted Wilson, Gaspar and May Ellen Colon, Juan and Belkis Prestol, and Karen and Mike Porter to study Russian in 2D12, a large room at the General Conference headquarters. "It was six to seven hours a day, every day of the week for about four months," said Gaspar Colon. "Russian was a difficult language, but all of us had studied languages before and knew several languages. It required more effort than French or German. By the time we were ready to pack up and go we could understand it and were slightly conversant in Russian. We got immersed in it when we got there."

"The Russian people are correctly proud of their language," said Juan Prestol who went over as the treasurer of the division, "and when you speak publicly, officially, and you don't speak properly, they don't feel that comfortable. They feel better if you have a good translator. On a one-to-one-basis they love it when you talk to them in Russian. They welcomed that. Those are wonderful gestures that they really appreciate. So for me those seven hours a day all summer were worth it."

Highly Committed

"It was one of the toughest jobs we had tackled but one of the most rewarding. It was very hard to do anything there at that time. Some of the infrastructure of the country was challenging; telephone calls, travel, living conditions, food, all were difficult. It was a very challenging time in Russia because the Soviet system had collapsed. The economic situation was very challenging also," said Ted. "The Lord gave us wonderful opportunities."

The *Adventist Review* commented on their plans. "'Church leaders in the Euro-Asia Division are planning to have 158 evangelistic meetings this year conducted by expatriate evangelists,' says Ted N. C. Wilson, division president. 'Another 120 meetings will be conducted by national pastors.'"[297]

The Division voted to launch an outreach program in public schools. "'Thousands of schools are requesting moral and religious education to be taught by church and other groups,' says Wilson. 'We're excited about the prospects.' The effort will be financed by contributions from Adventists in Gentry, Arkansas."[298]

Ted kept this evangelistic momentum going and also stabilized a number of the institutions that had been started there prior to his arrival. He provided guidance to Zaoksky Theological Seminary, which later became a university, and the Source of Life Publishing House, and the Voice of Hope Media Center.

"We also did considerable reorganization of the field in dividing the Russian Union into two unions because the Russian Union was covering eleven time zones. (In the USA we only have four time zones). So we created the East Russian Union Mission and the West Russian Union Conference," Ted said. "Since that time they have divided things even more. We also created a unit that took in the Caucasus countries, and created the Caucasus Mission because of some of the challenges with the systems and relationships.

"We had a development and construction service in the first two years or so which helped to build, with some very fine donations from the General Conference and individuals, hundreds of churches. This development and construction service was run by an Australian who spoke Russian, Peter Koolik, and some others who assisted him, and it was an incredible blessing because property at that time was absolutely so inexpensive, providing many opportunities to purchase and renovate buildings or build new churches. There was a window of time that we could do many things and probably much more should have been done.

"We also developed leaders. We used to have leadership meetings with our voted leaders and training sessions for all the people. I remember we had two very large 'administrative and departmental leadership councils,' and we would spend the whole week with all these people from all over the division to help them understand what it meant to be a church administrator or departmental director, explaining to them how the church works. I spent time personally with the leaders of the church at other times as well maybe taking a half a day or a day going through key case studies that we put together. A lot of leadership development was taking place. That helped to set the foundation because the church had been separated for decades from the organized church in the world field. It was one of the biggest challenges to try to help reestablish a normal church, a regular church organizational structure and relationship."

Another very big item the Lord helped Ted Wilson with was the establishment of a representative division office in Moscow. They had looked at many, many properties. Some had wanted to find something outside of Moscow with a more country atmosphere. There were several things that made it very difficult. Property ownership was very unclear at that time. Records and titles were all very nebulous. Another problem was that very few of the workers had cars, and they were dependent on public transportation. If they had gone too far out, it would've made it more difficult for the workers to access. And there was also a perception that Adventists needed to be in the city.

Eventually, they were able to find a three-story, partially-completed kindergarten building on the northeastern edge of Moscow near Ring Road, which encircled the city and gave access to major airports. The president of the country had ordered that no kindergartens were to be sold to anybody. But since this had never been used as a kindergarten, the Lord worked a miracle and allowed the building to be sold to the Adventists. The property was in a residential neighborhood. It was just a shell with very few interior walls and in a great state of disrepair. After removing more than thirty truckloads of rubbish from the site, the heating system was repaired, and walls were constructed on the inside. Peter Koolik selected some Australian contract supervisors who assisted many specialized tradespeople from Moldova, Uzebekistan, and other places in the Euro-Asia Division.

Workers stayed in cramped living quarters in a nearby school building leased for that purpose. A temporary kitchen was provided, and three Ukrainian wives provided all the meals. The building supplies were difficult to obtain, and the antiquated building equipment often broke down. One morning eleven police with bulletproof vests and automatic weapons were there to meet the workers as they arrived. The workers were told that if they tried to get away they would be shot. The militia asked to see their passports and residency permits, and nine of the workers were taken to jail and put in a 9'x12' cell. The ceiling sagged, blood stained the floor, and the smell of urine permeated the place. The workers prayed for their release, and by lunchtime, after paying a substantial sum of money, they were released.

The bureaucracy was unbelievable. Permits were required from more than fifteen government departments. A fourth floor was added that provided twelve to fourteen apartments and guest rooms for division employees and visitors. On March 22, 1995, the official certificate of title and deed for the new division office was signed.[299]

Schooling for the Children

Bradley Booth and his wife, Ruthi, from Cedar Rapids, Iowa, were asked to come to Russia to teach the children. An elementary education major, Brad developed into a creative teacher and principal when he returned to his home state of Iowa after graduating from Union College.

The union paper shared several creative hands-on projects that Brad and his students participated in while he was their teacher. One showed him grinding sprouted wheat to put into bread, a project that raised more than $3,000 for the school. Another article showed a "rockathon" where the students secured pledges toward each hour they would activate rocking chairs. The rockathon along with a one-day-a-week bakery project directed by Ruthi Booth raised funds to purchase a cassette recorder and some needed gymnastic equipment.[300] In 1988 this creative husband-and-wife team were contacted to go to the Ivory Coast to start a special school for the children of the expatriate workers. Later they would be called to Russia to teach the children.

Brad tells the story. "My wife, Ruthi, was the other teacher in this two teacher school. We soon found out that we couldn't leave our little kids at home. So then Ruthi stayed home, and we got a student task force person to serve as a teacher. But soon our kids were big enough to join us, and she became one of the teachers again. In Abidjan the school operated in a little church in Deux Plateaux (the two levels). The kids rode to the school in a van. Classes went from 7:30 in the morning to 12:30 in the afternoon every day, and then they went home for a two-hour siesta. Grades 5 to 8 would come back from 2:30 until 4:30 in the afternoon.

"There were about twenty kids in grades one through twelve. I was used to doing multi-grades. I was determined to give the kids a comparable education as to what they would get in the States. I even brought the Iowa test of basic skills series with me, and I tested them every year. Those kids were smart. Their parents were all professionals and dedicated Christians, and that's where it starts. It seemed like every kid was a genius. They didn't have TVs and no video games over there, and it was much easier for them to focus. I did a lot of very innovative stuff so that made school fun. Most of the kids were a grade or two grades ahead of where they were supposed to be at that age. Many of the children tested at the college level–grade fourteen–in the seventh and eighth grade. They just were very, very good.

Highly Committed

"One year we carved a full-sized wooden skeleton for science class. Another year we painted a twenty-five-foot wall mural of heaven. We designed it, and the children decided what they wanted in heaven, and I helped them paint it. With the skeleton everything was to scale. All the bones were in it. I don't know if you have ever seen the invisible man, a little see-through thing. We took the skeleton out and measured everything to scale and built a skeleton that was six-foot tall. We called him Dr. Bones. I still have that skeleton. My daughter said I can't throw it away. He's part of history. When my son and daughter got bigger and attended class, Dr. Bones was in their class, also.

"I taught all the subjects, and my specialty was contract teaching. I had to make special times for all the kids for all the subjects. I wanted them to have some control of their learning. I gave them all a one-sheet contract, which I put inside their folder for every subject, and every day something about that subject was on that sheet. Many of the subjects we did together like Bible.

"Let me say a little bit about the Wilson girls' personalities. Emilie, the oldest, was the quiet one. She was the bookworm, pretty serious. A sweet girl. Elizabeth, the second oldest, was busting out all over the place. Very animated. Elizabeth was the gregarious, vivacious, sanguine one. She was kind of a leader. Always getting everybody energized to do whatever we had to do. The youngest one, Catherine, followed the typical pattern for a third child. She was the creative one. She could create something out of nothing. She was independent in a quiet way and very creative. I was always impressed with her.

"One of Elizabeth's specialties was Christmas programs and talent shows. One year we did a Christmas play. We wanted to do something different. She came up with the idea of Herod's court. She was to be Herod's wife. And she greeted the people and the wise men when they came in. The show was quite good. We were never satisfied to do run-of-the-mill kinds of things. We had five languages in the classroom. So we just wrote into the script the parts that were in different languages.

"When Ted got the call to go to Russia, the family wasn't really that anxious to go. But the parents said, 'If we get Bradley Booth to go and teach the school, will you be interested?' The girls thought they might want to do that since they had had so much fun in Abidjan. We had nothing to start our school in Russia. I had to bring everything with me down to plywood, books, chemistry and experimental equipment for all of the sciences, and textbooks, computers. They didn't have anything over there. About three days before school started, I was running around trying to find carpet for the floor. I couldn't find any. They didn't have any desks. I went to a public school there, the Russian school, and bought them for a dollar apiece. I was surprised the preceptrice let them go at all and then so cheaply.

"The school was at the division office. We had many of the same families that were in Abidjan: the Colons, Wilsons. The Bowers and Porters joined us in Russia. We were renting an office building, which was zoned for green. Blue buildings were for retail stores. White buildings were for residences. Green was for business, I believe. We weren't supposed to be in there. It wasn't zoned for a school. I remember one time they came to my classroom and said, 'How would you like to go on a field trip today?' I said, 'Please, we have work to do.' They said, 'The authorities are coming to inspect the school today, and we're not supposed to have a school in here.' It was just another way the government collected money. So they took us for a field trip on that day.

"The organization of that school in Russia was pretty much the same as in Abidjan. We had five high school kids who were doing great. I didn't have to spend as much time with them as I did with the others. But algebra was a tough class. Everyone struggled with algebra and geometry. We usually did this one together. One year the eighth grade class wanted to take a trip to Turkey. We worked it out. They did some very outstanding things. They were always doing some very innovative things. About four boys used the Griggs University Home study course as their guide."

Regarding his service in the Euro-Asia Division, Ted Wilson feels that "one of the biggest things that I think we were able to do with God's power was to help regularize Christian stewardship practices and treasury receipting practices so that people would feel comfortable about their money. Once we began to proceed with a stewardship educational program, we saw God's incredible blessing on the church because of it. And when all of these regular accounting and accountability procedures were put into place and when we helped people understand the biblical principles of stewardship, of ownership of our time and our talent and abilities and our resources, the Lord just blessed incredibly, and tithes shot up so dramatically.

"One of the greatest challenges was to try to help our pastors become fully supported by the church as opposed to the former practice of just helping them out and expecting them to have another full-time job. So that really blessed incredibly, and we had received a gift, a donation from the people in the United States, and we used part of it to augment the salary. We asked that a stewardship director be appointed in every conference and in every union and of course we had one at the division. We would pay the salary of that full-time stewardship director at every union level and every conference level for two years from the division, and then they would have to phase things in after that. Each local organization was responsible for travel for their stewardship person. With that kind of very strong approach and God's enormous blessing, we saw tithes and offerings increased incredibly. Especially tithes, and we just praise the Lord for that. There were a lot of things, wonderful things and many, many miracles that took place."

Morning Consecration

When asked if he still kept Ellen White's quotation in his Bible, Ted responded, "Yes, I still keep her quotation which my father sent to me—'Consecrate yourselves to God in the morning'—in my main preaching Bible. I always carry with me a small pocket Bible and my daytimer. I've carried the daytimer since 1977. Nick Satlemajer and I went to a time management seminar in New Jersey when we were working with Metro Ministries back in 1977. It was run by Ted Engstrom and Ed Dayton. They were some of the driving forces behind World Vision, and they offered this course for pastors and others.

"It was an extremely helpful seminar, and out of that came this Daytimer, and I have used it ever since. Most people have moved to some form of digitized calendars, iPhones and so forth. The daytimer has proved to be very helpful to me. I use my computer and phone regularly. But I can be speedier with my appointments by using this handwritten calendar and looking at it all at the same time. You can't flip back and forth with these computerized programs as fast as I can with the handwritten daytimer. To look at an entire month and then check on the dates gives me a certain satisfaction. I know exactly what I need to have to make plans for the future. When I can't look at a complete month like that, I feel uneasy. Plus, you don't have to worry about it running out of electricity."

Juan Prestol, his treasurer in Russia, talks about those two items. "There are two things that are always in Ted's pocket—one is a tiny Bible and the second one is the daytimer. When he pulls out the daytimer you can see when he flips the pages that it is full of notes, some in black and some in red. I used to joke about that with him. I would say I would like to know why when you take notes some things are in black and some things you write are in red. One day you're going to tell me the meaning of the red and the black.

"He uses the daily page calendar. I never used the daily page. I used the weekly or the little monthly calendar. He is a great note taker. He takes copious notes, which helps him remember details. To me that makes all the difference, because when I go back after weeks and months and I begin with him on a conversation, it's all fresh in his mind. And that way his work is much easier. He's also a network person. His antenna is 360, and he connects with people of Europe, Africa, Latin America, the United States, China with the same kind of ease."

The Annual Spring Council, which met in April 1996, established and voted into operation an Office of Volunteerism. It nominated Ted N. C. Wilson as its first director. It seemed at first that the president of the Euro-Asia Division would accept this position. The Wilson girls were getting older, and one was ready for college. The May 1, 1996, General Conference Committee minutes recorded that "Ted N. C. Wilson has declined his election as Associate Secretary and Director of the Center for volunteerism."[301]

Robert Kinney who had been voted in as the sixteenth president at a specially called meeting of the Review and Herald board indicated his desire to retire.[302] The board met quickly and elected Ted N. C. Wilson as the seventeenth president of the Adventist church's oldest and largest publishing house, and he accepted the job.

In the November 6, 1996, year-end meeting Ted N. C. Wilson and Bob Kyte, president of the Pacific Press Publishing Association, presented the challenge of the declining magazine subscriptions published by the two houses. In his overhead presentation, Ted and Kyte solicited suggestions from the group as to how they could meet this challenge. Some magazines would be merged and some would be eliminated. Appreciation was expressed to presidents of both publishing houses for the production of Net 96 materials. "The employees of both houses felt they were directly involved in Net 96 since the printing went through their presses."[303]

Review Open House

Ted wanted the community and the church to know more about the church's oldest institution, and he initiated an open house to bring these publics onto his turf. "More than 1,200 visitors from local communities and surrounding states flocked to the Review and Herald to participate in the 150-year-old Adventist publishing company's first open house since its 1983 relocation to Hagerstown, Maryland.

"From guided tours and an art show to a 5K fun run, face painting, and giveaways, the open house greeted visitors with an endless variety of fun and educational activities to introduce them to the Review and Herald and its many Christian products.

"Beginning at 10:00 am, guided tours of the publishing house and manufacturing plant, conducted at five-minute intervals throughout the day, allowed some 750 visitors to follow the process books and magazines undergo as they're sent to press.

"Highlights of the tour included a display of several original paintings by renowned religious artist Harry Anderson, live demonstrations of an antique Linotype machine, and viewing of the massive four-color web presses in action.

"Crowds of bargain-hunting readers flooded the book sale to purchase discounted books and talk with authors....

"Outside, people bought vegetarian hot dogs and burgers and headed to the six yellow-and-white tents, where magazine editors offered activities ranging from blood pressure checks by *Vibrant Life* staff to a complementary color analysis at the *Women of Spirit* display....

"Event coordinator Bonnie Laing said, 'God blessed our efforts. People used to drive by this place every day on their way to work and had no idea what's going on here.'

"'The purpose of our open house is to increase community awareness and church awareness,' added Review and Herald president Ted N. C. Wilson. 'Our next Open House will be September 13, 1998.'"[304]

The Wilson family was happy to move back to their house in Maryland. The one-hour commute to Hagerstown gave Ted a great deal of time to think and plan. The publishing work had gone through some real challenging times. The impact of electronics and e-books had lessened the need and demand for printed materials. Ted tried to refine things as much as possible to save money. He had to reduce the workforce, which was not easy, and also reduce inventory

"We paid tithe on our profits. We saw God's blessings in many ways. We didn't see any phenomenal jumps in our income, but we felt we should do that and we did. In the distant past institutions used to tithe. I don't know about the Review itself. I suspect it may have. But somewhere along the line it was deemed that institutions were a part of the church and didn't really have to contribute tithe, but I felt convicted that that's what we ought to do. So that's what we did. We were in the black at least for one year, but it was not an easy thing. You have a lot of equipment challenges and needs. Healthcare becomes very expensive.

"We did have the George King Institute, which helped train young people for literature evangelism. That was a blessing, but after a while we had to phase that out because of financial challenges. We also tried to have some promotional activities to help increase our sales and visibility. The race, which originated with the open house, still goes on. I believe that's the only thing that's left.

"At Annual Council time we rented a bus that took interested delegates up to the Review. We served them a meal, took them on a tour, and gave them books usually from inventory that needed to be written down. It was an opportunity to share the Review.

"My work at the Review was a strong learning experience for me. I had never been in charge of an institution, and certainly not a publishing house. It gave me real insights on how an institution works and how to deal with certain challenges and problems. I did also try to get around the publishing house about once a week. I just walked through and visited the workers, greeting them, encouraging them, picking up any problems or challenges.

"I would spend time working in different departments. I went out to press rooms assisting as I could and would help in various places. I did not want to disrupt their work but at least be part of their setting. I worked in the bindery, in shipping, and I even got to drive the big lawnmower that we had. It was a huge tractor with an enclosed cabin. I think they were holding their breath because I could have had an accident, but everything came out fine. I tried to become part of different areas to help them know that we were interested in their work and trying to assist in any way I could."

On September 6, the Review and Herald Publishing Association board of directors named Robert S. Smith its eighteenth president. Smith replaced Ted Wilson who, after four years as president, moved to the General Conference as a general vice president. At 65, Smith was the first African American president for the 150-year-old publishing house.

C. D. Brooks comments again on the work Ted Wilson did as vice president at the GC. "I remember my father-in-law, Elder John Wagner, talking about good men at the General Conference, and he named Elder Neal Wilson's father, Nathaniel, as one of them. So you get the idea that these traits can flow through the DNA, the bloodline, or they are taught to the family members. I have seen in Ted some of what I saw in his dad, Neal, and what my father-in-law saw in his grandfather. And I'm not surprised at that. Let me give you a real-life experience.

"We had a very fine man who passed away. He worked for the church when he died. His family, of course, was broken and distressed. He had children and a lovely wife. Pastor Al Johnson was in charge of making the funeral arrangements, and his desire was to have the service in the General Conference auditorium. Pastor Johnson had already gotten permission to do it there. All of a sudden, while five of us were in his office putting it together, Pastor Johnson got a call, and we were told that a new policy had been implemented, and we couldn't use the auditorium. The word had already been sent out that the service was going to take place in the GC auditorium. This change would have brought great confusion to the widow in her bereavement.

Highly Committed

"I made a suggestion, 'Call Ted Wilson.' I was there when Pastor Johnson called him and explained the problem to Pastor Wilson. Wilson's response was, 'Don't do anything until I get back to you.' In about a half an hour the phone rang, and it was Ted. He said, 'Al, the service will be held in the auditorium.' And it was. How do I know? I was there. I thought about that seriously. There are some men who are just good men, and there are things we can pass along to our children if we would do what the Lord says."

On November 3, 2009, after the required posting, by order of the Circuit Court for Montgomery County, Domestic System, "Ted" was added officially to his name. His family and friends had called him Ted for so long that no one really knew him as Norman. For legal and personal reasons, he would now officially be Ted N. C. Wilson.

Ted and Nancy with their daughters "Emilie, Elizabeth and Catherine when they were serving as missionaries in Abidjan, Ivory Coast.

Abidjan, Russia, and the Review

During the 1990s the Wilson family served in Moscow, Russia, where Ted was president of the ESD Division.

Chapter Fifteen

Ted N. C. Wilson: World Church President

"Anyone can be great because anyone can serve." Church sign

Some people were beginning to speculate. The fifty-ninth General Conference session to be held in Atlanta, Georgia, in 2010 was still in the distant future, but already there was a buzz in the air. Church members knew that the incumbent president, Jan Paulsen, would be about 75 years old at that session. Questions swirled. Would he want to serve again? Would they reelect him at that age? If he retired, who would replace him?

Adventist Church governance is different from national politics. With Adventist elections there are no surveys. No gallop or quinnipiac polls can be taken to see who the favorite is. With church leadership no candidate can declare himself the most qualified in the organization and start campaigning for the presidency. Voicing such a boastful conviction, even if true, would immediately disqualify that person. There are no organized Adventist groups such as the Democratic, Republican, or independent parties that promote their candidate.

In American politics the candidate with the most money and the greatest following has an advantage in the power struggle. Money can acquaint people with a candidate's platform, abilities, and vision for the nation. Debates go on ad infinitum until one candidate in each party prevails and is ready to do battle with the candidate of the other party. Then the debating process begins all over again. This doesn't happen in the Adventist Church.

The Adventist election system is quiet, calm, and very spiritual. It is usually finished in a few hours. There is no power struggle for the presidency of the world church. Leaders who have proven themselves by serving as chief officer of a division or a vice president at the General Conference are usually considered first. It is rare for a pastor of a local church, no matter how effective his leadership has been, to rise to this level of leadership directly. Slowly over time, a leader must gain experience and prove himself spiritually and administratively by serving in different posts.

As the session approached, colleagues and workers clustered in little groups at lunchtime and after meetings to discuss this burning issue. Who would be the next GC president?

It would have been inappropriate for the *Adventist Review,* the official voice of the Seventh-day Adventist Church, to make predictions, but several years before the fifty-ninth session David Newman wrote an article in *Adventist Today*, an independent magazine, hypothesizing about the next president. "At the last General Conference Session in 2005, where Paulsen was up for re-election, four candidates were presented to the nominating committee for consideration. After the first round of balloting, Jere Patzer and Lowell Cooper dropped out. In the next round, Wilson received 91 votes to Paulsen's 98 with seven people absent or abstaining. The vote revealed that Wilson had a lot of support from the world field....

"In preparing for this article, I learned that three names surface more often than others in respect to who the next president might be: Lowell Cooper, Pardon Kandanga Mwansa, and Ted N. C. Wilson. All are general vice presidents of the General Conference....

"Ted Wilson comes from the United States, Lowell Cooper from Canada, and Pardon Mwansa from Zambia, Africa. Currently the membership of the Adventist Church in North America is 6.8 percent of the world membership. The membership of the Church in Africa is 33.9 percent of the world membership.... With North America making up less than 7 percent of the world membership, it is time for a non-North American to lead the world church."[305]

All thirteen divisions of Adventism make arrangements to send delegates to the church's largest meeting, which is convened every five years to select the person who will lead the flock for the ensuing quinquennium. Representation based on membership allows delegates from every nation where there is a church to gather together for their input. "The direction our church is headed is being steered not by a single individual (or a single country), but by a representative community of believers."[306]

After the delegates arrive, they first meet together as a division group to "caucus" or select the ones who will be a part of the 246-member nominating committee. It is in the nominating committee that the real work of selection is done. Many names are presented to the nominating committee, but only one name is placed before the session delegates on the floor to vote upon.

Late Thursday afternoon, June 24, 2010, the General Conference session officially began, and the thirteen world divisions each met together to select the members who would represent their part of the world on the nominating committee. The evening session began with Dr. Ella Simmons, the first woman to serve as a GC vice president, chairing the session. The delegates voted to approve the names that were brought from the caucuses to be on the nominating committee.

The main item of business that Thursday evening was the incumbent president's report. Paulsen summarized his activities during the past five years partly through a video documentary and partly through a sermon. He addressed the question about his retirement at the end of his speech. "I have not given an answer," he said to the delegates.

Paulsen indicated that he had been praying over the matter for some time. "If some of you get a word from the Lord in the next day or so, please let me know," he said with a smile. "Maybe this is the time to leave. We have struggled with this. We are not ready to give an answer at this very moment." Many felt that he was suggesting that he would be open to reelection should the possibility arise.

Room C304 was tucked away in a distant hallway on the top level of the sprawling Georgia World Congress Center. It was here that the nominating committee met behind closed doors to undertake the selection of the world church president on Friday morning, June 25.

"Before being allowed entry into the room, committee members representing all 13 world church regions lined up in single file to surrender their cell phones to a General Conference employee, who placed each device into its own clear plastic bag, which remained outside the hall.

"Acknowledging the age of rapid-fire texting, e-mailing, and Tweeting, the committee agreed during a late-night organizational meeting June 24 to ban phones.... After turning in their phones, members picked up their paper name tags and handed them to a volunteer security officer at the door, who then checked the names with the participants' badges before finally letting them into the room. Inside, members sat at tables with binders and handheld wireless devices to record their votes electronically."[307]

Several names were discussed. When the committee had narrowed it down to just a few, they had prayer and implored the Holy Spirit to guide them in their selection. After more prayer and discussion, the name of Ted N. C. Wilson was finally settled on. The mantle of leadership would fall on his shoulders if the main body approved of the nominating committee's choice.

Highly Committed

"Committee leaders then left the room and walked to the cavernous Georgia Dome, where they informed current president Jan Paulsen of the selection. The leadership then met in private with Wilson, who indicated he would accept if the nomination was approved by the session delegates.

"A security detail then escorted Wilson, Chairman Kyte, and other committee leaders to the backstage area of the platform.

"Wilson's name was brought before hundreds of delegates ..." sitting on the convention floor.[308]

The *Adventist Review* documents what happened next:

"ROBERT KYTE: Mr. Chairman, delegates and guests, it's a pleasure to be here this morning on behalf of the Nominating Committee, which represents each of you as delegates to this session. The meeting was formally organized last night, when I was selected to serve as chairman. I'm pleased to have a very good team working with me in the leadership of the committee. To my right is Dr. Delbert Baker, president of Oakwood University. Cindy Tutsch, an associate director for the Ellen G. White Estate, is the secretary for the committee, and Ismael Castillo, the president of Montemorelos University, is the assistant secretary for the Nominating Committee. Our committee convened this morning, and after devotions and prayers we felt led by the Spirit as we discussed the candidates for the office of president of the General Conference. We are here to submit a report on that one position, and Cindy Tutsch, our secretary, will make that presentation.

"CYNTHIA TUTSCH: Mr. Chair, for president of the Seventh-day Adventist World Church, the Nominating Committee presents the name of Elder Ted Wilson to serve for the next term of office. I so move.

"ARMANDO MIRANDA [chair of the business session]: We have a motion, and it has been seconded. Any comments or questions? So it seems to me that we are ready to proceed. All in favor, please take your yellow cards and lift them. Thank you. Opposed, the same sign. [A few yellow cards went up.] It is carried. Thank you very much. We would like to welcome Elder Ted Wilson as the General Conference president. Elder Ted Wilson and Mrs. Wilson. [They were received with a standing ovation.]

"TED N. C. WILSON: Nancy and I are deeply honored and humbled. We are humbled beyond words at the confidence and the encouragement of our people. This is not just a regular organization. This is not just another denomination. This is God's remnant church. It is that which He has supreme regard for, and to be requested to serve as a servant leader is something that truly brings us to our knees. I know personally that I do not know everything, I do not have the answers for everything, and so we must seek the wisdom of counselors; we must, as Scripture says, fall on our knees before the Lord and ask for wisdom; we must seek counsel in the holy Word of God; and we must follow the counsel of the Spirit of Prophecy. And let me tell you, brothers and sisters, the Spirit of Prophecy is one of the greatest gifts God has given to the Seventh-day Adventist Church. It is applicable not only for the past but for the present and for the future, for, brothers and sisters, we are going home soon.

"Each of you in your own languages knows that precious phrase 'Jesus is coming soon.' I hope to learn it in many different languages.

"Jesus is coming soon. And this church needs, beyond anything else, to fall on its knees, to ask for God's guidance, to recognize that we need to humble ourselves, to ask for forgiveness from the Lord, to ask the Holy Spirit to bring us revival and reformation, so that the latter rain will fall and the work will go forward in a powerful way. In the book *Selected Messages*, book 1, page 121, the servant of the Lord says that our greatest need is a revival of true godliness, and that to seek this should be our first work. And I pledge by God's grace that we will work together to humble ourselves personally, and corporately, to ask the Lord to lead us into the kingdom. I think of a beautiful text that is one of my favorites, Joel 2:21: 'Fear not, O land; be glad and rejoice: for the Lord will do great things.' And I want to claim that for each of us here at the fifty-ninth session of the

General Conference. Don't be afraid for the future. Don't shrink back from the task God has given to us—the proclamation of the three angels' messages of Revelation 14—that we are a called-out people. Revelation 12:17 tells us who we are. Know who you are! By God's grace, let us move forward under the direction of the Holy Spirit as we humbly bow before Him.

"And on behalf of Nancy, my precious wife, and me—let me tell you, wives are so important. Our spouses are so important. This wonderful woman is a spiritual backbone for me. She loves the Lord. She loves the Bible. She loves the Spirit of Prophecy. And I honor her today. And I thank God for her.

"We cannot lead in any way without the united camaraderie of each of you. And so I ask that you will join us in a special humbling of ourselves as we seek God's guidance and revival and reformation in our own lives and in the Seventh-day Adventist Church so that we can truly see God do great things.

"I also want to add a word of deep appreciation for those who have been serving during this past quinquennium. I want to pay honor and tribute to Elder Paulsen and to those who have associated with him. There will be opportunity to say additional words in the future, but it is always good to show appreciation for those things that have happened that will uplift the church. So by God's grace we will fulfill the task that you have assigned, and we will do it with humility, and I ask and covet your prayers for this precious, precious church and for the mission that it has and for the task that you have assigned to us. Thank you very much."[309]

Post Election

Things happened fast after his election. Edwin Garcia summed it up. "U.S. President Barack Obama enjoyed a 77-day transition period from election to inauguration. Pacific Union College president Heather J. Knight took 81 days to prepare for her new job.

"But when Pastor Ted N. C. Wilson was elected leader ... on Friday, he was given less than two hours to leave his old job and settle into the new one ... The speedy time frame may seem incredibly brief for a job with such a significant responsibility, but it's also part of a well-established practice at every General Conference session, and church officials are confident that the process works.

"Presidents aren't the only ones who undergo a quick transition. Dozens of church leaders elected during the 10-day session ... start their new jobs—or continue in their positions, in the case of incumbents—effective immediately after a vote of the delegates.

"But nowhere is the transition more fast-paced than in the presidency, where the newly elected leader's life changes dramatically in a matter of minutes.

"He's instantly assigned a security detail that zips him from place to place, sometimes through secret passages to avoid crowds. He's suddenly the top leader at the early-morning planning meeting where he was merely a participant the day before. He gets to exert influence over the Nominating Committee, which selects the leaders who work with him for the next five years.

"Oh, and if there's time, his scheduler carves out as many appointments as possible with former president Jan Paulsen to help ease the transition during Wilson's first whirlwind week in office.

"'Everything moves at warp speed, oh my, it's unbelievable,' said former president Robert S. Folkenberg.

"'It's sensory overload, spiritual overload, and information overload,' added Folkenberg, the church's top leader from 1990 to 1999, who recalled how he shifted from being Carolina Conference president to General Conference president in a matter of minutes.

"Those who know Wilson say he's up to the challenge, thanks to his background and experience ...

"'He is pretty well acquainted with some of the issues that will have to be dealt with,' said Orville D. Parchment, assistant to President Paulsen since 2003, and, as of the end of June, the assistant to President Wilson.

Highly Committed

"The new General Conference president would wake up before sunrise for his personal devotions, and then would attend the 6:45 a.m. Steering Committee meeting, where he'd sit at the head of a rectangular conference table, surrounded by vice presidents and other officers who help set the session agenda for the day....

"After the morning gathering, Wilson would slip into back-to-back meetings, some of them in a temporary, cubicle-paneled office that was assembled for him in the Georgia World Congress Center, which is nearly identical to an office from where the soon-to-retire Paulsen worked across the hall.

"It was not uncommon for Wilson to attend late-night meetings after the evening program in the Georgia Dome, which typically let out after 9:00 p.m.

"After the session concluded, Wilson returned to Silver Spring, Maryland, and moved into the president's office about 40 feet down the hall from his previous office.

"His invitation calendar would begin to fill. And fast.

"'The new president will start taking appointments, and his appointments in a little while—I would say within a month or two—will stretch into two, three years,' Parchment said. 'There's no honeymoon period.'"[310]

Following a long-established tradition the newly elected president presented the sermon on the second Sabbath to the 70,000 plus attendees in Atlanta's Georgia Dome.

Shortly after Ted Wilson's (TW) election, Pat Humphrey (PH), associate communication director for the Southwestern Union and associate editor of the *Record*, talked with the new president about his vision for the church. Following are some excerpts from that conversation.

"PH: What is your vision for the church? What do you want to see happen in this church under your leadership?

"TW: One of the greatest challenges that we face is to try to humble ourselves before the Lord. We must ask the Lord to bring us into a condition where we are revived, and then allow a true reformation in our lives to set the stage for the latter rain. The Spirit of Prophecy has told us that our greatest need is a revival of true godliness. That's our greatest need! So I think that probably is highest on my agenda for the church itself.

"When it comes to the way we do our mission outreach, one of the greatest challenges that we face is the use of media. How do we reach the millions of people in areas that are very difficult to penetrate? How do we use the Internet? How do we use television, radio, print media, and all these various facets of technical outreach? How do we reach—and this is one of the greatest challenges that we have—the 50 percent of the population of this world who now live in the large cities? How do we break into those cities? We're going to be giving strong emphasis to urban evangelism, urban ministry, and how to work in these great cities.

"We also need to utilize the tremendous resource of our young people. I'm not just talking about putting them on committees and that kind of thing, which has been a source of concern on the floor and, certainly, there is a place for that. But you don't necessarily accomplish things in committees. The committees can help to guide, but you accomplish things out where the people are. And that's where young people shine the most. They are just full of energy, and they are willing to dedicate their lives, and we've got to harness that power in an even greater way. There are a lot of things we're going to be looking at. I have a long list, but I really hope that with the spiritual approach, the Holy Spirit will be able to set free the creative ideas that young people have, that women have, that men have, that everybody has, so that (together) we can finish this great work that God has entrusted to His people.

"PH: What are some of the other major challenges we are facing as the Seventh-day Adventist Church today?

"TW: I would say that one of the biggest challenges we're going to have is the discussion and dispute that is occurring now, and that will occur, on the authoritative voice of God in Scripture. (Dealing with the question of) Is the Word of God truly an authoritative source? Unfortunately, the tendency in much of the world theologically and, gladly, not that much in Adventist circles, is the tendency to use what is called higher criticism, where the individual is the arbiter as to what is inspired and what is not. Whereas the Spirit of Prophecy tells us that we are to read the Scripture as it is. When the Lord says He created the earth in six days and rested on the seventh day, that is a literal understanding and not some allegorical, figurative allusion. So I think attacks on the credibility of Scripture—the authoritative aspect of Scripture—is probably one of the most important situations that we will face.

"Another thing is the Spirit of Prophecy, which, I believe, is one of the greatest gifts God has given to the Seventh-day Adventist Church. We could not be a people as we are today if it were not for the Spirit of Prophecy. I would just appeal to people—because obviously, I am a great believer in the Spirit of Prophecy—to, rather than to criticize it or to ignore it, I would just urge them to read it and let the Holy Spirit speak to them as they read it. Read the *Testimonies,* books on health and education, and you will see that it is God-inspired. And, it's a blessing to the church.

"PH: What kind of progress are we making as a church in resolving some of the concerns people have expressed—such issues as the role of women, and youth in the church, and Creation?

"TW: I think we're making progress. Obviously, there will always be differences of opinion. And I would hope we would not get into highly divisive fractious fighting that will make people bitter, because that is counterproductive. I think one has to simply use the Word of God as the first line of understanding and defense. Let me put it this way. Our church started out with people coming together who had divergent views about various doctrinal ideas, and they simply prayed together; they knelt, they agonized with the Lord and as they did that, the Lord revealed, either through the ministry of Ellen White or the impact of the Holy Spirit, a more general consensus about a particular doctrine. And when we come together in a prayerful, respectful way, I believe the Holy Spirit, as Scripture says, will lead us into all truth. It doesn't mean, I suppose, that we will always all agree, but I just have the hope that as Jesus prayed in John 17 that His people might be one, that we will submit ourselves to the leading of the Holy Spirit so that truly we can become one.

"PH: How did you feel when you were asked to take the helm of the world church? Tell me about your leadership style and your philosophy of leadership.

"TW: Obviously, when I was told, I just felt this heaviness that almost smothers you. You realize that this is a job beyond any human ability, and fortunately, this is not a job that is only focused on the president. We have a committee system in our church. We do not have a presidential system. It is not just the 'CEO' who 'calls all the shots.' We work together in a collegial way. That responsibility is shared with other leaders and with other individuals who can help shoulder the burden. You don't know how reassuring it's been for me. I've received scores and scores and scores of e-mails, and practically the one thing that I hear from almost everybody is, 'We are praying for you.' And let me tell you, that is so reassuring and I need prayers more than anything else. I need the wisdom of God. I try to claim James 1:5 every morning to ask God for wisdom, because I don't have it. It's an incredible, humbling experience, and I cannot do it on my own and I covet your prayers.

"In terms of leadership style, I like to be rather informal. I like to get participation. I like to hear people's views. I like to come to a consensus. I believe in servant leadership. I like for people to feel that I'm accessible and that other leaders are accessible. I like to have a balanced approach in which we listen carefully to people, we are fair with people, and we don't brush people off. Leadership involves a lot of listening, a lot of praying, and then careful analysis and asking the Lord to guide us in the right way. And if we make a mistake, we shouldn't be too proud to say, 'Well, maybe we ought to try this way.' You need to be flexible and open, and in the long run, to realize that leadership really is to depend wholly on the Lord. I absolutely believe that. He will not leave us without direction. This is the object of His supreme regard—this precious church—and I have every confidence that God will give us the answers to the challenges we face."[311]

Ted N. C. Wilson is indeed a servant leader. He is quick to tackle big jobs and doesn't mind working unseen and silently behind the scenes. In addition to all of his other responsibilities at the session, he was chair of the music committee, which started operating years before the GC session of 2010 and continued all during the session. The job included finding an appropriate theme song, choosing hymns that would inspire the audience, arranging for the music for Sabbaths, planning for large choirs, orchestras, and other musical groups, organizing the mini concerts, and coordinating the lectures on church music.

There were five subcommittees that began screening the hundreds of different applicants who wanted to perform. "One of the highlights of the GC session is praising and glorifying God through music," Wilson told *Adventist Review*. "The plethora of international musicians from around the world is a wonderful blessing to the church."[312]

Ted Wilson left Atlanta with a growing vision of what needed to be done to "finish the work." His vision sharpened, and he began to implement his goals at the General Conference headquarters building. In his first address as president to the employees at the church's world headquarters on July 28, 2010, shortly after leaving Atlanta, he introduced his priorities for the denomination for the next five years. "The belief that Christians cannot 'hasten or delay' the Second Coming is a misconception, Wilson said. While the 'manufacture' of programs or activities at church headquarters cannot 'force' Christ's return, a 'revival of true godliness' and 'humble submission to God' among Christians can ... 'You are dedicated, educated, consecrated people' ... 'but if we're not praying in humility ... our talents are worth virtually nothing.'"[313]

He announced that he was setting up a Revival and Reformation Committee and urged the employees to join together in praying for the work of the Holy Spirit. He presented one of his favorite projects to the workers by challenging them to distribute Ellen White's book *The Great Controversy* to every household in the postal area surrounding the headquarters.

The response to his vision and to the book project was overwhelming. Employees donated more than $38,000—approximately 40 percent more than was needed—to fund the printing and mailing of *The Great Controversy* to the 22,000 homes in the 20904 zip code (Silver Spring, Maryland) in which the headquarters building was located. Money raised above the basic costs went toward sending copies of the book to the adjacent geographical areas.

In a follow-up e-mail after the launch of the project at the GC, President Ted Wilson wrote, "The Publishing Ministries Department has a plan to engage the whole church and all departments in launching a huge distribution of millions of copies of *The Great Controversy* around the world in 2012…. Our people are excited to distribute the book Ellen White said she wished was distributed above all [her] other books."[314]

After challenging the workers at the General Conference, Ted Wilson challenged the world fields to undertake a massive worldwide distribution of the book. In North America a nationwide effort is underway to distribute copies of the book to an estimated 116 million homes. Each paperback copy of *The Great Controversy* costs about $1.25 to print, package, and ship. When church members save the mailing expenses by personally giving the book to their neighbors and friends, the cost can be cut drastically. Each copy of *The Great Controversy* includes an invitation card for a Bible correspondence course, an unobtrusive way to encourage Bible study.

Ted Wilson's challenge was based on Revelation 18:1–"And after these things I saw another angel come down from heaven, having great power; and the earth was lightened with his glory"–that describes how God will illuminate the world with the gospel of Jesus Christ and on the admonition of Ellen White to give this book an unparalleled distribution: "*The Great Controversy* should be very widely circulated. It contains the story of the past, the present, and the future.... I am more anxious to see a wide circulation for this book than for any others I have written; for in *The Great Controversy*, the last message of warning to the world is given more distinctly than in any of my other books."[315]

Each division and their publishing houses were challenged to make plans for printing this book in large quantities and in the most inexpensive manner possible. It was recommended that the cost per volume not exceed U.S. $1.00 per copy to make it affordable for church members to purchase multiple copies. Each member was also encouraged to make the reading of the book a part of their personal study.

"'In 2011 we're encouraging all Adventist members to read it and become reacquainted with it,' stated DelbertW. Baker, a general vice president of the Seventh-day Adventist world church and chair of the Great Controversy Project Committee. 'But in 2012 and 2013 we want to distribute millions of copies around the world field.' Both Pacific Press and Review and Herald are working closely with the NAD for a national distribution program."[316]

The Great Hope

The South American Division set a goal to distribute 70 million copies of *The Great Hope*, an eleven-chapter abridged version of *The Great Controversy*. On October 29, 2011, hundreds of South American Adventists began a smaller distribution of what then developed into a massive distribution on March 24, 2012, when 25 million copies were distributed on that Sabbath across the division. They hope to distribute millions more during 2012 and 2013. The current total of what will be distributed worldwide during 2012 and 2013 by all thirteen divisions is about 175 million copies of various versions of the book. The Holy Spirit will lead many souls into the church because of the distribution of this inspired book.

Ted Wilson's next step was to bring his vision of revival and reformation to the leaders and representatives of the Adventist Church assembled at the world headquarters for the October 2010 Annual Council. The main item on the agenda was revival and reformation. Delegates shared how God had impacted their lives and how they longed to see Christ return. They prayed together and asked for an outpouring of the Holy Spirit and then voted an amazing document called "God's Promised Gift: An Urgent Appeal for Revival, Reformation, Discipleship, and Evangelism." Following are a few of the opening paragraphs of the document.

"We give thanks to our great and awesome God for His faithfulness and abundant blessings to His Church since its inception. The rapid worldwide expansion of His Church in both its membership and institutions is nothing short of a miracle of God. Although we praise Him for marvelously working to fulfill His purposes through His church, and thank Him for the godly leaders who have guided His people in the past, we humbly acknowledge that because of our human frailties even our best efforts are tainted by sin and in need of cleansing through the grace of Christ. We recognize that we have not always placed priority on seeking God through prayer and His Word for the outpouring of the Holy Spirit in latter-rain power. We humbly confess that in our personal lives, our administrative practices, and committee meetings we too often have labored in our own strength. Too often God's mission of saving a lost world has not taken first place in our hearts. At times in our busyness doing good things we have neglected the most important thing–knowing Him. Too often petty jealousies, ambitions, and fractured personal relationships have crowded out our longing for revival and reformation and caused us to labor in our human strength rather than in His divine power.

Highly Committed

"We accept the clear instruction of our Lord that 'the lapse of time has wrought no change in Christ's parting promise to send the Holy Spirit as His representative. It is not because of any restriction on the part of God that the riches of His grace do not flow earthward to men. If the fulfillment of the promise is not seen as it might be, it is because the promise is not appreciated as it should be. If all were willing, all would be filled with the Spirit' (*The Acts of the Apostles*, p. 50).

"We are confident that all heaven is waiting to pour out the Holy Spirit in infinite power for the finishing of God's work on earth. We acknowledge that the coming of Jesus has been delayed and that our Lord longed to come decades ago. We repent of our lukewarmness, our worldliness, and our limited passion for Christ and His mission. We sense Christ calling us to a deeper relationship with Him in prayer and Bible study and a more passionate commitment to share His last-day message with the world. We rejoice that 'it is the privilege of every Christian, not only to look for, but to hasten the coming of the Saviour' (*The Acts of the Apostles*, p. 600)....

"We especially recognize that God is going to use children and youth in this last mighty revival and encourage all of our young people to participate in seeking God for spiritual revival in their own lives and the empowerment of the Holy Spirit to share their faith with others.

"We appeal to each church member to unite with church leaders and millions of other Seventh-day Adventists seeking a deeper relationship with Jesus and the outpouring of the Holy Spirit at 7:00 each morning or evening, seven days a week. This is an urgent call to circle the globe with earnest intercession. This is a call to total commitment to Jesus and to experience the life-changing power of the Holy Spirit that our Lord is longing to give now.

"We believe that the purpose of the outpouring of the Holy Spirit in latter-rain power is to finish Christ's mission on earth so He can come quickly. Recognizing that our Lord will only pour out His Spirit in its fullness on a Church that has a passion for lost people, we determine to place and maintain revival, reformation, discipleship, and evangelism at the top of all our church business agendas. More than anything else we long for Jesus to come.

"We urge every church administrator, departmental leader, institutional worker, health worker, literature evangelist, chaplain, educator, pastor, and church member to join us in making revival, reformation, discipleship, and evangelism the most important and urgent priorities of our personal lives and our areas of ministry. We are confident that as we seek Him together, God will pour out His Holy Spirit in abundant measure, the work of God on earth will be finished, and Jesus will come. With the aged apostle John on the Isle of Patmos we cry out, 'Even so, come, Lord Jesus' (Revelation 22:20)."[317]

Knowing that Ted Wilson had worked in New York for around seven years, I asked him if he was still interested in that city. He replied, "Yes, I am still interested in New York. New York is a symbol of how all the rest of the world should be worked and how we should do urban evangelism. More than 50 percent of the world's population is found in the cities. The Adventist Church has never completely fulfilled what the Spirit of Prophecy has outlined.

"So I'm very interested in urban evangelism and its companion—medical missionary work. I'm not talking about what our large institutions are doing but how can the average church member use the principles of health to help somebody and witness to their neighbor with their own health habits so that people can become healthier. Medical missionary work is the last work we can do. When it's impossible for us to preach, we can do medical missionary work.

"Churches are doing great things, but the whole picture has not been implemented: vegetarian restaurants, reading rooms, retreats, and outpost centers. I believe the spirit of prophecy talked about centers of influence outside of the cities from which people would come into the cities and work and then go back to them. We have never seen that model function in a regular and consistent way. I want to believe that counsel will still help us in the future."

At the Annual Council in 2011 Wilson took his plan for the cities and his great interest in urban areas to the delegates. He told them, "Much work has been done in New York, but we have yet to see that city become 'a symbol of the work the Lord desires to see done in the world.'

"Some people love New York and others hate it. Graffiti I saw in New York captures the challenge of living and working in the large cities of the world. It said, 'Concrete jungle: A hard life.' There are many good and bad things about New York, like any big city, but the people are there ... people who need Christ and the hope of the Advent message. Since the time that I lived in New York, I have always had a strong burden for the cities and New York City in particular. So much is yet to be done.

"I want every administrator here and around the world to feel a heavy burden for the cities. God will bless our evangelism plans for the cities as we allow the Holy Spirit to lead in those plans and follow biblical and Spirit of Prophecy counsel. It is the reason for revival and reformation ... for intense prayer ... for humility before the Lord. Let us never ignore God's pleading with us about the work for the cities.

"As president of the General Conference today, I do not want to be accused by the Lord of dishonoring Him by ignoring the cities. I humble myself before Him and ask that I might be completely converted to God's plans for the people of the cities. Today, along with me, I want you to share that great burden of Jesus for the people of the cities. I have had in my office ever since I worked in New York City, the powerful picture of 'Christ of the City.' Since New York, it has hung in my offices in Abidjan, Silver Spring, Moscow, Hagerstown, in Silver Spring again, and now in my current office. I also have the same picture facing me every day as I sit at my home desk. Let our hearts cry out to God on behalf of the millions in the cities of the world–in your division, in your union, in your conference, in your mission, or in your field. As leaders, never ignore our great task using every means possible for our 'Mission to the cities.'

"Tomorrow morning, during the Council of Evangelism and Witness, we will present the unprecedented 'Mission to the Cities.' Of course, our church is currently doing many good things in the cities of the world, but in the year 2013 we will launch a very specific, comprehensive, sustained evangelistic approach for the world beginning in New York City. We are calling, through the leading of the Holy Spirit, for a comprehensive approach that will continue until Jesus comes ... not a hit and run approach to evangelism, but a long-term, sustained, Spirit-filled approach.

"We want to start with New York City since Ellen White indicated that it should be a symbol as to how the rest of the world should be worked. Since large cities are made up of many smaller communities and neighborhoods, we expect to have approximately 150 to 200 evangelistic meetings in the metropolitan New York area from June 7-29, 2013. Many preparatory outreach activities by church members will take place in a comprehensive manner that will lead up to the June 2013 evangelistic meetings. We are working closely with the North American Division, Atlantic Union, Columbia Union, Greater New York Conference, Northeastern Conference, New Jersey Conference, and the Allegheny East Conference in the detailed planning for the evangelistic meetings in New York....

"Let us pledge ourselves to pray for these leaders, their pastors, church workers, and church members. By God's grace, I pledge myself and Nancy to hold one of those 200 evangelistic meetings in New York City in June 2013.

"We have worked with the thirteen division presidents to send expert evangelists from their divisions to New York City to join us in holding meetings. Many of my fellow GC officers and colleagues will be holding

Highly Committed

some of these evangelistic meetings. Many from the Atlantic and Columbia unions, including local pastors in the New York area, will be actively involved. Pastor Mark Finley will lead an evangelistic field school of evangelism during those meetings. By God's grace, there will be a marvelous harvest of souls in metropolitan New York and a continued, sustained evangelistic work....

"This is only the beginning. Evangelists from the various divisions who will have been with us in New York will return to their home divisions to hold evangelistic series and field schools of evangelism for union and conference workers in a division-selected major city. Unions will then select a city to hold a major evangelistic series and field school. Then each conference or local field will select and hold an evangelistic series and field school in a major city....

"Our humble goal, by God's grace, will be to reach approximately 650 major cities of the world before the next General Conference session in 2015, all based on the power of the Holy Spirit through revival and reformation. The 777-prayer initiative should focus our attention on the incredible 'Mission to the Cities.' Please pray like never before for God's work in the great cities of the world. We are powerless except as we rely on our Chief Urban Evangelist who, as He looked over Jerusalem, wept!...

"When the cities are worked as God would have them, the result will be the setting in operation of a mighty movement such as we have not yet witnessed.... I have full confidence that God will fulfill His promise as we humbly submit our plans to Him and follow His instruction in the Bible and the Spirit of Prophecy. Let us plead with the Holy Spirit for the power to accomplish the task entrusted to us. What a day it will be when Jesus returns and we join with those who have been saved from the large cities and the rural areas to ascend with the Lord to our eventual homes for eternity—homes in the New Jerusalem and homes in the country in the new earth. Let us dedicate ourselves to God's comprehensive plans for 'Mission to the Cities.'"

As our last interview was coming to an end, I asked Ted Wilson, "What is your favorite text?"

"I have a lot of favorite scriptures, texts that I love," he answered. "One that is particularly meaningful to me now and a great encouragement is found in Joel 2:21: 'Fear not, O land; be glad and rejoice: for the Lord will do great things.' In some versions of the Bible, the text suggests that 'the Lord *is* doing marvelous things.' Right now.

"This text supports my strong belief in God's providence and how He leads us to what the Holy Spirit wants us to do. If we just trust and humbly submit, the Lord will do marvelous things to His glory and not for our own glory. The great things are not for us; they're for the church, for His cause, for His ultimate glory and triumph. It's a text that has meant a lot to me over many years now."

In addition to his favorite text, his favorite hymn is "The Church Has One Foundation, 'Tis Jesus Christ her Lord."

Ted Wilson sits back in his chair. Our visit is over. He wants to pray for me and my family before I leave. I am quietly touched by this thoughtfulness. His prayer ends with his longing for Christ to come soon. He wants to do all he can, using all of the resources of the church to finish the work. I know that these are not just shallow words. It is not just talk. There is an urgency to his words. He expects the Lord to do great things through him as He did through his great grandfather, his grandfather, and his father who all looked forward to that final glorious day. He has set in motion a call for repentance, revival, and reformation and a comprehensive strategy to reach the lost all over the world, especially in the great metropolitan areas such as New York City.

I leave his office knowing that the Adventist Church is in very good hands.

Presidents of the General Conference of Seventh-day Adventists

1.	John Byington	1863–1865	11.	W. A. Spicer	1922–1930
2.	James White	1865–1867	12.	C. H. Watson	1930–1936
3.	J. N. Andrews	1867–1869	13.	J. L. McElhany	1936–1950
4.	James White	1869–1871	14.	W. H. Branson	1950–1954
5.	George I. Butler	1871–1874	15.	R. R. Figuhr	1954–1966
6.	James White	1874–1880	16.	Robert H. Pierson	1966–1979
7.	George I. Butler	1880–1888	17.	**Neal C. Wilson**	**1979–1990**
8.	O. A. Olsen	1888–1897	18.	R. S. Folkenberg	1990–1999
9.	G. A. Irwin	1897–1901	19.	Jan Paulsen	1999–2010
10.	A. G. Daniells	1901–1922	20.	**Ted N. C. Wilson**	**2010–**

Interesting Facts about the Presidents of the Adventist Church

Since the election of John Byington as our first General Conference president (1863–1865), a total of seventeen men have held that office. All but four have been born in the continental United States. O. A. Olsen (1888–1897) was born in Norway but brought to America by his parents when only five, while C. H. Watson (1930–1936), born in Australia, came as an adult. Jan Paulsen was also born in Norway. Robert Folkenberg was born in Puerto Rico to American missionary parents.

The most unusual election took place in 1922. That year W. A. Spicer who had been secretary of the General Conference from 1903–1922, became president. A. G. Daniells, who had been president for twenty-one years, was elected secretary. Thus Elders Spicer and Daniells became the only men to serve as both president and secretary of the General Conference.

No General Conference treasurer has ever been chosen president.

The first man with no previous mission experience to achieve the office was O. A. Olsen. In fact, Elder Olsen became president while not present at the session that elected him, being in Europe. W. C. White, son of James and Ellen White, served as acting president for six months until Elder Olsen could finish up his work there and get back to the United States. The last president with no mission service was G. A. Irwin. Since 1901 every General Conference president has previously served the church overseas.

The General Conference chose James White as its first president, but he declined to serve because he had worked so hard for the church organization. John Byington was then asked to serve in his place. James White later accepted three terms (1865–1867, 1869–1871, and 1874–1880).

(cont.)

Highly Committed

A. G. Daniells (1901–1922) served as president for the longest perdiod; J. L. McElhany (1936–1950), the second longest. Two "firsts" served the shortest time: our first president, John Byington (1863–1865), and our first missionary, John N. Andrews (1867–1869).

The youngest man to serve as president, George I. Butler (1871–1874, 1880–1888), was only 37 when first elected. Two presidents were elected at age 64, our first president, John Byington, and Jan Paulsen.

Two presidents had the same birthday–January 3. J. L. McElhany was born in 1880, and Robert H. Pierson was born in 1911.

The only deceased president not buried in the United States is C. H. Watson. After his retirement he returned to his native Australia where he later died and was buried.

George Butler was converted to the Adventist faith by J. N. Andrews and later ordained to the ministry by James White. In 1910 another General Conference president, A. G. Daniells, ordained a future successor, young William H. Branson (1950–1954), to the ministry.

Neal Wilson, Robert Folkenberg, and Ted Wilson were all PKs—sons of Adventist ministers. Ted Wilson's grandfather was also a minister. Folkenberg is a fourth generation minister, and his son Robert is a minister.

George W. Brown was the only person nominated to the presidency who was non-Caucasian. Born in the Dominican Republic to an Antiguan father and Dominican mother (and a wife from Suriname), Brown declined the honor at the 1990 session in Indianapolis, saying he was 66 and couldn't make the needed changes in one term and didn't feel his health and that of his family could support two terms.

Robert Folkenberg is a licensed pilot, qualified to fly jet planes and helicopters. He rides a motorcycle.

Ted Wilson, Ph.D. (Religious Education, New York University, New York, 1981) and Jan Paulsen (University of Tubingen) are the only two presidents to earn doctoral degrees.

Neal C. Wilson and Ted N. C. Wilson are the only father and son to have served as president. Nathaniel C. Wilson was the only minister to have both his son (Neal C. Wilson) and his grandson (Ted N.C. Wilson) to serve as president of the General Conference.

(Some of this information came from the Adventist Review, July 2, 1985, p. 13.*)*

Our Mission Fields

The largest cities in the world, each with a population of at least 10 million, are arranged in alphabetical order:

Beijing, China
Buenos Aries, Argentina
Cairo, Egypt
Delhi, India
Dhaka, Bangladesh
Guangzhou, China
Istanbul, Turkey
Jakarta, Indonesia
Karachi, Pakistan
Kolkata, India
Los Angeles, United States
Manila, Philippines
Mexico City, Mexico
Moscow, Russia
Mumbai, India
New York, United States
Osaka-Kobe, Japan
Rio de Janeiro, Brazil
Sao Paulo, Brazil
Shanghai, China
Tokyo, Japan

Highly Committed

Past president Jan Paulsen and his wife welcome newly elected president Ted Wilson and his wife.

Ted and Nancy Wilson look confidently toward the future.

Ted N. C. Wilson: World Church President

Ted and Nancy Wilson with their three grown daughters, their spouses and grandchildren.
(back row, left to right): David Wright, Elizabeth Wright, Ted Wilson, Nancy Wilson,
Catherine Renck, Robert Renck, Jr., Emilie DeVasher, Kameron DeVasher.
(Front row, left to right): Matthew Wright, Lauren Wright, Henry DeVasher, Charlotte Rose Renck.

Where are the Wilson's daughters now?

- The Wilson's eldest daughter, Emilie, is a nurse but is currently a stay-at-home mom to little 9-month-old son, Henry. She is married to Kameron DeVasher, a pastor in Avon Park, Florida (Edward Evans DeVasher, was born October 2, 2012).
- Their second daughter, Elizabeth, is also a nurse and stay-at-home mom to their three little ones: Lauren, 4, Matthew, 2, and Maryanne, who was born April 1, 2011. Elizabeth is married to David Wright, a pastor in north Georgia.
- Catherine, their youngest daughter, is a physical therapist and stay-at-home mom to 8-month-old daughter, Charlotte Rose. She is married to Robert Renck, Jr., a dentist in Hagerstown, Maryland.

—Source: Gina Wahlen, The Journal, a Shepherdess International resource for ministry spouses; volume 28, third-quarter, 2011, p. 17.

Endnotes

1. Information from the interview tapes of W. Bruce Wilson, son of Nathaniel and Hannah Wilson. Recorded in the early 1980s and transcribed by Gwen Woodward-Schmidt on February 2, 2011.
2. This is not a direct quote from Mrs. White.
3. N. C. Wilson, "Memories of Ellen White," *Adventist Review*, September 20, 1979, p. 2. The mini-camp meeting was arranged by a group of local churches. It was not an official conference-sponsored camp meeting.
4. For about three years the family lived in Canada. The 1891 Canadian census shows them living in the province of Ontario and notes their religion as being Methodist. Since about 1892, they had resided in California.
5. To view a picture of the Healdsburg Church, visit their Web site: http://healdsburg.adventistfaith.org/church-bld.
6. A letter from Nathaniel Carter Wilson to Elder Herbert Ford, vice president of alumni affairs, Pacific Union College, November 11, 1984.
7. "Lodi Normal Academy Notes," *Pacific Union Recorder*, January 26, 1911, p. 7; February 23, 1911, p. 5.
8. J. N. Loughborough, "Obituaries," *Pacific Union Recorder*, February 16, 1911, pp. 6, 7.
9. Psalms 17:15.
10. Mr. and Mrs. W. G. Wilson, "Mountain View," *Pacific Union Recorder*, October 13, 1910, p. 5.
11. Lotta E. Bell, "Lodi Normal Academy Notes," *Pacific Union Recorder*, June 8, 1911, p. 6.
12. Information from a written report prepared by Kenneth Wilson for his 50th wedding anniversary.
13. *The Story of Our Church* (Mountain View, CA: Pacific Press Publishing Association, 1956), pp. 470-477.
14. "A Visit to Lake County," *The Educational Messenger*, July 24, 1908, p. 5.
15. E. A. S., "Nashville Agricultural and Normal Institute," *Southern Union Worker*, July 20, 1911, p. 229.
16. Mr. and Mrs. W. G. Wilson, "Notes from Georgia," *Echoes from the Field*, December 11, 1912, p. 2.
17. M. Bessie DeGraw, "Items Concerning the Self-Supporting School Work," *Southern Union Worker*, November 20, 1913, p. 1.
18. M. Bessie DeGraw. "News from the Nashville Agricultural and Normal Institute, *Southern Union Worker*, June 25, 1914, p. 202.
19. "Notes and Items," *Echoes from the Field*, December 31, 1913, p. 4.
20. J. E. Hansen, "New Southland Workers," *Field Tidings*, July 22, 1914, p. 5.
21. This book is available from TEACH Services.
22. Information from an interview with Janet Wilson-Kahler, the granddaughter.

Endnotes

23 W. C. White, "Reeves School Farm," *Southern Union Worker*, April 27, 1916, pp. 138, 139.
24 "Rural School Day at Madison," *The Madison Survey*, April 23, 1923, p. 66.
25 "Items of News," *The Madison Survey*, January 1, 1925, p. 4.
26 "News Items," *The Madison Survey*, August 3, 1932, p. 120.
27 "Don't Worry About Tomorrow—God is Already There," *Southern Tidings*, October 1995, p. 7.
28 General Conference Committee Minutes, April 28, 1924, p. 637.
29 *The Madison Survey*, October 8, 1924, p. 152.
30 "About the Place," *The Madison Survey*, December 3, 1924, p. 184.
31 "Around and About the Place," *The Madison Survey*, February 6, 1924, p. 27.
32 "Obituaries," *Southern Tidings*, March 1989, p. 23.
33 "Tennessee River News Notes," *Southern Union Worker*, March 19, 1925, p. 4.
34 A letter from W. H. Branson, president of the work in Africa, to N. C. Wilson, Nashville Agricultural Normal Institute, Madison, Tennessee, October 22, 1924.
35 A letter to N. C. Wilson at the Nashville Agricultural and Normal Institute, March 18, 1925.
36 "Madison News," *Southern Union Worker*, April 23, 1925, p. 2.
37 "Report of the Autumn Council of the General Conference Committee," *The Advent Review and Sabbath Herald*, December 4, 1924, pp. 3, 4.
38 "Report of the Autumn Council of the General Conference Committee: Week of Sacrifice," *The Advent Review and Sabbath Herald*, December 4, 1924, p. 4.
39 "The Autumn Council Calls for Help," *The Advent Review and Sabbath Herald*, November 12, 1925, p. 4.
40 Bertha D. Martin, "Heed Ye the Call," *The Advent Review and Sabbath Herald*, December 4, 1924, p. 1.
41 B. E. Beddoe, "1925 Advance Into Foreign Fields," *The Advent Review and Sabbath Herald*, January 7, 1926, p. 1.
42 B. E. Beddoe, "A Cable From Africa," *The Advent Review and Sabbath Herald*, May 14, 1925, p. 24.
43 Hannah Myrtle Wallin Wilson was born on February 24, 1898, in Roseau, Minnesota, and died on March 18, 1995. She was interred next to her husband, Nathaniel, in the Montecito Memorial Park in Loma Linda. Hannah was the sixth of twelve children. Her father, Lewis P Wallin, was born in Sweden in 1844, an important date for Seventh-day Adventists. Lewis left home at 16 years of age for America, where he became a farmer and lay preacher of the Seventh-day Adventist Church. In 1889 he married Anna Pierson who was born in Maine to Swedish immigrant parents. Hannah and Nathaniel's marriage was one of love and dedicated service to the Lord that lasted for seventy-three years.
44 W. A. Spicer, "The African Division Council," *The Advent Review and Sabbath Herald*, August 27, 1925, p. 4.
45 H. E. Lysinger, "Mission Offerings," *Southern Union Worker*, October 13, 1926, p. 5.

Highly Committed

[46] N. C. Wilson, "In North Rhodesia, Africa," *The Advent Review and Sabbath Herald*, January 13, 1927, pp. 8, 9.

[47] *The Story of Our Church* (Mountain View, CA: Pacific Press Publishing Association, 1956), pp. 289-297.

[48] "Brother Konigmacher Finds Five Companies," *The Advent Review and Sabbath Herald*, June 9, 1926, p. 12.

[49] J. I. Robinson, "Problem Forty-Four," *Review and Herald*, February 7, 1957, p. 6.

[50] N. C. Wilson, "The Southeast African Union," *The Advent Review and Sabbath Herald*, June 27, 1929, pp. 20, 21.

[51] *The Advent Review and Sabbath Herald*, December 20, 1928, p. 8; June 20, 1929, p. 15; October 23, 1930, p. 32; December 11, 1930, p. 18. *The Southern African Division Outlook*, June 15, 1955, pp. 4-6.

[52] N. C. Wilson, "Medical Work in Southeast African Union Mission," *The Advent Review and Sabbath Herald*, October 4, 1928, pp. 9, 10.

[53] W. H. Branson, "In Nyasaland," *The Advent Review and Sabbath Herald*, August 9, 1928, p. 24.

[54] "A Farewell Gathering," *The African Division Outlook*, March 10, 1930, p. 3.

[55] C. E. Dudley, *Thou Who Hast Brought us Thus Far on Our Way*, book 3, vol. 3 (Nashville, TN: Dudley Publications, 2000), p. 125.

[56] B. W. Abney, "Work in the Cape Colored Field of South Africa," *The Advent Review and Sabbath Herald*, November 16, 1933, p. 19.

[57] A letter from Southern African Division Treasurer A. E. Nelson to Pastors M. E. Kern and W. H. Williams, May 1934.

[58] A report based on the physician's examination, November 27, 1924, Madison, Tennessee.

[59] A letter from J. F. Wright to H. T. Elliott, June 13, 1934; filed in C. E. Wheeler folder.

[60] M. E. Kern, "Short Message From a Division President," *The Advent Review and Sabbath Herald*, June 13, 1935, p. 12.

[61] "Missionary Sailings," *The Advent Review and Sabbath Herald*, May 23, 1935, p. 24.

[62] "In Love With One's Environment," *The Advent Review and Sabbath Herald*, September 5, 1935, p. 4.

[63] David Sukumaran, Ph.D., "India-100 Years," *Adventist Review*, September 30, 1993, p. 10.

[64] N. C. Wilson, "Make Public Evangelism Foremost," *The Ministry*, December 1937, pp. 7, 8.

[65] R. W. Schwarz, *Light Bearers to the Remnant* (Mountain View, CA: Pacific Press Publishing Association, 1979), pp. 500, 501.

[66] N. C. Wilson, "The General Conference," *The Advent Review and Sabbath Herald*, July 23, 1936, p. 24.

[67] "Eighth Meeting," *The Advent Review and Sabbath Herald*, June 2, 1936, p. 97.

[68] Alonzo L. Baker, "Progress in Men and Methods," *The Advent Review and Sabbath Herald*, June 8, 1936, p. 1.

Endnotes

69 R. H. Pierson, "Carol Singing in Bombay," *Eastern Tidings*, January 1, 1938, p. 7.

70 "Wedding," *Eastern Tidings*, February 15, 1936, p. 8.

71 M. S. Vedarathnam, "Baptisms at the Council," *Eastern Tidings*, January 15, 1937, p. 5.

72 A letter from the Appointees' Committee, signed by A. W. C, November 8, 1940.

73 J. F. Wright, "An Open Letter," *The Southern African Division Outlook*, September 1, 1941, p. 1.

74 Milton Robison, "C. W. Bozarth Division President," *The Southern African Division Outlook*, May 1 1942, p. 1.

75 T. J. Michael, "Organization of the Wyoming Conference," *The Advent Review and Sabbath Herald*, September 6, 1945, pp. 18, 19.

76 "Omaha Home Missionary Convention," *The Advent Review and Sabbath Herald*, December 10, 1942, p. 17.

77 N. C. Wilson, "A Tower of Strength," *Central Union Reaper*, June 22, 1943, pp. 6, 7.

78 J. R. Ferren, "Central Union Evangelistic Institute," *The Advent Review and Sabbath Herald*, February 17, 1944, p. 17.

79 H. M. Walton, M.D., "Boulder Sanitarium Jubilee," *The Advent Review and Sabbath Herald*, April 6, 1944, p. 20.

80 Alten A. Bringle, "Mission to the Blind," *Central Union Reaper*, June 11, 1957, p. 1.

81 Louis Halswick, "Japanese Workers' Council in Colorado," *The Advent Review and Sabbath Herald*, February 8, 1945, p. 18.

82 Lora E. Clement, "A Preview of the Session," *The Advent Review and Sabbath Herald*, June 6, 1946, p. 2.

83 N. C. Wilson, "Union Presidents' Symposium: North American Division," *The Advent Review and Sabbath Herald*, January 9, 1947, p. 14.

84 Norman Reitz, "ASI: Vision for Outreach," *Adventist Review*, March 17, 2010. ASI Web site: www.asiministries.org.

85 A. V. Olson, "Shipwreck in the South Seas," *Review and Herald*, June 14, 1951, pp.15, 16. A. V. Olson, "Shipwrecked on a Coral Reef," *Junior Guide*, June 2, 1954, pp. 3, 21.

86 Ellen G. White, *Testimonies for the Church*, vol. 9 (Mountain View, CA: Pacific Press Publishing Association, 1902), pp. 112, 113.

87 N. C. Wilson, "The Advent Message on the Move in Indonesia", *The Advent Review and Sabbath Herald*, October 7, 1954, p. 20.

88 A letter from N. C. Wilson, May 1, 1955. Addressed from Takoma Hospital and Sanitarium, Greeneville, Tennessee. Addendum to the Bradleys, May 11.

89 Glen and Ethel Coon, "Greeneville Meetings Yield Good Results," *Southern Tidings*, May 29, 1957, p. 12.

90 N. C. Wilson, "Soul-Winning in Greeneville," *Southern Tidings*, October 12, 1955, p. 12.

91 M. Donovan Oswald, "Well Done!" *Southern Tidings*, February 20, 1957, pp. 6, 7.

Highly Committed

92 N. C. Wilson, "Operation Dixie in 1960," *Southern Tidings*, December 23, 1959, p. 12.
93 N. W. Dunn, "Michigan Holds Biennial Session in Centennial Year," *Review and Herald*, June 22, 1961, p. 20.
94 Morton Juberg, "Michigan Camp Meeting Celebrates Centennial," *Review and Herald*, September 7, 1961, p. 16.
95 Don Hawley, "A Gift to Nigerian Minister of Education," *Review and Herald*, August 12, 1965, p. 22.
96 Donald E. Mansell, "The Day in Detroit," *Review and Herald*, June 26, 1966, p. 2.
97 E. N. Wendth, "24,000 Pairs of Shoes," *Review and Herald*, December 15, 1966, p. 16.
98 "Baptism," *Pacific Union Recorder*, July 31, 1967, p. 2. "Four Youths Are Baptized at Healdsburg Services May 11," *Pacific Union Recorder*, June 24, 1968, p. 3. *Pacific Union Recorder*, January 16, 1967, p. 6. "Nutshell News From Northern," *Pacific Union Recorder*, November 13, 1967, p. 3.
99 "Berkshire Hosts General Conference Jewish Retreat," *The Atlantic Union Gleaner*, October 10, 1972, p. 12.
100 "Southern Asia Division Reunion Is Planned for Sunday, April 27," *Pacific Union Recorder*, April 16, 1973, p. 5.
101 N. C. Wilson, "Cheer and Encouragement," *Review*, January 9, 1975, p.10.
102 *The Australian Record*, June 28, 1971, p. 13, shared a letter that Pastor A. G. Stewart received "from Pastor N. C. Wilson, now living in California, who was president of the Australian division in the early 1950s. In a gracious gesture, Pastor Stewart invites the Record readers to share the letter with him."
103 "Recollections of My Early Life" is an unpublished paper written by Hannah Myrtle Wallin Wilson.
104 Corina Piercey of the Hermanus SDA Church, Bloemfontein, South Africa, shared her memories of the Wilsons.
105 Jim Joyner, "The Journeys of Neal Wilson," *The Free-Press*, October 10, 1990, pp. 13-15.
106 William G. Johnsson, *Embrace the Impossible* (Hagerstown, MD: Review and Herald Publishing Association, 2008), pp. 64, 65.
107 *Seventh-day Adventist Encyclopedia*, vol. 10 (Washington, D.C.: Review and Herald Publishing Association, 1976), p. 1555.
108 A letter from Neal C. Wilson, March 30, 1940, sent from Salisbury Park, Poona, India.
109 Myrna Tetz, *Leadership Lessons from the Life of Neal C. Wilson* (Nampa, ID: Pacific Press Publishing Association, 2011), pp. 15, 16.
110 "Vincent Hill News," *Eastern Tidings*, November 1, 1939, p. 8.
111 "Vincent Hill News," *Eastern Tidings*, December 1, 1939, p. 8.
112 "Vincent Hill News," *Eastern Tidings*, December 15, 1939, pp. 7, 8.
113 "Poona Paragraphs," *Eastern Tidings*, January 1, 1940. General Conference service record.
114 "Chronicle Campaign Opens," *Pacific Union Recorder*, September 24, 1941, p. 5.

Endnotes

115 Ron Osborn, "An Immigrant's Tale," *Adventist Review*, February 17, 2000, p. 16.

116 Ibid., p. 17

117 Information from personal communication with Ivanette Miklos Osborn—niece of Elinor Wilon, daughter of Sue Neumann Miklos, and mother of Ron Osborn.

118 Information from Ivanette Osborn.

119 "Students Conduct Efforts," *Pacific Union Recorder*, February 11, 1942, p. 2.

120 R. H. Pierson, "Tamil Mission Building Work," *Eastern Tidings*, January 15, 1942, p. 6.

121 A letter from W. I. Smith, April 20, 1942.

122 T. S. Copeland, "News Notes," *Southern Tidings*, May 20, 1942, p. 5.

123 Myrna Tetz, *Leadership Lessons from the Life of Neal C. Wilson* (Nampa, ID: Pacific Press Publishing Association, 2011), p. 17.

124 E. H. Oswald, "Summer Evangelistic Efforts," *Central Union Reaper* July 7, 1942, p. 4.

125 A letter from General Conference Associate Secretary T. J. Michael to Neal Wilson.

126 A letter from Neal Wilson, August 11, 1942, sent from Sheridan, Wyoming.

127 General Conference Committee Minutes, April 5, 1942, p. 378.

128 General Conference Committee Minutes, April 7, 1942, p. 394.

129 General Conference Committee Minutes, April 23, 1942, p. 414.

130 General Conference Committee Minutes, April 30, 1942, pp. 425, 426.

131 General Conference Committee Minutes, July 13, 1942, p. 512.

132 General Conference Committee Minutes, August 17, 1942, p. 544.

133 General Conference Committee Minutes, August 20, 1942, p. 550.

134 A letter from E. D. Dick to Neal Wilson, August 20, 1942.

135 A letter from E. D. Dick, August 20, 1942.

136 A letter from Nathaniel C. Wilson, president of the Central Union Conference, September 8, 1942.

137 General Conference Committee, July 20, 1942.

138 George Keough, *Austrtalasian Record*, April 8, 1918, p. 8.

139 A letter from Nathaniel Wilson to H. W. Vollmer, M.D, September 13, 1942.

140 A letter from T. J. Michael to Nathaniel Wilson, September 30, 1942.

141 Neal C. Wilson, "Cleveland Evangelistic Effort," *The Advent Review and Sabbath Herald*, November 25, 1943, pp. 17, 18.

142 J. R. Spangler, "Tribute to Roy Allan Anderson," *Canadian Union Messenger*, March 1986, p. 21.

143 Letters from Roger Alman to Neal Wilson in Cleveland, Ohio, December 8, 1943, February 10, 1944, and February 28, 1944.

144 General Conference Committee Minutes, July 19, 1943.

145 General Conference Committee Minutes, January 13, 1944.

146 General Conference Committee Minutes, March 2, 1944.

147 T. J. Michael, "Ordination Service at Washington Missionary College," *The Advent Review and*

Sabbath Herald, April 6, 1944, p. 17.

[148] *Ibid.*

[149] *Seventh-day Adventist Encyclopedia*, vol. 10 (Washington, D.C.: Review and Herald Publishing Association, 1976), p. 179.

[150] A letter from Elder T. J. Michael of the General Conference to Mr. J. Neumann of Chicago, Illinois, July 27, 1944.

[151] A letter from Neal Wilson to Elder T. J. Michael, August 21, 1944.

[152] Charles F. Ward, *Australasian Record*, March 5, 1979, p. 3.

[153] Information from a telephone interview with Evelyn Zytkoskee.

[154] Information from a telephone interview with Dr. Richard and Veda Lesher.

[155] Neal C. Wilson, "Protect the Lord's Land," *Middle East Messenger*, August–September 1948, p. 73.

[156] Ibid., p. 75.

[157] A letter from Nathaniel Wilson to Elder W. H. Anderson, December 21, 1947.

[158] *Seventh-day Adventist Encyclopedia*, vol. 10 (Washington, D.C.: Review and Herald Publishing Association, 1976), pp. 351-352.

[159] E. L. Branson, "Our Mission Work in Bible Lands," *The Advent Review and Sabbath Herald*, January 6, 1949, pp. 19, 20.

[160] Neal C. Wilson, "Is It Worth While?" *Middle East Messenger*, October 1948, p. 92.

[161] Edwin G. Essery, "Medical Work in the Middle East," *The Advent Review and Sabbath Herald*, April 3, 1947, pp. 14, 15.

[162] E. L. Branson, "The Middle East Union," *The Advent Review and Sabbath Herald*, December 2, 1948, p. 15.

[163] A. G. Zytkowski, "Egypt Mission," *Middle East Messenger*, April 1949, p. 3.

[164] Alger Francis Johns, "Baptism in the Middle East," *The Advent Review and Sabbath Herald*, September 13, 1945, pp. 15, 23.

[165] Alger Francis Johns, "Evangelistic Council in the Middle East," *The Advent Review and Sabbath Herald*, November 8, 1945, p. 13.

[166] Miriam Wood, "A Word Portrait," *Adventist Review*, December 20, 1979, p. 8.

[167] "Camp Meetings in Egypt," *Middle East Messenger*, August-September 1948, pp. 71, 72.

[168] "Egypt," *Eastern Tidings*, June 15, 1948, p. 7.

[169] General Conference Committee Minutes, March 6, 1950, p. 1800.

[170] General Conference Committee Minutes, July 23, 1950, p. 36. It was voted that the East Mediterranean Division be divided into two union missions to be known as the Middle East Union, comprising Turkey, Lebanon-Syria, Iraq, Kuwait, Oman Hadramut, Cyprus, and the Neutral Territory between Iraq and Transjordan; and the Nile Union, comprising Egypt, Libya, Angola-Egyptian Sudan, Saudi Arabia, Aden, Yemen, and Transjordan.

[171] J. I. Robison, "Recent Missionary Departures," *The Advent Review and Sabbath Herald*,

December 28, 1950.

172 Wadie Farag, "We Witnessed the Horrors of War," *The Advent Review and Sabbath Herald*, May 23, 1957, p. 16

173 "Here and There," *Middle East Messenger*, Second Quarter 1957, p. 7.

174 A letter from Geo. J. Appel to Elder W. P. Bradley, December 9, 1951.

175 "An Afternoon With the Unattached Missions," *The Advent Review and Sabbath Herald*, July 17, 1950. p. 144.

176 "Largest Baptism in Egypt," *The Advent Review and Sabbath Herald*, August 20, 1953, p. 32.

177 "Upper Egypt Mission," *Middle East Messenger*, Fourth Quarter, 1955, p. 11.

178 "Nile Union," *Middle East Messenger*, Second Quarter 1956, p. 8.

179 Farris B. Bishai, "Into All the World—And Now to the Sudan," *Middle East Messenger*, Third Quarter 1954, p. 4.

180 Neal C. Wilson, "Opening Our Work in Khartoum, Sudan," *The Advent Review and Sabbath Herald*, September 3, 1953, p. 14.

181 *Ibid.*

182 *Ibid.*, pp. 14, 15.

183 A letter from Neal C. Wilson to Pastor D. E. Rebok at the General Conference, May 12, 1953.

184 A letter from Neal C. Wilson to Elder and Mrs. Roenfelt, January 7, 1954.

185 Chafic Srour and Ormond K. Anderson, "Surveying New Fields," *Middle East Messenger*, Third Quarter 1954, pp. 5, 7.

186 "Here and There," *Middle East Messenger*, First Quarter 1955, p. 8.

187 "Egypt," *Middle East Messenger*, Third Quarter 1960, p. 7.

188 George J. Appel, "Hospital Opened in Libya," *The Advent Review and Sabbath Herald*, July 19, 1956, pp. 1, 25.

189 Neal C. Wilson, "Thank You, Takoma Hospital," *Southern Tidings*, March 7, 1956, p. 2..

190 A letter from Neal Wilson to Pastor C. L. Torrey, treasurer, General Conference, September 15, 1954.

191 H. M. Tippett, "Our Reporters Story for June 25," *The Advent Review and Sabbath Herald*, June 26, 1958, page 132.

192 D. L. Chappell, "From Tripoli to Tehran," *The Atlantic Union Gleaner*, June 20, 1966, pp. 1, 2.

193 General Conference Committee Minutes, November 26, 1958, p. 180.

194 "Nile Union News," *Middle East Messenger*, First Quarter 1959, p. 6.

195 General Conference Committee Minutes, March 6, 1958, p. 1125.

196 D. E. Venden, "N. C. Wilson Joins Central's Staff," *Pacific Union Recorder*, March 23, 1950, p. 7.

197 A letter from Neal Wilson, Central California Conference, to Elder N. W. Dunn, Washington, D.C., March 10, 1959.

198 D. E. Venden, N. C. Wilson, "How Willing Are You?", *Pacific Union Recorder*, February 1, 1960, p. 7.

Highly Committed

[199] Neal C. Wilson, "In Central—Make It at Least Sixty-two Cents," *Pacific Union Recorder*, February 1, 1960, p. 7.

[200] D. A. Roth, "Neal Wilson Appointed to Union Staff," *Columbia Union Visitor*, January 21, 1960, p. 1.

[201] L. E. Lenheim, "Church Accepts Gift of Eight-Million-Dollar Hospital," *The Advent Review and Sabbath Herald*, December 17, 1959, p. 16.

[202] "Kettering Hospital Proposal Accepted by Union," *Columbia Union Visitor*, November 26, 1959, p. 12.

[203] Neal Wilson, "Key to Kettering Given in Ceremony," *Columbia Union Visitor*, May 25, 1961, p. 1.

[204] This information was recorded during a private conversation with Don A. Roth in May 2011.

[205] Neal C. Wilson, "A Message From Your Union Conference President," *Columbia Union Visitor*, October 11, 1962, p. 1

[206] D. A. Roth, "Elder Neal Wilson Elected Union President," *Columbia Union Visitor*, August 2, 1962, p. 12.

[207] Neal C. Wilson, "Eleven-Million-Dollar Hospital Gift to Adventists," *Review and Herald*, March 5, 1964, p. 21.

[208] A letter from Neal C. Wilson to Theodore Carcich, February 8, 1966.

[209] Morton Juberg, "Church Officers Attend Human Relations Sessions," *Columbia Union Visitor*, March 10, 1966, p. 2.

[210] Arthur H Roth, "Dateline Washington," *Review and Herald*, March 12, 1970, p. 20.

[211] S.E. Gooden, "Leader of the North American Division Visits South Atlantic Conference", *Southern Tidings*, April, 1973, page 6.

[212] Neal C. Wilson, "Action Taken to Strengthen Black Work in N.A.," *Review*, October 27, 1977, p. 32.

[213] "N. C. Wilson Elected to New Post," *Columbia Union Visitor*, July 14, 1966, p. 2.

[214] Miriam Wood, "A Word Portrait," *Adventist Review*, December 20, 1979, p. 8

[215] "N. C. Wilson Elected to New Post," *Columbia Union Visitor*, July 14, 1966, p. 2

[216] "GC president issue statements on racism, peace, home and family, and drugs," *Adventist Review*, June 30, 1985, p. 2.

[217] "General Conference president announces retirement," *Adventist Review*, October 26, 1978, p. 1.

[218] General Conference Committee Minutes, October 17, 1978, pp. 78-327.

[219] Neal C. Wilson, "It's Harvest Time," *Adventist Review*, November 2, 1978, pp. 1, 4.

[220] "May the days not be prolonged: A response by Robert H. Pierson to Neal C. Wilson's address accepting the General Conference presidency," *Adventist Review*, November 2, 1978, pp. 4, 5.

[221] J. Robert Spangler, "A Tribute to Elder Pierson," *Ministry*, December 1978, p. 18.

[222] Neal C. Wilson, "The Challenge of the Cities," *Adventist Review*, June 7, 1979, p. 3.

[223] Neal C. Wilson, "A Letter from my father," *Adventist Review*, August 2, 1979, p. 3.

[224] The program and poems were found in the General Conference archives.

[225] William G. Johnsson, *Embrace the Impossible* (Hagerstown, MD: Review and Herald Publishing Association, 2008), p. 112.

Endnotes

[226] Lawrence Maxwell, "The Day in Dallas," *Adventist Review*, April 20, 1980, p. 10.

[227] Herbert Douglass, "The Day in Dallas," *Adventist Review*, May 1, 1980, p. 7.

[228] Miriam Wood, "The Day in Review" *Adventist Review*, June 30, 1985, p. 9.

[229] Leo R. Van Dolson, "Annual Council 1079," *Adventist Review*, November 8, 1979, p. 4.

[230] William G. Johnsson, "Wilson's Road to Nairobi," *Adventist Review*, October 25, 1988, p. 11.

[231] William G. Johnsson, "Church Pays Tribute to Robert H. Pierson," *Adventist Review*, February 9, 1989, p. 6.

[232] Ronald Graybill, "The Making of a General Conference President, 1990" *Spectrum*, 20:5, August 1990, pp. 10–15.

[233] *Ibid.*, p. 12.

[234] Douglas Hackleman, *Who Watches? Who Cares?* (Morrison, CO: Members for Church Accountability, 2008), pp. 226, 227.

[235] "Third Business Meeting: Fifty-fifth General Conference Session, July 6, 1990, 2:00 p.m.," *Adventist Review*, July 9, 1990, pp. 12, 13.

[236] William G. Johnsson, *Embrace the Impossible* (Hagerstown, MD: Review and Herald Publishing Association, 2008), p. 114.

[237] William G. Johnsson, "Neal C. Wilson—Church Statesman," *Adventist Review*, July 8, 1990, p. 4.

[238] William G. Johnsson, *Embrace the Impossible* (Hagerstown, MD: Review and Herald Publishing Association, 2008), p. 114.

[239] General Conference Committee Minutes, May 16, 1991, pp. 91–197.

[240] General Conference Committee Minutes, May 16, 1991, pp. 91–197.

[241] Myrna Tetz, *Leadership Lessons From the Life of Neal C. Wilson* (Nampa, ID: Pacific Press Publishing Association, 2011), p. 94.

[242] The Library of Congress, Congressional Record, 102nd Congress (1991-1992).

[243] Myrna Tetz, *Leadership Lessons From the Life of Neal C. Wilson* (Nampa, ID: Pacific Press Publishing Association, 2011), p. 90.

[244] Jamie Arnall, "Historic Adventist Village Opens," *Adventist Review*, http://www.adventistreview.org/2000-1539/news.html (accessed June 24, 2012).

[245] "Proceedings. Tenth Business Session," *Adventist Review*, July 13, 2000, p. 22.

[246] "Proceedings: Fourth Business Meeting," (57th General Conference Session, July 2, 2000, 9:30 a.m.) *Adventist Review*, GC Session Bulletin 4, pp. 25, 26.

[247] *Ibid.*

[248] *Ibid.*

[249] *Ibid.*

[250] "Session Actions: 57th General Conference Session, July 2, 2000, 9:30 a.m.," *Adventist Review*, http://www.adventistreview.org/2000-bulletin4/actions-proceedings.html (accessed June 24, 2012).

Highly Committed

[251] "Former GC President Witnesses Unveiling Of New Gandhi Statue," *Adventist Review*, http://www.Adventistreview.org/2000-1549/news.html (accessed June 24, 2012).

[252] Mark A. Kellner, "Ireland: Wilson Evangelizes Ancestral Island," Adventist News Network, http://news.adventist.org/archive/articles/2004/06/15/ireland-wilson-evangelizes-ancestral-island (accessed June 24, 2012).

[253] *Ibid.*

[254] *Ibid.*

[255] *Ibid.*

[256] "Session Snapshot," *Adventist Review*, July 3, 2005, p. 10.

[257] "I Remember Neal," Letters, John McConnell, Citrus Heights, California, *Adventist Review*, April 14, 2011.

[258] "Students address G. C.," *Sligonian*, October 16, 1969, p. 1.

[259] Ellen G. White, *Steps to Christ* (Mountain View, CA: Pacific Press Publishing Association, 1893), p. 70.

[260] Don Hawley, "New York Catacombs Invite Youth to Consider Christ," *Review*, September 23, 1971, p. 15.

[261] Arthur McLarty, "The Catacombs Pay—A Family Is Reunited, Two Prepare for Baptism," *The Atlantic Union Gleaner*, January 11, 1972, p. 8.

[262] Emma Kirk, "Atlantic Union," *Review*, September 19, 1974, p. 20.

[263] "General Conference Leaders Assist in Patchogue," *The Atlantic Union Gleaner*, May 13, 1975, p. 10.

[264] D. E. Kenyon, "Drug Seminar," *The Atlantic Union Gleaner*, April 8, 1975, pp. 10, 11.

[265] D. E. Kenyon, "Three Churches Organized," *The Atlantic Union Gleaner*, March 23, 1976, pp. 13-15.

[266] *Seventh-day Adventist Encyclopedia*, vol. 10 (Washington, D.C.: Review and Herald Publishing Association, 1976), p. 440.

[267] Helen F. Smith, "An Adventist Lighthouse in the Heart of New York," *The Advent Review and Sabbath Herald*, December 6, 1956, pp. 1, 25. "Grand Opening of New York Center," *The Atlantic Union Gleaner*, November 26, 1956, pp. 1, 2.

[268] Ellen G. White, *Evangelism* (Washington, D.C.: Review and Herald Publishing Association, 1946), pp. 384, 385.

[269] D. A. Roth, "Evangelistic Lectures in New York Center to Begin November 18," *Columbia Union Visitor*, November 1, 1956, p. 1.

[270] Neal C. Wilson, "Metro Ministry Leaders Appointed," *Review*, October 21, 1976, p. 24.

[271] Eric W. Hon, "Metro Ministry Takes On the Challenge of New York", *Review*, July 21, 1977, pp. 17, 18.

[272] Annual Council Minutes, October 17, 1976, pp. 76-104.

[273] Nikolaus Satelmajer, "Linketts Outsell Hot Dogs at Coliseum," *Review*, September 1, 1977, p. 26.

[274] "Metro Ministries Medical Director Featured on "Health Fair of the Air," *The Atlantic Union Gleaner*, January 1979, p. 2.

Endnotes

[275] *Ibid,* "New personnel at N.Y. Metro Ministry".

[276] "New personnel at N.Y. Metro Ministry," *Adventist Review,* January 4, 1979, p. 27.

[277] "1978 Greater New York Ordination Service," *The Atlantic Union Gleaner,* October 24, 1978, pp. 8, 9.

[278] General Conference Committee Minutes, September 18, 1969, pp. 69–1648.

[279] General Conference Committee Minutes, August 16, 1979, pp. 79–196.

[280] "Metro Offices and Departments Relocated," *The Atlantic Union Gleaner,* December 25, 1979, p. 19.

[281] "Union President Visits Metropolitan Ministries," *The Atlantic Union Gleaner,* August 28, 1979, pp. 17, 18.

[282] General Conference Committee Minutes, March 27, 1980, pp. 80–94.

[283] "'Ted' N. C. Wilson Appointed Director of Metro Ministries," *The Atlantic Union Gleaner,* December 12, 1978, p. 8.

[284] "To New Posts," *Adventist Review,* December 10, 1981, p. 22.

[285] R. J. Kloosterhuis, "Amazing Accomplishments," *Adventist Review,* July 2, 1985, p. 24.

[286] A letter from Ted Wilson to Elder J. R. Spangler, ministerial and stewardship association, General Conference of SDA, April 27, 1982.

[287] R. J. Kloosterhuis, "Amazing Accomplishments," *Adventist Review,* July 2, 1985, pp. 24, 25.

[288] James L. Fly, "Africa-Indian Ocean Division sets the pace for Harvest '90," *Adventist Review,* October 10, 1985, pp. 26, 27.

[289] "Zaire Crusade Nets 145 Baptisms," *Adventist Review,* August 11, 1988, p. 6.

[290] "SDAs Attend Ivory Coast Reception," *Adventist Review,* February 27, 1986, p. 6.

[291] *Adventist Review,* January 6, 1983 page 19 and April 25, 1985 page 20.

[292] Neal C. Wilson, "New African Division Dedicates New Offices," *Adventist Review,* August 13, 1987, pp. 18, 20.

[293] William G. Johnsson and Delbert W Baker, "Adventist Team Scales Mount Kilimanjaro," *Adventist Review,* December 1, 1988, p. 18.

[294] William G. Johnsson, "A Remarkable Council," *Adventist Review,* November 23, 1989, p. 4.

[295] J. R. Spangler, "The Soviet Union: a Decade of Destiny," *Adventist Review,* February 7, 1991, pp. 8, 9.

[296] Shirley Burton, "Soviet division is re-named during annual council," *Visitor,* November 15, 1991, p. 11.

[297] "Euro-Asia Maps Evangelistic Strategy," *Adventist Review,* February 18, 1993, p. 6.

[298] "Euro-Asia to Launch Public School Outreach," *Adventist Review,* March 25, 1993, p. 6.

[299] Peter Koolik, "God Guides in the Development of the New Division Office," *Adventist Review,* May 25, 1995, p. 20.

[300] Norma Howell, "Mason City School 'Rock,'" *The Mid-America Adventist Outlook,* January 1988, p. 23. Picture with caption, *The Mid-America Adventist Outlook,* December 5, 1985, p. 5.

Highly Committed

[301] General Conference Committee Minutes, May 1, 1996, pp. 96-33.

[302] "Newsbreak," *Adventist Review*, May 16, 1996, p. 22.

[303] General Conference Committee Minutes, November 6, 1996, pp. 96–197.

[304] "Review and Herald Open House Builds Community Awareness," *Adventist Review*, November 20, 1997, pp. 20, 21.

[305] J. David Newman, "The Next General Conference President?" *Adventist Today*, September-October 2008, pp. 6-8.

[306] Sari Fordham, "Why GC Sessions?" *Adventist Review*, June 25, 2010, p. 10.

[307] Edwin Manuel Garcia, "Behind the Scenes of a President's Appointment," *Adventist Review*, June 28, 2010, http://www.adventistreview.org/article/3528/archives/issue-2010-1521/behind-the-scenes-of-a-president-s-appointment (accessed July 3, 2012).

[308] *Ibid*.

[309] "Second Business Meeting: Fifty-ninth General Conference session, June 25, 2010, 9:15 a.m.," *Adventist Review*, http://www.adventistreview.org/article.php?id=3522 (accessed July 3, 2012).

[310] "The Swift Transition of a New Church President," *Adventist Review*, July 8, 2010, http://www.adventistreview.org/article.php?id=3636 (accessed July 3, 2012).

[311] Pat Humphrey, "A Vision for the Church," *Tidings*, August 2010, pp. 8, 9.

[312] Sandra Blackmer, "Hitting the Right Note," *Adventist Review*, http://www.adventistreview.org/article/3598/archives/issue-2010-1525/hitting-the-right-note (accessed July 3, 2012).

[313] Elizabeth Lechleitner, "New Adventist President Envisions a Church Marked by Prayer, Revival," Adventist News Network, http://news.adventist.org/en/archive/articles/2010/07/28/new-adventist-president-envisions-a-church-marked-by-prayer-revival (accessed July 3, 2012).

[314] Adventist News Network staff, "Adventist Headquarters' Neighbors to Get Book Mailing," *Adventist Review*, http://www.adventistreview.org/article/3661/archives/issue-2010-1527/27cn-adventist-headquarters-neighbors-to-get-book-mailing (accessed July 3, 2012).

[315] Ellen G. White, *Colporteur Ministry* (Mountain View, CA: Pacfic Press Publishing Association, 1953), p. 127.

[316] Karen Pearson, "Sharing the Great Hope with the World," Pacific Press Publishing Association Media Release, December 14, 2011.

[317] "Annual Council Action: God's Promised Gift," *Adventist Review*, http://www.adventistreview.org/article/3823/archives/issue-2010-1532/32cn-revival-document (accessed July 3, 2012).

Index

Abney, Benjamin W., Sr. 48
Ackerman, Dorothy Evans 182
Altman, Roger 101
Anderson, Roy Allan 101, 233
Anderson, Shirley Wilson iii, 164
Anderson, W. H. 29, 35, 109, 111, 234
Andrews, John Nevins 31, 172, 190
ASI 67, 123, 231
Australasian Division 71, 73-74, 83, 123
Baker, Delbert 200, 214
Banks, Rosa 161
Barbawy, Hilmy 115
Beach, Bert B. iv, 113, 157
Berlitz Language School 197
Birkenstock, C. F. 46
Bishai, Ferris 115
Blue Mountain Academy 127, 131
Booth, Bradley iv, 205-206
Botswana 36
Bradford, Charles E. 160
Branch, Mabel 45
Branson, Ernest 104
Branson, W. H. 30-31, 47, 96, 104, 134, 223, 229-230
Broadview Adventist Academy 92
Brooks, Charles D. iv, 127-128
Brown, George 145-146
Buckman, W. M. 79
Cairo City Evangelistic Center 119
Carcich, Theodore 127, 133-134, 236
Carlisle, Sir James 154
Central California Conference 122, 172, 235
Cheatham, Wendell iv, 174
Christian Record Services for the Blind 65
Civil Rights Movement 125, 128

Claremont Union College 87
Cleveland, E. E. 48, 197
Clinton, President Bill 156
Colón, Gaspar iv, 188
Columbia Union College (CUC) 173
Commission on Chemical Dependency and the Church 155-156
Congressional Record 153, 237
Conley, J. B. 58
Coolidge, L. E. 76
Coon, Susan 79
Cooper, Lowell 212-213
Cornell, Roy S. 117-118
Cossentine, E. E. 71
Crane, Dianne and Don 166
Dabrowski, Ray (Rajmund) 178
David, Ezra 153
Davis, Jerome iv, 173
Delafield, Mrs. D. A. 175
Dick, E. D. 90, 96, 98, 233
division office in Moscow 204
Douglass, Herbert 143, 237
Druillard, Nellie H. 17
Dudley, Charles E. 146
Dunbar, Eldine 92
Dunbar, Richard 92
Dunn, Dr. Robert H. 185
Egyptian Mission 104, 108
Eisenhower, President 76
Elternhaus 157-159, 164, 166, 168
Esteb, Adlai 141
Eunice Girls School 87
Evans, I. H. 65, 134
Evans, Irving M. 182
Evans, L. C. 182

Highly Committed

Fagal, Bill 167
Figuhr, R. R. 79, 124-125, 132-133, 183, 223
Folkenberg, Robert 145-146, 223-224
Fraser, Trevor H. iv, 186
funeral service 144
Gallagher, Jiggs iv, 173, 190, 192
Gallagher, Mayor Shaun 157
Gandhi, Mahatma 156
Georgia Cumberland Academy 23
Georgia-Cumberland Conference 23, 75, 77, 83, 93, 182
Geraty, Dr. Tom and Hazel 178
Gifford, Stephen 145
Gilbert, Don 153
Graybill, Ronald 145, 237
Greenville district 75-76
Grey College 87-88
Gurubatham, Joseph 173
Handysides, Allan 155
Hanson, E. D. 88
Harvey, Paul 78
Hawley, Don 176, 232, 238
Hayner, Bill 174
Healdsburg Church 8-9, 83, 228
"Heed Ye the Call" (Bertha D. Martin) 33, 229
Heinrich, Oscar 126
Helderberg College 87
Henri, C. D. 141
Hodge, Benito 126
Hon, Eric 184, 186
Human Relations Committee 127
Humphrey, Pat 216, 240
Hunt, William 39-40
Hurlbutt farm 16
Hurlbutt, Emeline Carter 18
Hurlbutt, Nathaniel W. 19
Ibrahim, Kahlil 99
Imoke, S. E. 79

infantile paralysis (polio) 89
Institute of Alcoholism and Drug Dependency 155
Interesting Facts about the Presidents of the Adventist Church 223
Japanese Workers' Council 65, 231
Jewish Christians 80
Johns, Alger F. 102
Johnson, Mrs. Lyndon 79
Johnson, Pastor Al 209
Johnsson, William iv, 89, 143, 160, 200
Kennedy School of Missions 96-98
Keough, George D. 99
Kettering, Charles 123, 125
King, Martin Luther 126, 156, 174
Kinney, Robert 208
Kisekka, Samson 144
Kloosterhuis, Robert J. 196
Knight, Heather J. 215
Konigmacher, S. M. 42
Koolik, Peter 204-205, 239
Kretchmar, Dr. 30
Kruger, Mrs. 110
Kulakov, Pastor M. P. 182
Kuzma, Dr. Kay 178
La Sierra College 173, 191
Landless, Peter 157
largest cities in the world 225
Laurence, Professor J. P. 180
Lee, Willie 126
Lenheim, L. E. 123, 236
Lesher, Richard 107, 143, 188
Lindsay, Ron 126
Lodi Academy 10, 12, 23, 35, 86, 88
Lodi Normal Academy 10, 14, 228
Londonderry, Northern Ireland 157
Loughborough, J. N. 11, 39, 228
Lowry, Roscoe S. 157

Index

Luwazi Mission 45
Lysinger, H. E. 23, 41, 229
Madison College iv, 12, 17, 19, 22-24, 41, 53, 66-67, 76, 83, 86, 99, 182
Magan, Percy T. 17
Malamulo Mission 45-47
Malinki, James 45
Marple, Chaplain A. C. 175
Martin, Bertha D. ("Heed Ye the Call") 33, 229
Mashburn, Dr. Donald 175
Matadani Mission 47
McClure, Al 154
McElhany, J. L. 63, 66, 134, 223-224
McFarland, J. Wayne 67, 179, 182
McKee, A. C. 102
McNeilus, Garwin 202
Mercy Home 110
Meyers, Melva LaVern 23
Michael, T. J. 96, 100, 102, 105, 231, 233-234
Michigan Conference 77-79, 82-83, 133, 163
Miklos, Sue Neumann 92, 233
Miller, Harry 34
Minchen, E. L. 174
Moffitt, L. L. 30
Morella, Constance A. 153
Mostert, Tom 145
Mount Kilimanjaro 143, 153, 165, 200-201, 239
Mountain View School 14
Murrill, Ruth 112, 170
Mwami Mission 46
Mwansa, Pardon Kandanga 212
"My Favorite Text" 82
Myers, C. K. 31
Nash, G. R. 75
Neslund, Thomas 156
Neumann, Joseph 91
Neumann, Theresa 91
New York Center 175, 183-184, 186-188, 238

New York Metro Ministries 139
New York University 188-189, 191, 224
Nile Union Mission 114, 120
Nixon, Bob iv, 158
Nortey, Jacob J. 200
North American Division Presidents 134
Nyasaland 40, 43-47, 83, 230
Olson, A. V. 71, 231
Operation Dixie Crusade 77
ordination 65, 102, 163, 186, 201
   ten men 102
Osborn, Dick 173
Osborn, Ivanette Miklos 181, 233
Osborn, Ken 182
Oswald, E. H. 93, 233
Parchment, Orville 160
Patchogue 178-180, 183, 191, 238
Patzer, A. J. 140
Paulien, Jonathan K. 186
Paulsen, Jan 145, 160-161, 212, 214-215, 223-224
Paulson, David 16
Pearson, R. G. 45
Peeke, Victor 172-173
Piercey, Corina 87, 232
Pierson, Elder 132, 137-141, 143-144, 236
Pierson, R. H. 57, 79, 133, 174, 231, 233
pledge 11, 16, 46, 65, 81, 156, 214, 221
Presidents of the General Conference of Seventh-day Adventists 223
Prestol, Juan iv, 203, 207
PREXAD 127-128, 136-137
Reading Rehab Center 181
Reed, Ambassador Joseph Verner 160, 162
Reeves, Benjamin 145
"Reflections on a Lifelong Friendship" 190
Reiger, Bob 167
Reile, Lloyd 178
Return of the Jews 110

Highly Committed

Review and Herald 39, 41, 65, 82, 96, 101-102, 132, 136, 192, 208-209, 219, 230-232, 234, 236-238, 240
Rice, George 153, 160
Robison, J. I. 43, 234
Rock, Calvin 137, 143, 145
Rodriquez, J. J. 198
Romeom Tony iv, 176
Romney, George 78-79, 133
Roth, Don iv, 124
Russell, Malcolm 173
Sanitarium Health Food Company 74
Satelmajer, Nikolaus iv, 179-180, 184, 186, 238
Scharffenberg, Lloyd 176
Scott, Lida Funk 17
Service Record for Nathaniel Carter Wilson 83
Sessions of the General Conference of Seventh-day Adventists 68-70
Shaw, J. L. 30-31
Shorter, Rick and Gwen 176
Simmons, Dr. Ella 213
Simons, Don 128-129
Singleton, H. D. 127
Singleton, Ken iv, 172
Slater Dr. James 162
Smith, Robert S. 209
Spangler, J. Robert 101, 136, 236
Spicer, W. A. 32, 34, 57, 223, 229
statement on June 27, 1985, regarding racism 134
Sutherland, Edward A. 16
Tatum, Roger 173
Tetz, Myrna 153, 232-233, 237
The Catacombs 176-177, 238
The Great Controversy 8, 154, 177, 218-219
The Great Hope 219
The Layman Foundation iv, 77
Thekerani Mission 47
Thompson, G. Ralph 140, 145, 153, 160
Tong, Archie 31, 34
Tymeson, Miriam 172
Valenca, Marco A. 186
Vandeman, George 154
Vincent Hill School 57, 59, 74, 89-90, 93, 144
Vollmer, Donald Evans 182
Vollmer, Dr. Donald 158, 182
Vollmer, Dr. Donald Henry 182
Vollmer, Dr. Henry W. 182
Vollmer, Dr. James Merl 183
Vollmer, Dr. Jim 158
Vollmer, Mary Louise Evans 182
Vollmer, Pastor Don 158
Vollmer, Mary Lou 158
Wagner, Elder John 209
Wallin, Enos 35
Wallin, Hannah 35
Wallin, Inez 35
Ward, Eric 197
Wedgewood Trio 183
Wellman, S. A. 65
Weniger, Charles 100
Werderich, Theresa 91
Wessels, Pieter 40
'Whispers of Hope' 95
White, Ellen 7, 9, 23, 132, 138, 147, 154, 188, 207, 217-219, 221, 223, 228
White, J. Edson 17
White, W. C. 17-18, 223, 229
Whiting, Albert 156
Wilson, Bill 24
Wilson, Dr. Bruce 167
Wilson, Elinor Esther Neumann 168
    age 91, passed 168
Wilson, Isabella Scott 7, 11
Wilson, J. H. C. 39
Wilson, Ken 172
Wilson, Kenneth 21, 228

Wilson, Nancy iii, 159, 181, 186

Wilson, Neal C. 78, 93-94, 97, 102, 104, 112-114, 116-118, 120, 124, 127-128, 132-134, 137, 140, 143-144, 146-147, 152-153, 156-157, 160, 162, 167, 180, 223-224, 232-239
   accomplishments during Neal C. Wilson's presidency 147

Wilson, Neal Clayton 86, 160, 170
   died on December 14, 2010 160
   memorial service 160

Wilson, Ted iii, 155, 157, 160, 170, 173, 175, 178, 180-182, 186-187, 190, 196, 199, 201, 203-204, 207, 209-210, 213-214, 216, 218-220, 222, 224, 239
   baptism (May 19, 1962) 174
   his teachers 170
   ordination service 186
   "Ted" was added officially to his name (November 3, 2009) 210

Wilson, William Henry iii, 7-8, 11, 13
   baptized 8

Wilson's daughters 227

Wilson-Kahler, Janet 21, 228

Wood, Kenneth H. 157

Wood, Miriam 133, 234, 236-237

Wright, Henry 126

Wright, J. F. 63-64, 230-231

Wright, Ron 198-199

Yezidis 114

Zaoksky Theological Seminary 202, 204

Zytkoskee, A. Gordon 102

Zytkoskee, Evelyn iv, 107, 113, 171, 234

We invite you to view the complete
selection of titles we publish at:

www.TEACHServices.com

Scan with your mobile
device to go directly
to our website.

Please write or email us your praises, reactions, or
thoughts about this or any other book we publish at:

TEACH Services, Inc.
P U B L I S H I N G
www.TEACHServices.com

P.O. Box 954
Ringgold, GA 30736

info@TEACHServices.com

TEACH Services, Inc., titles may be purchased in bulk for
educational, business, fund-raising, or sales promotional use.
For information, please e-mail:

BulkSales@TEACHServices.com

Finally, if you are interested in seeing
your own book in print, please contact us at

publishing@TEACHServices.com

We would be happy to review your manuscript for free.

www.ingramcontent.com/pod-product-compliance
Lightning Source LLC
Chambersburg PA
CBHW082114230426
43671CB00015B/2702